# Have Dog Will Travel—

## California Edition

### Comprehensive guide to over 2,200 dog-friendly accommodations

Barbara Whitaker

Ginger & Spike Publications
Wilsonville, Oregon

Printed in the United States of America.
First printing

## Publisher's Cataloging-in-Publication
### *(Provided by Quality Books, Inc.)*


Whitaker, Barbara.
    Have dog will travel : comprehensive guide to over
2,200 dog-friendly accommodations / Barbara
Whitaker. – California ed.
    p. cm.
    Includes index.
    ISBN 0-9660544-7-4

    1. Hotels–Pet accommodations–California–
Directories.  2. Dogs–Housing–California–Directories.
3. Pets and travel–California.   I. Title.
TX907.3.C2W45 2005          917.9406'154
                    QBI04-200248

Cover and interior illustrations by Kristin Johnson and Bob Sleeper

Ginger & Spike Publications
PO Box 937, Wilsonville OR  97070-0937
Phone 503-625-3001, Fax 503-625-3076
Email barbw@havedogwilltravel.com
Web www.havedogwilltravel.com

# Acknowledgments

I want to express my appreciation for all the wonderful people who helped me to bring this fifth volume in the *Have Dog Will Travel* series to completion.

Heartfelt thanks to my dear friends Susan Foster, Randi Goodrich and Bonnie Vorenberg for their never-flagging encouragement and support, and for keeping me focused (and sane!) throughout the long process. Kudos also to Carol Beck, Celeste Elliott, Curtis May and Craig Piland for their help during the research stage.

Special thanks to my husband Linn for his ongoing encouragement and support. And of course, I must acknowledge my four-footed buddies Ginger and Spike, whose companionable presence, as I sat at my computer day after day, motivated me to finish this *California Edition*.

I couldn't have done it without you—many thanks, one and all!

In loving memory of
Brujo, Jack, Kala, Jeremiah,
Kaka, Irish, and Almond—
faithful companions, all.

# Table of Contents

## 4: The Well-Behaved Traveler On the Road

## 5: First Aid for Your Traveling Dog

## 6: Emergency Clinics

California's 24 hour and "after-hours"
emergency veterinary clinics

## 7: If Your Dog Gets Lost

## 8: Dog-Friendly Lodgings

Over 2,200 dog-friendly hotels, motels, B & Bs,
cabins and vacation homes throughout California

## A: Business Name Index

Remember a lodging's name but not which
city it's located in? Look it up here!

## B: Topics Index

Check here for the page number of any topic
mentioned in chapters 1 through 7

# 1: Touring With Your Well-behaved Traveler

So you plan to travel in California by car, and you want to take your dog along? Well, you're in good company—lots of dogs travel with their owners. Ginger, my German Shepherd/Norwegian Elkhound, certainly does. After all, she's part of the family, and a vacation just wouldn't be the same without her.

Traveling with a well-behaved dog can be great fun and a minimum of fuss. But it does involve some advance planning and effort on your part. It also requires extra consideration for your fellow travelers and for the friendly people who provide your accommodations.

Chapters 1–7 in this book are packed with common-sense information you can use to transform your dog into a well-behaved traveler—making your trips more fun for both of you. There's even a common-sense first aid guide, with a list of 24-hour emergency veterinary clinics in each state, for your pet's safety and your own peace of mind.

In Chapter 8 you'll find detailed listings for more than 2,200 hotels, motels, and bed & breakfast inns throughout California where you and your well-behaved dog are welcome guests.

At the back of the book you'll find two separate indexes:

- A: Business Name Index—alphabetical list of all the business names, cross-referenced to their detailed listings in Chapter 8

- B: Topics Index—alphabetical list of the pet travel topics that are discussed in Chapters 1 through 7

# How to have fun and get invited back

The numbers of hotels, motels, cabins and B & Bs that accept pets have dwindled in recent years. This unfortunate trend is due largely to a few irresponsible dog owners who allow their dogs to damage furnishings and landscaping, or behave aggressively toward other guests and their pets. Or, they fail to make sure their pet, his travel bed, and his cleanup towels are freshly washed in preparation for their trip.

As responsible dog owners, we can all help to reverse this trend. Preparing in advance and taking appropriate equipment along not only ensures more enjoyable trips for ourselves and our dogs—it also provides positive examples of well-behaved traveling dogs, to help encourage more establishments to accept pets.

This book will help you prepare for a great trip with your dog, by following these easy but important steps:

- Attend obedience training classes with your dog *before* you travel. When you are both familiar with the basic commands for good behavior, you'll be ready when the unexpected happens. (And believe me, it *does* eventually happen!)

- Prepare a canine first aid kit and learn (in advance) how to handle a medical emergency

- Pack the appropriate pet travel supplies

- Call ahead to reserve a dog-friendly room—be aware that most of the hotels, motels and bed-and-breakfast inns included in this book allow dogs in some, but not all, of their rooms

- Always pay attention to your dog's impact on other guests and on the facilities, both indoor and outdoor, where you're staying—in short, be well-behaved travelers!

# When to bring your dog—and when NOT to

Obviously you want your dog to travel with you, or you wouldn't be reading this book. But also ask yourself whether or not he *wants* to come along.

Your dog will probably enjoy the trip if:

🐕 You're traveling by car

🐕 Driving time will be fairly short, so he won't be in the car for hours

🐕 You've planned lots of activities that your dog can share, like hiking or walking on the beach

But consider traveling *without* your dog when:

🐕 Adverse weather conditions would make him miserably hot or cold

🐕 You'd be traveling by plane or train—these are more of an ordeal for your pet than a vacation

🐕 Most of your time would be spent in activities that your dog could not share—after all, would *you* want to spend your entire vacation locked in an empty car or motel room while your companion attended meetings all day long?

# And now, a word from Spike

The feline member of our family ("He Who Must Be Obeyed") wants to point out that he definitely prefers to stay home while Ginger goes traveling. Call him a homebody if you like, but Spike insists that most cats would much rather stay behind in their own familiar surroundings. On Spike's advice, then, this book focuses on traveling with dogs only.

Obviously you'll be making arrangements for your cats to be properly cared for in your absence. So, you can rest assured that they will be just fine while you're gone. Though it may hurt to admit it, they probably won't even miss you.

As Spike puts it, "I'm staying here. And as long as I'm properly fed and admired, my servants *[that's us mere humans]* can go wherever they like!"

# 2: Puppy, Pack Your Bags

It has been said that every successful vacation begins with careful packing. This is just as true for your dog as for yourself—you need to bring along the proper pet supplies. Use the handy checklist on page 21 to be sure nothing important gets left behind.

Many of these supplies are as close as your local pet store. You can also check in dog magazines at your library or newsstand for the names of mail order pet supply houses and write, telephone or go online to request their catalogs. You'll be amazed at the variety of new gadgets available to make traveling with your pet easy and fun.

## Collar and leash

Every dog should wear a sturdy leather or woven collar at all times, with the appropriate license, identification and rabies tags attached.

**Don't use a choke collar as a permanent collar!** Properly used, it can be helpful during training sessions, but if left on your dog all the time, the choke collar could snag on a low branch or other obstruction. Don't let your beloved pet become one of the sad stories of dogs who choked to death when their owners were not there to rescue them.

If your dog is really hard to control, check with a reputable trainer about using a *prong collar* during your training sessions. This type of collar has blunt metal prongs that momentarily pinch the dog's neck when he pulls against the leash or when you administer a correction. Again, this is for use during training sessions only; don't leave it on your dog all the time!

You'll need a 1-ft to 6-ft long leash for walking with your dog close to your side. Woven nylon or leather works better than metal chain, which is noisy and harder to hold onto. Also check out the new retractable leashes that extend to 16 feet or more so your pet can investigate his surroundings without dragging you every which way, then they retract fully for walking close to your side.

🐾 Attending a basic obedience class with your dog is one of the very best ways to help him master the fine art of walking on leash.

# All the proper ID tags

As important as your dog's license and ID tags are at home, they're even more vital when you travel. If you and your pet lose track of each other, those ID tags will enable his finders to contact you.

Any number of companies can create ID tags for you. Veterinary offices often have brochures from several of them. Dog magazines are full of ads for this service—check your library or newsstand. Some mail order catalogs also offer custom tags. Do-it-yourself tag-making machines are starting to appear in malls and pet stores. Dog shows and pet fairs and even holiday bazaars often include a booth where they'll make your tags "while you wait."

**Dog license tag**—Among the many good reasons for licensing your dog, one of the best is that the license number and phone number of your county dog control department appears on the tag. Those numbers offer yet another way to trace your dog back to you if he becomes lost.

**Permanent identification tag**—This should include your name, home address and phone number, and perhaps your dog's name. (Ginger's tag even lists her veterinarian's phone number.) If you don't want to reveal your full street address, just list your city and state. Ideally, this information should be permanently engraved or stamped onto a metal tag. The rectangular style of tag that fastens flat to the collar will stay cleaner and doesn't add to the jingling of the other tags.

**Rabies tag**—Provided by your veterinarian. This tag shows a serial number that can be traced back to the veterinarian and then to the dog's owner. There could be dire consequences if your dog were to get picked up as a stray and not have proof of current rabies vaccination.

**Travel tag**—Very important! This tag shows where you can be reached *during your vacation*. Several styles are available; one is a two-part set consisting of a round cardboard tag that you write on, which then fits inside a clear plastic snap-together case. Another type consists of a tiny metal barrel that unscrews to hold a rolled-up slip of paper—just be sure to tighten the two halves together *very securely* to keep them from jiggling loose.

Write or type the name, street address, city and phone number where you're staying. If your trip includes several destinations, either list them all or make a separate tag for each destination. As an alternative, list the name and phone number of someone who can receive messages for you. You may also want to add "Reward Offered" (no specific dollar amount) and "Call collect" on the tag.

# Microchip ID system

Microchipping is one of the newest and most promising ways to identify a lost pet. While tags or collars can fall off or be removed, a microchip stays with your pet forever. Each chip is programmed with a unique ID code that can be detected by a hand-held scanning device, similar to the UPC scanners used in retail stores to read product barcodes.

Your veterinarian can implant the microchip, no bigger than a grain of rice, beneath your pet's skin in a safe, quick office procedure. Then all you have to do is register your pet's unique code and your contact information with the national database agency to receive coverage anywhere you travel in the USA.

Microchip scanners are now used at thousands of animal control agencies, shelters and veterinary clinics across the country. Once the chip's code has been retrieved, the staff simply calls it in to the national database agency, which is accessible 24 hours a day, 365 days a year via a toll-free number. The database agency then notifies you that your dog has been found.

The cost of implanting the microchip and the onetime fee to register your pet in the database add up to about $50—pretty inexpensive insurance for your dog's safe return if he should ever get lost. Pet fairs or veterinary associations sometimes sponsor low-cost microchip clinics.

# Health certificate and vaccinations

Get this certificate from your veterinarian not more than 10 days before beginning your trip. Effective for 30 days, it states that your pet is in good health, and also includes a list of his current vaccinations. While not strictly required when traveling by car, you'll *definitely* need this if you plan to travel by air (even just within your state) or to enter Canada. Before traveling to any other countries, check with their embassies for specific vaccinations and other requirements.

If your pet takes medication or has other health problems, get a copy of his medical records along with the certificate. Make sure the paperwork includes your veterinarian's name, address and phone number, in case follow-up information is needed.

The most well known canine vaccination is for rabies. In fact, you can't get a dog license without proof of a current rabies vaccination. And as a caring, responsible pet owner, *of course* you license your dog, right?

In addition, your pet should be immunized against distemper, hepatitis, parainfluenza, leptospirosis and possibly parvovirus. Depending on where you'll be traveling, your veterinarian may also recommend a preventive for heartworm or Lyme disease.

Also ask about annual booster shots for corona and bordetella. These safeguard your pet against kennel cough and other infectious diseases he might be exposed to from contact with other dogs, and are often required before your dog can attend obedience classes or stay in a boarding kennel.

**Bottom line on vaccinations:** Your traveling dog is exposed to many new health hazards at rest stops, parks and other public areas. Along with the stress of drinking unfamiliar water and meeting new dogs, these factors add up to very real dangers for the non-vaccinated dog. So be safe—vaccinate!

---

🐕 Some vaccines can take up to 30 days to develop their full protective strength, so check with your veterinarian and *plan ahead!*

# First aid kit

A basic first aid kit is easy to put together and enables you to deal with emergencies until you can get to a local veterinarian. You'll find a list of the items that belong in your first aid kit on pages 38–39.

Of course you'll also bring along any special medication your veterinarian may have prescribed. If fleas are a problem in the area you're visiting, you may want to include flea-and-tick spray or powder— just be sure to apply it to your dog only when outdoors, never in your motel room. Or ask your veterinarian about the monthly flea and tick treatments that protect your pet "from the inside out."

# Travel crate

Many trainers, breeders and veterinarians recommend using a portable kennel, or *crate,* when your dog travels in the car. Obviously, this is more practical with small dogs than with larger ones—it is much easier to fit a Beagle-sized crate into the back seat than one for a Rottweiler.

Several types of crate are available, from collapsible wire mesh panels, to soft-sided carriers, to rigid molded plastic. A wire crate works well in the flat back of a van or station wagon, while the plastic carriers often fit better into the back seat of a sedan. Of course, when traveling by plane, your dog *must* be in an airline-approved travel crate.

The crate should be large enough for your dog to turn around, lie down, and stand or sit up without hitting his head. If he's still a puppy, get a crate that will be large enough for his full adult size. Think of this as his den—*cozy* and *secure*—so don't get anything larger than your adult pet will need. To cushion and provide traction underfoot, place a folded blanket on the bottom of the crate. Better yet, cut a thick piece of carpet to fit snugly without slipping—ask your local carpet dealer for a remnant or sample square.

# Restraints and safety barriers

If a travel crate isn't the answer for your situation, not to worry—there are a number of other safety options you can use instead.

**Seat belts**—Available for dogs of all sizes, these consist of a chest harness and a strap that fastens to the car seat or to the regular seat belt. These allow your dog to sit up or lie down as he chooses, yet prevent him from being thrown forward in the event of a sudden stop. Various sizes and types are available. And it keeps him from jumping around in the car while you're trying to concentrate on safe driving.

**Metal barriers**—These allow you to close off the back seat or the back of a station wagon, and can be ordered for specific makes of cars, other models are adjustable to fit a variety of vehicles. Your dog can see and hear you through the barrier, but is securely restrained from jumping or being thrown into the front seat. Metal barriers may be either temporarily or permanently installed.

**Mesh barriers**—These stretchy nets create a temporary barrier between the front and back seats. Mesh nets are available in generic sizes and shapes to fit most car models.

**Collapsible window screens**—Made of strong plastic struts that expand like a child's safety gate, these fit securely into a partially opened car window. With screens in place on both sides of the car, there is plenty of air circulation but no danger of your dog jumping out—or of someone reaching into the parked car. When removed, the screens take up almost no space and fit easily under a car seat. Ginger's favorite is called a "Pet-Vent," made by Hamilton Products.

# Food

First and foremost, you'll need to bring along dog food and a bowl to serve it in. Unless you're absolutely certain that your dog's preferred brand of food is available wherever you plan to travel, you should pack enough dog food for the entire trip.

If your dog typically nibbles at his food without finishing it all right away, bring a bowl with a snap-on lid that can go back into your dog's tote bag without spilling kibble everywhere. The shallow containers used for whipped toppings or margarine work very well.

You may also want to bring along a vinyl placemat for catching spills under the food and water bowls. This is an item you can pick up for pennies at garage sales. Or you can buy fancy mats and bowls, decorated with pet pictures or paw prints, in pet stores or mail order catalogs.

Remember to pack a can opener for canned food, along with a serving spoon and a snap-on lid for covering any portion to be saved for the next meal. If your dog is accustomed to frequent dog treats or snacks, pack those too. A small cooler is helpful in hot weather for keeping drinking water and leftover canned food cool.

# Water

Pack a plastic gallon jug of water and an unbreakable bowl where they'll be accessible during your travels, since your dog will need a drink of water every few hours. Don't let him drink from streams or puddles, because drinking unfamiliar or polluted water can lead to stomach upsets or diarrhea.

Many veterinarians recommend bringing enough water from home to last at least halfway through your trip. By gradually mixing your own water with the local tap water, you can prevent an unpleasant digestive reaction. You can also buy distilled water for about a dollar a gallon at most grocery stores.

*Never* allow your dog to drink from the toilet in your motel room—some establishments put slow-release cleaning chemicals into the toilet tank, which could make him very sick.

# Bedding & towels

You should always travel with your dog's own bedding and cleanup towels. Your dog will thank you—and so will the hotel and motel managers, for sparing their furnishings. If your dog is accustomed to sleeping on the bed with you, or on other furniture, bring a clean sheet from home to protect bedspreads and upholstery. And do consider training your dog to stay off the furniture, at home *and* when traveling.

A travel crate, so useful in the car, also makes the perfect bed. It is reassuringly cozy and safe. If you're not using a crate, then bring along a *familiar* washable blanket or other bedding. Ginger travels with the same trusty sleeping bag that she sleeps on at home. Zipped up and folded in half, it makes a thick, soft bed. Opened out full length, it protects her favorite spot in the back seat of the car from dirt, mud and beach sand.

An absolute must is a pair of cleanup towels especially for your dog. Use these to rub down a wet coat or wipe muddy or sandy paws. If your dog is an enthusiastic drinker, spread one out under his water bowl.

You can spend a lot of money on "designer" travel supplies if you choose, but the sheet, dog towels, and bedding can also be found very inexpensively at garage sales, rummage sales, or secondhand stores. Ginger's sleeping bag cost us a dollar, and her towels were a quarter each. The tote bag which holds her travel supplies was another garage sale find—making the cost of her entire travel set less than three dollars.

# Grooming aids

Pack your dog's brush or comb, since you'll probably be going to fun places that will result in a happy but dirty or sandy pet! A quick brushing *before* going indoors will keep your motel room clean, and will endear you to the housekeeping staff—not to mention how much your pet probably enjoys being groomed. Ginger jumps up and down with delight at the mere sight of her brush.

Take care of major grooming chores *before* your trip—trim those too-long toenails and brush the loose hair out of his coat. And pack a bottle of pet shampoo if he has shown any tendency to roll in smelly things. I'll never forget the day that Jeremiah, my husband's 100-pound Great Pyrenees, found a dead seal on the beach—enough said!

# Cleaning up

Even seasoned canine travelers occasionally have car sickness accidents, so it's a good idea to pack supplies in the car for quick cleanups. Paper towels, pre-moistened towelettes, or just a wet washcloth in a plastic bag are all good. Stash them in an easy-to-reach spot in the car, such as under the front seat.

Many hotels and motels lay out free amenities such as shampoo and hand lotion. Wouldn't it be great if they offered guests with dogs the choice of a few disposable pooper scoopers or cleanup bags instead! In the meantime, however, it is up to us as dog owners to take full responsibility for cleaning up after our dogs.

*Please, please be considerate* of others by cleaning up after your dog's rest stops—whether in a park, on the motel grounds, or at a roadside rest area. You can use either disposable pooper scoopers, or a reusable scooper with disposable bags—plus another bag for storing the scooper between uses.

For a low cost, low tech method, use a plastic produce bag saved from a trip to the grocery store. Place your hand inside the bag and use this "glove" to pick up the doggy doo. With your other hand, turn the bag inside out, then twist the top shut and secure it with a knot. Properly dispose of the bag in a trash can.

Keep several clean, folded bags in your car, ready for the next rest stop. And *always* tuck one in your pocket when taking your dog out for a walk. Zip-top plastic bags also work well.

# Last but not least, a flashlight

You probably already have a flashlight stashed in your vehicle for emergencies. Keep another one in your dog's tote bag for those just-before-bedtime walks.

# Tote bag checklist

- First aid kit, health certificate/medical records
- Dog bed (sleeping bag or blanket) and towels
- Dog food, bowl, serving spoon, can opener and snap-on lid, vinyl placemat
- Jug of water, drinking bowl
- Dog brush or comb, shampoo
- Pooper scoopers (reusable or disposable) or a supply of plastic bags
- Paper towels, pre-moistened towelettes, or wet washcloth in a plastic bag
- Flashlight
- A favorite chew toy!

# 3: Good Behavior is a TEAM Effort

Which sort of pet would you rather vacation with: a barky, uncontrollable bundle of energy, or a well-behaved traveler? The answer is obvious, and basic obedience training is the key.

"Obedience" simply means that your dog is reliably under your control, both on and off the leash. Mastering just a few useful commands—and reviewing them often with your pet—can make all the difference in his behavior. The practice sessions can be a lot of fun, and they help to strengthen the bond between you and your dog.

## What commands are necessary?

According to noted dog trainer Bruce Sessions, only two commands are truly required for the traveling dog: *come* and *no*. Check your local library's archives for his excellent article "Training the RV Dog" in the September 1985 issue of *Trailer Life* magazine—he explains how to teach these vital commands in just 15 minutes a day for one week.

Ginger and I have also learned a few more commands in obedience class that come in very handy: *sit, down, stay* and *heel*. Does your dog absolutely have to know all these commands before he can travel with you? No, but they will definitely make your trips more relaxed. Compare the following two scenarios...

### Before obedience training...

It was early morning at the motel, and I had just let Ginger off her leash (my first mistake) in the designated corner of the motel grounds for a rest stop. Another guest and her dog suddenly appeared, and Ginger ran to investigate the newcomer, ignoring my call to *"Come back here right now!"* I had to chase after her to grab her collar. The other guest glared as our two dogs bristled and snarled at each other in the traditional "I'm a tougher dog than you are" dance. On the leash again, Ginger lunged along the path at full speed, dragging me behind her.

In the motel room, she ran back and forth between the window and the closed door, barking at the sounds of people and cars outside—in spite of my repeated scolding to *"Stop that barking and lie down."* Loaded down with luggage, I opened the door and she ran out ahead of me, nearly tripping another guest in her excitement.

### ...and after

Let's try this again now that Ginger and I have completed our obedience classes: I take her outside *on the leash* for her morning rest stop. If she moves toward an approaching dog, I tell her *"Heel"* and we walk in the opposite direction. If she makes any aggressive move or sound, I say *"No!"* sharply and we keep walking—without her pulling on the leash.

Back in the motel room, if Ginger barks at a sound outside, I say *"No!"* followed by *"Down."* She lies down quietly on her own bed. When checking out of the room, I put her on the leash *before* opening the door, tell her *"Heel"* and she walks politely beside me to the car. Once she's safely inside, I can finish loading the luggage.

### What a difference!

Feel the difference in stress levels between these two scenarios? And that's just the beginning of the day—imagine the whole vacation with an uncontrollable dog versus a well-behaved traveler.

# Obedience 101

You *can* learn about obedience training from books, and there are some excellent ones available. However, I definitely recommend that you and your dog attend at least a beginners' obedience class. A trained instructor can get you off to a great start, avoiding behavior problems before they begin.

Professional dog trainers usually offer both group and one-on-one sessions—check the Yellow Pages under "Dog Training" or ask for referrals at your veterinary clinic. Beginning, intermediate and advanced levels of obedience classes may also be available through your local school district or community college. Call the school office and ask about their Continuing Education or Community Education programs. Class schedules may also be available at your local bank, library or Post Office.

# Train BEFORE you travel

The time to begin obedience training is before your trip—so that your dog can learn the basic commands in a controlled area without distractions. Once he understands the commands, start practicing with him in a public area like a park, surrounded by people and other dogs. He'll soon learn that you expect the same good behavior wherever he goes, regardless of distractions in the background.

Relax and have fun with this training time. Your dog will love the extra attention and he'll try to please you. Be patient and upbeat even if he gets confused at first. If you reach a stumbling block, go back to an earlier command that he knows well, to get his confidence level back up before you try the more difficult command again.

Keep your training sessions short so that they don't turn into torture for either one of you. And always end with a few minutes of plain old playing—toss a ball for your dog to fetch, or lead him on a run around the yard to release any leftover tension. After all, good behavior is supposed to make your time together more fun, right?

# Basic commands

The following discussion is based on the collective expertise of a number of well-known trainers and authors. For more detailed information on obedience training, check your local bookstore or library.

**Come**—This is an easy command that most dogs pick up very quickly. You want to get your dog's attention in such an inviting way that there's nothing else he'd rather do than come running to you. While your dog is on a leash or long cord, call his name followed by the command *"Come."* As soon as he starts toward you, praise him lavishly. Giving a small food treat at first for every positive response helps to reinforce the idea that coming when called is a wonderful idea.

**No**—There is no specific routine for teaching this command. Just belt it out in a very firm tone of voice, whenever your dog is doing something you *really* don't want him to do. Don't overuse it though—save it for when he does something you absolutely will not tolerate; otherwise you risk losing its impact. The sudden loud command should startle him out of whatever he's doing. Then as soon as he begins to pay attention to you, praise him. You may even want to call him over to you for a pat on the head or a good ear-scratching.

**Sit**—With your dog on the leash, say his name and then *"Sit."* At the same time, pull up gently on the leash and push down on his hindquarters to guide him into the sit position. Praise him *("Good sit")* and then release him from this position with *"Okay"* or *"Release."* (Use the same word consistently.) Only after you give the release command is he allowed to stand up again. Then give lots of praise, both verbal and hands-on. Most dogs will be so delighted with themselves by this time that they'll happily repeat the exercise over and over as long as you keep telling them how wonderful they are.

**Down**—With your dog on the leash, say his name and the command *"Down"* while you pull downward on his leash. At first, you may also need to push down on his hindquarters or shoulders until he is lying down. Again, give lots of praise to reassure him that he's doing well. Use patience and lots of repetition here.

**Stay**—With your dog in the Sit or Down position, hold your hand in front of his face, palm toward him, while saying *"Stay."* Praise lavishly for even the shortest compliance, then release. Gradually increase the time your dog is expected to hold this position, then practice keeping him in the Stay position as you step further and further away. Always remember to release him from this position before going on to another command or ending the practice session, so he doesn't get the idea that *he* can decide when this command is over.

**Heel (walking on leash)**—Start with your dog sitting at your left side, leash in your left hand. Say his name and the command *"Heel"* just before you step out with your left foot. Take just a few steps the first time, then say *"Sit"* as you stop walking. You want him to learn to stay right at your side rather than rushing ahead of you, and to immediately sit down when you stop.

Say *"Heel"* and start walking again, and so on. He'll soon learn to follow your steps. In fact, he'll probably anticipate your takeoff and start too soon at first, so be patient. Once he catches on to the routine, stop giving the Sit command every time, so that he learns to do it automatically.

Try carrying a small food treat right in front of his nose to keep him at your side. Give him the treat after he has successfully walked a few steps and then stopped with you. And of course, give lots of praise. (If you think it's starting to sound like practice and praise are the secrets to successful obedience training, you're absolutely right!)

# Controlling aggression

If you intend to take your well-behaved traveler out in public, he must be reliably *not* aggressive toward people or dogs. Some dogs don't start out being comfortable with other dogs. Their reactions range from defensive postures, i.e., raised fur along the back of the neck and fierce stares, to outright barking or growling.

The best way to overcome defensive or aggressive tendencies is to socialize your dog at an early age, that is, to get him accustomed to being in the presence of other dogs. Simply attending obedience classes will go a long way toward helping him relax around dogs and people. Your instructor can also offer specialized help for problem dogs.

Dog behaviorists say that once you establish yourself as the "pack leader," your dog will follow your lead on whether to charge ahead or hold back. The most important step in preventing aggression is to *always* have your dog under your control—this means on the leash—whenever you venture outside your car or motel room.

# If your dog is a barker

Simply put, barking is *not* to be tolerated. A barking dog makes everyone around you miserable. You should train your dog to stop barking as soon as you give the all-purpose command *"No!"*

A really insistent barker may at first need more than a spoken command to break through his mental barriers. I've had good luck with plain water in a plastic squirt bottle. One good squirt in the face (aim for the forehead) doesn't hurt your dog, but it certainly interrupts his train of thought, especially when accompanied by a loud *"No!"* and followed with praise the minute he stops barking.

Of course, a dog left behind in a motel room, barking incessantly, is absolutely out. This kind of barking is a sign of stress, as in "They left me here all alone and I'm scared/bored/frustrated." It isn't fair to your dog or to the unfortunate neighbors who have to endure the noise.

*Never leave your dog alone in the motel room.* He should be going with you—isn't that why you brought him on the trip in the first place? If he can't be with you for a short time, such as while you're in a restaurant, then let him wait in your car, not in the room. (See page 32 for safety tips on briefly leaving your pet in a parked car.)

If you already use a travel crate, your dog should be accustomed to sitting or lying down quietly when he's inside it. Put him in the crate for a few minutes to calm down when he becomes upset and barky. Be sure to practice this "time-out in the crate" exercise at home before you travel, so that your dog knows exactly what is expected of him when he is put into his little den.

# Learning to love car rides

Many dogs just naturally love going anywhere in the car with you, but others have difficulty getting used to the sound and motion. Pacing back and forth, drooling, panting excessively or throwing up are all signs that your dog is anxious about being in the car. Some advance preparations will help to ensure a comfortable trip for all concerned.

**Getting used to the car**—Practice rides can help to reassure him that riding in the car can be fun rather than intimidating. In extreme cases, you may need to start by sitting quietly with him in the car, not even starting the engine. Ignore him for a few minutes—perhaps read a magazine article—then let him out of the car with a simple word of praise and a pat on the head.

Repeat this exercise until he can enter the car, sit quietly, and exit without any problems. Then try starting the car but not going anywhere. Next, try driving just around the block, and so on. By the time you've progressed to taking him with you on short errands, such as to the grocery store and back, he'll probably just take a nap while you drive.

Arrange some of your practice trips to include a fun destination or activity, like a brisk walk in the park. Ginger loves riding to the drive-up window at our bank, because the teller keeps a bowl of treats handy for canine customers.

**Avoiding a "nervous stomach"**—Stress can trigger car sickness, so don't give food or water for at least an hour before a practice ride. Allow time for a few minutes of exercise and a chance to relieve himself just before you leave. If he still gets carsick, see page 50 for some simple remedies.

**Riding politely**—Train your dog to sit or lie down quietly—no jumping around, and no barking in your ear or out the window. Consider using one of the safety restraints described on pages 17–18. Reassure him by remaining calm yourself. Don't keep asking anxiously if he's all right—he'll pick up on your tension and get even more nervous. Praise him for sitting politely, then ignore him as long as he behaves himself.

**Loading and unloading**—For his own safety, your dog *must* learn to wait for your command before getting into or out of the car. Never open the door without checking that the leash is attached to his collar, and that you have a firm grasp on the other end of the leash. Losing control of an excited dog in unfamiliar territory can be disastrous—so use the Stay command to keep him safely in the car until you are ready for him to get out.

# Reviewing what your dog already knows

A brief practice session makes a great exercise break during your trip. It also helps to reinforce the idea that obedience is expected even when surrounded by unfamiliar distractions. Start by walking your dog on the leash. Pause periodically to practice the Sit or Down command, then release him and continue your walk. Or tell him to Sit and Stay while you walk ahead a few steps—still holding the leash, of course. Then call him to you once more, with lots of praise.

A few minutes of this activity at each rest stop will leave you with a happy dog who settles down comfortably as soon as you resume driving.

# 4: The Well-Behaved Traveler On the Road

Okay, you've faithfully completed your dog's obedience training, assembled his first aid kit (see page 38) and packed his food, water, and other traveling supplies. You've made your advance room reservations, you're ready to go, and your ecstatic pet is running in circles around the car. This is the payoff for all your preparations—it's time to hit the road!

## Tips for traveling in the car

The safest way for a smaller dog to ride in the car is in a travel crate. This protects him in case of a sudden stop and keeps him from jumping around in the car or getting underfoot while you're trying to drive. If your pet is too large for a travel crate, consider using a doggy seat belt that offers similar protection but still allows him to sit or stand up, as he chooses. Ginger's designated travel spot is on her sleeping bag, which has been spread out across the back seat to protect the upholstery.

Take your dog's leash off once he's safely inside the car, and remember to put it on again *before* you let him out. Don't leave the leash attached to his collar while the car is in motion.

If you feel you must open a car window near him, roll it down just enough for your dog to put his nose into the fresh air, not his whole face. *Never* let him hang his head out the window of a moving car—not only could he squeeze his whole body out if he decided to chase something, but airborne objects such as insects or flying gravel could injure his ears and eyes. Or the force of the wind could actually give him an earache.

It goes without saying that your pet belongs *inside* the vehicle. A dog riding in the open bed of a pickup truck is an accident just waiting to happen. He's exposed to wind-borne hazards and harsh weather, and could be thrown out of the vehicle if you swerve or brake suddenly.

If you need to briefly leave your dog in the parked car—while you stop for lunch, for example—be sure he won't suffer from heat buildup in the car, which can lead to heatstroke or even death. Park in a covered lot, or at least in the shade. For cross-ventilation, open windows on both sides of the car and insert the safety screens described on page 18. Check frequently to be sure the temperature in the car is still comfortable. Or better yet, have an outdoor picnic lunch and let him lounge in the shade with you.

# Rest stop pointers

When traveling a long distance, stop every few hours to give both you and your pet a chance to stretch and relax. Keep him on the leash the whole time you're at the rest stop, and stay in the designated pet areas.

He'll probably be ready for a drink of water. Then give him a few minutes to relieve himself and walk around a bit. Be considerate of others by *always* cleaning up after your dog—use plastic bags or pooper scoopers, and properly dispose of the waste in a garbage can.

This is a great time for a short exercise break, especially if you combine it with a review of obedience commands. Try walking a short distance and have him sit or lie down, then walk for another minute and practice a different command, and so on. A few minutes of activity will have you both feeling refreshed and ready to continue your trip.

# Checking into your room

When you arrive at your overnight destination, be sure to remind the staff that your dog is traveling with you. Of course, you should already have stated this when making your advance reservation, but tell them again now that you have arrived. That way, they can be sure not to put you in a "no-pets" room by mistake—many establishments reserve certain rooms for guests who suffer from allergies. Sneaking a dog into a no-pets room hurts all dog owners by jeopardizing the management's willingness to accept dogs in the future.

Ask where on their grounds you can exercise your dog, whether or not they provide cleanup bags or pooper scoopers, and which trash cans you should use for disposal.

A growing number of California's parks and beaches either do not allow dogs, or only allow them at certain times. So when you check in, also ask for directions to the dog-friendly parks or beaches in the area.

# Room etiquette

Place your pet's bed on the floor in a corner of the room and show him where it is, then make sure that he uses his own bed and not the furniture. If your pet is accustomed to sleeping on your bed or other furniture at home, bring along a sheet to cover the motel furnishings— and resolve to begin breaking that habit as soon as your trip is over.

If your dog gets bored or rambunctious while in the room, offer him a favorite chew toy to play with. Watch that he doesn't damage the furnishings—remember, you are legally and financially responsible for any damage your dog does to motel property, both indoors and out.

While it's natural for dogs to bark at unfamiliar sounds, don't tolerate any barking in the room, no matter what's going on outside. Barking is the single most common reason given by managers for not allowing dogs to stay. *Never* leave your pet alone in the room when you go out, for example, to dinner. Take him along and let him wait for you in the car rather than in the room. He'll feel safer in that familiar place and should settle right down for a nap while you're gone. More and more establishments are offering onsite dogsitting services (for a fee), or can recommend local dogsitters or even "doggy day care" facilities.

Before you and your dog leave the room, make him sit down by the door while you put his leash on. He should remain sitting while you open the door and step outside, then he can follow you out. Don't let him charge through the door ahead of you.

When you and your pet return to the room, check him over before stepping inside. Use the dog towel you brought from home to wipe off any mud or sand on his feet. This small courtesy only takes a second, helps to keep the room clean, and has a positive effect on the manager's willingness to continue accepting pets as guests.

# Mealtime arrangements

Put the food and water bowls on your dog towel or vinyl placemat in the bathroom. If your pet is a messy eater, the placemat is easy to rinse off and drip-dry in the bathtub, and the smooth bathroom floor is much easier to clean than the bedroom carpet. Don't let him drink out of the toilet—cleaning chemicals that may have been added to the toilet tank could make him sick.

On checkout day, it's a good idea to withhold food and water at least an hour before starting a long drive. If your pet tends to suffer from car sickness, you may need to do this as much as six hours before departure—meaning, the night before if you plan to leave early the next morning.

# Walking on the grounds

Shortly after eating or drinking, your dog will need a walk outside, in the designated pet relief area. This is also true after he has been waiting in the car while you were out having your own dinner. And of course, just before bedtime is another important walking time. Be sure to always take along the pooper scooper or plastic bag for cleaning up after him.

Always keep your dog leashed while on the premises. And be courteous when taking him for a "relief walk"—use the designated pet area or at least go to the far end of the grounds, away from buildings, major footpaths and children's play areas, and of course, always clean up after him. Don't let him romp in landscaped flower beds, decorative ponds or streams. Be aware of your pet's energy level and potential for destruction, and seek out areas where he can play harmlessly.

# On the trail

When you go out for the day's activities, remember to bring along your dog's water jug and bowl, just as you would pack your own water bottle for a hike. And of course, the first aid kit should be in your car, not left behind in the room.

Pay attention to your pet's effect on other people and animals when you're out in public. You are responsible for making sure that he doesn't cause anyone else discomfort. If you're walking along a trail, for example, rein him in to walk closely beside you when you encounter other hikers. Don't let him monopolize the whole walkway or run up to greet them—or worse yet, to challenge their own pet.

Remember that although your dog is the apple of your eye, not everyone shares your enchantment. In fact, some people are uncomfortable around even the smallest, meekest dog. So keep your pet on the leash unless you're in a clearly marked "off-leash area."

Watch out for potential hazards underfoot: broken glass, nails or other sharp objects, burning hot pavement, melted road tar, chemical sprays or wet paint could all injure his feet or poison him when he licks his fur. Also remember to clean his feet after walking on snow or ice that may have been treated with salt or other de-icing chemicals.

# At the beach

Many dogs love playing in the ocean, and few scenes are more enjoyable to watch than a happy dog chasing waves up and down the beach. However, don't allow your pet to chase the shore birds, as that can cause them severe or even fatal stress. You can also be cited and fined for endangering the wildlife.

Keep a close eye on your pet while he's in the water—don't let him wade or swim out too far, as dangerous currents can arise unexpectedly and carry him away from the shore.

Also watch that he doesn't drink a lot of salt water, or else he may be throwing up later in the car. A little bit won't hurt him, and he'll soon learn that he doesn't like the taste after all. Offer him a drink of fresh water when he gets back to your parked car, and then wait a few minutes before bundling him inside—he may still need to throw up any salt water already in his stomach.

After walking your dog on the beach, brush off any sand clinging to his feet or coat. Salt water that dries on his skin can cause lasting irritation, so if he's been in the surf, rinse the salt away as soon as possible— definitely *before* returning to your room. This is where those dog towels you packed in his tote bag come in handy. And of course, the motel's towels should *never* be used on your dog!

# 5: First Aid for Your Traveling Dog

Whether your pet sustains a minor scratch or a life-threatening injury, you need to know what first aid measures to take. Then, for all but the most minor problems, your immediate next step is to get him to the nearest veterinary clinic. If you're not sure just how serious the problem is, call them—most clinics are happy to answer questions over the phone, and can give you exact directions for getting there if it becomes necessary.

## Before first aid is needed

Put together your dog's own first aid kit in advance (page 38) and *always* bring it (and this book) along when he travels with you. Keep it in your car when you're out and about, not in the motel room with the luggage.

Read through this chapter *now* to get a basic idea of what to do in an emergency, and how to use the supplies in the first aid kit.

Knowing your dog's healthy state will help you to recognize when something is wrong. Sit down on the floor with your dog—he'll love the attention—and listen to his breathing. Place your palm on his chest just behind his "elbow" and feel his heartbeat. Check the size and color of his pupils, the color of his gums and tongue, and how warm his body feels normally.

In an emergency, refer to specific sections in this chapter for the proper first aid steps to take. Or better yet, have another person read the steps aloud to you while you perform them on your pet. As soon as you complete the emergency procedures, take him to a veterinary clinic, or at least call the clinic for further instructions.

---

🐾 It's a good idea to identify nearby veterinary clinics at your vacation destination *before* the need arises. See the list of emergency clinics starting on page 55, or check the local Yellow Pages.

---

# Your dog's first aid kit

This list includes the emergency supplies you'll need until you can get to the clinic. All items are available from your veterinarian or local pharmacy. The dosage of some medicines varies according to body weight, so write your pet's correct dose on a piece of masking tape attached to each medicine container. Pack everything into a sturdy carrier, such as a fishing tackle box or cosmetics travel case.

**Travel papers**—copies of your dog's license, health certificate, veterinary records if he has special medical problems, and a master Lost-and-Found poster with extra photos of your dog as described on page 71; store all this paperwork in a zip-top plastic bag

**Any medication your dog takes**—and the written prescription

**Honey** packets (available in restaurants) or **small hard candies** such as butterscotch or fruit flavors (no chocolate)—for treating carsickness or upset stomach (page 50)

**Antibacterial ointment**—such as *Panalog* from your veterinarian, or *Neosporin* from any pharmacy, for treating wounds (page 48)

**Tranquilizers**—but *only* if prescribed by your veterinarian *and* you've tested the dosage on your pet before the trip. Please note that the ASPCA discourages tranquilizer use because the effects can be unpredictable.

**Plastic dosage spoon**—for measuring liquid medicines (available at any pharmacy, often for free)

**Paper** or **flexible plastic cup**—for administering liquid medicines; can be squeezed into the shape of a pouring spout

**Slip-on muzzle**—for restraining an injured dog (page 43)—the kind that fastens with hook-and-loop tape is especially easy to use

**Emergency stretcher**—flat piece of wood or cardboard stored in your car's trunk— for moving an injured dog (page 47)

**Kaopectate**—for treating diarrhea

**Hydrogen peroxide**, 3% solution—for treating poison (page 46) and cleaning wounds (page 48)

**Activated charcoal**—for treating poison (page 46)

**Olive oil**—for treating poison (page 46)

**Petroleum jelly**—for taking rectal temperature (see below)

**Sterile eye drops**—for rinsing eyes (page 49)

**Zip-top plastic bags**—for collecting a sample of poison (page 45)

**Sterile gauze pads**—for bandaging wounds and burns (page 44, 48)

**Adhesive tape** and **elastic bandages**—for wounds (page 44, 48)

**Cotton-tipped swabs**—for cleaning wounds (page 48–49)

**Rectal thermometer**—for taking rectal temperature (see below)

**Ice pack**—for treating heatstroke (page 52)

**Tweezers**—for removing foreign objects (page 49)

**Pliers**—for removing foreign objects (page 49, 50)

**Blunt-tipped scissors**—for bandaging wounds (page 44, 48)

# Taking your dog's temperature

Have another person restrain your dog while you take his temperature, if at all possible. Coat the rectal thermometer with a bit of petroleum jelly or hand lotion to make insertion easier.

Firmly grasp your dog's tail and very gently insert the thermometer about one inch while rotating it back and forth slightly. After one minute, remove it to read the temperature. Wash the thermometer with soap and *cool* water before returning it to its protective case. Normal canine body temperature is 100° to 101°—anything over 102.5° deserves a phone call to the veterinary clinic for further advice.

# What to do in a life-threatening emergency

Your pet is depending on you for the first aid that he needs to survive until you reach a veterinarian. Remain calm and focused on what you need to do. Speak to him reassuringly as you work.

Each step listed here is described in greater detail in the sections that follow—exact page numbers are indicated for each step.

1. *Do not move your dog* until you have checked his injuries. The only exception is when it's unsafe to leave him where he is, such as in the middle of a busy street.

2. Check for a heartbeat—if there is none, start cardiac massage *immediately* (page 42).

3. Check whether he is breathing—if not, begin artificial respiration *immediately* (page 42).

4. Muzzle and restrain him if he's in obvious pain, seems dazed or starts to struggle (page 43).

5. Check for obvious injuries; control severe bleeding (page 43-44).

6. Check for symptoms of internal bleeding (page 44).

7. Check for signs of poisoning—depending on the type of poison, induce vomiting or make him swallow an antidote (page 45–46).

8. Move him to your vehicle using a board, stiff cardboard or a blanket as a stretcher (page 47).

9. Treat for shock by keeping him warm (page 47).

10. Rush him to the nearest veterinary clinic. If possible, have another person call ahead so they can prepare for your pet's arrival.

# If your dog is choking

The traveling dog may encounter chicken bones at picnic areas, fishing line at the river's edge—even more dangerous if a fishhook is still attached—or any number of other choking hazards that can be potentially fatal unless you act quickly.

Signs of choking include violent pawing at his mouth or throat and loud gasping or gagging sounds. In his panic, he may even snap at your hand when you try to help.

If possible, have another person hold your pet while you open his mouth wide and pull his tongue out straight with your fingers or a cloth.

If you can see the entire object, pull it out. But *never* pull on a fishline that extends out of sight down his throat—there could be a hook at the other end. Instead, take him to a veterinary clinic for an x-ray.

If you can't see what he's choking on, place your hands on each side of his chest and squeeze in a sudden, forceful movement. The air expelled from his lungs may dislodge the object in his throat.

If he is still choking, head straight for the emergency clinic. Keep him as immobile as possible during the trip, and speak reassuringly to calm him.

# If your dog is drowning

If your pet is in the water and can't make it back to shore, *do not* swim out to him. Try to help him from shore by extending out a board, rope or any floating thing that he can hold or climb onto. If you still can't reach him, wade part of the way out and try again. If you absolutely must swim all the way out to him, bring something he can cling to other than your own body—otherwise you could be seriously clawed or even pulled under in his panic to get out of the water.

After you get him onto the shore, lift his back legs as high above his head as possible for fifteen seconds and give three or four downward shakes to drain his airway. Gently pull his tongue out straight, and clear any debris from his mouth with your hand or a cloth.

If his heart has stopped, start cardiac massage *immediately* (page 42).

If he has a heartbeat but is not breathing, give artificial respiration *immediately* (page 42).

Once he begins breathing on his own, dry him off and keep him warm. If he's willing to drink, give him warm liquids. If his body temperature doesn't quickly return to normal, check with a veterinarian for follow-up treatment.

# Cardiac massage

Place your palm on your dog's chest just behind the elbow. (Practice this at home until you can easily detect his normal heartbeat.) If his heart has stopped beating, you must restart it *immediately*. Gently lay your dog on his side with head extended—don't move him suddenly, as that can further deepen his shock. Pull his tongue out straight to clear the airway.

Place your hands on each side of his chest just behind the elbow. In a sudden forceful movement, squeeze your hands together to compress the chest, then release. Repeat once every second for one minute, then check for heartbeat again. If there still is none, repeat the steps above. As soon as his heart starts beating, give artificial respiration to restore his breathing.

# Artificial respiration

Check your pet's heartbeat before beginning this procedure. If his heart has stopped, you must perform cardiac massage (see above) before giving artificial respiration.

If your dog has swallowed water while drowning, or choked on vomit or other liquids, lift his back legs as high above his head as possible for fifteen seconds and give three or four downward shakes to drain his airway. Gently pull his tongue out straight and clear any debris from his mouth with your hand or a cloth.

Place your hands on both sides of his chest just behind the elbow. Squeeze hard, then release. Repeat once every five seconds for one minute. If the movement of air in and out of the lungs seems blocked, open his mouth wide to see if an object is lodged in his throat, and remove it.

If he doesn't start breathing within one minute, grasp his muzzle firmly to hold his mouth shut. Take a deep breath, place your mouth over his nose, forming a tight seal, and blow gently. You should see his chest rise as air enters his lungs.

Listen for air leaving the lungs, then repeat every five seconds for one minute (ten to fifteen breaths). Check to see if he's breathing on his own, then repeat for another ten to fifteen breaths, and so on.

Have someone drive you and your dog to the veterinary clinic while you continue helping him to breathe. Don't give up even if there is no immediate response—dogs have been successfully revived after extended periods of artificial resuscitation, as long as the heart continues beating.

# Restraining an injured dog

An injured dog is also frightened, disoriented and in pain. He may not recognize you and could even snap at your hand when you try to help him. Unless he's unconscious, you'll need to muzzle him before you can safely check his injuries.

Use the slip-on muzzle in your first aid kit or improvise one from a handkerchief, scarf, or his own leash—whatever is handy. Since a muzzle doesn't work well on a short-nosed dog, loosely place a coat or blanket over his head instead. Whatever you use, be sure not to restrict your dog's breathing. And be ready to remove the muzzle *immediately* if your dog starts to vomit or has obvious difficulty in breathing.

# Broken bones

If your dog is unable to move his leg (or tail) or holds it at an odd angle, the bone may be fractured. Muzzle and restrain him before checking for broken bones, and handle the injured leg as little as possible.

If the bone is protruding from an open wound, cover with a clean cloth and control the bleeding with direct pressure.

If you can find a rigid stretcher (page 47) for moving your dog, don't waste time applying a splint. But if you have to jostle him in a blanket stretcher or carry him in your arms, you should immobilize the broken ends of the bone before moving him.

To apply a temporary splint, wrap a clean cloth around the leg for padding. Fold a newspaper, magazine or piece of cardboard in a U-shape around the leg or lay a strip of wood alongside it. Hold it all in place with adhesive tape or strips of cloth. The splint should extend beyond the joints above and below the fracture in order to hold the broken bones still.

# External bleeding

Your first concern is to stop any major bleeding. Minor wounds that are losing only a small amount of blood can wait for the veterinarian. But if blood is either spurting out or flowing steadily, you must act *now*.

Cover the wound with a sterile gauze pad or clean cloth if possible, or just place your hand directly over the wound. Apply firm, steady pressure until the bleeding stops. Secure with adhesive tape or an elastic bandage.

If the wound is on the leg (or tail) and you cannot slow down the blood loss after a few minutes of direct pressure, you must apply a tourniquet. This may result in having to amputate the limb, so use this method only as a last resort—always try direct pressure first. And *never* place the tourniquet over a joint or a fractured bone.

Wrap a handkerchief or other strip of cloth in a loose loop around the leg about one inch above the wound. Tie it with a double knot, then place a strong, short stick in the loop. Twist the stick to tighten the loop until the blood flow stops.

Now take him to the emergency clinic *fast*. On the way there, you *must* loosen the tourniquet every ten minutes to allow some blood to flow through the limb. Apply direct pressure to the wound to prevent further bleeding, and tighten the tourniquet again only if absolutely necessary.

# If you suspect internal bleeding

Hidden bleeding inside your dog's body can result from a fall or other traumatic blow or from certain kinds of poison. Even if he has no visible wounds, his internal organs may be seriously damaged. He may go into fatal shock without immediate veterinary care.

Signs of internal bleeding include: pale skin, gums and tongue; bleeding from ears, mouth or anus; bloody vomit or stool; difficulty breathing; or extreme sleepiness from which you cannot rouse him. Symptoms may appear immediately after the accident or hours later, even if he seemed fine initially.

Use a rigid stretcher (page 47) if at all possible to move your dog to and from your car on the way to the emergency clinic. Keep him warm and try not to jostle him any more than you absolutely have to.

# Poisoning

Your dog can be poisoned by eating or drinking a toxic substance, inhaling it, licking it off his coat or paws or absorbing it through his skin. Poisons that your pet might encounter when traveling include spilled antifreeze, toxic bait intended for insects or rodents (or their dead bodies), garbage that contains poisonous substances, or chemical sprays that have been applied to plants that your dog chews or rolls in. Even your own prescription medicine can poison your pet if he discovers it in your luggage and accidentally swallows some while playing with this new "rattle toy."

Signs of poisoning include: drooling or difficulty swallowing; trembling; vomiting; shallow rapid breathing; twitching; seizure or coma.

## Contact poisoning

Rinse his coat immediately with lots of water—fresh water, sea water, mud puddle by the side of the road, whatever it takes to dilute the chemical and wash it away. Wear rubber gloves, if available, to avoid getting the toxic chemicals on your own skin. Then wash him with mild hand soap or shampoo and rinse thoroughly with clean water. Repeat until all traces of the chemicals are removed.

See or call a veterinarian for further instructions.

## Swallowed poisons

Depending on the type of poison, you must choose between two very different first aid treatments—for **corrosive chemicals (Method A)** or **noncorrosive substances (Method B)**.

Your first step is to determine what kind of poison your pet has swallowed. If the product container is available, it may identify the ingredients, the antidote and whether or not to induce vomiting.

If you can't identify the type of poison, check inside your dog's mouth and throat. If the tissues look burned or raw as if from a corrosive substance, use Method A. Otherwise use Method B.

Bring the poison container itself if at all possible, or else try to collect a sample of the poison in a zip-top plastic bag from your first aid kit. Also, collect any material your dog vomits up. These samples can help the veterinarian identify the exact antidote that your dog will need.

**Method A. When the poison is CORROSIVE, such as an acid, alkali, or petroleum product:**
**NEUTRALIZE THE POISON**
**BUT DO NOT INDUCE VOMITING!**

These poisons will injure your dog's mouth and throat even further if he throws up. Instead, rinse his mouth thoroughly with water to wash away any remaining chemicals. Then make him swallow two to three tablespoons of olive oil or up to one cup of milk.

Keep him warm with a blanket or coat while you rush him to the nearest veterinary clinic.

**Method B. When the poison is NOT corrosive:**
**INDUCE VOMITING IMMEDIATELY!**

Mix equal parts of hydrogen peroxide and water. Make him swallow 1½ tablespoonfuls of this mixture for each ten pounds of body weight.

Example: the dose for a 60-lb dog would be 6 x 1½ = 9 tablespoons

If he doesn't vomit within ten minutes, repeat this dosage, but not more than three doses altogether.

After he vomits, make him swallow a mixture of three to four tablespoonfuls of activated charcoal in a cup of warm water. Wrap him in a blanket or coat while you rush him to the nearest veterinary clinic.

# A special warning about antifreeze

Every year, dogs die from ingesting antifreeze that has dripped from leaking car radiators. This coolant has a sweet smell and taste that attracts many pets to drink it—but even a tiny spoonful can be deadly.

If your dog has swallowed even the tiniest amount of antifreeze, induce vomiting *immediately* and then rush him to a veterinarian for an antidote injection—but you must work *fast*. Minutes can make the difference between losing him or saving his life.

🐕 Pet-safe antifreeze is now available at auto supply stores and service centers—ask for it the next time your car's radiator fluid is changed.

# Moving an injured dog

The safest way to move your pet is on a *stretcher,* a flat rigid surface that won't flex under his weight. A piece of wood or heavy cardboard will do, or even an air mattress blown up as firm as you can make it. If that's unavailable, use a blanket, tarp or piece of clothing that you can carry by its corners to make as flat a surface as possible.

Slide your dog onto the stretcher without twisting or shaking him. If possible, have a helper lift his hindquarters and abdomen at exactly the same moment that you lift his head and shoulders.

If you are alone and can't find a rigid stretcher, you'll have to carry him in your arms. Place one arm around his hindquarters and the other around his front legs at the shoulder, supporting his head on your arm. Keep his spine as straight as possible.

# Treating for shock

"Shock" refers to a sudden collapse of your dog's circulatory system, which can be brought on by serious injury or other trauma. All his bodily functions are shutting down. You must be very careful not to jostle or quickly move him, because any rapid movement can bring on the *fatal* stages of shock.

Symptoms of shock include: extreme muscle weakness; loss of bladder and bowel control; shallow, rapid breathing and pulse; pale or whitish gums and mouth; he feels cold to the touch; he appears asleep or semiconscious.

Pull his tongue out straight to clear the airway—but be very cautious, as even the most gentle dog may bite when dazed from great pain or fear. Try to get his head lower than his body to encourage circulation, unless he has a head injury, in which case you should keep his head level with his body.

Cover him with a blanket or coat to stabilize his body temperature; the only exception would be if his temperature is already too high (as in heatstroke). Now take him to a veterinary clinic for follow-up care. If possible, call ahead so the staff can prepare for the emergency procedures that your pet will need as soon as he gets there.

# Treating burns

Watch for hazards that can lead to your dog being accidentally burned—sparks from a beach bonfire, hot liquids spilled from a tiny kitchen unit, licking meat juices from a hot barbecue grill or brushing against a space heater.

Chewing on an electrical cord can lead to burns in the mouth as well as unconsciousness, shock, and even death. Be sure to *unplug the cord* before touching your dog.

If the burned skin is red but not broken, gently run cold water over the affected area or cover it with an ice pack or a cold wet towel.

If the burned area is heavily blistered, raw, weeping or bleeding, blackened or whitish, *do not apply ice or water*—just cover with a sterile gauze pad or clean cloth. Treat for shock (page 47) and take your dog to the nearest veterinarian *immediately.*

# Minor cuts and scrapes

When Ginger is hot on the trail of a squirrel (though she never catches one), she'll gleefully charge into the thickest blackberry patch. She eventually comes back covered with thorns and scratches, grinning like a fool and enormously pleased with herself. So I've gotten plenty of practice at removing stickers and cleaning up her scrapes and scratches.

Rinse away any dirt in your pet's wound with clean water, then swab with hydrogen peroxide. If the wound is still bleeding, cover with a gauze pad and apply pressure until the bleeding stops. Then lightly apply an antibiotic ointment such as *Panalog* or *Neosporin*.

If the wound is more than just a scratch, or your dog just won't leave it alone, cover the area with a gauze pad held in place with adhesive tape or an elastic wrap bandage. Elastic bandages are much easier to work with than sticky tape, especially after your dog starts fiddling with it and you have to readjust things.

And of course, for anything more than a minor scratch or scrape, you should have a veterinarian take a look at it.

# Removing foreign objects

Use common sense on whether or not to try removing an embedded object such as a burr or porcupine quill. In some cases, incorrect removal can do more harm than if you just keep your dog as motionless as possible while you drive him to the nearest clinic, to let the veterinarian do the job right.

## From the ears

Use tweezers to gently remove seeds or burrs from the *outer* ear canal. If your dog still shakes his head or scratches repeatedly at his ear, seeds or other tiny intruders may also be deeper inside the ear canal and must be removed by a veterinarian.

## From the eyes

If your pet paws at his eye or rubs his face along the ground, gently hold the eyelid open and check for seeds or debris. Use sterile eye drops or saline solution to wash away a loose object. Don't try to remove an object that is embedded into the surface of the eye. Instead, take him to the nearest veterinary clinic *right away.*

## From everywhere else

You're already familiar with this routine if your dog loves to crash through the underbrush like Ginger does. Run your hands gently over his face, body and feet to check for thorns. If he's limping or holding up his paw, he has already zeroed in on the problem for you.

Use tweezers to pull out embedded thorns or splinters. When a foreign object is buried too deeply to find, either soak the affected body part in salt water (one teaspoon salt per cup of lukewarm water) several times a day until the object works its way up to the surface where you can remove it, or else have a veterinarian remove it.

Sharp objects such as porcupine quills or a fishhook can be removed with pliers. First use the wire cutter notches at the center of the pliers to clip off the tip of each porcupine quill or the barbed point of the fishhook *if it is exposed.* But if the fishhook point is hidden below the skin surface, or if your dog won't submit to having the objects pulled out, take him straight to a veterinarian.

When finished, rinse all wounds with hydrogen peroxide.

## Watch out for ticks

Examine your dog closely after outdoor activities, especially his head, shoulders and feet. Forget the old wives' tales about using a match to burn the tick off, applying gasoline or petroleum jelly to loosen its grip, and so on. Dousing the tick with alcohol or nail polish remover *may* make it easier to remove.

Use tweezers to grab the tick by its head, very close to the dog's skin, and firmly pull it out. Don't squeeze its fat abdomen—doing so might force disease-carrying blood back into the bite wound. Above all, *don't use your fingers.* Ticks can carry Lyme disease and Rocky Mountain spotted fever, both of which are dangerous to humans.

Swab the bite area with hydrogen peroxide. If the skin becomes red or irritated, see a veterinarian for follow-up treatment.

# Treating an upset stomach

Car sickness is one of the most common complaints for the traveling dog—whether it's because he's fearful of the car, or just overly excited about coming along. Try reducing his stress level with practice rides as described on page 28. Don't give him food or water for at least an hour before traveling. And always allow him a few minutes of exercise and a last-minute chance to relieve himself before loading him back into the car.

If your dog still gets carsick, try giving him a small spoonful of honey, a piece of hard candy or a spoonful of plain vanilla ice cream to calm his stomach. *However, you should never give your dog any food containing chocolate, as it can be toxic!*

If these simple remedies don't help, ask your veterinarian about stronger medicines for motion sickness.

An upset stomach can also be caused by eating unfamiliar or spoiled food, or drinking unfamiliar water—contaminants in the water or a different mineral content can throw your pet's system for a loop. Give him two teaspoons of Kaopectate for each ten pounds of body weight, once every four hours.

If the problem doesn't clear up within 24 hours, this may be a symptom of a more serious illness—see a veterinarian.

# Treating diarrhea

This may be a temporary upset caused by the stress of unfamiliar surroundings, food or water, or a symptom of a more serious illness. Give two teaspoons of Kaopectate for each ten pounds of body weight, once every four hours.

See a veterinarian if the diarrhea doesn't clear up within 24 hours or if other symptoms appear, such as labored breathing, bloody stool, either a rise or a drop in body temperature, listlessness or loss of appetite.

# Dealing with heat problems

Summer can mean added hazards for your pet. Shorthaired dogs can become sunburned just as easily as people can. Older or overweight pets are more prone to heat problems, as are short-nosed breeds and dogs who are taking certain medications. Heat problems are even more likely if the humidity is also high.

When walking your dog, pay special attention to the surface underfoot— if it's too hot for your bare feet, then it's too hot for your dog's paws as well.

Heatstroke can be caused by too much exercise in the hot sun, not drinking enough water, or simply from sitting in a hot car. On a sunny 80° day, the temperature inside your parked car (even with the windows partly rolled down) will climb well above 100° in just minutes, putting your pet in danger of permanent damage to the brain and internal organs, and even death.

## Recognizing the danger signs

Symptoms of heatstroke may include some or all of the following: frenzied barking; a vacant expression or wild-eyed stare; rapid or heavy panting; rapid pulse; dizziness or weakness; vomiting or diarrhea; deep red or purple tongue and gums (the normal color is light pink, except in breeds where the gums and tongue are naturally black); twitching, convulsions or coma.

Use a rectal thermometer to check your dog's body temperature. Normal body temperature is 100° to 101°—but it can rise to 106° or more with heatstroke.

### Treating for heatstroke

First, get your dog out of the sun. Then cover him with towels soaked in cool water, or pour cool water over him every few minutes. *Do not* immerse him in ice water or apply ice directly to his skin, but an ice pack is okay if wrapped in a towel.

Give him a small amount of cool water to drink, or let him lick ice cubes or a bit of plain vanilla ice cream. (Remember—no chocolate!) As soon as his body temperature begins to come down, take him to the nearest veterinarian for follow-up care.

# Keeping your pet safe in cold weather

Many dogs, Ginger included, love outdoor activities in the snow. But don't assume that your dog is as safe and comfortable as you are in your insulated boots and down-filled clothing. Wintertime hazards include hypothermia, frostbite, and irritation from road salt and other de-icing chemicals.

After playing outside, wash off any remaining ice or road salt and towel him dry. Then give him a well-deserved rest in a warm place—but not too close to a fireplace or space heater. If he's really chilled, he could burn himself without even feeling the heat.

### Treating for hypothermia

Smaller or older dogs are most likely to suffer from hypothermia. However, exposure to the cold *when he's wet* can be extremely hazardous for any dog, especially if immersed in icy water for even a few minutes. When your pet starts to lag behind you instead of bounding ahead, that's the signal to get him back indoors and warmed up. If he becomes listless, ignores your calls or just wants to lie down in the snow, you've definitely stayed out too long—you need to warm him up right away.

Dry him off and boost his circulation by rubbing vigorously with a towel. Wrap him in a warm blanket and offer warm (not hot) water if he's willing to drink it. If his body temperature has dropped below 98.5° take him to a veterinarian *immediately.*

## Treating for frostbite

When the weather turns windy, check frequently to see if your dog's feet, ears, and tail are getting pale or numb. If so, bring him indoors right away.

Massage the affected areas *very gently* to encourage circulation—rough handling can bruise damaged tissues. Soak frostbitten paws or tail in lukewarm (90°) water to gradually restore circulation. Keep him warm and check with a veterinarian for follow-up care.

# 6: Emergency Clinics

Time is a critical factor when your pet needs emergency medical care. Your best bet for quickly finding a veterinary clinic is the local phone book. Always call ahead, even during their posted office hours. That gives their staff a chance to prepare so that any lifesaving procedures that the doctor may deem necessary will be ready the minute your pet arrives. They can also give directions so that you don't waste time or get lost along the way.

It is also a good idea to glance through the local Yellow Pages when you first arrive at your vacation destination, to see what veterinary clinics are located near you. And remember that even though the nearest clinic in your area may not be open at the moment, many do offer 24-hour "on call" emergency service. When you phone them after normal business hours, their answering service takes down your name, the nature of the emergency, and the phone number you're calling from. That information is immediately relayed to the doctor who is "on call" at the time. He or she then calls you back with either instructions for handling the situation yourself or directions for meeting the doctor at the clinic.

Some of the emergency clinics listed on the following pages are open 24 hours/day, every day of the year. Several more are "after-hours" clinics, meaning that they are open all night on weeknights, and around the clock on weekends and holidays.

# California's Emergency Veterinary Clinics

| Anaheim | **East Hills Animal Hospital**<br>8285 E Santa Ana Canyon Rd Suite 150<br>714-921-2500<br>24 hours/day, 365 days/year |
|---|---|

Arroyo Grande

**Central Coast Pet Emergency**
1558 W Branch St
805-489-6573

Monday–Thursday 6 PM–8 AM
Friday 6 PM–Monday 8 AM
Holidays 24 hours/day

Atascadero

**Atascadero Pet Center**
9575 El Camino Real
805-466-3880

24 hours/day, 365 days/year

Bakersfield

**Animal Emergency & Urgent Care**
4300 Easton Dr # 1
661-322-6019

Monday–Friday 5:30 PM–8 AM
Saturday Noon–Monday 8 AM
Holidays 24 hours/day

Bellflower

**Animal Care Clinic**
10404 Rosecrans Ave
562-920-1795

24 hours/day, 365 days/year

Bellflower

**VCA Lakewood Animal Hospital**
17801 Lakewood Blvd
562-633-8126

24 hours/day, 365 days/year

Berkeley

**Pet Emergency Treatment Service**
1048 University Ave
510-548-6684

Monday–Thursday 6 PM–8 AM
Friday 6 PM–Monday 8 AM
Holidays 24 hours/day

| | |
|---|---|
| Berkeley | **Special Veterinary Service**<br>at Berkeley Dog & Cat Hospital<br>2126 Haste St<br>510-848-5041<br>24 hours/day, 365 days/year |
| Cameron Park | **Mother Lode Pet Emergency Clinic**<br>4050 Durock Rd<br>530-676-9044<br>Monday–Thursday 6 PM–8 AM<br>Friday 6 PM–Monday 8 AM<br>Holidays 24 hours/day |
| Campbell | **United Emergency Animal Clinic**<br>1657 S Bascom Ave<br>408-371-6252<br>Monday–Thursday 6 PM–8 AM<br>Friday 6 PM–Monday 8 AM<br>Holidays 24 hours/day |
| Capitola | **Pacific Veterinary Emergency**<br>1980 41st Ave<br>831-476-2584<br>Monday–Thursday 6 PM–8 AM<br>Friday 6 PM–Monday 8 AM<br>Holidays 24 hours/day |
| Carmichael | **Sacramento Animal Medical Group**<br>4990 Manzanita Ave<br>916-331-7430<br>24 hours/day, 365 days/year |
| Chico | **North Valley Veterinary Service**<br>2525 Dominic Dr<br>530-899-1720<br>Monday–Friday 5:30 PM–8 AM<br>Saturday Noon–Monday 8 AM<br>Holidays 24 hours/day |
| Chula Vista | **A Cat & Dog Emergency Clinic**<br>3438 Bonita Rd<br>619-427-2881<br>24 hours/day, 365 days/year |

| Concord | **Veterinary Emergency Clinic**<br>1410 Monument Blvd<br>925-798-2900<br>24 hours/day, 365 days/year |
|---|---|
| Corona | **Aacacia Animal Hospital**<br>939 W 6th St<br>951-371-1002<br>24 hours/day, 365 days/year |
| Diamond Bar | **East Valley Emergency Pet Clinic**<br>938 N Diamond Bar Blvd<br>909-861-5737<br>Monday–Friday 6 PM–8 AM<br>Saturday Noon–Monday 8 AM<br>Holidays 24 hours/day |
| Dublin | **Emergencies–Vetcare**<br>7660 Amador Valley Blvd<br>925-556-1234<br>24 hours/day, 365 days/year |
| El Monte | **Emergency Pet Clinic**<br>3254 Santa Anita Ave<br>626-579-4550<br>Monday–Friday 6 PM–8 AM<br>Saturday Noon–Monday 8 AM<br>Holidays 24 hours/day |
| Encinitas | **North Coast Veterinary**<br>414 Encinitas Blvd<br>760-632-1072<br>24 hours/day, 365 days/year |
| Escondido | **Animal Urgent Care–Escondido**<br>2430 S Escondido Blvd # A<br>760-738-9600<br>Monday–Thursday 6 PM–8 AM<br>Friday 6 PM–Monday 8 AM<br>Holidays 24 hours/day |

| | |
|---|---|
| Fair Oaks | **Greenback Veterinary Hospital**<br>8311 Greenback Lane<br>916-725-1541<br>24 hours/day, 365 days/year |
| Fairfield | **Solano Pet Emergency Clinic**<br>4437 Central Pl Suite B3<br>707-864-1444 or 707-554-6311<br>Monday–Thursday 6 PM–8 AM<br>Friday 6 PM–Monday 8 AM<br>Holidays 24 hours/day |
| Fountain Valley | **All-Care Animal Referral Center**<br>18440 Amistad St # E<br>714-963-0909 or 800-944-PETS<br>24 hours/day, 365 days/year |
| Fremont | **American Animal Hospital**<br>37177 Fremont Blvd<br>510-791-0464<br>24 hours/day, 365 days/year |
| Fremont | **Ohlone Veterinary Emergency**<br>1618 Washington Blvd<br>510-657-6620<br>Monday–Thursday 6 PM–8 AM<br>Friday 6 PM–Monday 8 AM<br>Holidays 24 hours/day |
| Fresno | **Veterinary Emergency Service**<br>1639 N Fresno St<br>559-486-0520<br>24 hours/day, 365 days/year |
| Fullerton | **Airport Animal Hospital**<br>2433 W Commonwealth Ave<br>714-879-4531<br>24 hours/day, 365 days/year |

| | |
|---|---|
| Garden Grove | **Orange County Emergency Pet Clinic**<br>12750 Garden Grove Blvd<br>714-537-3032<br>Monday–Friday 6 PM–8 AM<br>Saturday Noon–Monday 8 AM<br>Holidays 24 hours/day |
| Granada Hills | **Chatoak Emergency Veterinary Clinic**<br>17659 Chatsworth St<br>818-368-5150 or 818-363-7444<br>24 hours/day, 365 days/year |
| Grand Terrace | **Animal Emergency Clinic**<br>12022 La Crosse Ave<br>909-825-9350<br>Monday–Thursday 6 PM–8 AM<br>Friday 6 PM–Monday 8 AM<br>Holidays 24 hours/day |
| La Habra | **North Orange County Pet Clinic**<br>1474 S Harbor Blvd<br>714-441-2925<br>Monday–Thursday 6 PM–8 AM<br>Friday Noon–Monday 8 AM<br>Holidays 24 hours/day |
| La Mesa | **A Pet Emergency & Specialty Center**<br>5232 Jackson Dr # 105<br>619-462-4800<br>24 hours/day, 365 days/year |
| Laguna Niguel | **Crown Valley Animal Care Center**<br>28892 Crown Valley Pkwy<br>949-495-1123<br>24 hours/day, 365 days/year |
| Lancaster | **Animal Emergency Clinic**<br>1055 W Avenue M # 101<br>661-723-3959<br>Monday–Friday 6 PM–8 AM<br>Saturday Noon–Monday 8 AM |

| | |
|---|---|
| Loomis | **Loomis Basin Veterinary Clinic**<br>3901 Sierra College Blvd<br>916-782-9797<br>24 hours/day, 365 days/year |
| Los Altos | **Adobe Animal Hospital**<br>396 1st St<br>650-948-9661<br>24 hours/day, 365 days/year |
| Los Angeles | **Animal Specialty Group**<br>4641 Colorado Blvd<br>818-244-7977<br>Monday–Thursday 2 PM–8 AM<br>Friday 2 PM–Monday 8 AM<br>Holidays 24 hours/day |
| Los Angeles | **Animal Surgical Emergency Center**<br>1535 S Sepulveda Blvd<br>310-473-1561 or 310-473-5906<br>24 hours/day, 365 days/year |
| Los Angeles | **Eagle Rock Emergency Pet Clinic**<br>4252 Eagle Rock Blvd<br>323-254-7382<br>Monday–Friday 6 PM–8 AM<br>Saturday Noon–Monday 8 AM<br>Holidays 24 hours/day |
| Los Angeles | **VCA West Los Angeles Animal Hospital**<br>1818 S Sepulveda Blvd<br>310-473-2951<br>24 hours/day, 365 days/year |
| Mission Viejo | **Animal Urgent Care–South Orange**<br>28085 Hillcrest<br>949-364-6228<br>Monday–Friday 6 PM–8 AM<br>Saturday Noon–Monday 8 AM<br>Holidays 24 hours/day |

| | |
|---|---|
| Modesto | **Veterinary Emergency Clinic**<br>1800 Prescott Rd<br>209-527-8844<br>Monday–Thursday 6 PM–8 AM<br>Friday 6 PM–Monday 8 AM<br>Holidays 24 hours/day |
| Monterey | **Monterey Peninsula–Salinas Veterinary**<br>2 Harris Ct # A1<br>831-373-7374<br>Monday–Thursday 5:30 PM–8 AM<br>Friday 5:30 PM–Monday 8 AM<br>Holidays 24 hours/day |
| Murrieta | **California Veterinary Specialists**<br>25100 Hancock Ave # 116<br>951-600-9803<br>24 hours/day, 365 days/year |
| Newport Beach | **Central Orange County Emergency Animal Clinic**<br>3720 Campus Dr # D<br>949-261-7979<br>Monday–Friday 6 PM–8 AM<br>Saturday Noon–Monday 8 AM<br>Holidays 24 hours/day |
| Norwalk | **Crossroads Animal Emergency and Trauma Center**<br>11057 Rosecrans Ave<br>562-863-2522<br>Monday–Friday 6 PM–8 AM<br>Saturday 4 PM–Monday 8 AM<br>24 hours/day, 365 days/year |
| Palo Alto | **South Peninsula Veterinary**<br>3045 Middlefield Rd<br>650-494-1461<br>Monday–Friday 6 PM–8 AM<br>Saturday Noon–Monday 8 AM<br>Holidays 24 hours/day |

| | |
|---|---|
| Pasadena | **Animal Emergency Clinic**<br>2121 E Foothill Blvd<br>626-564-0704<br>Monday–Friday 6 PM–8 AM<br>Saturday Noon–Monday 8 AM ➤<br>Holidays 24 hours/day |
| Poway | **Animal Emergency Clinic**<br>12775 Poway Rd<br>858-748-7387<br>Monday–Thursday 6 PM–8 AM<br>Friday 6 PM–Monday 8 AM<br>Holidays 24 hours/day |
| Rancho Santa Fe | **Criticare Veterinary Specialty Hospital**<br>6525 Calle Del Nido<br>858-759-2255<br>24 hours/day, 365 days/year |
| Reseda | **McClave Veterinary Hospital**<br>6950 Reseda Blvd<br>818-881-5102<br>24 hours/day, 365 days/year |
| Rohnert Park | **Animal Care Center–Sonoma County**<br>6470 Redwood Dr<br>707-584-4343<br>24 hours/day, 365 days/year |
| Roseville | **Atlantic Veterinary Hospital &<br>Pet Emergency Center**<br>1100 Atlantic St<br>916-783-4655<br>24 hours/day, 365 days/year |
| Sacramento | **Emergency Animal Clinic of Sacramento**<br>9700 Business Park Dr Suite 404<br>916-362-3111<br>24 hours/day, 365 days/year |
| Sacramento | **Mueller Pet Medical Center**<br>6420 Freeport Blvd<br>916-428-9202<br>24 hours/day, 365 days/year |

| | |
|---|---|
| Sacramento | **Sacramento Emergency Veterinary Clinic**<br>2201 El Camino Ave<br>916-922-3425<br>Monday–Thursday 6 PM–8 AM<br>Friday 6 PM–Monday 8 AM<br>Holidays 24 hours/day |
| San Diego | **A Animal ER of San Diego**<br>5610 Kearny Mesa Rd<br>858-569-0600<br>Monday–Friday 6 PM–8 AM<br>Friday 6 PM–Monday 8 AM<br>Holidays 24 hours/day |
| San Diego | **Emergency Animal Clinic**<br>2317 Hotel Circle South # A<br>619-299-2400<br>24 hours/day, 365 days/year |
| San Francisco | **All Animals Emergency Hospital**<br>1333 9th Ave<br>415-566-0531<br>Monday–Thursday 6 PM–8 AM<br>Friday 6 PM–Monday 8 AM<br>Holidays 24 hours/day<br>24 hours/day, 365 days/year |
| San Jose | **Emergency Animal Clinic**<br>5440 Thornwood Dr<br>408-578-5622<br>Monday–Thursday 6 PM–8 AM<br>Friday 6 PM–Monday 8 AM<br>Holidays 24 hours/day |
| San Leandro | **Animal Medical Emergency**<br>655 Lewelling Blvd # 302<br>925-261-9111<br>24 hours/day, 365 days/year |

| | |
|---|---|
| San Leandro | **Bay Area Veterinary Medical Group**<br>14790 Washington Ave<br>510-352-6080<br>Monday–Thursday 6 PM–8 AM<br>Friday 6 PM–Monday 8 AM<br>Holidays 24 hours/day |
| San Marcos | **California Veterinary Specialists**<br>100 N Rancho Santa Fe Rd # 133<br>760-734-4433<br>24 hours/day, 365 days/year |
| San Mateo | **Northern Peninsula Veterinary**<br>227 N Amphlett Blvd<br>650-348-2575 or 650-348-2576<br>Monday–Thursday 5:30 PM–8 AM<br>Friday 5:30 PM–Monday 8 AM<br>Holidays 24 hours/day |
| San Rafael | **Pet Emergency & Specialty–Marin**<br>901 Francisco Blvd E<br>415-456-7372<br>Monday–Thursday 5:30 PM–8 AM<br>Friday 5:30 PM–Monday 8 AM<br>Holidays 24 hours/day |
| Santa Barbara | **C.A.R.E. Hospital**<br>301 E Haley St<br>805-899-2273<br>24 hours/day, 365 days/year |
| Santa Barbara | **Pacific Emergency Pet Hospital**<br>2963 State St<br>805-682-5120<br>Monday–Thursday 6 PM–8 AM<br>Friday 6 PM–Monday 8 AM<br>Holidays 24 hours/day |
| Santa Cruz | **Santa Cruz Veterinary Hospital**<br>2585 Soquel Dr<br>831-475-5400<br>24 hours/day, 365 days/year |

| | |
|---|---|
| Santa Monica | **North Bay Animal Emergency**<br>1304 Wilshire Blvd<br>310-451-8962<br><div align="right">Monday–Friday 6 PM–8 AM<br>Saturday 6 PM–Monday 8 AM<br>Holidays 24 hours/day</div> |
| Santa Rosa | **Emergency Animal Hospital**<br>1946 Santa Rosa Ave<br>707-544-1647<br><div align="right">Monday–Thursday 6 PM–8 AM<br>Friday 6 PM–Monday 8 AM<br>Holidays 24 hours/day</div> |
| Santa Rosa | **Pet Care Veterinary Hospital**<br>1370 Fulton Rd<br>707-579-5900<br><div align="right">24 hours/day, 365 days/year</div> |
| Sherman Oaks | **Emergency Animal Clinic**<br>at Beverly Oaks Animal Hospital<br>14302 Ventura Blvd<br>818-788-2022<br><div align="right">24 hours/day, 365 days/year</div> |
| South Pasadena | **TLC Pet Medical Center**<br>1412 Huntington Dr<br>626-441-8555<br><div align="right">24 hours/day, 365 days/year</div> |
| Stockton | **Associated Veterinary Emergency Medical Services**<br>3008 E Hammer Lane # 115<br>209-952-8387<br><div align="right">Monday–Thursday 6 PM–8 AM<br>Friday 6 PM–Monday 8 AM<br>Holidays 24 hours/day</div> |

| | |
|---|---|
| Studio City | **Animal Emergency Center**<br>11740 Ventura Blvd<br>818-760-3882<br>Monday–Thursday 6 PM–8 AM<br>Friday 5 PM–Monday 8 AM<br>Holidays 24 hours/day |
| Temecula | **Emergency Pet Clinic**<br>27443 Jefferson Ave<br>951-695-5044<br>Monday–Thursday 6 PM–8 AM<br>Friday 6 PM–Monday 8 AM<br>Holidays 24 hours/day |
| Thousand Oaks | **Pet Emergency Clinic**<br>2967 N Moorpark Rd<br>805-492-2436<br>24 hours/day, 365 days/year |
| Thousand Palms | **Animal Emergency Clinic**<br>72374 Ramon Rd<br>760-343-3438<br>Monday–Friday 5 PM–8 AM<br>Saturday Noon–Monday 8 AM<br>Holidays 24 hours/day |
| Torrance | **Animal Emergency Medical Center**<br>3511 Pacific Coast Hwy # A<br>310-325-3000<br>24 hours/day, 365 days/year |
| Torrance | **Emergency Pet Clinic–South Bay**<br>2325 Torrance Blvd<br>310-320-8300<br>Monday–Friday 6 PM–8 AM<br>Saturday Noon–Monday 8 AM<br>Holidays 24 hours/day |
| Tustin | **Advanced Critical Care**<br>3021 Edinger Ave<br>949-654-8950<br>24 hours/day, 365 days/year |

| | |
|---|---|
| Tustin | **Advanced Veterinary Specialty**<br>2965 Edinger Ave<br>949-653-9300<br><br>24 hours/day, 365 days/year |
| Upland | **Emergency Pet Clinic–Inland**<br>10 W 7th St<br>909-931-7871<br><br>Monday–Friday 6 PM–8 AM<br>Saturday Noon–Monday 8 AM<br>Holidays 24 hours/day |
| Upland | **VCA Central Animal Hospital**<br>281 N Central Ave<br>909-981-2855<br><br>24 hours/day, 365 days/year |
| Ventura | **Pet Emergency Clinic**<br>2301 S Victoria Ave<br>805-642-8562<br><br>Monday–Thursday 6 PM–8 AM<br>Friday 6 PM–Monday 8 AM<br>Holidays 24 hours/day |
| Victorville | **Animal Emergency Clinic**<br>15532 Bear Valley Rd<br>760-962-1122<br><br>Monday–Thursday 6 PM–8 AM<br>Friday 6 PM–Monday 8 AM<br>Holidays 24 hours/day |
| Visalia | **Tulare–Kings Veterinary Service**<br>4946 W Mineral King Ave<br>559-739-7054<br><br>Monday–Thursday 5 PM–8 AM<br>Friday 5 PM–Monday 8 AM<br>Holidays 24 hours/day |
| Westwood | **California Animal Hospital**<br>1736 S Sepulveda Blvd<br>310-479-3336<br><br>24 hours/day, 365 days/year |

Woodland Hills    **Animal Emergency Clinic**
20051 Ventura Blvd
818-887-2262

Monday–Thursday 6 PM–8 AM
Friday 6 PM–Monday 8 AM
Holidays 24 hours/day

# 7: If Your Dog Gets Lost

You've heard the saying "carry an umbrella and you'll never get rained on." Hopefully, being prepared in case your dog gets lost will work the same way for you. And it will remind you of how important—and easy—it is to *prevent* losing him.

The basic prevention measures (you've seen all these before) include:

- Make sure your dog is *always* wearing his collar with ID tags attached. (See page 15 for information on proper travel tags.)

- Attach the leash to his collar *before* letting him out of your car or motel room—and hold onto the other end!

- *Never* leave him alone and unrestrained—he should be in his travel crate or at least inside your car, with adequate ventilation and shade.

That said, if by some chance you and your dog do get separated, don't panic. Your cool-headed actions now, plus a few advance preparations that you wisely made before leaving home, will maximize your chances of finding him as quickly as possible.

## Preparing a Lost Dog poster

Your first advance effort should be in creating a master lost-and-found poster, complete with your dog's photo and detailed description. Feel free to copy the fill-in-the-blanks poster on the following page and use it to create your own poster. (Enlarge it to 8.5" x 11" or even bigger for better visibility.)

First, write a brief description of your pet. Include his name, age, breed, sex (and if neutered or spayed), coat and eye color, height (at top of head or ears when standing), weight, and any special characteristics, such as a crooked ear or a limp.

# LOST DOG

Name:

Breed:

Age:

Sex:

Ht:                Wt:

Eye color:

Coat color & length:

Collar & ID tags:

Distinctive markings or behaviors:

Last seen at:

Owners:

Home address:

Home Phone (call COLLECT!):

Staying locally at:

Dates at this location:

Local phone:

(Call collect or leave message and we will reimburse you.)

## REWARD!

```
┌ ─ ─ ─ ─ ─ ─ ─ ─ ┐
│                 │
│                 │
│  Attach photo here  │
│                 │
│                 │
│                 │
└ ─ ─ ─ ─ ─ ─ ─ ─ ┘
```

Second, find a recent close-up photo of your pet, or take a new one right now. It should clearly show his color, any distinctive markings and his relative size. For example, photograph your dog standing beside a person or a car—if you personally appear in the photo alongside your dog, that also provides visual proof of ownership.

List your home phone number (for leaving a message) and a cell phone number, if you'll have that phone with you on your travels; if not, include another number that will be answered by a live person who can receive and relay messages for you. Leave blank spaces for the name, address and phone number of your motel. You'll add that information if and when you actually use the poster.

Store the poster and photo with your dog's other travel papers, which I recommend keeping in a plastic bag inside his first aid kit. Also tuck in a broad tipped marking pen.

## Searching for your lost dog

As soon as you realize your pet is missing, begin searching the immediate area in an ever-widening spiral pattern. Keep calling your dog's name—if he's within the sound of your voice, *he'll* most likely find *you.* Try to enlist the aid of other people in your search.

It's important to search *on foot,* not in your car, for several reasons. First, if you're walking, your dog is more likely to catch your scent and come back to you. Second, if you're cruising along in the car, your pet may hear you call him, but by the time he runs to that location, you could be a block—or a mile—away, missing him altogether.

## When to call for reinforcements

If you've already searched for an hour or two without finding your dog, it's time to move on to public announcements. Phone the police or county sheriff's office, the dog pound or humane society, and the local veterinary clinics to see if anyone has already found your pet.

Remember to tell them if your dog has been implanted with an identification microchip (see page 15 for more information).

Leave your phone numbers with everyone you speak to, and check back with them periodically. Also ask if any local radio or TV station broadcasts lost pet announcements as a public service. (Then after you find your dog, be sure to let everyone know, so they don't continue to broadcast the alert.)

# Putting up Lost Dog posters

If you've already checked with the local authorities and still haven't found your dog, you'll need to start posting "Lost Dog" notices around the area. That way, when someone does find him, they'll know how to contact you.

Get out your master poster. Attach your pet's photo and fill in the name, address, and phone number of the place where you're staying. Then take it to the local quick print shop and run off *color copies* for posting around town. If you can't find a print shop, pharmacies and "one-stop shopping" stores are also likely to have copy machines available, though you may have to settle for black-and-white rather than color copies.

Beginning at the location where your dog was last seen and spiraling outward again, start putting up your posters wherever people congregate:

- On bulletin boards in parks, shopping malls, or in front of convenience stores

- In store windows—be sure to ask for permission first!

- At bus stops or parking lot entrances

- On street signs or light posts, especially where cars are likely to be stopping or moving slowly

- Near schools or churches

Since your motel's phone number appears alongside your own phone numbers on each poster, notify them of your situation right away. If you can, have a family member stay by the phone in your room in case that all-important "Found Dog" call comes in while you're out searching. If not, see if the folks at the front desk can take messages for you.

Continue to check back periodically at the place where your dog disappeared, in case he returns there. By the end of the day, he'll be hungry, thirsty, and anxious about being separated from you. Leave a handful of his food there, along with something that has your scent on it, such as a dirty sock. Finding this sign of you during the night may encourage him to stay there until you come back in the morning.

Stay in the local area as long as possible. Even if you don't find your pet right away, he may well turn up after another day or two. A local person may take him in overnight, then deliver him to the local dog pound or animal shelter the next day.

If you do have to leave town without him, be sure to leave your home phone number with everyone—motel management, police, dog pound, local veterinarians—along with instructions to call you "COLLECT" if necessary.

And of course, check your home phone often for messages. If your dog is picked up and traced by his license number, rabies tag number or microchip ID, you'll be contacted at your *permanent* address and phone number, so keep that line of communication open as well.

## May your dog never be lost

Your pet is a beloved member of your family, and I sincerely hope you never lose him. Please, spend just a minute or two reviewing the simple steps at the beginning of this chapter to prevent losing him in the first place.

# Happy travels to you and your dog from Ginger—and Spike too!

# 8: Dog-Friendly Lodgings

This directory chapter is organized by state, then city, then business name. If you know the business name but not the city, see the cross-referenced Business Name Index, beginning on page 379. All the lodgings listed here have reported that they allow dogs in some, but not necessarily all, of their units. Always call ahead to specifically request a dog-friendly unit. Please be aware that some of these establishments accept dogs "by manager's approval only," meaning they reserve the right to refuse overly dirty, large or out-of-control pets.

California is a leader in eliminating smoking in public places, so the majority of these dog-friendly lodgings are either completely nonsmoking (indoors) or at least offer nonsmoking pet-friendly rooms on request. Therefore, this directory only mentions the smoking policy if dogs are restricted to smoking rooms exclusively.

The room rates shown here represent a range from off-season lows to peak-season highs. In most cases, these are the "before tax" prices; all are accurate as of the time each business was contacted during the preparation of this book. However, as in most industries, all prices shown are "subject to change without notice"—so be sure to ask about the current rates when you call to reserve your pet-friendly room.

If you don't see one of your favorite establishments listed here, don't despair. Some managers said that although they do accept dogs, they didn't wish to "go public" with that information in this directory. However, most of them also said they will continue to accept customers who have stayed there with their well-behaved dogs in the past.

## Abbreviations used in this directory

In order to include as much useful information as possible in each listing, some abbreviations became necessary. A "legend" appears at the top of each even-numbered page to explain all these abbreviations.

| C = coffee<br>CB = continental<br>    breakfast<br>F = refrigerator<br>FB = full breakfast<br>FR = fitness room | GP = guest pass to<br>    fitness center<br>IP = indoor pool<br>IS = in-room spa<br>K = full kitchen<br>(k) = kitchenette | L = lounge<br>M = microwave<br>OP = outdoor pool<br>R = restaurant<br>S = sauna/steam<br>T = spa or hot tub | # of units)<br>& rates | food<br>& drink | pool, sauna<br>& hot tub |
|---|---|---|---|---|---|

# California's Dog-Friendly Lodgings

## Adin

| | | | |
|---|---|---|---|
| **Juniper Tree Motel**  530-299-3300<br>Hwy 299 & Hwy 139<br>grassy area for walking dogs | (7)<br>$37 | M/F | |

## Ahwahnee

| | | | |
|---|---|---|---|
| **Yosemite's Apple Blossom Inn B & B**<br>44606 Silver Spur Trail        559-642-2001<br>www.sierratel.com/appleblossominn    888-687-4281<br>well-behaved dogs by advance reservation only,<br>rooms and3 bdrm vacation home, on 5 acres with<br>orchard, open field and walking trails | (4)<br>$85–<br>$135 | FB<br>CB | OP<br>T |

## Alameda

| | | | |
|---|---|---|---|
| **Alameda Islander Motel**       510-865-2121<br>2428 Central Ave       pet fee $20/stay<br>2½ miles to fenced off-leash dog park | (62)<br>$50 | K | |

## Albion

| | | | |
|---|---|---|---|
| **Fensalden Inn**           707-937-4042<br>33810 Navarro Ridge Rd       800-959-3850<br>www.fensalden.com<br>dogs allowed with advance reservation only in<br>bungalow that sleeps 6, on 8 acres for walking dogs | (8)<br>$215–<br>$225 | K | |

## Altaville

| | | | |
|---|---|---|---|
| **Angels Inn Motel**         209-736-4242<br>600 N Main St            888-753-0226<br>www.centralsierralodging.com      pet fee $10/day<br>open walking area, 1½ miles to park, 3 miles to lake | (58)<br>$49–<br>$69 | CB<br>M/F | OP |

## Alturas

| | | | | |
|---|---|---|---|---|
| **Best Western Trailside Inn**<br>343 N Main St<br>www.bestwestern.com/alturas<br>open walking area, ¼ mile to park | 530-233-4111<br>pet fee $5/day | (38)<br>$63–<br>$75 | CB<br>M/F | OP |
| **California Pines Lodge**<br>750 Shasta View Dr<br>next to lakeside walking trail | 530-233-5842<br>pet fee $10/stay | (28)<br>$45–<br>$65 | K<br>R/L | OP |
| **Drifters Inn**<br>Hwy 395<br>large open walking area | 530-233-2428<br>pet fee $3/day | (19)<br>$33–<br>$46 | K<br>M/F | |
| **Essex Motel**<br>1216 N Main St<br>grassy walking area | 530-233-2821<br>each pet $5/day | (16)<br>$40–<br>$60 | | |
| **Frontier Motel**<br>1033 N Main St<br>open walking areas, near park and wildlife refuge | 530-233-3383 | (11)<br>$35–<br>$50 | K | |
| **Hacienda Motel**<br>201 E 12th St<br>open walking area, 5 blocks to park | 530-233-3459<br>each pet $5/day | (18)<br>$35–<br>$55 | C<br>M/F | |
| **Rim Rock Motel**<br>Hwy 299<br>www.rimrockmotel.com<br>dogs by owner's approval only, next to park | 530-233-5455 | (14)<br>$46–<br>$55 | C<br>F | |
| **Super 8 Motel**<br>511 N Main St<br>www.super8.com<br>open walking area, 10 blocks to park | 530-233-3545 | (48)<br>$58–<br>$64 | CB<br>M/F | |
| **Wagon Wheel Motel**<br>308 W 12th St　open walking area, 1 mile to park | 530-233-5866 | (6)<br>$40 | C<br>F | |

## Amador City

| | | | | |
|---|---|---|---|---|
| **Mine House Inn B & B**<br>14125 Hwy 49<br>www.minehouseinn.com<br>well-behaved dogs by manager's approval only,<br>historic 1870s and 1930s buildings, walking paths | 209-267-5900<br>800-646-3473<br>pet fee $10/day | (13)<br>$95–<br>$245 | FB<br>M/F | OP<br>T |

| C = coffee<br>CB = continental<br>    breakfast<br>F = refrigerator<br>FB = full breakfast<br>FR = fitness room | GP = guest pass to<br>    fitness center<br>IP = indoor pool<br>IS = in-room spa<br>K = full kitchen<br>(k) = kitchenette | L = lounge<br>M = microwave<br>OP = outdoor pool<br>R = restaurant<br>S = sauna/steam<br>T = spa or hot tub | (# of units)<br>& rates | food<br>& drink | pool, sauna<br>& hot tub |
|---|---|---|---|---|---|

## Anaheim

| | | | | |
|---|---|---|---|---|
| **Anaheim Plaza Hotel & Suites**<br>1700 S Harbor Blvd<br>www.anaheimplazahotel.com<br>dogs in smoking rooms only, grassy walking area,<br>15 minute drive to park | 714-772-5900<br>800-228-1357 | (300)<br>$49–<br>$99 | C<br>M/F<br>R | OP<br>T |
| **Best Western Anaheim Hills**<br>5710 E La Palma Ave<br>www.bestwesterncalifornia.com<br>across street to park | 714-779-0252<br>800-346-6662<br>pet fee $15/day | (101)<br>$64–<br>$99 | CB<br>K | OP<br>T<br>FR |
| **Best Western Anaheim Stardust**<br>1057 W Ball Rd<br>www.anaheimstardust.com<br>dogs in smoking rooms only, ½ mile to park | 714-774-7600<br>800-222-3639<br>pet fee $10/day | (95)<br>$54–<br>$99 | FB<br>CB<br>M/F | OP<br>T |
| **Calico Motel**<br>500 S Beach Blvd<br>1 block to park | 714-826-9598<br>pet fee $10/day | (18)<br>$40–<br>$50 | | |
| **Clarion Hotel**<br>616 W Convention Way<br>www.choicehotels.com<br>lawn area, 1 mile to park | 714-750-3131<br>800-228-5151<br>pet fee $10/day<br>$25 cleaning fee | (284)<br>$60–<br>$150 | R/L | OP |
| **Coast Anaheim Hotel**<br>1855 S Harbor Blvd<br>www.coasthotels.com          lawn area, 2 miles to park | 714-750-0169 | (499)<br>$71–<br>$195 | C<br>F | OP<br>T<br>FR |
| **Econo Lodge**<br>1126 W Katella Ave<br>www.econolodgeatthepark.com          each pet $10/day<br>1 block to park | 714-533-4505<br>888-533-4505 | (35)<br>$50–<br>$150 | CB<br>M/F | OP |
| **Embassy Suites Anaheim North**<br>3100 E Frontera St<br>www.embassysuitesanaheim.com<br>dogs under 50 lbs only, lawn, riverbed walking trail | 714-632-1221<br>pet fee $50/stay | (222)<br>$119–<br>$189 | FB<br>R | IP<br>T |

| | | | | |
|---|---|---|---|---|
| **Hilton Anaheim** | 714-750-4321 | (1,572) | CB | IP |
| 777 W Convention Way | 800-445-8667 | $79– | (k) | OP |
| www.anaheim.hilton.com | | $299 | M | S/T |
| dogs under 50 lbs only, ½ mile to park and trail | | | R | FR |
| **La Quinta Inn & Suites Anaheim/Disneyland** | | (129) | FB | OP |
| 1752 S Clementine St | 714-635-5000 | $89– | M/F | T |
| www.lq.com | 800-992-4884 | $105 | | FR |
| small to medium dogs only, 1½ miles to park | | | | |
| **Mardi Gras Motel** | 714-776-7660 | (8) | K | OP |
| 2245 W Lincoln Ave | pet fee $5/day | $43– | | |
| open walking area | | $45 | | |
| **Motel 6 Fullerton East** | 714-956-9690 | (94) | C | |
| 1440 N State College Blvd | 800-466-8356 | $46– | | |
| www.motel6.com | | $56 | | |
| walking area behind building, 2 miles to park | | | | |
| **Quality Inn Maingate** | 714-750-5211 | (66) | CB | OP |
| 2200 S Harbor Blvd | 800-479-5210 | $59– | | T |
| www.visitmickey.com | pet fee $25/stay | $89 | | |
| lawn walking area, ½ mile to park | | | | |
| **Ramada Ltd Maingate North** | 714-999-0684 | (91) | CB | OP |
| 921 S Harbor Blvd | 800-235-3399 | $50– | M/F | |
| www.ramadamaingatenorth.com | pet fee $20/stay | $69 | R | |
| lawn walking area, 1 mile to park | | | | |
| **Red Roof Inn** | 714-520-9696 | (235) | C | OP |
| 100 W Disney Way | 800-733-7663 | $52– | M/F | T |
| www.redroof.com | | $89 | | |
| open walking area | | | | |
| **Residence Inn Anaheim/Disneyland** | | (200) | CB | OP |
| 1700 S Clementine St | 714-533-3555 | $99– | K | T |
| www.marriott.com | 800-331-3131 | $129 | | GP |
| pet fee $10/day plus $60 cleaning fee | | | | |
| pet relief area | | | | |
| **Sheraton Anaheim** | 714-778-1700 | (475) | K | OP |
| 900 S Disneyland Dr | 800-325-3535 | $95– | M/F | T |
| www.sheratonanaheim.com | pet fee $25/day | $200 | R | FR |
| dogs under 80 lbs only, pet basket with food/bowls/ sleeping mat, courtyard, lawn area, 2 miles to park | | | | |

| C = coffee<br>CB = continental<br>   breakfast<br>F = refrigerator<br>FB = full breakfast<br>FR = fitness room | GP = guest pass to<br>   fitness center<br>IP = indoor pool<br>IS = in-room spa<br>K = full kitchen<br>(k) = kitchenette | L = lounge<br>M = microwave<br>OP = outdoor pool<br>R = restaurant<br>S = sauna/steam<br>T = spa or hot tub | (# of units)<br>& rates | food<br>& drink | pool, sauna<br>& hot tub |
|---|---|---|---|---|---|

## Anaheim (continued)

| | | | | |
|---|---|---|---|---|
| **Staybridge Suites**<br>1855 S Manchester Ave<br>www.staybridge.com<br>Mon–Thur evening beverages and appetizers,<br>lawn walking area | 714-748-7700<br>800-238-8000<br>pet fee $150/stay | (143)<br>$130–<br>$200 | FB<br>R | OP<br>T<br>FR |
| **Towneplace Suites by Marriott**<br>1730 S State College Blvd<br>www.towneplacesuites.com<br>1 dog under 25 lbs only, gravel area, 3 blocks to trail | 714-939-9700 | (141)<br>$69–<br>$129 | K | OP<br>T<br>FR |
| **Travelodge Anaheim at the Park**<br>1166 W Katella Ave<br>www.anaheimatthepark.com<br>grassy walking area, 1½ blocks to park | 714-774-7817<br>800-578-7878<br>pet fee $10/day | (57)<br>$65–<br>$105 | CB<br>M/F | OP<br>T |
| **Vagabond Inn**<br>2145 S Harbor Blvd<br>www.vagabondinn.com<br>sidewalk areas for walking dogs, 1 mile to park | 714-971-5556<br>800-220-4820<br>pet fee $10/day | (60)<br>$49–<br>$69 | CB | OP<br>T<br>IS |

## Anderson

| | | | | |
|---|---|---|---|---|
| **Amerihost Inn**<br>2040 Factory Outlet Dr<br>www.amerihostinn.com<br>open field, 1 mile to park | 530-365-6100<br>800-434-5800<br>pet fee $10/stay | (61)<br>$69–<br>$84 | CB<br>M/F | IP<br>T<br>FR |
| **Best Western Knights Inn**<br>2688 Gateway Dr<br>dogs by manager's approval only, open field | 530-365-2753<br>800-528-1234 | (40)<br>$64 | F<br>R | OP |
| **Valley Inn Motel**<br>2861 McMurray Dr<br>open field, short drive to park | 530-365-2566<br>pet fee $6/day | (62)<br>$52–<br>$60 | CB<br>F | OP |

## Angels Camp

| | | | |
|---|---|---|---|
| **Best Western Cedar Inn & Suites**   209-736-4000<br>444 S Main St   800-937-8376<br>www.bestwesternangelscamp.com   pet fee $10/day<br>adult dogs allowed in ground floor rooms only,<br>open walking area and trails, short drive to parks | (38)<br>$85–<br>$164 | CB<br>M/F | OP<br>T |
| **Cooper House B & B**   209-736-2145<br>1184 Church St   800-225-3764 ext 326<br>cat-friendly dogs by owner's approval only, suite<br>with outside entrance and deck, complimentary wine<br>and appetizers, close to creek and off-leash dog park | (3)<br>$125 | CB | |

## Angelus Oaks

| | | | |
|---|---|---|---|
| **Lodge at Angelus Oaks**   909-794-9523<br>37825 Hwy 38   pet fee $5/day<br>dogs by advance reservation only, cabins sleep 2–6,<br>surrounded by national forest, dogs must be leashed | (7)<br>$50–<br>$70 | K | |
| **Seven Oaks Mountain Cabins**   909-794-1277<br>40700 Seven Oaks Rd   pet fee $5/day<br>rustic cabins sleep up to 6, fishing creek, walking<br>area with wildlife so dogs must be leashed | (6)<br>$70 | K | |

## Antioch

| | | | |
|---|---|---|---|
| **Best Western Heritage Inn**   925-778-2000<br>3210 Delta Fair Blvd   800-422-2340<br>www.bestwesterncalifornia.com   pet fee $15/stay<br>small dogs only, small grassy area, 1 mile to college | (73)<br>$90–<br>$100 | CB<br>M/F<br>R | OP<br>T<br>IS |
| **Ramada Inn**   925-754-6600<br>2436 Mahogany Way   800-900-9100<br>www.ramada.com   pet fee $50/stay<br>lawn walking area, 1 block to park | (116)<br>$59–<br>$125 | CB<br>M/F | OP<br>T<br>GP |

## Apple Valley

| | | | |
|---|---|---|---|
| **Apple Valley Lodge**   760-242-5658<br>19599 Hwy 18   each pet $5–$10/day<br>1 mile to park   depending on size of dog | (30)<br>$50–<br>$55 | C<br>F | OP |

| | | | | | | | |
|---|---|---|---|---|---|---|---|
| C = coffee | GP = guest pass to | L = lounge | | | | | |
| CB = continental | fitness center | M = microwave | | | | | |
| breakfast | IP = indoor pool | OP = outdoor pool | | | | | |
| F = refrigerator | IS = in-room spa | R = restaurant | | (# of units) & rates | food & drink | pool, sauna & hot tub | |
| FB = full breakfast | K = full kitchen | S = sauna/steam | | | | | |
| FR = fitness room | (k) = kitchenette | T = spa or hot tub | | | | | |

## Applegate

| | | | | |
|---|---|---|---|---|
| **Applegate Inn** | 530-878-7770 | (30) | M/F | |
| 17855 Lake Arthur Rd | | $39– | | |
| small dogs by advance approval only, rooms/cabins, | | $59 | | |
| open and wooded areas, close to parks/lakes/trails | | | | |

## Aptos

| | | | | |
|---|---|---|---|---|
| **Apple Lane Inn B & B** | 831-475-6868 | (5) | FB | |
| 6265 Soquel Dr | 800-649-8988 | $120– | F | |
| www.applelaneinn.com | pet fee $25/day | $200 | | |
| pet-friendly room with outside entrance, garden and | | | | |
| lawn walking area, 1 mile to state park and beaches | | | | |
| **Bayview Hotel B & B** | 831-688-8654 | (12) | FB | |
| 8041 Soquel Dr | 800-422-9843 | $109– | R | |
| www.bayviewhotel.com | | $269 | | |
| ½ block to park, short walk to dog-friendly beach | | | | |
| **Rio Del Mar Beach House** | 831-239-2736 | (1) | K | |
| 120 Marina Ave | | $150– | | |
| www.vrbo.com/42200 | | $250 | | |
| 3 bdrm house sleeps 8, courtyard, ½ block to beach | | | | |

## Arcadia

| | | | | |
|---|---|---|---|---|
| **Motel 6** | 626-446-2660 | (87) | C | OP |
| 225 Colorado Pl | 800-466-8356 | $54– | | |
| www.motel6.com | large garden, walking area | $66 | | |
| **Residence Inn** | 626-446-6500 | (120) | | |
| 321 E Huntington Dr | 800-331-3131 | $100– | | |
| www. residenceinn.com | pet fee $75/stay | $175 | | |

## Arcata

| | | | | |
|---|---|---|---|---|
| **Best Western Arcata Inn** | 707-826-0313 | (62) | CB | IP |
| 4827 Valley West Blvd | 888-646-6514 | $60– | | OP |
| www.bestwesterncalifornia.com | each pet $10/day | $115 | | T |
| open walking area, ¼ mile to park, 1 mile to trails | | | | |

| | | | | |
|---|---|---|---|---|
| **Comfort Inn**<br>4701 Valley West Blvd<br>www.comfortinnredwoods.com<br>1 dog under 20 lbs, open area, short drive to park | 707-826-2827<br>888-411-2827<br>pet fee $5/day | (57)<br>$55–<br>$120 | CB<br>M/F | IP<br>T<br>GP |
| **Hotel Arcata**<br>708 9th St<br>www.hotelarcata.com<br>90-year old Victorian hotel, 15 minute walk along bay<br>to bird sanctuary, ¾ mile to park | 707-826-0217<br>800-344-1221<br>each pet $5/day | (32)<br>$79–<br>$150 | CB<br>R | GP |
| **Motel 6**<br>4755 Valley West Blvd<br>www.motel6.com | 707-822-7061<br>800-466-8356<br>small pet relief area | (86)<br>$46–<br>$52 | C | OP |
| **Quality Inn**<br>3535 Janes Rd<br>www.qualityinnarcata.com<br>1–2 dogs only, open pasture, ½ mile to park | 707-822-0409<br>800-549-3336<br>pet fee $10/day | (64)<br>$59–<br>$149 | CB<br>M/F | OP<br>T |
| **Super 8 Motel**<br>4887 Valley West Blvd<br>www.super8.com<br>open walking area, 5 miles to park | 707-822-8888<br>800-800-8000<br>each pet $5/day | (60)<br>$53 | CB<br>F | |

### Arnold

| | | | | |
|---|---|---|---|---|
| **Ebbett's Pass Lodge**<br>1173 Hwy 4<br>rooms/2 bdrm cabin, wooded area, 5 miles to park | 209-795-1563<br>each pet $5/day | (15)<br>$43–<br>$110 | C<br>(k)<br>M/F | |
| **Meadowmont Lodge**<br>2011 Hwy 4 & Country Club Dr<br>pet fee $10–$20/day<br>dogs by manager's advance approval only, close to<br>hiking trails, 1 mile to state park | 209-795-1394<br>888-538-1222 | (19)<br>$59–<br>$125 | C<br>K | FR |
| **Sierra Vacation Rentals**<br>908 Moran Rd<br>www.sierravacationrentals.com | 209-795-2422<br>800-995-2422<br>cabins sleep 10 | (30)<br>$115–<br>$160 | K | OP |

### Arrowbear

| | | | | |
|---|---|---|---|---|
| **Deep Creek Motel**<br>2312 Blue Jay Lane<br>dogs by owner's approval only, open field | 909-867-2312<br>800-282-2312 | (27)<br>$60–<br>$100 | CB | |

| C = coffee<br>CB = continental<br>  breakfast<br>F = refrigerator<br>FB = full breakfast<br>FR = fitness room | GP = guest pass to<br>  fitness center<br>IP = indoor pool<br>IS = in-room spa<br>K = full kitchen<br>(k) = kitchenette | L = lounge<br>M = microwave<br>OP = outdoor pool<br>R = restaurant<br>S = sauna/steam<br>T = spa or hot tub | (# of units)<br>& rates | food<br>& drink | pool, sauna<br>& hot tub |
|---|---|---|---|---|---|

## Arroyo Grande

| | | | | |
|---|---|---|---|---|
| **Best Western Casa Grande**<br>850 Oak Park Blvd<br>www.pismobeachca.net<br>walking area, ½ mile to park, short drive to beach | 805-481-7398<br>800-459-9777<br>pet fee $10/day | (114)<br>$59–<br>$189 | CB | OP<br>S<br>T<br>FR |
| **Premier Inns Pismo Beach**<br>555 Camino Mercado<br>www.premierinns.com<br>pet relief area, 5 minute drive to beach | 805-481-4774<br>888-339-6161 | (100)<br>$44–<br>$82 | CB<br>F | OP<br>T |

## Atascadero

| | | | | |
|---|---|---|---|---|
| **Motel 6**<br>9400 El Camino Real<br>www.motel6.com    lawn walking area, 1 mile to park | 805-466-6701<br>800-466-8356 | (117)<br>$44–<br>$65 | C | OP |
| **San Palo Inn**<br>4900 San Palo Rd<br>small dogs by manager's approval, 2 miles to park | 805-462-1670 | (11)<br>$140–<br>$165 | K | |

## Auburn

| | | | | |
|---|---|---|---|---|
| **Best Western Golden Key**<br>13450 Lincoln Way<br>www.bestwesterncalifornia.com    each pet $15/stay<br>open walking area, ½ mile to park | 530-885-8611<br>800-201-0121 | (68)<br>$63–<br>$115 | CB<br>M/F | OP<br>T |
| **Foothills Motel**<br>13431 Bowman Rd<br>www.thefoothillsmotel.com    pet fee $10/day<br>dogs in smoking rooms only, open field, ¼ mile to<br>park, ½ mile to riverside trail | 530-885-8444<br>800-292-5694 | (62)<br>$55–<br>$90 | CB | OP<br>T |
| **Holiday Inn**<br>120 Grass Valley Hwy<br>www.holiday-inn.com    pet fee $20/stay<br>dogs under 30 lbs allowed in first floor rooms only,<br>5 minute drive to park | 530-887-8787<br>800-814-8787 | (96)<br>$98–<br>$107 | R | OP<br>T |

| Motel 6 | 530-888-7829 | (57) | C | OP |
|---|---|---|---|---|
| 1819 Auburn Ravine Rd | 800-466-8356 | $56– | | T |
| www.motel6.com | | $68 | | |
| dogs under 20 lbs only, lawn area, 1 mile to park | | | | |

| Power's Mansion Inn B & B | 530-885-1166 | (10) | FB | |
|---|---|---|---|---|
| 164 Cleveland Ave | pet fee $10/day | $129 | | |
| 1898 mansion, 2 pet-friendly rooms with outside | | | | |
| entrances, pet relief area, short drive to park | | | | |

| Travelodge | 530-885-7025 | (77) | CB | OP |
|---|---|---|---|---|
| 13490 Lincoln Way | 877-885-7025 | $59– | M/F | T |
| www.auburntravelodge.com | pet fee $10/day | $99 | | |
| grassy walking area, 2 miles to park | | | | |

## Avalon

| Best Western Catalina Canyon Resort & Spa | | (75) | CB | OP |
|---|---|---|---|---|
| 888 Country Club Dr | 310-510-0325 | $90– | R | T |
| www.bestwesterncalifornia.com | 888-478-7829 | $340 | | FR |
| | pet fee $50/stay | | | |
| well-behaved dogs under 50 lbs, garden courtyard | | | | |
| and open walking areas | | | | |

| Edgewater Hotel | 310-510-0347 | (8) | CB | IS |
|---|---|---|---|---|
| 415 Crescent Ave | 866-462-2825 | $110– | M/F | |
| www.edgewaterbeachfronthotel.com | pets $50/stay | $425 | | |
| beachfront location, grassy walking area in nearby | | | | |
| nursery, short walk to dog-friendly beaches | | | | |

## Baker

| Bun Boy Motel | 760-733-4363 | (20) | C | |
|---|---|---|---|---|
| 72139 Baker Blvd | | $39– | | |
| open desert area for walking dogs | | $49 | | |

| Motel Will's Fargo | 760-733-4477 | (30) | C | OP |
|---|---|---|---|---|
| 72252 Baker Blvd | | $37– | | |
| small to medium dogs only, lawn and open desert | | $53 | | |

| Royal Hawaiian Motel | 760-733-4326 | (43) | C | OP |
|---|---|---|---|---|
| 200 W Baker Blvd | | $37– | F | |
| grassy shaded walking area, ½ mile to park | | $49 | | |

| C = coffee | GP = guest pass to | L = lounge | | | |
| CB = continental | fitness center | M = microwave | | | |
| breakfast | IP = indoor pool | OP = outdoor pool | | | |
| F = refrigerator | IS = in-room spa | R = restaurant | | | |
| FB = full breakfast | K = full kitchen | S = sauna/steam | | | |
| FR = fitness room | (k) = kitchenette | T = spa or hot tub | (# of units) & rates | food & drink | pool, sauna & hot tub |

## Bakersfield

| | | (# of units) & rates | food & drink | pool, sauna & hot tub |
|---|---|---|---|---|
| **Best Inn** 200 Trask St www.bestinn.com open walking area, 20 minute drive to park | 661-764-5221 pet fee $5/day | (53) $39–$59 | CB M/F | OP |
| **Best Value Inn** 818 Real Rd www.bvhotel.com small dogs only, grassy courtyard, 1 mile to park | 661-324-6666 | (165) $49–$89 | CB M/F | OP |
| **Best Western Crystal Palace Inn** 2620 Buck Owens Blvd dogs under 30 lbs only next to river walk | 661-327-9651 800-424-4900 each pet $10/day | (195) $69–$98 | FB M/F R/L | OP T FR |
| **Best Western Heritage Inn** 253 Trask St www.bestwesterncalifornia.com small dogs only, grassy walking area | 661-764-6268 800-780-7234 pet fee $10/day | (47) $72–$90 | CB | OP T IS |
| **Best Western Hill House** 700 Truxtun Ave www.bestwestern.com/hillhouse dogs under 50 lbs only, lawn walking area | 661-327-4064 800-300-4230 pet fee $10/day | (100) $69–$99 | CB F R/L | OP |
| **Days Inn & Golf** 4500 Buck Owens Blvd www.the.daysinn.com courtyard and lawn, 2 miles to park and bike trail | 661-324-5555 800-329-7466 pet fee $20/stay | (205) $59–$89 | CB (k) | OP T |
| **Doubletree Hotel** 3100 Camino Del Rio Ct www.doubletree.com courtyard and open walking area | 661-323-7111 800-222-8733 pet fee $15/stay | (262) $79–$159 | | OP T FR |
| **E-Z8 Motel** 2604 Buck Owens Blvd www.ez8motels.com riverside walking trails | 661-322-1901 | (100) $38–$45 | C F | OP T |

| | | | | |
|---|---|---|---|---|
| **E-Z8 Motel** 5200 Olive Tree Ct www.ez8motels.com 1 dog under 20 lbs, open walking area, ½ mile to park | 661-392-1511 | (101) $37– $80 | C F | OP T |
| **Holiday Inn Select** 801 Truxtun Ave www.holidayinnbakersfield.com small gravel and grass walking areas, ½ mile to park | 661-323-1900 | (258) $79– $119 | C R | OP T FR |
| **Howard Johnson** 2700 White Lane www.hojo.com          lawn walking area, 3 miles to park | 661-396-1425 800-446-4656 | (149) $55– $75 | CB M/F | OP T |
| **La Quinta Inn** 3232 Riverside Dr www.lq.com          next to bike trail and park | 661-325-7400 800-531-5900 | (129) $67– $91 | CB F | OP T |
| **Liberty Inn** 8230 E Brundage Lane          pet fee $5/day lawn walking area, 2 miles to park | 661-366-1630 | (40) $40– $50 | C M/F | IP T |
| **Motel 6 East** 8223 E Brundage Lane www.motel6.com  open walking area, 4 miles to park | 661-366-7231 800-466-8356 | (109) $42– $46 | C | OP |
| **Motel 6 North** 5241 Olive Tree Ct www.motel6.com          small lawn and vacant lot | 661-392-9700 800-466-8356 | (109) $38 | C | OP |
| **Motel 6 South** 2727 White Lane www.motel6.com          lawn area, 1 mile to park | 661-834-2828 800-466-8356 | (100) $45– $52 | C | OP |
| **Motel 6 Convention Center** 1350 Easton Dr www.motel6.com   lawn walking area, 2 miles to park | 661-327-1686 800-466-8356 | (106) $43– $46 | C | OP |
| **Quality Inn** 1011 Oak St www.choicehotels.com          each pet $10/day small dogs only, lawn area, short walk to parks | 661-325-0772 800-221-6832 | (89) $62– $72 | FB | OP T FR |
| **Ramada Ltd Central** 830 Wible Rd www.ramada.com          each pet $5/day lawn walking area, 2 miles to park | 661-831-1922 800-272-6232 | (52) $50– $80 | CB M/F | OP T |

| | (# of units) & rates | food & drink | pool, sauna & hot tub |
|---|---|---|---|
| C = coffee   GP = guest pass to fitness center   L = lounge   M = microwave<br>CB = continental breakfast   IP = indoor pool   OP = outdoor pool<br>F = refrigerator   IS = in-room spa   R = restaurant<br>FB = full breakfast   K = full kitchen   S = sauna/steam<br>FR = fitness room   (k) = kitchenette   T = spa or hot tub | | | |

## Bakersfield (continued)

| | | (# of units) & rates | food & drink | pool, sauna & hot tub |
|---|---|---|---|---|
| **Red Lion Hotel**<br>2400 Camino Del Rio Ct<br>www.bakersfieldredlion.com<br>close to riverside walking trail | 661-327-0681<br>800-430-7627<br>pet fee $25/stay | (162)<br>$79–<br>$89 | C<br>M/F<br>R/L | OP<br>T<br>FR |
| **Residence Inn**<br>4241 Chester Lane<br>www.residenceinn.com<br>pet relief area, 2 miles to park | 661-321-9800<br>800-331-3131<br>each pet $6/day<br>$75 cleaning fee | (114)<br>$129–<br>$179 | CB<br>K | OP<br>T<br>FR |
| **Rio Bravo Resort**<br>11200 Lake Ming Rd<br>www.riobravoresort.com<br>dog must be in travel crate if alone in room, 40 acres | 661-872-5000<br>888-517-5500<br>pet fee $15/day | (110)<br>$95–<br>$250 | C<br>K | OP<br>T |
| **Roadrunner Inn & Suites**<br>2619 Buck Owens Blvd<br>open area behind building, 5 minute drive to park | 661-323-3727 | (48)<br>$36–<br>$40 | C | |
| **Royal Oak Inn**<br>889 Oak St<br>each pet $5–$20/day (depending on size)<br>small grassy walking area, 1 mile to park | 661-324-9686<br>887-203-1464 | (42)<br>$40–<br>$45 | CB<br>M/F | OP |
| **Super 8 Motel**<br>901 Real Rd<br>www.super8.com<br>lawn area, 3 blocks to park | 661-322-1012<br>800-800-8000<br>each pet $10/day | (87)<br>$54–<br>$60 | C<br>M/F | OP<br>T |
| **Vagabond Inn**<br>6100 Knudsen Dr<br>www.vagabondinn.com<br>empty lot for walking dogs, 5 minute drive to park | 661-392-1800<br>800-522-1555<br>pet fee $5/day | (154)<br>$44–<br>$53 | CB | OP |
| **Vagabond Inn**<br>6501 Colony St<br>www.vagabondinn.com<br>open walking area behind hotel, ½ mile to park | 661-831-9200<br>800-522-1555<br>each pet $5/day | (134)<br>$46–<br>$56 | CB<br>M/F | OP |

## Baldwin Park

| | | | | |
|---|---|---|---|---|
| **Motel 6** <br> 14510 Garvey Ave <br> www.motel6.com | 626-960-5011 <br> 800-466-8356 <br> 1 mile to park | (73) <br> $46– <br> $60 | C | OP |

## Banning

| | | | | | |
|---|---|---|---|---|---|
| **Super 8 Motel** <br> 1690 W Ramsey St <br> www.super8.com <br> lawn and open walking area behind building | 909-849-8888 <br> 800-800-8000 <br> pet fee $10/day | (51) <br> $60– <br> $90 | CB <br> M/F | OP | |
| **Travelodge** <br> 1700 W Ramsey St <br> www.travelodge.com <br> well-behaved dogs only | 909-849-1000 <br> 800-578-7878 | (42) <br> $54– <br> $68 | CB | OP | |

## Barstow

| | | | | | |
|---|---|---|---|---|---|
| **American Inn** <br> 1350 W Main St <br> www.americaninnbarstow.com <br> 1 block to park | 760-256-8921 <br> pet fee $5/stay | (40) <br> $36– <br> $45 | CB | OP | |
| **Best Motel** <br> 1281 E Main St <br> dirt walking area, ½ mile to park | 760-256-6836 <br> pet fee $5/day | (28) <br> $36– <br> $40 | CB <br> M/F | OP | |
| **Best Western Desert Villa Inn** <br> 1984 E Main St <br> www.bestwesterncalifornia.com <br> small lawn walking area, 3 miles to park | 760-256-1781 <br> 877-498-1652 <br> pet fee $10/stay | (95) <br> $62– <br> $99 | CB <br> M/F | OP <br> T | |
| **Brant's Motel** <br> 921 E Main St <br> lawn walking area, ½ mile to park | 760-256-9331 <br> pet fee $5/day | (15) <br> $25 | M/F | | |
| **Budget Inn** <br> 1111 E Main St <br> grass and sandy walking areas, 1½ miles to park | 760-256-1063 <br> pet fee $5/day | (40) <br> $30– <br> $40 | C <br> M/F | OP | |
| **Days Inn** <br> 1590 Coolwater Lane <br> www.daysinn.com <br> lawn walking area, 3 blocks to park | 760-256-1737 <br> 800-329-7466 <br> each pet $10/day | (112) <br> $43– <br> $59 | CB <br> M/F | OP | |

| Key | | | | | (# of units) & rates | food & drink | pool, sauna & hot tub |
|-----|-----|-----|-----|-----|-----|-----|-----|

C = coffee
CB = continental breakfast
F = refrigerator
FB = full breakfast
FR = fitness room
GP = guest pass to fitness center
IP = indoor pool
IS = in-room spa
K = full kitchen
(k) = kitchenette
L = lounge
M = microwave
OP = outdoor pool
R = restaurant
S = sauna/steam
T = spa or hot tub

## Barstow (continued)

| Listing | Contact | (# of units) & rates | food & drink | pool, sauna & hot tub |
|---|---|---|---|---|
| **Desert Inn Motel** 1100 E Main St ground floor pet rooms, grassy area, ½ mile to park | 760-256-2146 | (95) $24–$38 | C M/F | OP |
| **Econo Lodge** 1230 E Main St gravel walking area | 760-256-2133 800-553-2666 pet fee $7/day | (50) $40–$55 | CB M/F | OP |
| **Economy Inn** 1243 E Main St dirt and grass walking areas, 1 mile to park | 760-256-5601 pet fee $5/day | (65) $31–$45 | CB M/F | OP |
| **Executive Inn** 1261 E Main St small gravel walking area, ¾ mile to park | 760-256-7581 pet fee $5/day | (33) $27–$45 | CB (k) M/F | OP |
| **Gateway Motel** 1630 E Main St empty lot for walking dogs, 1½ miles to park | 760-256-8931 each pet $10/stay | (33) $36–$40 | M/F | OP |
| **Holiday Inn Express–Barstow Historical Rt 66** 1861 W Main St www.hiexpress.com ⅓ mile to park | 760-256-1300 800-465-4329 | (65) $75–$89 | CB M/F | OP FR |
| **Holiday Inn Express–Outlet Center** 2700 Lenwood Rd www.hiexpress.com surrounded by open desert area, 4 miles to parks | 760-253-9200 800-465-4329 | (110) $99–$159 | FB M/F | OP T FR |
| **Motel 6** 150 Yucca Ave www.motel6.com small lawn, ½ mile to park | 760-256-1752 800-466-8356 | (121) $35 | C | OP |
| **Nites Inn** 1261 W Main St gravel walking area, 2 blocks to park | 760-255-1838 pet fee $5/day | (28) $33 | C M/F | OP |

| | | | | |
|---|---|---|---|---|
| **Pennywise Inn** 2980 E Main St dogs allowed in smoking rooms only, open field, 2 miles to park | 760-252-8268 | (67) $35– $45 | C M/F L | OP |
| **Quality Inn** 1520 E Main St dogs in smoking rooms only   pet fee $10/stay pet relief area, 2 blocks to school sports field | 760-256-6891 800-228-5151 | (100) $50 | CB M/F | OP FR |
| **Ramada Inn** 1511 E Main St www.ramada.com   pet fee $20/stay lawn walking area, 2 miles to park | 760-256-5673 800-272-6232 | (148) $69– $99 | CB M/F | OP T GP |
| **Red Roof Inn** 2551 Commerce Pkwy www.redroof.com dogs allowed in first floor rooms with outside entrances, open desert area, 2 miles to park | 760-253-2121 800-733-7663 | (110) $55– $65 | C M/F | OP T |
| **Route 66 Motel** 195 W Main St   each pet $5/day small dogs only, open desert area, 2 miles to park | 760-256-7866 | (20) $33– $35 | | |
| **Sage Motel** 220 W Main St open desert walking area | 760-256-2116 | (15) $28 | | |
| **Stardust Inn** 901 E Main St   pet fee $5/stay dogs in smoking rooms only, 1 mile to park | 760-256-7116 | (24) $32– $38 | C M/F | OP |
| **Super 8 Motel** 170 Coolwater Lane www.super8.com   each pet $5/day pet relief area, 3 miles to park | 760-256-8443 800-800-8000 | (108) $58– $66 | C M/F | OP |

## Bear Valley

| | | | | |
|---|---|---|---|---|
| **Basecamp Lodge** 148 Bear Valley Rd www.basecamplodge.com   pet fee $5/day well-behaved dogs by advance reservation, rustic lodge rooms, close to woods, lakeside trails | 209-753-2344 | (14) $20– $65 | R/L | |

| | | | |
|---|---|---|---|
| C = coffee<br>CB = continental<br>  breakfast<br>F = refrigerator<br>FB = full breakfast<br>FR = fitness room | GP = guest pass to<br>  fitness center<br>IP = indoor pool<br>IS = in-room spa<br>K = full kitchen<br>(k) = kitchenette | L = lounge<br>M = microwave<br>OP = outdoor pool<br>R = restaurant<br>S = sauna/steam<br>T = spa or hot tub | (# of units) & rates | food & drink | pool, sauna & hot tub |

## Bear Valley (continued)

| | | | |
|---|---|---|---|
| **Lake Alpine Lodge**          209-753-6358<br>4000 Hwy 4<br>www.lakealpinelodge.com<br>dogs allowed in canvas tent cabins that sleep 4,<br>bathhouse, woods, lakefront trails | (12)<br>$40 | R/L | |
| **Powderbears Log Cabin**          209-753-2136<br>222 Toll Gate Rd<br>modern cabin sleeps 8, woods for off-leash walking | (1)<br>$150–<br>$300 | K | |

## Beaumont

| | | | |
|---|---|---|---|
| **Best Value Inn**          909-845-2185<br>625 E 5th St                    pet fee $3/day<br>lawn walking area, 2 blocks to park | (23)<br>$50–<br>$80 | CB<br>F | OP |
| **Best Western El Rancho Motel**     909-845-2176<br>480 E 5th St                    800-528-1234<br>www.bestwesterncalifornia.com     pet fee $8/day<br>open walking area, 2 blocks to park | (52)<br>$65–<br>$85 | CB<br>M/F | OP<br>FR |
| **Windsor Motel**          909-845-1436<br>1265 E 6th St          pet fee $5–$10/day<br>www.motelwindsor.com<br>1 dog only, grass and dirt areas, 6 miles to park | (16)<br>$60–<br>$70 | C<br>M/F | OP |

## Belden

| | | | |
|---|---|---|---|
| **Belden Town Resort & Lodge**     530-283-9662<br>14785 Belden Town Rd<br>cabins sleep up to 6, lawn, riverside woods, trails | (12)<br>$65–<br>$125 | K<br>R/L | |

## Bell Gardens

| | | | |
|---|---|---|---|
| **Vagabond Inn LA/Bell Gardens**     323-560-8221<br>6344 Eastern Ave                  800-522-1555<br>www.vagabondinn.com            pet fee $10/day<br>small dog only, parking lot relief area, ½ mile to park | (32)<br>$65–<br>$89 | CB<br>M/F | |

## Bellflower

| | | | |
|---|---|---|---|
| **Motel 6** 562-531-3933 17220 Downey Ave 800-466-8356 www.motel6.com 1 small dog only, small gravel walking area | (154) $46 | C | OP |

## Belmont

| | | | |
|---|---|---|---|
| **Motel 6** 650-591-1472 1101 Shoreway Rd 800-466-8356 www.motel6.com · pet fee $10/day 1 dog only, sleeping rooms and suites, walking trail | (71) $55 | K | OP T |

## Ben Lomond

| | | | |
|---|---|---|---|
| **Econo Lodge** 831-336-2292 9733 Hwy 9 800-424-6423 www.stayintheredwoods.com pet fee $25/stay lawn and gravel areas, walking path through woods | (23) $70– $150 | CB M/F | OP |

## Benicia

| | | | |
|---|---|---|---|
| **Best Western Heritage Inn** 707-746-0401 1955 E 2nd St 800-327-9321 www.bestwesterncalifornia.com pet fee $25/stay lawn walking area | (100) $70– $99 | CB M/F | OP T |
| **Inn at Benicia Bay** 707-746-1055 145 E D St pet fee $5/day www.theinnatbeniciabay.com cat-friendly dogs by advance approval only, 1 block to greenway, 3 blocks to bayside walking area, 5 miles to dog park | (9) $119– $249 | FB | IS |
| **Union Hotel** 707-746-0110 401 1st St 1 block to waterfront park | (12) $95– $175 | FB CB M/F | GP IS |

## Benton

| | | | |
|---|---|---|---|
| **Inn at Benton Hot Springs** 760-933-2287 55137 Hwy 120 866-466-2824 www.395.com/oldhouse hot tubs fed by natural hot spring, high desert area, close to trails and Boundary Peak | (6) $75 | FB F | T FR |

| C = coffee<br>CB = continental<br>   breakfast<br>F = refrigerator<br>FB = full breakfast<br>FR = fitness room | GP = guest pass to<br>   fitness center<br>IP = indoor pool<br>IS = in-room spa<br>K = full kitchen<br>(k) = kitchenette | L = lounge<br>M = microwave<br>OP = outdoor pool<br>R = restaurant<br>S = sauna/steam<br>T = spa or hot tub | (# of units)<br>& rates | food<br>& drink | pool, sauna<br>& hot tub |
|---|---|---|---|---|---|
| **Berkeley** | | | | | |
| **Beau Sky Hotel**    510-540-7688<br>2520 Durant Ave    800-990-2328<br>www.citysearch.com/sfo/beauskyhotel<br>7 blocks to dog park | | | (20)<br>$89–<br>$129 | CB | IS |
| **Doubletree Hotel Berkeley Marina** 510-548-7920<br>200 Marina Blvd    800-333-3333<br>www.doubletree.com<br>1 dog under 25 lbs only, next to park, jogging trails | | | (375)<br>$119–<br>$218 | CB<br>R | OP<br>FR |
| **Golden Bear Inn**    510-525-6770<br>1620 San Pablo Ave    800-525-6770<br>www.goldenbearinn.com    pet fee $10/day<br>lawn walking area, 2 blocks to park | | | (46)<br>$69–<br>$89 | C<br>(k) | |
| **Berry Creek** | | | | | |
| **Lake Oroville B & B**    530-589-0700<br>240 Sunday Dr    800-455-5253<br>www.lakeoroville.com/lakeoroville    ea pet $10/day<br>rural walking area, wildlife so dogs must be leashed | | | (6)<br>$125–<br>$165 | FB | IS |
| **Beverly Hills** | | | | | |
| **Avalon Hotel of Beverly Hills**    310-277-5221<br>9400 W Olympic Blvd    800-535-4715<br>www.avalonbeverlyhills.com<br>lawn walking area, 6 blocks to park | | | (86)<br>$235 | R/L | OP<br>FR |
| **Beverly Crescent Hotel**    310-247-0505<br>403 N Crescent Dr    pet fee $25/day<br>www.crescentbh.com<br>dogs under 15 lbs only, 1 block to park | | | (35)<br>$165–<br>$250 | R/L | |
| **Beverly Hilton**    310-274-7777<br>9876 Wilshire Blvd # 1    800-445-8667<br>www.beverlyhills.hilton.com    pet fee $25/day<br>dogs under 25 lbs only, next to park and jogging trail | | | (581)<br>$165–<br>$299 | CB<br>M/F<br>R/L | OP<br>FR |

| | | | |
|---|---|---|---|
| **Loews Beverly Hills** 310-277-2800<br>1224 S Beverwil Dr<br>www.loewshotels.com<br>petwalking/petsitting/in-home boarding services,<br>lawn and residential neighborhood, close to parks | (137)<br>$195–<br>$210 | C<br>M/F<br>R | OP<br>FR |
| **Luxe Hotel Rodeo Drive** 310-273-0300<br>360 N Rodeo Dr 800-589-3411<br>www.luxehotels.com pet fee $200/stay<br>10 blocks to park | (86)<br>$149–<br>$259 | CB<br>F | FR |
| **Mosaic Hotel Beverly Hills** 310-278-0303<br>125 S Spalding Dr<br>www.mosaichotel.com<br>small dogs only, residential area, 1 block to park | (49)<br>$269–<br>$289 | C<br>F<br>R/L | OP<br>FR |
| **Peninsula Beverly Hills** 310-551-2888<br>9882 S Santa Monica Blvd 800-462-7899<br>www.peninsula.com pet fee $35/day<br>walking map of local area, dogwalking service | (196)<br>$395–<br>$3,500 | | |
| **Raffles L'Ermitage Beverly Hills** 310-278-3344<br>9291 Burton Way 800-800-2113<br>www.raffles-lermitagehotel.com pet fee $150/stay<br>gourmet pet menu, sidewalk for walking dogs | (123)<br>$345–<br>$405 | F<br>R/L | OP<br>T<br>FR |
| **Regent Beverly Wilshire Hotel** 310-275-5200<br>9500 Wilshire Blvd 800-421-4354<br>www.regenthotels.com/beverlywilshire<br>dogs under 10 lbs only, dog biscuits/bowls/toys,<br>dogwalking service, pet relief area, ½ mile to park | (399)<br>$425 | | |

### Bieber

| | | | |
|---|---|---|---|
| **Bieber Motel** 530-294-5454<br>100 Hwy 299 E<br>lawn walking area, 1 mile to wildlife refuge | (18)<br>$44 | C<br>M/F | |

### Big Bear City

| | | | |
|---|---|---|---|
| **Cienaga Creek Ranch** 909-584-1147<br>43630 Rainbow Lane 888-336-2891<br>www.mountaincottage.com each pet $10/day<br>cottages sleep up to 4, on 50 acre ranch for off-leash<br>walking, surrounded by national forest | (5)<br>$119–<br>$299 | K | IS |

| C = coffee  GP = guest pass to  L = lounge  CB = continental  fitness center  M = microwave  breakfast  IP = indoor pool  OP = outdoor pool  F = refrigerator  IS = in-room spa  R = restaurant  FB = full breakfast  K = full kitchen  S = sauna/steam  FR = fitness room  (k) = kitchenette  T = spa or hot tub | (# of units) & rates | food & drink | pool, sauna & hot tub |
|---|---|---|---|

## Big Bear City (continued)

| Gold Mountain Manor Cabins  1117 Anita Ave  www.goldmountainmanor.com  5 minute drive to national parks | 909-585-6997  800-509-2604 | (17)  $150–  $250 | K | T |
|---|---|---|---|---|
| Inn Der Bach  1351 Midway Blvd  www.innderbach.com  lodge rooms/apartment sleeps up to 7, fenced yard,  on 33 wooded acres for walking dogs | 909-585-3702  pet fee $15/stay | (14)  $165 | C  K  F | |
| Nature's Inn  932 Greenway  www.naturesinnatbigbearlake.com  dogs allowed by advance reservation only, open  walking area, 2 blocks to park | 909-585-2226  877-585-2226 | (8)  $40–  $110 | C  K  M/F | |

## Big Bear Lake

| All Seasons Resort Rentals  41348 Big Bear Blvd  www.allseasonsbigbear.com  pet fee $50/stay  1 bdrm cabins to 5 bdrm lakefront vacation homes,  wooded residential walking areas, resident wildlife  so dogs must be leashed | 909-866-5851  800-752-4020 | (50)  $85–  $500 | K | T |
|---|---|---|---|---|
| Alpine Getaway Resort Rentals  40019 Big Bear Blvd  www.alpinegetaway.com  vacation homes, woods and hiking trails, close to  national forest and ski areas | 909-866-5711  800-822-5946 | (48)  $100–  $150 | K | S |
| Alpine Village Suites  546 Pine Knot Ave  www.2avs.com  suites/cabins sleep up to 6, lakeside walking area,  hiking trails in woods | 909-866-5460 | (8)  $89–  $269 | C  K | IS |

| | | | | |
|---|---|---|---|---|
| **Bear Country Resorts** 909-866-4650<br>40055 Big Bear Blvd  877-822-0212<br>www.bigbear-rentals.com<br>homes/cabins, residential neighborhoods, trails | (40)<br>$150–<br>$185 | K | T | |
| **Bear Lake Resort Rentals** 909-866-7750<br>42007 Fox Farm Rd # 4  800-533-7368<br>www.bearlakeresortrentals.com<br>cabins/vacation homes, residential areas, trails | (65)<br>$85–<br>$500 | K | | |
| **Best Western Big Bear Chateau** 909-866-6666<br>42200 Moonridge Rd  800-232-7466<br>www.bestwestern.com/bigbearchateau<br> pet fee $30/1st day, $15/each additional day<br>woods and hiking trails, short drive to parks | (80)<br>$79–<br>$179 | C<br>R/L<br>FR | OP<br>S<br>T | |
| **Big Bear Cabin 4U** 818-247-8704<br>on Villa Grove<br>www.vacationrentals411.com/vacation/5929.html<br>dogs under 40 lbs only, rustic 3 bdrm cabin sleeps 6,<br>pet cookies/bowls/leash, fenced yard, close to trails | (1)<br>$125–<br>$195 | K | | |
| **Big Bear Cabins–Lakeside** 909-866-2723<br>39774 Big Bear Blvd<br>rooms/cabins, lakeside area, ½ mile to trails | (15)<br>$69–<br>$169 | K | IS | |
| **Big Bear Cool Cabins** 909-866-7374<br>www.bigbearcoolcabins.com  800-550-8779<br>vacation homes/cabins/condominiums, surrounded<br>by national forest and walking trails | (65)<br>$100–<br>$250 | K | S | |
| **Big Bear Frontier Hotel Resort** 909-866-2232<br>40472 Big Bear Blvd  800-457-6401<br>www.bigbearfrontier.com  each pet $15/day<br>rooms/cabins sleep up to 12, lakeside walking<br>area, close to hiking trails | (63)<br>$97–<br>$500 | CB<br>K | OP | |
| **Big Bear Lakefront Lodge** 909-866-8271<br>40360 Lake View Dr  each pet $10/day<br>www.lakefrontlodge.com  1½ miles to park | (22)<br>$90–<br>$180 | (k) | IS | |
| **Big Bear Lake Inn** 909-866-3477<br>39471 Big Bear Blvd  800-843-0103<br>www.bigbearlakeinn.net<br>small dogs only, walking areas, 1 mile to trails | (50)<br>$49–<br>$189 | F | OP<br>T | |

| C = coffee<br>CB = continental<br>    breakfast<br>F = refrigerator<br>FB = full breakfast<br>FR = fitness room | GP = guest pass to<br>    fitness center<br>IP = indoor pool<br>IS = in-room spa<br>K = full kitchen<br>(k) = kitchenette | L = lounge<br>M = microwave<br>OP = outdoor pool<br>R = restaurant<br>S = sauna/steam<br>T = spa or hot tub | # of units)<br>& rates | food<br>& drink | pool, sauna<br>& hot tub |
|---|---|---|---|---|---|
| **Big Bear Lake (continued)** | | | | | |
| **Big Bear Lodge**        909-866-1779<br>40451 Big Bear Blvd    888-949-2327<br>www.bigbearlodge.com    pet fee $25/stay<br>dogs in smoking units only, cabins/vacation homes,<br>grassy and wooded walking areas, close to lake | | | (6)<br>$75–<br>$125 | C<br>M/F<br>R | OP |
| **Big Bear Mountain Resort Rentals**  909-878-2233<br>40729 Village Dr #2    800-966-9971<br>www.bigbear1.com    pet fee $20/day<br>1–5 bdrm vacation homes sleep up to 16, some with<br>fenced yards, close to hiking trails and parks | | | (100)<br>$99 | K | T |
| **Big Bear Vacations**        909-866-8200<br>40729-2 Village Dr    800-524-6600<br>    pet fee $10/day<br>vacation homes sleep up to 20, some with fenced<br>yards, short drive to lake and hiking trails | | | (250)<br>$200 | K | T |
| **Black Forest Lodge & Cabins**  909-866-2166<br>41121 Big Bear Blvd    800-255-4378<br>www.blackforestlodge.com<br>suites/cabins/vacation homes sleep up to 14,<br>on 3½ wooded acres for walking dogs | | | (74)<br>$75–<br>$800 | M/F<br>K | OP<br>IS |
| **Boulder Creek Resort**    909-866-2665<br>760 Blue Jay Rd #12    800-244-2327<br>www.800bigbear.com    pet fee $10/day<br>rooms/1–2 bdrm cabins, 4 bdrm chalet, next to park | | | (32)<br>$45–<br>$450 | K | OP<br>T |
| **Cal-Pine Chalets**        909-866-2574<br>41545 Big Bear Blvd    800-965-7463<br>www.cal-pine.com<br>studios/vacation homes/3 bdrm chalets sleep up to<br>10, wooded walking areas | | | (21)<br>$69–<br>$150 | K | |

| | | | |
|---|---|---|---|
| **Cozy Hollow Lodge** 909-866-9694 <br> 40409 Big Bear Blvd 800-882-44480 <br> www.cozyhollowlodge.com each pet $10/day <br> studio to 2 bdrm cabins, pet relief area, seasonal <br> stream and woods, residential streets to walk dogs | (13) <br> $50– <br> $169 | C <br> K <br> M/F | |
| **Creek Runner's Lodge** 909-866-7473 <br> 374 Georgia St <br> www.www.pineknot.com/~creekrunner <br> 1–3 bdrm cabins sleep 2–6, ¼ mile to lakeside park | (11) <br> $65– <br> $200 | K | IS |
| **Eagle's Nest B & B** 909-866-6465 <br> 41675 Big Bear Blvd 888-866-6465 <br> www.eaglesnestlodgebigbear.com <br> suite/2 bdrm cabin that sleeps 4, lawn, woods, trails | (11) <br> $115– <br> $175 | K <br> (k) | |
| **Escape For All Seasons Rentals** 909-866-7504 <br> 41935 Switzerland Dr <br> www.bigbearescape.com <br> pet-friendly 2 bdrm condominium (unit #62) sleeps 6, <br> deck, residential area, near national forest and trails | (55) <br> $100– <br> $190 | K | |
| **Fireside Lodge** 909-866-2253 <br> 40660 Lake View Dr 800-831-2253 <br> www.firesidelodge.net pet fee $25/stay <br> small lakeside park, 2 miles to hiking trails | (31) <br> $179– <br> $159 | CB <br> M/F | OP |
| **Gold Mine Lodge** 909-866-5118 <br> 42268 Moonridge Rd 800-641-2327 <br> dogs under 35 lbs only pet fee $35/stay <br> sleeping room/1 bdrm suite, park-like walking areas | (11) <br> $59– <br> $155 | CB <br> K | T |
| **Golden Bear Cottages** 909-866-2010 <br> 39367 Big Bear Blvd 800-461-1023 <br> www.goldenbear.net each pet $10/day <br> fenced patios or yards, open field, 3 blocks to water- <br> front, 1 mile to off-leash dog park and hiking trails | (27) <br> $79– <br> $109 | C <br> K <br> M/F | OP <br> T <br> IS |
| **Grey Squirrel Resort and Vacation Rentals** <br> 39372 Big Bear Blvd 909-866-4335 <br> www.greysquirrel.com 800-381-5569 <br> each pet $10/day <br> 1 bdrm cabins to 5 bdrm vacation homes sleep up to <br> 15, park-like setting, 2 miles to park and hiking trails | (48) <br> $85– <br> $650 | K | OP <br> T |

| C = coffee<br>CB = continental<br>　　breakfast<br>F = refrigerator<br>FB = full breakfast<br>FR = fitness room | GP = guest pass to<br>　　fitness center<br>IP = indoor pool<br>IS = in-room spa<br>K = full kitchen<br>(k) = kitchenette | L = lounge<br>M = microwave<br>OP = outdoor pool<br>R = restaurant<br>S = sauna/steam<br>T = spa or hot tub | (# of units)<br>& rates | food<br>& drink | pool, sauna<br>& hot tub |
|---|---|---|---|---|---|
| **Big Bear Lake (continued)** | | | | | |
| **Happy Bear Vacation Rentals**　909-866-7744<br>41592 Big Bear Blvd　　　　　800-766-9776<br>www.happybearrentals.com　　pet fee $50/stay<br>1–2 bdrm vacation homes sleep up to 6, some with<br>fenced yards, bike and walking path around lake | | | (10)<br>$100–<br>$200 | K | |
| **Honey Bear Lodge**　　　　　909-866-7825<br>40994 Pennsylvania Ave　　　800-628-8714<br>www.honeybearlodge.com　　pet fee $10/day<br>rooms/1–4 bdrm cabins/vacation homes sleep up to<br>20, woods and grassy areas, bike and walking trail,<br>2 blocks to lake | | | (22)<br>$39–<br>$559 | C<br>K<br>M/F | IS |
| **Lakeview Forest Resort Rentals**　909-866-8686<br>40715 Lakeview Dr　　　　　pet fee $25/stay<br>www.bigbearparadise.com<br>rooms/cabins sleep up to 12, lakefront and woods | | | (20)<br>$95–<br>$475 | C<br>K | IS |
| **Log Cabin Resort Rentals**　　909-866-8708<br>40679 Lakeview Dr　　　　　800-767-0205<br>www.logcabinresorts.com　　pet fee $10/day<br>studio to 4 bdrm cabins, 2 blocks to waterfront and<br>park, short drive to off-leash dog park | | | (12)<br>$135–<br>$600 | K<br>M/F | T |
| **Majestic Moose Lodge**　　　909-866-2435<br>39328 Big Bear Blvd　　　　　877-585-5855<br>www.majesticmooselodge.com　pet fee $10/day<br>pet relief area, 2 wooded acres, 5 minute walk to lake | | | (21)<br>$99–<br>$229 | C<br>M/F | OP<br>IS |
| **Moore's Motel**　　　　　　909-866-4804<br>560 Edgemoore Rd<br>cabins sleep up to 4, grassy and wooded walking<br>areas, 3 blocks to lake | | | (4)<br>$53–<br>$63 | K | |

| | | | | |
|---|---|---|---|---|
| **Motel 6** 909-585-6666 42899 E Big Bear Blvd 800-466-8356 www.motel6.com 1 dog only, pet cleanup bags, creekside walking area, ½ mile to walking trail, short drive to parks | (120) $46–$70 | C | OP |
| **Mountain Lodging Unlimited** 909-866-5500 www.bigbearmtnlodging.com cabins to 4 bdrm vacation homes | (4) $50–$600 | | |
| **Mountain Vista Resort** 909-585-7855 1288 Club View Dr 800-221-3143 www.mountainvistaresort.net pet fee $20/day dogs allowed in smoking rooms and 3 bdrm condo only, deck, wooded hillside, 2 miles to lake | (12) $150–$300 | K | |
| **Pine Haven Cottages** 909-866-2637 517 Knight Ave 1 small adult dog, fenced yard, 1 block to lake | (10) $70–$75 | C K | |
| **Pine Knot Guest Ranch** 909-866-6500 908 Pine Knot Ave 800-866-3446 www.pineknotguestranch.com each pet $10/day rooms/homes sleep up to 8, lawn and walking trails, 4 blocks to lake | (13) $89–$169 | C K (k) | IS |
| **Pine Tree Cottage** 818-314-8866 421 Crane Dr www.bigbear-cabin.com 3 bdrm cottage sleeps 10, fenced yard, hiking trails | (1) $150–$250 | K | T |
| **Russian Big Bear Cabins** 909-866-7633 586 Main St 323-974-6175 1 bdrm cabins, walking distance to lake and village | (9) $75–$120 | K | T IS |
| **Shore Acres Lodge** 909-866-8200 40090 Lakeview Dr 800-524-6600 www.bigbearvacations.com each pet $10/day cabins sleep 8, lakeside walking area, close to trails | (11) $125–$175 | K | OP |
| **Sleepy Forest Resort** 909-866-7444 426 S Eureka Dr 800-544-7454 www.sleepyforest.com each pet $25/day cabins sleep 10, 3 blocks to lakeside park | (25) $129–$229 | CB K M/F | IS |

|  | | |
|---|---|---|
| C = coffee | GP = guest pass to | L = lounge |
| CB = continental | fitness center | M = microwave |
| breakfast | IP = indoor pool | OP = outdoor pool |
| F = refrigerator | IS = in-room spa | R = restaurant |
| FB = full breakfast | K = full kitchen | S = sauna/steam |
| FR = fitness room | (k) = kitchenette | T = spa or hot tub |

## Big Bear Lake (continued)

| Listing | Phone | (# of units) & rates | food & drink | pool, sauna & hot tub |
|---|---|---|---|---|
| **Spencer Rental Services** 42139 Big Bear Blvd www.donsellersrentals.com 1–7 bdrm vacation homes, wooded walking areas | 909-866-2483 800-237-3725 | (90) $90– $600 | K | T |
| **Stage Coach Lodge** 652 Jeffries www.stagecoachlodge.com   each pet $10/day studio to 3 bdrm cabins sleep up to 16, close to parks, ¼ mile to lake, bike path across lake | 909-878-3088 800-756-9871 | (15) $103– $369 | CB K | IS |
| **Timber Haven Lodge** 877 Tulip Lane www.timberhavenlodge.com   pet fee $10/day 1–2 bdrm log cabin/cottage suites sleep up to 6, patios, wooded area, across street to national forest | 909-866-7207 888-282-3568 | (10) $99– $225 | CB K | T IS |
| **Timberline Lodge** 39921 Big Bear Blvd www.thetimberlinelodge.com   pet fee $10/day rooms/vacation homes sleep up to 8, marina, boat rentals, woods and meadow, near hiking trails | 909-866-4141 800-803-4111 | (21) $79– $300 | C K M/F | OP |
| **Village Reservation Services** 713 Pine Knot Ave www.villagereservations.net studio cabins to 6 bdrm homes, hiking trails | 909-866-8583 | (85) $99– $250 | K | T |
| **Vintage Inn Resort** 41066 Big Bear Blvd www.vintageresort.com   pet fee $10/day   lakeside walking area | 909-866-4978 | (35) $69– $89 | (k) | |
| **Wildwood Resort** 40210 Big Bear Blvd www.wildwoodresort.com   each pet $10/day rooms/suites/cabins sleep up to 10, ½ mile to lake | 909-878-2178 888-294-5396 | (29) $85– $100 | CB K M/F | OP T |

## Big Bend

| | | | |
|---|---|---|---|
| **Forest Springs Getaway**    530-337-6704 <br> pet fee $10–$25/day <br> www.forest-springs-getaway.com <br> rooms in log house, guesthouse with outdoor sitting area, private lake, fields, forest and miles of trails | (4) <br> $120 | K <br> R | |

## Big Pine

| | | | |
|---|---|---|---|
| **Big Pine Motel**    760-938-2282 <br> 370 S Main St    pet fee $5/day <br> 1–2 dogs only, pet relief area, park-like picnic area | (15) <br> $44– <br> $85 | K <br> M/F | |
| **Bristlecone Motel & Market**    760-938-2067 <br> 101 N Main St <br> small dogs only, vacant lot, 1 block to park | (17) <br> $40– <br> $68 | C <br> M/F | |

## Big Sur

| | | | |
|---|---|---|---|
| **Gorda by the Sea**    805-927-4600 <br> Hwy 1 <br> www.bigsurgordasprings.com <br> dogs under 25 lbs allowed in 2 cabins only, lawn and gardens, close to hiking trails, 1 mile to beach | (11) <br> $175– <br> $250 | C <br> F | |

## Bishop

| | | | |
|---|---|---|---|
| **Best Western Bishop Holiday Spa Lodge** <br> 1025 N Main St    760-873-3543 <br> small dogs only, open walking area    800-576-3543 | (89) <br> $80– <br> $95 | CB <br> M/F | OP <br> T |
| **Bishop Creek Lodge & Parchers Resort** <br> 2100 S Lake Rd    760-873-4484 <br> www.bishopcreekresorts.com    pet fee $10/day <br> modern or rustic cabins sleep up to 8, high desert walking area | (26) <br> $90– <br> $235 | CB <br> K <br> R/L | |
| **Bishop Village Motel**    760-872-81556 <br> 286 W Elm St    888-668-554 <br> www.bishopvillagemotel.com    pet fee $10/day <br> lawn walking area, 3 blocks to park, close to trails | (17) <br> $49– <br> $79 | C <br> (k) <br> M/F | OP |

| C = coffee<br>CB = continental<br>    breakfast<br>F = refrigerator<br>FB = full breakfast<br>FR = fitness room | GP = guest pass to<br>    fitness center<br>IP = indoor pool<br>IS = in-room spa<br>K = full kitchen<br>(k) = kitchenette | L = lounge<br>M = microwave<br>OP = outdoor pool<br>R = restaurant<br>S = sauna/steam<br>T = spa or hot tub | (# of units)<br>& rates | food<br>& drink | pool, sauna<br>& hot tub |
|---|---|---|---|---|---|

## Bishop (continued)

| | | | | | |
|---|---|---|---|---|---|
| **Chalfant House B & B**<br>213 Academy St<br>www.chalfanthouse.com<br>dogs by advance reservation in cottage that sleeps 4,<br>fenced yard, 3 blocks to park, new dog park will be<br>completed soon | 760-872-1790<br>800-641-2996<br>pet fee $10/day | | (7)<br>$100–<br>$105 | FB | |
| **Comfort Inn**<br>805 N Main St<br>www.choicehotels.com<br>open field, 1 block to park | 760-873-4284<br>800-576-4080<br>each pet $5/day | | (54)<br>$59–<br>$89 | CB<br>M/F | OP<br>T |
| **Days Inn**<br>724 W Line St<br>www.daysinn.com<br>dogs allowed in smoking rooms only, open field | 760-872-1095<br>800-329-7466<br>pet fee $7–$10/day | | (73)<br>$70–<br>$80 | CB<br>M/F | OP |
| **Holiday Inn Express**<br>636 N Main St<br>www.holidayinnbishop.com<br>dogs by advance reservations only, next to park | 760-872-2423<br>877-395-2395<br>pet fee $20/day | | (66)<br>$80–<br>$150 | CB<br>M/F | OP<br>S<br>T<br>FR |
| **Joseph House Inn B & B**<br>376 W Yaney St<br>www.josephhouseinn.com<br>dogs by advance reservation in 3 rooms with outside<br>entrances, 3 garden acres, waterfront walking area | 760-872-3389 | | (5)<br>$125–<br>$165 | FB | |
| **Motel 6**<br>1005 N Main St<br>www.motel6.com<br>grassy area, 1½ blocks to park | 760-873-8426<br>800-466-8356 | | (52)<br>$50–<br>$90 | C<br>F | OP |
| **Paradise Resort**<br>7997 Lower Rock Creek Rd<br>cabins sleep 4, creekside walking trails, described by<br>owner as "paradise for people and pets" | 760-387-2370<br>each pet $10/stay | | (20)<br>$85–<br>$134 | K<br>R | |

| | | | | |
|---|---|---|---|---|
| **Ramada Inn** 760-872-1771 155 E Elm St 800-272-6232 www.bishopramadalimited.com    each pet $15/day pet relief area, 1½ blocks to city park | (52) $80– $110 | CB M/F | OP T |
| **Rodeway Inn** 760-873-3564 150 E Elm St 800-356-3221 www.choicehotels.com small lawn walking area, 1 block to city park | (55) $55– $130 | CB M/F | OP |
| **Starlite Motel** 760-873-4912 192 Short St 877-873-4912 open fields and dirt walking area    pet fee $7/day | (25) $39 | C M/F | OP |
| **Sunrise Motel** 760-873-3656 106 MacIver Lane large grassy walking area, 2 blocks to park | (9) $59 | C K | |
| **Thunderbird Motel** 760-873-4215 190 W Pine St 888-828-2473 pet fee $4/day open walking area, 1 block to pool, 1½ blocks to park | (23) $44– $79 | CB M/F | OP |
| **Town House Motel** 760-872-4541 625 N Main St 888-399-1651 small dogs only, grassy walking area, 1 block to park | (34) $45– $55 | C M/F | OP |
| **Trees Motel** 760-873-6391 796 W Line St    each pet $10/day open walking areas, 1½ miles to city park | (16) $48– $70 | K F | |
| **Vagabond Inn** 760-873-6351 1030 N Main St 800-522-1555 www.vagabondinn.com    each pet $5/stay lawn walking area, 2 blocks to city park | (80) $70– $100 | CB M/F | OP T |

## Blairsden

| | | | |
|---|---|---|---|
| **Camp Layman Resort** 530-836-2356 512 Camp Layman Rd    pet fee $10/day dogs by advance reservation only, cabins sleep 2–10, riverfront woods and walking trails | (13) $70– $150 | K | |
| **Feather River Inn** 530-836-2623 65899 Hwy 70 888-324-6400 www.featherriverinn.com    pet fee $10/stay rustic cabins, on 100 acres, fishing pond and trails | (35) $69 | FB R | OP |

| C = coffee  GP = guest pass to  L = lounge<br>CB = continental       fitness center  M = microwave<br>  breakfast  IP = indoor pool  OP = outdoor pool<br>F = refrigerator  IS = in-room spa  R = restaurant<br>FB = full breakfast  K = full kitchen  S = sauna/steam<br>FR = fitness room  (k) = kitchenette  T = spa or hot tub | (# of units)<br>& rates | food<br>& drink | pool, sauna<br>& hot tub |
|---|---|---|---|
| **Blairsden (continued)** | | | |
| **Feather River Park Resort**     530-836-2328<br>Hwy 89 Box 37 (Hwy 89 & A14)     pet fee $8/day<br>www.featherriverparkresort.com<br>1–2 bdrm log cabins, open May 1-Oct 10, 160 acres<br>with meadows, trails, canyons, streams and lakes | (35)<br>$125–<br>$225 | K | OP |
| **Gray Eagle Lodge**     530-836-2511<br>Gold Lake Rd Box 38     800-635-8778<br>www.grayeaglelodge.com     each pet $20/day<br>rustic cabins sleep up to 6, breakfast and dinner<br>included in daily rate, miles of hiking trails | (19)<br>$190–<br>$235 | FB<br>F<br>R | |
| **Blythe** | | | |
| **Best Value Inn**     760-922-5145<br>850 W Hobsonway     each pet $5/day<br>www.bestvalueinn.com<br>large lawn walking area | (50)<br>$49–<br>$54 | CB<br>M/F<br>R/L | OP |
| **Best Western Sahara Inn**     760-922-7105<br>825 W Hobsonway     800-528-1234<br>www.bestwesterncalifornia.com<br>lawn, close to park | (46)<br>$54–<br>$79 | CB<br>M/F | OP<br>T |
| **Blue Line Motel & Trailer Park**     760-922-3151<br>950 E Hobsonway     877-209-6777<br>1 dog in smoking rooms only, vacant lot to walk dogs | (17)<br>$33–<br>$36 | F | |
| **Blythe Inn**     760-922-2184<br>401 E Hobsonway     each pet $3/day<br>lawn and vacant lot to walk dogs, 4 blocks to park | (64)<br>$40–<br>$299 | C<br>M/F<br>R | OP<br>FR |
| **Comfort Suites**     760-922-9209<br>545 E Hobsonway     866-804-4549<br>www.choicehotels.com     pet fee $10/day<br>small lawn, 3 blocks to park | (67)<br>$55–<br>$89 | CB<br>M/F | OP<br>T<br>FR |

| | | | | |
|---|---|---|---|---|
| **Desert Winds Motel**  9090 E Hobsonway  dogs in smoking rooms only, lawn, 3 miles to park | 760-922-0273  pet fee $5/day | (23)  $27 | M/F | |
| **Dunes Motel**  9820 E Hobsonway  dogs in smoking rooms only, open walking area | 760-922-4126  each pet $5/day | (30)  $38 | C  M/F | OP |
| **Hampton Inn**  900 W Hobsonway  www.hiblythe.com  dogs in smoking rooms only, 2 miles to park | 760-922-9000  800-426-7866  pet fee $10/stay | (59)  $69–  $149 | FB  M/F | OP  T  FR |
| **Holiday Inn Express**  600 W Donlon St  www.hieblythe.com  lawn and gravel walking areas, 1 block to park | 760-921-2300  800-465-4329  pet fee $10/day | (66)  $89 | CB  M/F | IP  T |
| **Legacy Inn**  903 W Hobsonway  dogs in smoking rooms only, grass and gravel areas | 760-922-4146  877-737-5342 | (48)  $46–  $86 | CB  M/F | OP  T |
| **Motel 6**  500 W Donlon St  www.motel6.com | 760-922-6666  800-466-8356  lawn, 1½ blocks to park | (92)  $46–  $52 | C | OP |
| **Super 11 Inn**  1020 W Hobsonway  small to medium dogs only, large field | 760-922-3161 | (46)  $45–  $95 | CB  M/F | OP |
| **Super 8 Motel**  550 W Donlon St  www.super8.com  lawn and gravel walking areas, 1 block to park | 760-922-8881  866-425-9843  pet fee $5/day | (79)  $44–  $89 | CB  M/F | OP |
| **Travelers Inn Express**  1781 E Hobsonway  large lawn, 2 miles to park | 760-922-3334 | (35)  $59–  $129 | C  M/F | OP  T |

## Bodega Bay

| | | | | |
|---|---|---|---|---|
| **Bodega Coast Inn**  521 Cost Hwy 1  www.bodegacoastinn.com  dogs allowed in 2 ground floor rooms with outside  entrances, cliffside walking area overlooking ocean | 707-875-2218  800-346-6999  pet fee $30/stay | (44)  $169–  $279 | CB  F | T |

| C = coffee  GP = guest pass to  L = lounge<br>CB = continental  fitness center  M = microwave<br>breakfast  IP = indoor pool  OP = outdoor pool<br>F = refrigerator  IS = in-room spa  R = restaurant<br>FB = full breakfast  K = full kitchen  S = sauna/steam<br>FR = fitness room  (k) = kitchenette  T = spa or hot tub | (# of units) & rates | food & drink | pool, sauna & hot tub |
|---|---|---|---|

## Bolinas

| | | | |
|---|---|---|---|
| **Dog's Inn**  415-868-2110<br>20 Mesa Rd<br>½ acre fenced yard overlooking Bolinas Lagoon,<br>pet-friendly small town, walking areas, close to<br>off-leash dog beach | (4)<br>$130–<br>$220 | FB<br>F | OP |

## Boonville

| | | | |
|---|---|---|---|
| **Boonville Hotel**  707-895-2210<br>14050 Hwy 128  pet fee $15/day<br>www.boonvillehotel.com<br>historic hotel, cottages, quiet street for walking dogs,<br>8 miles to park | (10)<br>$215–<br>$250 | CB<br>F<br>R | |
| **The Other Place**  707-894-5322<br>www.sheepdung.com<br>1–2 bdrm cottages, breakfast supplies, on 550 acre<br>ranch, off-leash areas, trails, swimming pond | (3)<br>$175–<br>$300 | C<br>K | |

## Boron

| | | | |
|---|---|---|---|
| **Best Boron Motel**  760-762-5229<br>26881 Twenty Mule Team Rd<br>small dogs allowed in smoking rooms only, large<br>open walking area, 3 blocks to park | (35)<br>$50–<br>$69 | C<br>M/F | OP |

## Borrego Springs

| | | | |
|---|---|---|---|
| **Borrego Springs Resort**  760-767-5700<br>1112 Tilting T Dr  888-826-7734<br>www.borregospringsresort.com<br>dogs under 15 lbs only, open area, 5 miles to park | (100)<br>$119–<br>$135 | CB<br>M/F | OP<br>T<br>FR |
| **Borrego Valley Inn**  760-767-0311<br>405 Palm Canyon Dr  800-333-5810<br>www.borregovalleyinn.com  each pet $25/stay<br>on 10 acres for walking dogs | (15)<br>$455–<br>$220 | CB<br>K<br>M/F | OP<br>T |

| | | | | |
|---|---|---|---|---|
| **Stanlunds Resort Inn & Suites** | 760-767-5501 | (21) | CB | OP |
| 2771 Borrego Springs Rd | pet fee $10/day | $55– | K | T |
| www.stanlunds.com | | $100 | M/F | |
| private patios, desert and walking trails, state park | | | | |
| **Whispering Sands Motel** | 760-767-4760 | (8) | CB | OP |
| 2376 Borrego Springs Rd | each pet $5/day | $55– | (k) | |
| www.thewhisperingsands.net | | $85 | | |
| community kitchen, open areas, 2 blocks to park | | | | |

## Boulder Creek

| | | | | |
|---|---|---|---|---|
| **Merrybrook Lodge** | 831-338-6813 | (10) | C | |
| 13420 Big Basin Way | pet fee $15/day | $120– | K | |
| www.showhotel.com | | $150 | F | |
| rooms/cottages, creek and redwoods, gravel walking area, 7 miles to park | | | | |

## Brawley

| | | | | |
|---|---|---|---|---|
| **Townhouse Lodge Motel** | 760-344-5120 | (40) | C | |
| 135 Main St | 888-820-5120 | $54– | M/F | |
| lawn, 5 minute walk to park | pet fee $15/stay | $58 | | |

## Brea

| | | | | |
|---|---|---|---|---|
| **Homestead Studio Suites Hotel** | 714-528-2500 | (133) | K | |
| 3050 E Imperial Hwy | pet fee $25/day | $53– | | |
| www.homesteadhotels.com | | $77 | | |
| pet relief area, ½ mile to park | | | | |
| **Hyland Motel** | 714-990-6867 | (26) | C | |
| 727 S Brea Blvd | | $55 | M/F | |
| small dogs only, lawn area | | | | |
| **Woodfin Suites** | 714-579-3200 | (88) | FB | OP |
| 3100 E Imperial Hwy | 800-966-3346 | $99– | K | T |
| www.woodfinsuitehotels.com | pet fee $5/day | $139 | | GP |
| small lawn, ¾ mile to park | | | | |

## Bridgeport

| | | | | |
|---|---|---|---|---|
| **Best Western Ruby Inn** | 760-932-7241 | (30) | CB | T |
| 333 Main St | 800-937-8376 | $120– | M/F | |
| www.bestwestern.com/rubyinn | | $160 | | |
| pet relief area | | | | |

| C = coffee<br>CB = continental<br>　　breakfast<br>F = refrigerator<br>FB = full breakfast<br>FR = fitness room | GP = guest pass to<br>　　fitness center<br>IP = indoor pool<br>IS = in-room spa<br>K = full kitchen<br>(k) = kitchenette | L = lounge<br>M = microwave<br>OP = outdoor pool<br>R = restaurant<br>S = sauna/steam<br>T = spa or hot tub | # of units)<br>& rates | food<br>& drink | pool, sauna<br>& hot tub |
|---|---|---|---|---|---|
| ### Bridgeport (continued) | | | | | |
| **Redwood Motel**<br>425 Main St<br>www.redwoodmotel.net<br>clean well-behaved dogs welcome, pet relief area,<br>lots of walking trails | 760-932-7060<br>888-932-3292<br>pet fee $5/day | | (20)<br>$45–<br>$110 | C<br>M/F | |
| **Silver Maple Inn**<br>310 Main St<br>www.silvermapleinn.com<br>large walking area, next to park | 760-932-7383 | | (20)<br>$75–<br>$95 | C<br>F | |
| **Twin Lakes Resort**<br>10316 Twin Lakes Rd<br><br>1–3 bdrm housekeeping cabins sleep up to 12,<br>waterfront and walking trails in national forest area | 760-932-7751<br>877-932-7751<br>pet fee $25/stay | | (8)<br>$110–<br>$147 | K | |
| **Walker River Lodge**<br>100 Main St<br>www.walkerriverlodge.com<br>open mid-May to Mid-November, lawn walking area | 760-932-7021<br>800-688-3351 | | (36)<br>$55–<br>$200 | CB<br>M/F | OP<br>T |
| ### Brisbane | | | | | |
| **Homewood Suites**<br>2000 Shoreline Ct<br>www.homewoodsuites.com<br>dogs under 75 lbs only, Mon–Thur beverages and<br>light dinner, waterfront path, free shuttle to parks | 650-589-1600<br>800-226-5466<br>pet fee $75/stay | | (177)<br>$89–<br>$149 | CB<br>K | IP<br>FR |
| ### Brownsville | | | | | |
| **Brownsville Motel**<br>8592 La Porte Rd<br>open and wooded areas for walking dogs | 530-675-2480 | | (14)<br>$55–<br>$66 | | |

## Buellton

| | | | | |
|---|---|---|---|---|
| **A Country Lane Motel** | 805-688-4181 | (14) | M/F | |
| 412 Avenue of the Flags | pet fee $10/day | $49– | | |
| lawn walking area, across street to park | | $120 | | |
| **Motel 6** | 805-688-7797 | (59) | C | OP |
| 333 McMurray Rd | 800-466-8356 | $48– | | |
| www.motel6.com   pet relief area, 5 blocks to park | | $62 | | |
| **Rancho Santa Barbara Marriott** | 805-688-1000 | (149) | CB | OP |
| 555 McMurray Rd | pet fee $50/stay | $110– | R/L | |
| www.santaynezhotels.com   lawn, 3 miles to park | | $239 | | |
| **Rodeway Inn** | 805-688-0022 | (60) | CB | |
| 630 Avenue of the Flags | 888-424-6423 | $50– | M/F | |
| www.buelltonrodewayinn.com   pet fee $25/stay | | $120 | | |
| large lawn walking areas | | | | |

## Buena Park

| | | | | |
|---|---|---|---|---|
| **Best Western Inn & Suites** | 714-522-7360 | (177) | CB | OP |
| 7555 Beach Blvd | 888-522-5885 | $69– | M/F | T |
| www.bestwesterncalifornia.com   pet fee $25/stay | | $99 | | IS |
| dogs under 25 lbs only, gravel walking area | | | | |
| **Colony Inn** | 714-527-2201 | (90) | CB | OP |
| 7800 Crescent Ave | 800-982-6566 | $40– | | |
| | pet fee $2/day | $65 | | |
| **Covered Wagon Motel** | 714-995-0033 | (19) | C | OP |
| 7830 Crescent Ave | pet fee $7/day | $55 | M/F | |
| lawn walking area | | | | |
| **Motel 6** | 714-522-1200 | (187) | C | OP |
| 7051 Valley View St | 800-466-8356 | $44– | | |
| www.motel6.com   small grassy area, close to park | | $48 | | |
| **Red Roof Inn** | 714-670-9000 | (131) | C | OP |
| 7121 Beach Blvd | 800-733-7663 | $50– | M/F | T |
| www.redroof.com   dogs under 50 lbs only | | $70 | | GP |

## Burbank

| | | | | |
|---|---|---|---|---|
| **Coast Anabelle Hotel** | 818-845-7800 | (47) | C | OP |
| 2011 W Olive Ave | 800-663-1144 | $129 | F | FR |
| www.coasthotels.com   3 blocks to park | | | R | |

| C = coffee<br>CB = continental<br>breakfast<br>F = refrigerator<br>FB = full breakfast<br>FR = fitness room | GP = guest pass to<br>fitness center<br>IP = indoor pool<br>IS = in-room spa<br>K = full kitchen<br>(k) = kitchenette | L = lounge<br>M = microwave<br>OP = outdoor pool<br>R = restaurant<br>S = sauna/steam<br>T = spa or hot tub | # of units)<br>& rates | food<br>& drink | pool, sauna<br>& hot tub |
|---|---|---|---|---|---|
| **Burbank (continued)** | | | | | |
| **Graciela Burbank**   818-842-8887<br>322 N Pass Ave   888-956-1900<br>www.thegraciela.com   pet fee $150/stay<br>dogs allowed in ground floor rooms with outside<br>entrances and private patios, residential streets | | | (101)<br>$157–<br>$173 | FB<br>CB<br>L | S<br>T |
| **Hilton Burbank**   818-843-6000<br>2500 N Hollywood Way   800-840-6450<br>www.burbankairport.hilton.com   pet fee $25/day<br>dogs under 50 lbs, lawn areas, 5 minute drive to park | | | (180)<br>$200 | F<br>R/L<br>T | OP<br>S<br>FR |
| **Holiday Inn Burbank Media Center**<br>150 E Angeleno Ave   818-841-4770<br>www.holiday-inn.com   800-465-4329<br>small lawn walking areas   each pet $10/day | | | (480)<br>$123–<br>$149 | C<br>F<br>R | OP<br>FR |
| **Safari Inn**   818-845-8586<br>1911 W Olive Ave   800-782-4373<br>residential street for walking dogs, 3 blocks to park | | | (55)<br>$92 | C<br>F | OP<br>FR |
| **Burlingame** | | | | | |
| **Crowne Plaza Airport Burlingame**   650-342-9200<br>1177 Airport Blvd   800-411-7275<br>www.sfocp.com<br>next to fenced off-leash dog park | | | (309)<br>$79–<br>$99 | R/L | OP<br>T<br>FR |
| **Doubletree Hotel San Francisco Airport**<br>835 Airport Blvd   650-344-5500<br>www.doubletree.com   800-222-8733<br>park and open field   pet fee $20/stay | | | (390)<br>$89–<br>$179 | CB<br>R/L | OP<br>FR |
| **Embassy Suites Hotel**   650-342-4600<br>150 Anza Blvd   800-362-2779<br>www.embassyburlingame.com   pet fee $50/stay<br>1 bdrm suites sleep up to 6, bayside walking trail,<br>1 block to fenced off-leash dog park | | | (340)<br>$99–<br>$179 | FB<br>(k) | IP<br>S<br>T<br>FR |

| | | | |
|---|---|---|---|
| **Red Roof Inn San Francisco Airport** <br> 777 Airport Blvd            650-342-7772 <br> www.redroof.com            800-733-7663 <br> lawn walking area, jogging path, 300 yards to park | (213) <br> $49– <br> $59 | C <br> R | OP <br> GP |
| **San Francisco Airport Marriott**    650-692-9100 <br> 1800 Old Bayshore Hwy            800-228-9290 <br> www.marriott.com <br> small dogs only, next to dog-friendly beach | (668) <br> $159– <br> $179 | C <br> R/L | |
| **Sheraton Gateway**            650-340-8500 <br> 600 Airport Blvd            800-325-3535 <br> www.sheratonsfo.com    walking trail around bay | (404) <br> $59– <br> $169 | F <br> R/L | IP |
| **Vagabond Inn**            650-692-4040 <br> 1640 Bayshore Hwy            800-522-1555 <br> www.vagabondinn.com    each pet $10/day <br> small grassy walking area | (93) <br> $69 | CB <br> M/F | |
| **Burney** | | | |
| **Burney Motel**            530-335-4500 <br> 37448 Main St    pet fee $7/day <br> lawn and gravel walking areas, 11 miles to state park | (10) <br> $49– <br> $69 | C <br> M/F | |
| **Charm Motel**            530-335-2254 <br> 37363 Main St <br> pet fee $5/day up to 25 lbs, $10/day over 25 lbs <br> lawn area and walking trails | (42) <br> $61– <br> $80 | CB <br> M/F | OP |
| **Green Gables Motel**            530-335-2264 <br> 37385 Main St <br> www.greengablesmotel.com <br> pet fee $5/day up to 25 lbs, $10/day over 25 lbs <br> large lawn area, close to walking trails | (26) <br> $47– <br> $78 | CB <br> M/F | OP |
| **Shasta Pines Motel**            530-335-2201 <br> 37386 Main St    each pet $8/day <br> www.shastapinesmotel.com <br> 1 dog by advance reservation, gravel walking area | (30) <br> $39– <br> $129 | C <br> M/F | OP <br> S <br> T |
| **Sleepy Hollow Lodge**            530-335-2285 <br> 36898 Main St    pet fee $5/day <br> www.users.snowcrest.net/simivstk.com <br> ground floor rooms with outside entrances, across <br> street to woods and large open walking area | (10) <br> $50– <br> $58 | C <br> M/F | |

| C = coffee<br>CB = continental breakfast<br>F = refrigerator<br>FB = full breakfast<br>FR = fitness room | GP = guest pass to fitness center<br>IP = indoor pool<br>IS = in-room spa<br>K = full kitchen<br>(k) = kitchenette | L = lounge<br>M = microwave<br>OP = outdoor pool<br>R = restaurant<br>S = sauna/steam<br>T = spa or hot tub | (# of units)<br>& rates | food<br>& drink | pool, sauna<br>& hot tub |
|---|---|---|---|---|---|
| **Buttonwillow** | | | | | |
| **Homeland Inn**<br>20688 Tracy Ave<br>www.homelandinn.com | 661-764-5207<br>pet fee $2/day<br>vacant lot for walking dogs | | (23)<br>$33–<br>$35 | C | OP |
| **Motel 6**<br>20638 Tracy Ave<br>www.motel6.com | 661-764-5153<br>800-466-8356<br>grassy walking area | | (120)<br>$36 | C | OP |
| **Super 8 Motel**<br>20681 Tracy Ave<br>www.super8.com | 661-764-5117<br>800-800-8000<br>lawn, field, 3 miles to park | | (86)<br>$37–<br>$47 | CB | OP<br>T |
| **Willow Inn & Suites**<br>20645 Tracy Ave<br>grassy walking area, 4 miles to park | 661-764-5121<br>pet fee $5–$10/stay | | (82)<br>$38–<br>$85 | CB<br>M/F | OP |
| **Calexico** | | | | | |
| **Hollie's Hotel**<br>801 S Imperial Ave<br>small dogs only, grassy areas, 5 blocks to park | 760-357-3271<br>800-446-5543 | | (57)<br>$62 | FB<br>M/F | OP |
| **Villa Sur Motel**<br>304 E 4th St<br>small grassy walking area | 760-357-3112 | | (44)<br>$43–<br>$51 | C<br>F | OP |
| **Calimesa** | | | | | |
| **Calimesa Inn Motel**<br>1205 Calimesa Blvd<br>½ mile to park | 909-795-2536<br>pet fee $7/day | | (36)<br>$55–<br>$65 | CB<br>F | OP |
| **Calipatria** | | | | | |
| **Calipatria Inn & Suites**<br>700 N Sorensen Ave<br>www.calipatriainn.com<br>open walking area, 5 blocks to park | 760-348-7348<br>800-830-1113<br>pet fee $10/day | | (40)<br>$68 | CB<br>M/F<br>R | OP<br>T |

## Calistoga

| | | | | |
|---|---|---|---|---|
| **Alpine Inn of Napa Valley** 707-942-4080<br>1706 Adele Ave<br>small dogs by advance reservation only, patio,<br>special meals available by advance arrangement,<br>fields and quiet streets for walking dogs | (4)<br>$80–<br>$225 | CB<br>M<br>K | T |
| **Bear Flag Inn** 707-942-5534<br>2653 Foothill Blvd 800-670-2860<br>www.bearflaginn.com<br>dogs allowed in cottage that sleeps 4, open field,<br>1 mile to park | (5)<br>$175–<br>$250 | FB | OP<br>T |
| **Chateau De Vie** 707-942-6446<br>3250 Hwy 128 877-558-2513<br>www.chateaudv.com<br>dog may be left alone in room if kept in travel crate,<br>gated formal gardens and vineyard for walking dogs | (3)<br>$189–<br>$279 | FB<br>F | T |
| **Calistoga Enchanted Cottage** 707-942-9463<br>800-963-9463<br>pet fee $10/day<br>freshly bathed dog only, suite/cottage sleep up to 8,<br>private porch, patio, photo gallery of innkeeper's art,<br>½ acre wooded hillside, 2 blocks to park, near trails | (2)<br>$78–<br>$258 | CB<br>K<br>M/F | GP |
| **Croak Creek Cottage** 707-942-5380<br>3051 Foothill Blvd pet fee $15/day<br>www.jocelynaudette.com<br>studio cottage sleeps 3, deck overlooking seasonal<br>creek, vineyard and gardens, private country lane | (1)<br>$140 | K | |
| **Elms B & B** 707-942-9476<br>1300 Cedar St 888-399-3567<br>www.theelms.com pet fee $30/stay<br>lawn walking area, next to park, close to hiking trails | (7)<br>$150–<br>$245 | FB | T |
| **Fanny's B & B** 707-942-9491<br>1206 Spring St<br>www.fannysnapavalley.com<br>dogs by advance approval only, lawn walking area | (2)<br>$125–<br>$180 | FB | |

| | | # of units) & rates | food & drink | pool, sauna & hot tub |
|---|---|---|---|---|
| C = coffee<br>CB = continental<br>  breakfast<br>F = refrigerator<br>FB = full breakfast<br>FR = fitness room | GP = guest pass to<br>  fitness center<br>IP = indoor pool<br>IS = in-room spa<br>K = full kitchen<br>(k) = kitchenette | L = lounge<br>M = microwave<br>OP = outdoor pool<br>R = restaurant<br>S = sauna/steam<br>T = spa or hot tub | | |

## Calistoga (continued)

| | | | | |
|---|---|---|---|---|
| **Hillcrest B & B** <br>3225 Lake County Hwy <br>www.bnbweb.com/hillcrest <br>dogwalking/dogsitting services, swimming lake, <br>off-leash walking area, 40 acres of hiking trails | 707-942-6334 <br>each pet $10/day | (6) <br>$69–<br>$175 | CB | T <br>IS |
| **Meadowlark Country House B & B** <br>601 Petrified Forest Rd <br>www.meadowlarkinn.com <br>rooms/guesthouse sleeps 5, 20 acres, large meadow | 707-942-5651 <br>800-942-5651 | (8) <br>$165–<br>$265 | FB | |
| **Nance's Hot Springs** <br>1614 Lincoln Ave <br>www.nanceshotsprings.com <br>breakfast on weekends only, field, ¼ mile to park | 707-942-6211 | (24) <br>$77–<br>$125 | CB | |
| **Pink Mansion** <br>1415 Foothill Blvd <br>www.pinkmansion.com <br>residential streets, 1 mile to park | 707-942-0558 <br>800-238-7465 <br>each pet $30/day | (6) <br>$165–<br>$345 | FB | OP <br>T |
| **Trailside Inn B & B** <br>4201 Silverado Trail <br>www.trailsideinn.com <br>dogs with advance approval only, breakfast supplies, <br>patios, 2 landscaped acres, 1½ miles to park | 707-942-4106 | (3) <br>$145–<br>$185 | C <br>K | |
| **Washington Street Lodging** <br>1605 Washington St <br>www.washingtonstreetlodging.com  pet fee $15/stay <br>cottages, riverside decks, close to parks and trails | 707-942-6968 <br>877-214-3869 | (5) <br>$95–<br>$140 | C <br>K <br>(k) | |

## Camarillo

| | | | | |
|---|---|---|---|---|
| **Motel 6** <br>1641 E Daily Dr <br>www.motel6.com | 805-388-3470 <br>800-466-8356 <br>3 blocks to park | (82) <br>$52–<br>$61 | C | OP |

## Cambria

| | | | | |
|---|---|---|---|---|
| **Cambria Pines Lodge** | 805-927-4200 | (126) | FB | IP |
| 2905 Burton Dr | 800-445-6868 | $109– | R/L | T |
| www.cambriapineslodge.com    each pet $25/day | | $359 | | FR |
| pet treats, landscaped grounds and walking areas | | | | |
| **Cambria Shores Inn** | 805-927-8644 | (24) | CB | |
| 6276 Moonstone Beach Dr | 800-433-9179 | $85– | M/F | |
| www.cambriashores.com    each pet $10/day | | $180 | | |
| afternoon appetizers and cookies, lawn, 2 blocks to | | | | |
| off-leash dog park, 6 miles to dog-friendly beach | | | | |
| **Creekside Inn** | 805-927-4021 | (23) | C | |
| 2618 Main St | 800-269-5212 | $69– | | |
| www.moonstonehotels.com    each pet $10/day | | $129 | | |
| pet supplies, *Fido Friendly Magazine,* creekside park | | | | |
| **Fog Catcher Inn** | 805-927-1400 | (60) | FB | OP |
| 6400 Moonstone Beach Dr | 800-425-4121 | $139– | M/F | T |
| www.fogcatcherinn.com    each pet $25/day | | $319 | | |
| dogs allowed on beachfront boardwalk in front of | | | | |
| hotel, 1 mile to park, 10 miles to dog-friendly beach | | | | |
| **Mariners Inn** | 805-927-4624 | (26) | CB | T |
| 6180 Moonstone Beach Dr | pet fee $10/day | $79– | F | |
| www.marinersinncambria.com | | $165 | | |
| across street to grassy walking area | | | | |
| **Sea Otter Inn** | 805-927-5888 | (25) | CB | OP |
| 6656 Moonstone Beach Dr | 800-965-8347 | $79– | | |
| www.moonstonehotels.com    each pet $25/day | | $199 | | |
| beachfront boardwalk, 10 miles to dog-friendly beach | | | | |

## Cameron Park

| | | | | |
|---|---|---|---|---|
| **Best Western Cameron Park Inn** | 530-677-2203 | (65) | CB | OP |
| 3361 Coach Lane | 800-601-1234 | $69– | M/F | T |
| www.bestwesterncalifornia.com    pet fee $10/day | | $149 | | FR . |
| lawn walking area, 1 mile to park and lake | | | | |

## Camino

| | | | | |
|---|---|---|---|---|
| **Camino Hotel B & B** | 530-644-7740 | (9) | FB | |
| 4103 Carson Rd | 866-644-7440 | $86– | | |
| www.caminohotel.com    2 blocks to park and trails | | $119 | | |

| C = coffee<br>CB = continental<br>breakfast<br>F = refrigerator<br>FB = full breakfast<br>FR = fitness room | GP = guest pass to<br>fitness center<br>IP = indoor pool<br>IS = in-room spa<br>K = full kitchen<br>(k) = kitchenette | L = lounge<br>M = microwave<br>OP = outdoor pool<br>R = restaurant<br>S = sauna/steam<br>T = spa or hot tub | (# of units)<br>& rates | food<br>& drink | pool, sauna<br>& hot tub |
|---|---|---|---|---|---|
| **Camp Nelson** | | | | | |
| **Pierpoint Springs Resort**     559-542-2423<br>801 Hwy 190<br>surrounded by national forest, lots of walking trails | | | (5)<br>$65 | C | |
| **Campbell** | | | | | |
| **Campbell Inn**     408-374-4300<br>675 E Campbell Ave     800-582-4449<br>www.campbell-inn.com     pet fee $50/stay<br>16 mile long walking and bike path | | | (95)<br>$99–<br>$129 | FB<br>F | OP<br>T<br>GP |
| **Motel 6**     408-371-8870<br>1240 Camden Ave     800-466-8356<br>www.motel6.com     1 block to park | | | (49)<br>$62–<br>$66 | C | |
| **Residence Inn San Jose/Campbell**   408-559-1551<br>2761 S Bascom Ave     800-331-3131<br>www.residenceinnsanjose.com     pet fee $75/stay<br>studio/1 bdrm suites, Mon–Thur light dinner and<br>beverages, lawn walking area | | | (80)<br>$99–<br>$169 | FB<br>K | OP<br>T<br>GP |
| **Canoga Park** | | | | | |
| **Canoga House Motor Hotel**     818-341-9700<br>7435 Winnetka Ave     pet fee $10/day<br>next to park | | | (48)<br>$50 | C<br>F | OP |
| **Motel 6**     818-346-5400<br>7132 De Soto Ave     800-466-8356<br>www.motel6.com     small dogs only, 1 block to park | | | (64)<br>$55 | C | OP |
| **Canyon Country** | | | | | |
| **Super 8 Motel**     661-252-1722<br>17901 Sierra Hwy     800-800-8000<br>www.super8.com     large walking area | | | (50)<br>$55–<br>$60 | CB | OP<br>T |

## Canyon Lake

| | | | |
|---|---|---|---|
| **Canyon Lake Resort Inn** 31820 Railroad Canyon Rd lawn walking area | 909-244-1164 pet fee $10/day | (30) $59 | C M/F |

## Canyondam

| | | | |
|---|---|---|---|
| **Plumas Pine Resort** 3000 Almanor Dr W www.plumaspinesresort.com dogs allowed May 1–Nov 1 only, 2 bdrm cabins sleep 4, wooded lakeside area, 10 mile paved trail | 530-259-4343 | (6) $100 | R/L |
| **Wilson's Camp** 2932 Lake Almanor Dr W www.camp-prattville.com    10 mile long walking trail | 530-259-2267 | (7) $75– $125 | K R |

## Capay

| | | | | |
|---|---|---|---|---|
| **Capay Valley B & B** 15875 Hwy 16 www.capayvalleybedandbreakfast.com dogs by owner's approval only    pet fee $25/day cottages sleep up to 6, fenced yards, 142 acre ranch | 530-796-3738 866-227-2922 | (6) $89– $250 | (k) CB | OP T |

## Capitola

| | | | | |
|---|---|---|---|---|
| **Best Western Capitola by-the-Sea Inn & Suites** 1435 41st Ave www.bestwesterncapitola.com dogs over 1 year old only    pet fee $10/day dogsitting service, open walking areas, 8 blocks to dog-friendly beach | 831-477-0607 800-621-8115 | (54) $89– $209 | CB M/F | OP T FR |
| **Capitola Inn** 822 Bay Ave dogs under 25 lbs only    pet fee $20/stay large lawn, 1 mile to beach | 831-462-3004 800-660-2713 | (56) $63– $175 | CB | OP |
| **Monarch Cove** 620 El Salto Dr www.monarch-cove-inn.com well-mannered dogs by manager's advance approval only, cabins/Victorian bungalows overlooking ocean, garden and trails for walking dogs | 831-464-1295 | (10) $185– $275 | CB K | T |

| C = coffee<br>CB = continental<br>   breakfast<br>F = refrigerator<br>FB = full breakfast<br>FR = fitness room | GP = guest pass to<br>   fitness center<br>IP = indoor pool<br>IS = in-room spa<br>K = full kitchen<br>(k) = kitchenette | L = lounge<br>M = microwave<br>OP = outdoor pool<br>R = restaurant<br>S = sauna/steam<br>T = spa or hot tub | (# of units)<br>& rates | food<br>& drink | pool, sauna<br>& hot tub |
|---|---|---|---|---|---|
| **Carlsbad** | | | | | |
| **Four Seasons Resort**   760-603-6800<br>7100 Four Seasons Point   pet fee $100/stay<br>www.fourseasons.com<br>dogs under 15 lbs only, lawn, trail around lagoon | | | (320)<br>$295–<br>$520 | M/F<br>R/L | OP<br>S<br>T |
| **Inns of America–San Diego North**<br>751 Raintree Dr   760-931-1185<br>www.innsofamerica.com   pet fee $5/day<br>pet relief area and walking paths, ⅓ mile to beach,<br>10 miles to dog park | | | (125)<br>$69–<br>$129 | CB<br>M/F<br>R/L | OP |
| **Motel 6 Downtown**   760-434-7135<br>1006 Carlsbad Village Dr   800-466-8356<br>www.motel6.com<br>grassy courtyards, 4 blocks to dog-friendly beach | | | (109)<br>$56–<br>$70 | C | OP |
| **Motel 6 South**   760-431-0745<br>750 Raintree Dr   800-466-8356<br>www.motel6.com<br>well-behaved dogs only, lawn walking area, 1 mile to<br>beach, 7 miles to fairgrounds | | | (160)<br>$50–<br>$65 | C | OP |
| **Red Roof Inn**   760-438-1242<br>6117 Paseo Del Norte   800-733-7663<br>www.redroof.com<br>1 dog only, lawn walking area, pet cleanup bags,<br>short drive to park, 1 mile to beach | | | (142)<br>$65–<br>$72 | C | OP |
| **Residence Inn San Diego/Carlsbad** 760-431-9999<br>2000 Faraday Ave   800-331-3131<br>www.carlsbadri.com   pet fee $75/stay<br>courtyard and grassy area, 10 minute drive to park | | | (121)<br>$159–<br>$213 | FB<br>(k) | OP<br>T<br>FR |
| **Travel Inn Motel**   760-729-4941<br>3666 Pio Pico Dr   800-900-0275<br>dogs in smoking rooms only   pet fee $35/stay<br>vacant lot, 2 blocks to park | | | (40)<br>$45–<br>$65 | C | OP |

## Carmel

| | | | |
|---|---|---|---|
| **Best Western Carmel Mission Inn**  831-624-1841<br>3665 Rio Rd  800-348-9090<br>www.carmelmissioninn.com  each pet $35/stay<br>pet-friendly ground floor rooms, open walking<br>areas, 5 miles to off-leash dog beach | (165)<br>$79–<br>$339 | C<br>F<br>R | OP<br>T |
| **Briarwood Inn**  831-626-9056<br>5th Ave & San Carlos St  800-999-8788<br>www.briarwood-inn-carmel.com  pet fee $25/day<br>complimentary evening port and sherry, pet relief<br>area, 6 blocks to beach | (12)<br>$250–<br>$550 | CB<br>K | |
| **Carmel Country Inn**  831-625-3263<br>Dolores St & 3rd Ave  800-215-6343<br>www.carmelcountryinn.com  each pet $20/day<br>studios/1–2 bdrm suites, small lawn area, close to<br>trails/dog-friendly beaches/off-leash dog beach | (6)<br>$150–<br>$295 | CB<br>F | |
| **Carmel Fireplace Inn**  831-624-4862<br>San Carlos & 4th  866-626-1171<br>www.carmelfireplaceinn.com  pet fee $25/day<br>dogs under 25 lbs only, complimentary evening port<br>and sherry, patio, 2 blocks to park, 7 blocks to<br>dog-friendly beach | (18)<br>$145–<br>$325 | CB<br>F | |
| **Carmel Garden Court Inn**  831-624-6926<br>4th Ave & Torres St  800-313-7770<br>www.carmelgardencourtinn.com  pet fee $50/stay<br>rooms with outside entrances and private patios,<br>small lawn, 7 blocks to dog-friendly beach | (10)<br>$150–<br>$245 | CB<br>M/F | |
| **Carmel River Inn**  831-624-1575<br>Hwy 1 at Oliver Rd  800-882-8142<br>www.carmelriverinn.com  each pet $10/day<br>cottages sleep up to 6, pet supplies, on 14 acres of<br>meadow and woods, 2 miles to dog-friendly beach | (43)<br>$79–<br>$399 | C<br>K | OP |
| **Carmel Tradewinds Inn**  831-624-2776<br>Mission St & 3rd Ave  800-624-6665<br>www.tradewindsinn.com  each pet $25/day<br>2 blocks to park, 7 blocks to dog-friendly beach | (28)<br>$195–<br>$425 | CB<br>F | IS |

| | C = coffee<br>CB = continental<br>    breakfast<br>F  = refrigerator<br>FB = full breakfast<br>FR = fitness room | GP = guest pass to<br>    fitness center<br>IP = indoor pool<br>IS = in-room spa<br>K  = full kitchen<br>(k) = kitchenette | L  = lounge<br>M = microwave<br>OP = outdoor pool<br>R  = restaurant<br>S  = sauna/steam<br>T  = spa or hot tub | (# of units)<br>& rates | food<br>& drink | pool, sauna<br>& hot tub |
|---|---|---|---|---|---|---|
| **Carmel (continued)** | | | | | | |
| **Casa de Carmel**<br>Monte Verde St & Ocean Ave<br>www.casadecarmel.com<br>    pet fee $20/day for 1 dog, $30/day for 2 dogs<br>breakfast basket, pet cleanup bags, streets and parks<br>for walking dogs, short walk to off-leash dog beach | | 831-624-7738<br>800-262-1262 | (7)<br>$125–<br>$165 | CB<br>M/F | |
| **Coachmans Inn**<br>San Carlos St & 7th Ave<br>www.coachmansinn.com    pet fee $20/day<br>large patio, evening sherry and cookies, quiet<br>residential walking area, 5 blocks to dog beach | | 831-624-6421<br>800-336-6421 | (30)<br>$115–<br>$205 | CB<br>M/F | S<br>T |
| **Cypress Inn**<br>NE Corner of Lincoln at 7th<br>www.cypress-inn.com<br>    pet fee $25/day for 1 dog, $40/day for 2 dogs<br>afternoon tea and appetizers, pet cleanup bags,<br>dirt walking path, 5 blocks to dog-friendly beach | | 831-624-3871<br>800-443-7443 | (44)<br>$100–<br>$495 | CB<br>L | |
| **Edgemere Cottages**<br>San Antonio Ave & Santa Lucia    pet fee $25/day<br>www.edgemerecottages.com<br>dogs by advance reservation, 1920s French Tudor<br>cottages sleep up to 5, 1 block to dog-friendly beach | | 831-624-4501 | (4)<br>$150–<br>$225 | CB<br>K | |
| **Forest Lodge Cottages**<br>Ocean Ave & Torres St    each pet $10/stay<br>www.carmelbythesea.com/forestlodge.htm<br>cottages sleep up to 6, garden, 9 blocks to dog beach | | 831-624-7023 | (4)<br>$110–<br>$300 | CB<br>K<br>M/F | |
| **Lamplighters Inn**<br>Ocean Ave & Camino Real    $20/day for 1 dog<br>www.carmellamplighter.com    $30/day for 2 dogs<br>rooms/suites, pet cleanup bags, close to several<br>parks, 6 blocks to off-leash beach | | 831-624-7372 | (6)<br>$159–<br>$359 | C<br>K | |

| | | | | |
|---|---|---|---|---|
| **Lincoln Green Inn** | 831-624-1880 | (4) | K | |
| 26200 Carmelo St | 800-262-1262 | $205– | | |
| (between 15th & 16th Sts) | | $285 | | |
| www.vagabondshouseinn.com/cottages.html | | | | |
| pet fee $20/day for 1 dog, $30/day for 2 dogs | | | | |
| 1 bdrm cottages, 3 blocks to dog-friendly beach | | | | |
| **Sunset House** | 831-624-4884 | (4) | CB | IS |
| Camino Real & Ocean Ave | 877-966-9100 | $210– | F | |
| www.sunsethousecarmel.com   each pet $25/stay | | $230 | K | |
| patios, 3 blocks to off-leash dog beach | | | | |
| **Vagabond's House Inn** | 831-624-7738 | (13) | FB | |
| Dolores St & 4th Ave | 800-262-1262 | $145– | K | |
| www.vagabondshouseinn.com   pet fee $20–$30/day | | $265 | M/F | |
| pet cleanup bags, short walk to off-leash dog beach | | | | |
| **Wayside Inn** | 831-624-5336 | (22) | CB | IS |
| Mission St & 7th Ave | 800-433-4732 | $149– | K | |
| www.ibts-waysideinn.com | | $199 | M/F | |
| 1 block to park, 7 blocks to dog-friendly beach | | | | |

## Carmel by the Sea

| | | | | |
|---|---|---|---|---|
| **Hofsas House** | 831-624-2745 | (38) | CB | OP |
| San Carlos St & 4th Ave | 800-221-2548 | $85– | K | S |
| www.hofsashouse.com   pet fee $20/day | | $250 | F | |
| rooms/2 bdrm suites, pet bed, wooded walking area | | | | |
| **Stonehouse Inn** | 831-624-4569 | (8) | FB | |
| 8th & Monte Verde | 800-748-6618 | $99– | | |
| www.carmelstonehouse.com | | $189 | | |
| dogs by owner's approval only, complimentary | | | | |
| cheese and wine social hour, freshly baked cookies, | | | | |
| 3½ blocks to off-leash dog beach | | | | |

## Carmel Valley

| | | | | |
|---|---|---|---|---|
| **Blue Sky Lodge** | 831-659-2256 | (27) | C | OP |
| 10 Flight Rd | 800-733-2160 | $69– | K | T |
| www.blueskylodge.com | | $139 | | |
| 1–2 dogs only, rooms/1–2 bdrm suites, enclosed | | | | |
| patios, lawn and open field, close to walking trails | | | | |

| C = coffee          GP = guest pass to   L = lounge |
| CB = continental            fitness center   M = microwave |
|    breakfast       IP = indoor pool   OP = outdoor pool |
| F = refrigerator   IS = in-room spa   R = restaurant |
| FB = full breakfast   K = full kitchen   S = sauna/steam |
| FR = fitness room   (k) = kitchenette   T = spa or hot tub |

|  | (# of units) & rates | food & drink | pool, sauna & hot tub |
|---|---|---|---|

## Carmel Valley (continued)

| **Carmel Valley Lodge** 831-659-2261 | (31) | CB | OP |
|---|---|---|---|
| 8 Ford Rd                800-641-4646 | $169– | K | S |
| www.valleylodge.com      each pet $10/day | $339 | F | T |
| rooms/2 bdrm cottages, lawn, 2 miles to dog park | | | FR |

| **Gardiner's Resort** 831-659-2207 | (17) | FB | OP |
|---|---|---|---|
| 114 Carmel Valley Rd          800-453-6225 | $350 | R | S |
| www.gardiners-resort.com      each pet $20/day | | | T |
| cottages sleep 4, rate includes 3 gourmet meals daily, | | | FR |
| lawn, 1½ miles to park and hiking trails | | | |

| **Los Laureles Lodge** 831-659-2233 | (31) | CB | OP |
|---|---|---|---|
| 313 W Carmel Valley Rd         800-533-4404 | $105– | F | |
| www.loslaureles.com      each pet $20/day | $135 | R/L | |
| rooms/3 bdrm house with yard, across street to | | | |
| huge regional park with off-leash pet area and trails | | | |

## Carpinteria

| **Coastal Escapes** 805-566-0185 | (35) | K | IS |
|---|---|---|---|
| www.coastalescapes.com          800-292-2222 | $200– | | |
| pet fee $250/stay | $798 | | |
| 1–6 bdrm private homes, some with yards, within | | | |
| walking or driving distance to parks and beaches | | | |

| **Holiday Inn** 805-566-9499 | (108) | CB | OP |
|---|---|---|---|
| 5606 Carpinteria Ave          888-409-8300 | $109– | M/F | T |
| www.holiday-inn.com      each pet $10/day | $129 | | FR |
| lawn, 5 minute walk to beach | | | |

| **Motel 6 North** 805-684-6921 | (124) | C | OP |
|---|---|---|---|
| 4200 Via Real               800-466-8356 | $54– | M/F | |
| www.motel6.com      open area, 1 mile to park | $72 | | |

| **Motel 6 South** 805-684-8602 | (138) | C | OP |
|---|---|---|---|
| 5550 Carpinteria Ave          800-466-8356 | $53– | M/F | |
| www.motel6.com      open area, 1 mile to park | $74 | | |

## Cassel

| | | | |
|---|---|---|---|
| **Burney Mountain Guest Ranch**    530-335-4087<br>22800 Hat Creek Powerhouse 2    pet fee $5/day<br>www.burneymtn.com<br>rooms/suites/cabins sleep up to 4, rate includes 3<br>meals daily, working ranch with livestock so dogs<br>must be leashed, open walking areas | (7)<br>$150–<br>$250 | CB<br>F | OP |
| **Clearwater House**    530-335-5500<br>21568 Cassel Rd<br>www.clearwatertrout.com<br>well-trained dogs by advance arrangement only,<br>fly- fishing lodge, rate includes 3 meals daily, lawn,<br>hiking trails and creek | (7)<br>$185 | FB | |

## Castaic

| | | | |
|---|---|---|---|
| **Comfort Inn**    661-295-1100<br>31558 Castaic Rd    800-424-6000<br>www.comfortinn.com    pet fee $10/stay<br>back yard, walking distance to park | (120)<br>$55–<br>$75 | CB<br>F | OP |
| **Days Inn**    661-295-1070<br>31410 Castaic Rd    800-329-7466<br>www.daysinn.com    each pet $15/day<br>dogs in smoking rooms only, lawn, open field, park | (54)<br>$69–<br>$124 | CB<br>M/F | OP<br>T |

## Castella

| | | | |
|---|---|---|---|
| **Best in the West Resort**    530-235-2603<br>26987 Sims Rd<br>www.eggerbestwest.com<br>well-behaved dogs only, 1–2 bdrm modern cabins<br>sleep up to 14, creek, livestock on property so dogs<br>must be under control at all times, woods and open<br>walking area | (8)<br>$55–<br>$200 | K | |

## Castro Valley

| | | | |
|---|---|---|---|
| **Holiday Inn Express**    510-538-9501<br>2532 Castro Valley Blvd    800-465-4329<br>www.hiexpress.com/castrovalley    pet fee $20/day<br>patio and paved area to walk dogs, 1 mile to park | (62)<br>$79–<br>$139 | CB<br>M/F | OP<br>IS |

| | | | (# of units) & rates | food & drink | pool, sauna & hot tub |
|---|---|---|---|---|---|
| C = coffee | GP = guest pass to | L = lounge | | | |
| CB = continental | fitness center | M = microwave | | | |
| breakfast | IP = indoor pool | OP = outdoor pool | | | |
| F = refrigerator | IS = in-room spa | R = restaurant | | | |
| FB = full breakfast | K = full kitchen | S = sauna/steam | | | |
| FR = fitness room | (k) = kitchenette | T = spa or hot tub | | | |

## Cathedral City

| | | | | |
|---|---|---|---|---|
| **Comfort Suites of Rancho Mirage** | 760-324-5939 | (97) | CB | OP |
| 69151 E Palm Canyon Dr | 800-892-5085 | $79– | K | T |
| www.palmsprings.com | pet fee $10/stay | $139 | | |
| dogs under 20 lbs only, 3 miles to park | | | | |
| **Desert Palms Inn** | 760-324-3000 | (28) | R/L | OP |
| 67580 Jones Rd | 800-801-8696 | $69– | | T |
| | pet fee $10/day | $139 | | |
| small dogs, open lot, 10 minute drive to dog park | | | | |
| **Doral Desert Princess Resort** | 760-322-7000 | (460) | R/L | OP |
| 67-967 Vista Chino | 888-386-4677 | $97– | | T |
| www.doralpalmsprings.com | pet fee $50/stay | $139 | | FR |
| small dogs only, grassy area, 3 miles to dog park | | | | |
| **Franconia Court Hotel** | 760-324-4521 | (22) | C | OP |
| 69375 Ramon Rd | | $80– | F | |
| driving range, on 20 acres with 1 acre lawn, 1 block | | $125 | | |
| to park, 3 miles to off-leash dog park | | | | |
| **Villa Mykonos** | 760-321-2898 | (10) | K | OP |
| 67590 Jones Rd | 800-471-4753 | $190– | | T |
| www.villamykonos.com | | $250 | | |
| 2 bdrm condos sleep 5, patios, open field | | | | |
| **Villa Resort** | 760-328-0660 | (43) | C | OP |
| 67670 Carey Rd | 800-845-5265 | $69– | R/L | T |
| www.thevilla.com | | $149 | | FR |
| dogs under 35 lbs only, lawn and open desert area | | | | |

## Cayucos

| | | | | |
|---|---|---|---|---|
| **Cayucos Beach Inn** | 805-995-2828 | (36) | CB | |
| 333 S Ocean Ave | 800-482-0555 | $85– | M/F | |
| www.cayucosbeachinn.com | | $125 | | |
| pet fee $10/1st day, $5 each additional day | | | | |
| 1–3 dogs only, dogwashing facility and kennel, pet | | | | |
| relief area, 1½ blocks to dog-friendly beach | | | | |

| | | | | |
|---|---|---|---|---|
| **Cypress Tree Motel** 125 S Ocean Ave www.cypresstreemotel.com grassy walking area, 1 block to beach access | 805-995-3917 800-241-4289 pet fee $10/stay | (12) $52– $72 | C M/F | |
| **Dolphin Inn** 399 S Ocean Ave www.thedolphininn.com rooms/cottages sleep up to 5, 1 block to dog-friendly beach | 805-995-3810 800-540-4276 pet fee $10/stay | (19) $49– $109 | CB M/F | IS |
| **Estero Bay Motel** 25 S Ocean Ave www.esterobaymotel.com lawn walking area, short walk to dog-friendly beach | 805-995-3614 800-736-1292 pet fee $15/day | (12) $49– $165 | C M/F | |
| **Shoreline Inn** 1 N Ocean Ave www.cayucosshorelineinn.com beachfront walking area | 805-995-3681 800-549-2244 pet fee $10/stay | (29) $80– $125 | CB M/F | |

## Cecilville

| | | | | |
|---|---|---|---|---|
| **Doyle's Camp** 30001 Cecilville Rd rustic hunting cabins sleep up to 4, historic mining town, pastures and creekside trails | 530-462-4685 | (3) $38 | K R/L | |

## Cedarville

| | | | | |
|---|---|---|---|---|
| **Drew Hotel** 581 Main St rooms/suite sleep up to 8, grassy area behind building, vacant lot with creek for walking dogs | 530-279-2423 pet fee $10/day | (14) $47 | C K M/F | |
| **Sunrise Motel** State Route 299 W on 4 acres with open walking areas | 530-279-2161 pet fee $5/day | (14) $52 | C F | |

## Ceres

| | | | | |
|---|---|---|---|---|
| **Howard Johnson** 1672 Herndon Rd www.hojo.com undeveloped walking area, close to park | 209-537-4821 800-446-4656 pet fee $5/day | (51) $60– $70 | CB M/F | OP |

| C = coffee  GP = guest pass to  L = lounge<br>CB = continental     fitness center  M = microwave<br>    breakfast  IP = indoor pool  OP = outdoor pool<br>F = refrigerator  IS = in-room spa  R = restaurant<br>FB = full breakfast  K = full kitchen  S = sauna/steam<br>FR = fitness room  (k) = kitchenette  T = spa or hot tub | (# of units)<br>& rates | food<br>& drink | pool, sauna<br>& hot tub |
|---|---|---|---|
| **Ceres (continued)** | | | |
| **Microtel Inns & Suites**     209-538-6466<br>1760 Herndon Ave     800-771-7171<br>www.microtelinn.com    lawn, short drive to park | (59)<br>$64–<br>$89 | CB<br>M/F | OP<br>T |
| **Cerritos** | | | |
| **Sheraton Cerritos at Town Center**   562-809-1500<br>12725 Center Court Dr S<br>www.sheraton.com/cerritos<br>dogs under 50 lbs only, park-like walking area | (203)<br>$99–<br>$239 | R/L | OP<br>T<br>FR |
| **Chatsworth** | | | |
| **Ramada Inn**     818-998-5289<br>21340 Devonshire St     pet fee $10/day<br>www.ramada.com<br>dogs under 15 lbs, grassy area, open field and<br>walking path across street | (74)<br>$88–<br>$98 | CB<br>F | OP<br>T |
| **Staybridge Suites**     818-773-0707<br>21902 Lassen St     800-782-9274<br>www.staybridge.com     pet fee $150/stay<br>1–2 bdrm suites, Tues-Thur evening beverages and<br>appetizers, grassy walking area | (115)<br>$133 | FB<br>K | OP<br>T |
| **Chester** | | | |
| **Cedar Lodge Motel & RV Park**   530-258-2904<br>Junction Hwy 89 & Hwy 36<br>dogs allowed by manager's approval only,<br>rooms/suites, picnic area, pet relief area, woods and<br>hiking trails | (13)<br>$48–<br>$70 | C<br>K<br>M/F | OP |
| **Chester Manor Motel**     530-258-2441<br>306 Main St     888-571-4885<br>www.chestermanor.com    each pet $10/day<br>lawn and wooded walking area, 2 miles to lake | (18)<br>$72–<br>$99 | C<br>M/F | |

| | | | |
|---|---|---|---|
| **Seneca Motel** 530-258-2815<br>545 Martin Way pet fee $10/day<br>1–2 dogs allowed with manager's approval only,<br>open field, 6 blocks to park, closed in winter | (11)<br>$58–<br>$68 | C<br>(k) | |
| **Timber House Lodge** 530-258-2729<br>505 Main St (Hwy 36) pet fee $5/day<br>undeveloped walking area behind building | (16)<br>$50–<br>$65 | | |

### Chicago Park

| | | | |
|---|---|---|---|
| **Rollins Lakeside Inn Resort** 530-273-0729<br>18145 Rollins View Dr<br>www.rollinslake.net<br>dogs by advance approval only, cabins sleep 4 to 8,<br>wooded hillside and walking trail to lake | (9)<br>$130–<br>$200 | K | OP |

### Chico

| | | | |
|---|---|---|---|
| **Budget Motel** 530-898-0134<br>2566 Esplanade lawn area, 4 miles to park | (15)<br>$44 | M/F | |
| **Deluxe Inn** 530-342-8386<br>2507 Esplanade pet fee $10/day<br>walking area in parking lot, 2 miles to park | (36)<br>$45–<br>$53 | CB<br>M/F | OP |
| **Heritage Inn Express** 530-343-4527<br>725 Broadway St 800-660-1417<br>www.heritageinnexpresschico.com pets $20/stay<br>rooms/2 bdrm suites sleep up to 4, ½ block to park | (39)<br>$50–<br>$88 | CB<br>M/F | OP<br>IS |
| **Holiday Inn Chico** 530-345-2491<br>685 Manzanita Ct 800-310-2491<br>www.holiday-inn.com/chicoca pet fee $25/stay<br>lawn and quiet street to walk dogs, 2 miles to park | (172)<br>$89 | CB<br>R/L | OP<br>T<br>FR |
| **Matador Motel** 530-342-7543<br>1934 Esplanade<br>lawn walking area, 1½ miles to park | (31)<br>$41–<br>$51 | C<br>(k)<br>F | OP |
| **Motel 6** 530-345-5500<br>665 Manzanita Ct 800-466-8356<br>www.motel6.com large lawn, 1 mile to park | (78)<br>$48–<br>$66 | C | OP |
| **Music Express Inn** 530-891-9833<br>1145 El Monte Ave pet fee $2.50/day<br>www.now2000.com/musicexpress lawn, near park | (9)<br>$76–<br>$106 | FB | OP<br>IS |

| C = coffee | GP = guest pass to | L = lounge |
|---|---|---|
| CB = continental | fitness center | M = microwave |
| breakfast | IP = indoor pool | OP = outdoor pool |
| F = refrigerator | IS = in-room spa | R = restaurant |
| FB = full breakfast | K = full kitchen | S = sauna/steam |
| FR = fitness room | (k) = kitchenette | T = spa or hot tub |

| | (# of units) & rates | food & drink | pool, sauna & hot tub |
|---|---|---|---|

## Chico (continued)

| Oxford Suites<br>2035 Business Lane<br>www.oxfordsuites.com<br>1–2 dogs under 25 lbs only, evening beverages and<br>appetizers, pet relief area, baseball field and park | 530-899-9090<br>800-870-7848<br>pet fee $25/stay | (183)<br>$85–<br>$95 | FB<br>M/F | OP<br>S<br>FR |
|---|---|---|---|---|
| Regal Inn<br>2324 Esplanade<br>gazebo, park-like grounds for walking dogs,<br>less than 1 mile to park | 530-342-7555 | (30)<br>$33–<br>$55 | C<br>M/F | |
| Safari Inn<br>2352 Esplanade<br><br>dogs allowed in smoking rooms only,<br>lawn walking area, 1½ miles to park | 530-343-3201<br>800-624-9166<br>pet fee $15/stay | (47)<br>$36–<br>$55 | C<br>M/F | OP |
| Super 8 Motel<br>655 Manzanita Ct<br>www.super8chico.com<br>lawn walking area, 1½ miles to park | 530-345-2533<br>877-345-2533<br>each pet $4/day | (52)<br>$55–<br>$60 | CB<br>M/F | OP |
| Town House Motel<br>2231 Esplanade<br>open field, 2 miles to park | 530-343-1621<br>pet fee $5/day | (29)<br>$45–<br>$49 | CB<br>M/F | OP<br>IS |
| Vagabond Inn<br>630 Main St<br>www.vagabondinn.com<br>walking area in parking lot, 2 blocks to small park | 530-895-1323<br>800-522-1555<br>pet fee $10/day | (43)<br>$49–<br>$59 | CB<br>M/F | OP |

## Chino

| Motel 6 Chino/Los Angeles<br>12266 Central Ave<br>www.motel6.com<br>walking area in parking lot, 10 minute drive to park | 909-591-3877<br>800-466-8356 | (93)<br>$50–<br>$56 | C | OP |
|---|---|---|---|---|

## Chowchilla

| | | | | |
|---|---|---|---|---|
| **Days Inn** | 559-665-4821 | (30) | CB | OP |
| 220 E Robertson Blvd | 800-962-0777 | $48– | M/F | |
| www.daysinn.com | pet fee $10/day | $68 | | |
| gravel walking area | | | | |

## Chula Vista

| | | | | |
|---|---|---|---|---|
| **Chula Vista Travel Inn** | 619-420-6600 | (75) | CB | OP |
| 394 Broadway | 800-447-0416 | $55– | | T |
| www.travelinnsandiego.com | pet fee $5/day | $99 | | |
| 1 small dog only, parking lot and residential area | | | | |
| **La Quinta Inn** | 619-691-1211 | (142) | CB | OP |
| 150 Bonita Rd | 800-531-5900 | $99– | M/F | |
| www.lq.com | open field, 1 mile to walking trail | $139 | | |
| **Motel 6 San Diego/Chula Vista** | 619-422-4200 | (176) | C | OP |
| 745 E St | 800-466-8356 | $52– | | |
| www.motel6.com | lawn and dirt walking areas | $62 | | |

## Citrus Heights

| | | | | |
|---|---|---|---|---|
| **Olive Grove Suites** | 916-725-0169 | (80) | C | OP |
| 6143 Auburn Blvd | | $84 | K | T |
| dogs under 8 lbs only, 1 bdrm suites, lawn area | | | FR | |

## Claremont

| | | | | |
|---|---|---|---|---|
| **Ramada Inn** | 909-621-4831 | (121) | CB | OP |
| 840 S Indian Hill Blvd | 800-322-6559 | $69– | M/F | T |
| www.ramada.com | | $129 | R | |
| rooms with outside entrances, large grassy play area | | | | |

## Clearlake

| | | | | |
|---|---|---|---|---|
| **Linger Longer Resort** | 707-994-6427 | (6) | C | |
| 14235 Lakeshore Dr | | $75– | K | |
| www.lingerlongerresort.com | | $175 | | |
| rustic cabins, 1 block to small park, 2 blocks to lakefront park with small dog-friendly beach | | | | |
| **Trombetta's Resort** | 707-994-2417 | (5) | C | OP |
| 5865 Old Hwy 53 | | $60– | (k) | |
| small dogs only, cabins sleep 4, 350-ft fishing pier, 4 acre park-like resort near marsh and wildlife area | | | $85 | |

| C = coffee  GP = guest pass to  L = lounge<br>CB = continental  fitness center  M = microwave<br>breakfast  IP = indoor pool  OP = outdoor pool<br>F = refrigerator  IS = in-room spa  R = restaurant<br>FB = full breakfast  K = full kitchen  S = sauna/steam<br>FR = fitness room  (k) = kitchenette  T = spa or hot tub | (# of units)<br>& rates | food<br>& drink | pool, sauna<br>& hot tub |
|---|---|---|---|
| **Clearlake Oaks** | | | |
| **Blue Fish Cove Resort**          707-998-1769<br>10573 E Hwy 20          pet fee $20/1st day<br>www.bluefishcove.com          $5/additional day<br>1–2 bdrm cottages/duplexes/vacation rentals,<br>large grassy walking area, lakefront access | (10)<br>$50–<br>$140 | C<br>K<br>M/F | |
| **Lake Haven Motel & Resort**          707-998-3908<br>100 Short St          800-998-0106<br>waterfront walking area          pet fee $5–$10/day | (28)<br>$40–<br>$80 | M/F | |
| **Lake Marina Resort Motel**          707-998-3787<br>10215 E Hwy 20          pet fee $5/day<br>www.lakemarinaresort.com<br>cabins sleep 5, lakefront walking area, close to parks | (12)<br>$65–<br>$95 | (k) | |
| **Twenty Oaks Court**          707-998-3012<br>10503 E Hwy 20          888-662-4379<br>fenced yard, lakefront walking area   pet fee $5/day | (5)<br>$55–<br>$65 | C<br>M/F | |
| **Clio** | | | |
| **Lodge at Whitehawk Ranch**          530-836-4985<br>985 Whitehawk Dr          877-945-6343<br>www.lodgeatwhitehawk.com<br>dogs by advance approval, cabins, meadows, woods | (14)<br>$99–<br>$180 | FB<br>F<br>R/L | OP<br>T |
| **Molly's B & B**          530-836-4436<br>276 Main St          each pet $10/day<br>www.mollysbedandbreakfast.com<br>riverside walking area and hiking trails | (4)<br>$90–<br>$110 | FB | |
| **Cloverdale** | | | |
| **Abrams House Inn**          707-894-2412<br>314 N Main St<br>www.abramshouseinn.com<br>well-behaved small dogs by advance approval only,<br>Victorian inn, residential streets, 2 blocks to park | (4)<br>$75–<br>$145 | FB<br>F | |

| | | | | |
|---|---|---|---|---|
| **Garden Motel** 707-894-2594<br>611 N Cloverdale Blvd<br>lawn area, ½ mile to park and riverfront trails | (14)<br>$46–<br>$56 | C | | |
| **Vineyard Valley Inn** 707-894-0707<br>721 N Cloverdale Blvd         pet fee $10/day<br>www.vineyardvalleyinn.com     1 block to park | (15)<br>$49–<br>$109 | CB<br>M/F | | |

## Coalinga

| | | | | |
|---|---|---|---|---|
| **Baker House B & B** 559-934-1900<br>190 Mountain View Pl<br>only small dogs allowed indoors, larger pets must<br>stay in garage, close to school field for walking dogs | (4)<br>$65–<br>$75 | FB | | |
| **Best Western Big Country Inn** 559-935-0866<br>25020 W Dorris Ave              800-836-6835<br>www.bestwesterncalifornia.com   pet fee $10/stay<br>lawn walking areas | (48)<br>$74–<br>$109 | CB<br>M/F | OP | |
| **Cambridge Inn Motor Lodge** 559-935-1541<br>100 Cambridge Ave              pet fee $20/stay<br>lawn and parking lot walking areas, open field | (53)<br>$53–<br>$58 | C<br>F | OP | |
| **Harris Ranch Inn & Restaurant** 559-935-0717<br>24505 W Dorris Ave           800-942-2333 ext 682<br>www.harrisranch.com              each pet $10/day<br>landscaped gardens, lawn for walking dogs | (153)<br>$116 | C<br>F<br>R/L | OP<br>T<br>FR | |
| **Motel 6** 559-935-1536<br>25008 W Dorris Ave              800-466-8356<br>grass and dirt walking areas, 1 block to park | (122)<br>$46 | C | OP | |
| **Pleasant Valley Inn** 559-935-2063<br>25278 W Dorris Ave              pet fee $5/day<br>open field, ½ block to small park | (132)<br>$48 | C<br>M/F | OP | |
| **Royal Lodge** 559-935-1664<br>800 E Elm Ave                   pet fee $5/day<br>lawn and college campus for walking dogs | (24)<br>$35–<br>$45 | C<br>M/F | | |

## Cobb

| | | | | |
|---|---|---|---|---|
| **Eagle & Rose Inn** 707-928-5242<br>16695 Hwy 175                  pet fee $10/day<br>www.eagleandroseinn.com<br>lawn walking area and trails | (19)<br>$65–<br>$85 | C<br>M/F | OP<br>IS | |

| C = coffee  GP = guest pass to  L = lounge<br>CB = continental  fitness center  M = microwave<br>breakfast  IP = indoor pool  OP = outdoor pool<br>F = refrigerator  IS = in-room spa  R = restaurant<br>FB = full breakfast  K = full kitchen  S = sauna/steam<br>FR = fitness room  (k) = kitchenette  T = spa or hot tub | (# of units) & rates | food & drink | pool, sauna & hot tub |
|---|---|---|---|
| ### Coleville | | | |
| **Andruss Motel**    530-495-2216<br>106964 Hwy 395    pet fee $5/day<br>www.andruss.com<br>1950s knotty pine rooms, horse stables, large lawn | (13)<br>$46–<br>$64 | C<br>(k) | OP |
| **Toiyabe Motel**    530-495-2281<br>107045 Hwy 395    877-333-0059<br>www.yosemitearealodging.com   pet fee $5/day<br>1–2 dogs only, knotty pine rooms, teepees and Old<br>West memorabilia, large walking area, close to trails | (11)<br>$35–<br>$55 | C<br>M/F | |
| ### Colton | | | |
| **Days Inn**    909-788-9900<br>2830 S Iowa Ave    800-329-7466<br>www.daysinn.com    each pet $10/day<br>small grassy area, 5 miles to park | (149)<br>$59–<br>$65 | CB<br>F | OP<br>T<br>IS |
| **Hampton Inn & Suites**    909-824-3935<br>250 N 9th St    800-426-7866<br>www.hiscolton.com    pet fee $25/stay<br>small dogs, community kitchen, short drive to park | (83)<br>$99 | CB<br>M/F | OP<br>T<br>FR |
| ### Columbia | | | |
| **Columbia Gem Motel**    209-532-4508<br>22131 Parrotts Ferry Rd    866-436-6685<br>www.columbiagem.com<br>suites/cabins with private porches sleep up to 5,<br>1 acre landscaped gardens and lawn | (11)<br>$69–<br>$129 | C<br>M/F | |
| ### Concord | | | |
| **Best Western Heritage Inn**    925-686-4466<br>4600 Clayton Rd    800-622-6466<br>www.bestwesterncalifornia.com<br>dogs allowed in smoking rooms only, barkdust pet<br>relief areas in parking lot | (121)<br>$69–<br>$89 | CB<br>M/F | OP<br>T<br>GP |

| | | | | |
|---|---|---|---|---|
| **Holiday Inn** | 925-687-5500 | (198) | C | OP |
| 1050 Burnett Ave | 888-263-8555 | $70 | M/F | FR |
| www.holiday-inn.com/concordca   each pet $10/day | | | R/L | |
| dogs allowed in first floor rooms only, small grassy | | | | |
| walking area, short drive to park | | | | |
| **Premier Inns** | 925-674-0888 | (136) | CB | OP |
| 1581 Concord Ave | | $61– | M/F | T |
| www.premierinns.com | | $99 | | |
| lawn and dirt area, across highway to walking trail | | | | |

### Corcoran

| | | | | |
|---|---|---|---|---|
| **Budget Inn** | 559-992-3171 | (45) | CB | |
| 1224 Whitley Ave | pet fee $10/day | $49– | M/F | |
| www.corcoranbudgetinn.com | | $58 | | |
| dogs by manager's approval only, park across street | | | | |

### Corning

| | | | | |
|---|---|---|---|---|
| **Amerihost Inn** | 530-824-5200 | (60) | CB | IP |
| 910 Hwy 99 West | 800-434-5800 | $65– | M/F | T |
| vacant lot and lawn walking area | pet fee $10/day | $89 | | FR |
| **Best Western Corning Inn** | 530-824-2468 | (41) | CB | OP |
| 2165 Solano St | 800-221-2230 | $70– | M/F | |
| www.bestwesterncalifornia.com   pet fee $10/day | | $85 | | |
| freshly baked cookies in afternoon, gravel and | | | | |
| grassy walking areas, 1 mile to park | | | | |
| **Days Inn** | 530-824-2000 | (62) | CB | OP |
| 3475 99 West | 800-245-3655 | $60– | M/F | |
| www.daysinn.com | pet fee $5/day | $63 | | |
| lawn walking area | | | | |
| **Economy Inn** | 530-824-4322 | (18) | C | OP |
| 945 Hwy 99 West | pet fee $5/day | $40 | M/F | |
| small dogs only, small grass and gravel walking area | | | | |
| **Holiday Inn Express** | 530-824-2940 | (78) | CB | OP |
| 3350 Sunrise Way | 800-465-4329 | $79– | M/F | S |
| www.hiexpress.com/corningca   pet fee $10/day | | $89 | C | T |
| large lawn, 1 mile to riverside state park | | | | FR |

| C = coffee | GP = guest pass to | L = lounge | (# of units) & rates | food & drink | pool, sauna & hot tub |
|---|---|---|---|---|---|
| CB = continental | fitness center | M = microwave | | | |
| breakfast | IP = indoor pool | OP = outdoor pool | | | |
| F = refrigerator | IS = in-room spa | R = restaurant | | | |
| FB = full breakfast | K = full kitchen | S = sauna/steam | | | |
| FR = fitness room | (k) = kitchenette | T = spa or hot tub | | | |

### Corning (continued)

| | | | | |
|---|---|---|---|---|
| **Olive Tree Motel** 3040 Hwy 99 West dogs by manager's approval only, open field | 530-824-5339 | (10) $35– $40 | M/F | |

### Corona

| **Dynasty Suites** 1805 W 6th St www.dynastysuites.com dogs under 25 lbs allowed for AAA members only, 2 miles to park | 909-371-7185 pet fee $10/day | (56) $68– $120 | CB M/F | OP T |
|---|---|---|---|---|
| **Motel 6** 200 N Lincoln Ave www.motel6.com small grassy area, 1 mile to park | 909-735-6408 800-466-8356 | (149) $45 | C | OP |
| **Travelodge** 1701 W 6th St www.travelodge.com small well-behaved dogs only, ½ mile to park | 909-735-5500 pet fee $8/day | (46) $62– $72 | CB M/F | OP |

### Coronado

| **Coronado Inn** 266 Orange Ave www.coronadoinn.com lawn walking area, 9 blocks to dog-friendly beach | 619-435-4121 800-598-6624 pet fee $10/day | (31) $95– $165 | CB M/F | OP |
|---|---|---|---|---|
| **Coronado Island Inn** 301 Orange Ave www.coronadoinn.com lawn walking area, 9 blocks to dog-friendly beach | 619-435-0935 888-436-0935 pet fee $10/day | (14) $85– $120 | CB M/F | OP |
| **Coronado Island Marriott Resort** 2000 2nd St www.marriott.com lawn walking area, close to dog-friendly beaches | 619-435-3000 800-228-9290 | (300) $229– $264 | C R/L | OP S T |

| | | | | |
|---|---|---|---|---|
| **Coronado Victorian House**<br>1000 8th St<br>www.coronadovictorianhouse.com   pet fee $25/day<br>small dogs only, dinners/picnic baskets/private<br>dance lessons available by special arrangement,<br>3 blocks to off-leash dog beach | 619-435-2200<br>888-299-2822 | (7)<br>$250–<br>$1,000 | FB | |
| **Crown City Inn**<br>520 Orange Ave<br>www.crowncityinn.com   pet fee $8/day<br>afternoon refreshments, pet bowls/toys/treats,<br>lawn walking area, close to dog-friendly beaches | 619-435-3116<br>800-422-1173 | (35)<br>$100–<br>$120 | C<br>R/L | OP<br>IS |
| **El Rancho Motel**<br>370 Orange Ave   pet fee $20/day<br>www.elranchocoronado.com<br>small dogs only, 2 blocks to park | 619-435-2251 | (10)<br>$79–<br>$120 | C<br>M/F | |
| **Loews Coronado Bay Resort**<br>4000 Coronado Bay Rd<br>www.loewshotels.com<br>rooms/bungalows sleep up to 6, lawn walking area,<br>5 miles to off-leash dog beach | 619-424-4000 | (400)<br>$245–<br>$325 | F<br>R/L | OP<br>FR |

## Corralitos

| | | | | |
|---|---|---|---|---|
| **Corralitos Beach House**<br>811 Smith Rd<br>www.vrbo.com/46141<br>4 bdrm home sleeps 10, decks, on 5 acres with lush<br>garden, fields, wildlife, close to lake and hiking trails | 831-239-2736 | (1)<br>$150–<br>$250 | K | |

## Corte Madera

| | | | | |
|---|---|---|---|---|
| **Marin Suites Hotel**<br>45 Tamal Vista Blvd<br>www.marinsuites.com   pet fee $10/day<br>rooms/2 bdrm suites sleep up to 8, close to trails | 415-924-3608<br>800-362-3372 | (100)<br>$89–<br>$154 | CB<br>K | OP<br>S<br>FR |

## Costa Mesa

| | | | | |
|---|---|---|---|---|
| **Best Western Newport Mesa Inn**<br>2642 Newport Blvd<br>www.bestwesterncalifornia.com   pet fee $25/day<br>1 block to park | 949-650-3020<br>800-554-2378 | (98)<br>$99–<br>$109 | CB<br>M/F | OP<br>S<br>T<br>FR |

| | | # of units)<br>& rates | food<br>& drink | pool, sauna<br>& hot tub |
|---|---|---|---|---|
| C = coffee<br>CB = continental<br>    breakfast<br>F = refrigerator<br>FB = full breakfast<br>FR = fitness room | GP = guest pass to<br>    fitness center<br>IP = indoor pool<br>IS = in-room spa<br>K = full kitchen<br>(k) = kitchenette | L = lounge<br>M = microwave<br>OP = outdoor pool<br>R = restaurant<br>S = sauna/steam<br>T = spa or hot tub | | |

## Costa Mesa (continued)

| | | | | |
|---|---|---|---|---|
| **Comfort Inn**<br>2430 Newport Blvd<br>www.choicehotels.com     pet fee $10–$15/day<br>dogs under 35 lbs only, small lawn area, ¼ mile to<br>fairgrounds, 2 miles to park, 4 mi to beach | 949-631-7840<br>800-631-3363 | (58)<br>$59–<br>$99 | CB<br>F | OP<br>T |
| **Costa Mesa Marriott Suites**<br>500 Anton Blvd<br>www.marriott.com<br>small grassy area and lakeside walking trail,<br>15 minute drive to beach | 714-957-1100<br>800-627-7468 | (253)<br>$79–<br>$149 | C<br>R/L | OP<br>T<br>FR |
| **Hilton Costa Mesa**<br>3050 Bristol St         pet fee $25/stay<br>www.costamesa.hilton.com<br>dogs under 50 lbs only, quiet side street for walking<br>dogs, close to parks | 714-540-7000 | (486)<br>$89–<br>$159 | C<br>R/L | OP<br>T<br>FR |
| **La Quinta Inn**<br>1515 S Coast Dr<br>www.lq.com<br>dogs under 25 lbs only, small grassy walking area,<br>10 minute drive to park | 714-957-5841 | (163)<br>$91–<br>$126 | CB<br>M/F | OP<br>FR |
| **Motel 6**<br>1441 Gisler Ave<br>www.motel6.com<br>sidewalk for walking dogs | 714-957-3063<br>800-466-8356 | (94)<br>$61 | C | OP |
| **Ramada Ltd & Suites**<br>1680 Superior Ave<br>www.ramadalimitednewport.com<br>lawn walking area, 2 miles to dog park | 949-645-2221<br>800-345-8025 | (140)<br>$85–<br>$115 | CB<br>M/F | OP<br>T<br>FR |

| | | | |
|---|---|---|---|
| **Residence Inn** 714-241-8800<br>881 W Baker St 800-331-3131<br>www.costamesaresidenceinn.com pet fee $75/stay<br>studios/1 bdrm suites, Mon–Wed beverages and<br>snacks, pet relief area, near dog-friendly park, beach | (144)<br>$89–<br>$189 | FB<br>K<br>M/F | |
| **Vagabond Inn** 714-557-8360<br>3205 Harbor Blvd 800-554-8090<br>www.vagabondinn.com each pet $5/day<br>1–2 dogs only, lawn walking area | (125)<br>$63–<br>$82 | CB<br>M/F | OP<br>T |
| **Westin South Coast Plaza** 714-540-2500<br>686 Anton Blvd 800-937-8461<br>www.westin.com/southcoastplaza<br>"Heavenly Dog Bed" and other pet supplies, close to<br>park, 6 miles to dog-friendly beach | (392)<br>$109–<br>$199 | F<br>R | OP<br>GP |
| **Wyndham Garden Hotel** 714-751-5100<br>3350 Avenue of the Arts 800-889-8846<br>www.wyndham.com<br>pet fee $25/day plus $150 cleaning fee<br>lawn walking area, 3 miles to off-leash dog park | (238)<br>$89–<br>$289 | FB<br>CB<br>M/F<br>R/L | OP<br>T<br>FR |

## Cottonwood

| | | | |
|---|---|---|---|
| **Alamo Motel & RV Park** 530-347-3827<br>3818 Main St<br>small dogs only, large lawn | (10)<br>$47 | C<br>M/F | |
| **Travelers Motel** 530-347-3003<br>3910 Main St pet fee $10/day<br>small well-behaved dog with advance approval only,<br>open field, 1 mile to park | (9)<br>$40–<br>$65 | C<br>M/F | |

## Coulterville

| | | | |
|---|---|---|---|
| **Yosemite Gold Country Motel** 209-878-3400<br>10407 Hwy 49 800-247-9884<br>www.yosemitegoldcountry.com<br>dirt walking area, 10 to 15 minute drive to lakes | (9)<br>$58–<br>$62 | C<br>M/F | |

## Covelo

| | | | |
|---|---|---|---|
| **Wagon Wheel Motel** 707-983-6717<br>75860 Covelo Rd each pet $10/day<br>small lawn walking area | (17)<br>$65 | C<br>M/F | |

| C = coffee<br>CB = continental<br>　　breakfast<br>F = refrigerator<br>FB = full breakfast<br>FR = fitness room | GP = guest pass to<br>　　fitness center<br>IP = indoor pool<br>IS = in-room spa<br>K = full kitchen<br>(k) = kitchenette | L = lounge<br>M = microwave<br>OP = outdoor pool<br>R = restaurant<br>S = sauna/steam<br>T = spa or hot tub | # of units)<br>& rates | food<br>& drink | pool, sauna<br>& hot tub |
|---|---|---|---|---|---|

### Covina

| Evergreen Inn<br>20022 E Arrow Hwy | 626-331-8899 | (25)<br>$50 | | |
|---|---|---|---|---|

### Crescent City

| Anchor Beach Inn<br>880 Hwy 101 S<br>www.anchorbeachinn.com<br>small lawn walking area, across street to beach | 707-464-2600<br>800-837-4116<br>pet fee $10/day | (52)<br>$60–<br>$80 | CB<br>M/F | T |
|---|---|---|---|---|
| Best Value Inn<br>440 Hwy 101 N<br>www.bestvalueinn.com<br>lawn walking area, 1 mile to park, 1½ miles to beach | 707-464-4141<br>each pet $7/day | (61)<br>$49–<br>$69 | CB<br>F | S<br>T |
| Del Norte Motel<br>975 9th St<br>residential walking area, 6 blocks to beach | 707-464-4321 | (10)<br>$45–<br>$60 | C<br>M/F | |
| El Patio Motel<br>655 H St<br>residential street for walking dogs, ½ mile to beach | 707-464-5114<br>pet fee $5/day | (23)<br>$35–<br>$40 | (k)<br>M/F | |
| Gardenia Motel<br>119 L St<br>walking trail to beach | 707-464-2181<br>pet fee $5/day | (55)<br>$40–<br>$45 | C<br>M/F | |
| Hampton Inn<br>100 A St<br>www.hamptoninn.com<br>dogs under 30 lbs, lawn walking area, beach access | 707-465-5400<br>pet fee $25/stay | (53)<br>$89–<br>$107 | CB<br>M/F | IP<br>S<br>T<br>FR |
| Pacific Inn<br>220 M St<br>lawn walking area, 5 minute walk to park | 707-464-9553<br>pet fee $5–10/day | (25)<br>$47 | CB | |
| Royal Inn<br>102 L St<br>lawn and trail to beach | 707-464-4113<br>800-752-9610<br>pet fee $10/stay | (36)<br>$49–<br>$55 | C<br>M/F | |

| | | | | |
|---|---|---|---|---|
| **Super 8 Motel** | 707-464-4111 | (49) | CB | |
| 685 Hwy 101 S | 800-800-8000 | $50– | M/F | |
| www.super8.com | pet fee $10/day | $65 | | |
| harborside grassy walking area, 2 blocks to beach | | | | |
| **Town House Motel** | 707-464-4176 | (25) | C | |
| 444 Hwy 101 S | | $35– | M/F | |
| next to park, 1 block to beach | · | $45 | | |

### Crescent Mills

| | | | | |
|---|---|---|---|---|
| **Crescent Hotel** | 530-284-0879 | (6) | FB | |
| Hwy 89 | | $70– | R/L | |
| 1927 historic building, creekside walking area | | $80 | | |

### Crestline

| | | | | |
|---|---|---|---|---|
| **North Shore Inn** | 909-338-5230 | (10) | M/F | |
| 24202 Lake Dr | pet fee $25/stay | $46– | | |
| www.thenorthshoreinn.com | | $140 | | |
| across street from lake, walking trails | | | | |

### Cromberg

| | | | | |
|---|---|---|---|---|
| **Long Valley Resort** | 530-836-0754 | (9) | CB | |
| 59532 Hwy 70 | 800-887-6653 | $75– | K | |
| www.longvalleyresort.com | pet fee $7/day | $125 | | |
| cottages sleep up to 6, lawn and wooded areas for walking dogs, close to hiking trails | | | | |
| **Sierra Sky Lodge** | 530-836-2344 | (8) | C | OP |
| 58585 Hwy 70 | pet fee $8/day | $49– | K | |
| www.sierraskylodge.com | | $69 | M/F | |
| rooms sleep up to 6, lawn and wooded walking areas, close to parks and riverfront | | | | |
| **Twenty Mile House B & B** | 530-836-0375 | (7) | K | |
| www.graeagle.com | | $150– | | |
| dogs by owner's approval and advance reservation only, cabins sleep up to 6, private decks overlooking creek, dirt roads and wooded areas along riverside for walking dogs | | $175 | | |

| C = coffee　　　GP = guest pass to　L = lounge<br>CB = continental　　fitness center　M = microwave<br>　breakfast　　IP = indoor pool　OP = outdoor pool<br>F = refrigerator　IS = in-room spa　R = restaurant<br>FB = full breakfast　K = full kitchen　S = sauna/steam<br>FR = fitness room　(k) = kitchenette　T = spa or hot tub | # of units)<br>& rates | food<br>& drink | pool, sauna<br>& hot tub |
|---|---|---|---|
| **Crowley Lake** | | | |
| **Mono Sierra Lodge**　　　　760-935-4300<br>4135 Crowley Lake Dr　　　800-723-5387<br>　　　　　　　　　pet fee $10/day<br>dirt road to walk dogs, near lakes and hiking trails | (8)<br>$48–<br>$90 | C<br>K | |
| **Tom's Place Resort**　　　760-935-4239<br>8180 Crowley Lake Dr　　　pet fee $8/day<br>www.tomsplaceresort.com<br>1–2 pets allowed in 3 rustic cabins, wooded walking<br>area along creek | (12)<br>$60–<br>$100 | K<br>R/L | |
| **Culver City** | | | |
| **Four Points by Sheraton**　　310-641-7740<br>5990 Green Valley Cir　　　888-627-9051<br>www.fourpoints.com　　　pet fee $25/stay<br>parking area for walking dogs, ¼ mile to park | (199)<br>$79–<br>$95 | M/F<br>R/L | OP<br>FR |
| **Radisson Los Angeles Westside**　310-649-1776<br>6161 W Centinela Ave　　　800-333-3333<br>www.radisson.com/culvercityca　pet fee $50/stay<br>dogs allowed in first floor rooms by reservation only,<br>lawn walking area, 3 miles to beaches | (368)<br>$79–<br>$139 | C<br>F<br>R/L | OP<br>FR |
| **Cupertino** | | | |
| **Cypress Hotel**　　　　408-253-8900<br>10050 S De Anza Blvd　　　866-408-0704<br>www.thecypresshotel.com<br>pet toys/bowls/biscuits/ID tag provided, lawn<br>walking area, 5–10 minute walk to park | (214)<br>$109–<br>$219 | C<br>F | OP<br>IS<br>FR |
| **Cypress** | | | |
| **Homestead Studio Suites**　　714-761-2766<br>5990 Corporate Ave　　　888-782-9473<br>www.homesteadhotels.com　pet fee $25/day<br>small lawn walking area, 2 blocks to park | (134)<br>$70–<br>$120 | C<br>K | GP |

| | | | | |
|---|---|---|---|---|
| **Woodfin Suites** | 714-828-4000 | (142) | FB | OP |
| 5905 Corporate Ave | 888-433-9403 | $89– | K | T |
| www.woodfinsuitehotels.com | each pet $5/day | $129 | M/F | FR |
| dogs allowed in first floor rooms with outside | | | | |
| entrances, lawn and sidewalk for walking dogs | | | | |

## Dana Point

| | | | | |
|---|---|---|---|---|
| **Doubletree Guest Suites** | 949-661-1100 | (195) | C | OP |
| 34402 Pacific Coast Hwy | 800-486-1821 | $99– | M/F | S |
| www.dtdanapoint.com | pet fee $30/day | $169 | R/L | T |
| beach and garden area for walking dogs | | | | FR |
| **Laguna Cliffs Marriott Resort** | 949-661-5000 | (376) | FB | OP |
| 25135 Park Lantern | 800-228-9290 | $169– | CB | S |
| www.lagunacliffs.com | pet fee $75/stay | $269 | F | T |
| pet relief area, next to dog-friendly state park, | | | R/L | FR |
| 40 minute drive to dog-friendly beach | | | | |

## Dardanelle

| | | | | |
|---|---|---|---|---|
| **Dardanelle Resort** | 209-965-4205 | (12) | R | |
| Sonora Pass Hwy 108 | | $79– | K | |
| www.thedardanelleresort.com | | $149 | | |
| rooms/cabins, on 14 wooded acres for walking dogs, | | | | |
| children's play area and sports courts, winter access | | | | |
| by snowmobile only | | | | |

## Davis

| | | | | |
|---|---|---|---|---|
| **Aggie Inn** | 530-756-0352 | (33) | CB | S |
| 245 1st St | pet fee $10/day | $85– | M/F | T |
| www.stayanight.com/aggieinn | | $95 | | |
| creekside lawn area to walk dogs, 3 blocks to park | | | | |
| **Best Western University Lodge** | 530-756-7890 | (52) | CB | T |
| 123 B St | 800-528-1234 | $59– | M/F | FR |
| www.universitylodgeucd.com | pet fee $5/day | $89 | | |
| 2 blocks to park | | | | |
| **Davis Bed & Breakfast Inn** | | (9) | FB | |
| 422 A St | 530-753-9611 | $85– | | |
| www.davisbedandbreakfast.com | 800-211-4455 | $95 | | |
| room with outside entrance, across street to college | | | | |
| campus with lawns and sidewalks for walking dogs | | | | |

| C = coffee / CB = continental breakfast / F = refrigerator / FB = full breakfast / FR = fitness room — GP = guest pass to fitness center / IP = indoor pool / IS = in-room spa / K = full kitchen / (k) = kitchenette — L = lounge / M = microwave / OP = outdoor pool / R = restaurant / S = sauna/steam / T = spa or hot tub | (# of units) & rates | food & drink | pool, sauna & hot tub |
|---|---|---|---|

### Davis (continued)

| | | | |
|---|---|---|---|
| **Econo Lodge** 221 D St www.choicehotels.com 2 blocks to park | 530-756-1040 800-553-2666 pet fee $5/day | (26) $45– $70 | C M/F | |
| **Howard Johnson Hotel** 4100 Chiles Rd www.hojodavis.com on 5 acres with courtyard and lawn | 530-792-0800 800-446-4656 pet fee $10/day | (77) $73– $110 | FB M/F R | IP OP FR S/T |
| **Motel 6** 4835 Chiles Rd www.motel6.com 1 well-behaved dog only, lawn walking area, short drive to parks and greenbelt walking path | 530-753-3777 800-466-8356 | (103) $46– $52 | C | OP |
| **University Inn Bed & Breakfast** 340 A St www.davis411.com | 530-756-8648 800-756-8648 lawn walking area | (4) $65– $83 | CB M/F | |
| **University Park Inn & Suites** 1111 Richards Blvd www.universityparkinn.com lawn and walking path | 530-756-0910 each pet $10/stay | (45) $75 | CB M/F | OP |

### Death Valley

| | | | |
|---|---|---|---|
| **Amargosa Hotel** 101 Broadway www.amargosaoperahouse.com dogs allowed by manager's advance approval only, open desert walking area | 760-852-4441 | (14) $45– $60 | M | |
| **Stovepipe Wells Village** Hwy 190 www.stovepipewells.com inside national forest, desert area for walking dogs | 760-786-2387 | (83) $99 | F R/L | OP |

## Del Mar

| | | | |
|---|---|---|---|
| **Best Western Stratford Inn** 710 Camino Del Mar www.pacificahost.com grassy walking area, path to ocean bluff viewpoint | 858-755-1501 800-937-8376 pet fee $50/stay | (93) $129– $185 | C (k) F | OP T |
| **Clarion Del Mar Inn** 720 Camino Del Mar www.delmarinn.com dogs under 20 lbs allowed Oct–May only, lawn and open field, 5 blocks to beach access | 858-755-9765 800-451-4515 each pet $25/stay | (81) $114 | CB M/F | OP T GP |
| **Hilton San Diego/Del Mar** 15575 Jimmy Durante Blvd www.sandiegodelmarhilton.com lawn walking area, closest hotel to local dog beach, 1 mile to park and trails, 5 miles to off-leash dog park | 858-792-5200 800-833-7904 pet fee $40/stay | (257) $129– $249 | C R/L | OP T FR |
| **Les Artistes Inn** 944 Camino Del Mar www.lesartistesinn.com dogs by advance approval only, undeveloped walking area, residential streets, ½ mile to dog-friendly beach | 858-755-4646 pet fee $20/stay | (12) $85– $195 | CB M/F | IS |

## Delano

| | | | |
|---|---|---|---|
| **Comfort Inn** 2211 Girard St www.choicehotels.com pets allowed in smoking rooms only, open field | 661-725-1022 800-228-5150 pet fee $10/day | (45) $60– $70 | CB M/F | OP |
| **Hal-Mar Inn** 320 High St small dogs allowed by manager's approval only, open walking area | 661-725-3321 pet fee $5–$10/day | (8) $33– $38 | | |
| **Super 8 Motel** 2231 Girard St www.super8.com small grassy walking areas | 661-725-7551 800-800-8000 each pet $7/day | (48) $49– $79 | FB M/F | OP T |
| **Travel Inn** 405 Cecil Ave parking lot and grassy areas, 5 minutes to park | 661-725-3205 pet fee $4/stay | (60) $35– $45 | M/F | OP |

| C = coffee<br>CB = continental<br>    breakfast<br>F = refrigerator<br>FB = full breakfast<br>FR = fitness room | GP = guest pass to<br>    fitness center<br>IP = indoor pool<br>IS = in-room spa<br>K = full kitchen<br>(k) = kitchenette | L = lounge<br>M = microwave<br>OP = outdoor pool<br>R = restaurant<br>S = sauna/steam<br>T = spa or hot tub | (# of units)<br>& rates | food<br>& drink | pool, sauna<br>& hot tub |
|---|---|---|---|---|---|

## Desert Hot Springs

| | | | | |
|---|---|---|---|---|
| **Adobe Inn & Spa**    760-329-7292<br>66365 7th St<br>www.adobespa.com<br>enclosed yard and vacant lot to walk dogs, ½ block<br>to large park with swimming pool | (12)<br>$79–<br>$125 | K | T<br>GP |
| **Ambassador Resort Hotel & Spa**  760-329-1909<br>12921 Tamar Dr<br>natural hot springs swimming pool and hot pools,<br>sleeping rooms/1–2 bdrm suites, open desert<br>walking area, 2 blocks to park | (20)<br>$90–<br>$140 | C<br>K | OP<br>T |
| **Desert Hot Springs Spa Hotel**  760-329-6000<br>10805 Palm Dr             800-808-7727<br>www.dhsspa.com<br>grassy walking areas, 2 blocks to park, 20 minute<br>drive to dog park | (50)<br>$99–<br>$139 | R/L | OP<br>T<br>FR |
| **Emerald Springs Resort**    760-288-0071<br>68055 Club Circle Dr    pet fee $25/stay<br>www.emeraldsprings.net<br>mineral springs spas, open desert area, national park | (15)<br>$85–<br>$125 | CB<br>K | OP<br>S<br>T |
| **Flamingo Resort Hotel & Spa**  760-251-1455<br>67221 Pierson Blvd<br>hot springs pools, open desert area, 2 blocks to park | (32)<br>$90–<br>$120 | C | OP<br>T |
| **Highlander Lodge**    760-251-0189<br>68187 Club Circle Dr<br>www.highlanderlodge.com<br>hot mineral pool, open desert area | (18)<br>$98–<br>$110 | CB<br>K | OP<br>S<br>T |
| **The Last Resort**    760-902-3536 or<br>67780 Arena Blanca      760-322-8759<br>www.thelastresortcalifornia.com<br>eclectic 1–2 bdrm suites sleep up to 4, covered<br>patios, hot mineral water spa, natural desert area | (5)<br>$125–<br>$190 | K | T |

| | | | | |
|---|---|---|---|---|
| **Mineral Springs Resort** 11000 Palm Dr www.mineral-springs-resort.com small dogs only, mineral water spas, large lawn area | 760-329-6484 800-635-8660 | (93) $48– $119 | (k) R | OP |
| **Pyramid Spa Motel** 66563 5th St dogs by advance approval only, rooms with outside entrances and private yards, hot mineral water spas | 760-288-3732 | (18) $90– $145 | C (k) F | OP T |
| **Skyliner Spa Motel** 12840 Inaja St well-behaved dogs allowed with manager's approval only, studios and 1 bdrm suite with private sun deck, hot mineral water spa, natural desert walking area | 760-251-0933 | (4) $55– $75 | C K M/F | T |

## Dillon Beach

| | | | | |
|---|---|---|---|---|
| **Dillon Beach Property Mgt** PO Box 151 www.dillonbeach.com modern or old-fashioned vacation homes sleep up to 12, some with fenced yards or decks, near beaches | 707-878-2204 800-447-3767 pet fee $50/stay | (33) $200– $475 | K | T |
| **Seven Shells Beach House** 2 bdrm modern vacation home sleeps 6, deck, ocean views, 2 minute walk to off-leash dog beach | 805-962-7123 | (1) $150– $193 | K | |

## Dixon

| | | | | |
|---|---|---|---|---|
| **Best Western Inn Dixon** 1345 Commercial Way www.bestwesterncalifornia.com open field, ½ mile to park | 707-678-1400 800-937-8376 pet fee $10/stay | (105) $85– $95 | CB M/F | OP S T GP |
| **Dixon Motel** 805 N Adams St dogs allowed in smoking rooms only, walking area | 707-678-3332 | (13) $55– $60 | M/F | |
| **Super 8 Motel** 2500 Plaza Ct www.super8.com short drive to park | 707-678-3399 800-800-8000 pet fee $30/day | (55) $60– $75 | CB M/F | OP |

| | C = coffee<br>CB = continental<br>  breakfast<br>F = refrigerator<br>FB = full breakfast<br>FR = fitness room | GP = guest pass to<br>  fitness center<br>IP = indoor pool<br>IS = in-room spa<br>K = full kitchen<br>(k) = kitchenette | L = lounge<br>M = microwave<br>OP = outdoor pool<br>R = restaurant<br>S = sauna/steam<br>T = spa or hot tub | (# of units)<br>& rates | food<br>& drink | pool, sauna<br>& hot tub |
|---|---|---|---|---|---|---|

## Dorrington

| | | | |
|---|---|---|---|
| **Dorrington Inn & Chalets**<br>3450 Hwy 4<br>www.dorringtoninn.com<br>chalets sleep up to 4, 3 acres with large meadow | 209-795-2164<br>888-874-2164 | (9)<br>$99–<br>$159 | CB<br>(k)<br>M/F | |

## Dorris

| | | | | |
|---|---|---|---|---|
| **Elm Motel**<br>413 S Butte St<br>lawn walking area, 1½ blocks to park | 530-397-3051 | (9)<br>$26–<br>$32 | C<br>(k) | |
| **Golden Eagle Motel**<br>100 N Main St<br>www.goldeneagle.net<br>lawn, open field and wooded walking areas | 530-397-3114<br>pet fee $2/day | (19)<br>$37 | CB<br>M/F | |
| **Hospitality Inn B & B**<br>200 S California St<br>www.hospitalityinn.org<br>small dogs only, garden and open field, 10 minute<br>drive to wildlife refuge | 530-397-2097<br>800-397-2546 | (6)<br>$68 | CB<br>R | T |

## Douglas City

| | | | | |
|---|---|---|---|---|
| **Indian Creek Lodge**<br>5990 Hwy 299 W<br>www.iclodge.com          large riverside lawn | 530-623-6294 | (13)<br>$47–<br>$57 | C<br>M/F | OP |
| **Timber Lodge Motel**<br>100 Stainer Flat Rd<br>dogs by manager's approval, field, riverfront area | 530-623-6624 | (9)<br>$29–<br>$33 | C<br>M/F | |

## Downey

| | | | | |
|---|---|---|---|---|
| **Embassy Suites Hotel**<br>8425 Firestone Blvd<br>www.losangelesdowney.embsuites.com<br>lawn, 4 blocks to park          pet fee $25/day | 562-861-1900<br>800-362-2779 | (219)<br>$130–<br>$167 | FB<br>M/F | OP<br>T<br>FR |

## Downieville

| | | | |
|---|---|---|---|
| **Carriage House Inn** 530-289-3573<br>110 Commercial St  pet fee $15/day<br>www.downievillecarriagehouse.com<br>well-behaved dogs with advance approval only,<br>lawn and riverside walking area | (9)<br>$50–<br>$100 | CB<br>M/F | |
| **Downieville Inn** 530-289-3243<br>117 Main St  pet fee $10/stay<br>www.downievilleinn.com<br>lawn and sidewalk to walk dogs, close to hiking trails | (11)<br>$50–<br>$89 | C<br>(k) | |
| **Downieville River Inn & Resort** 530-289-3308<br>121 River St  800-696-3308<br>www.downievilleriverinn.com<br>dogs by advance reservation only, picnic area,<br>wooded riverside path, close to park and museum | (13)<br>$89–<br>$99 | CB | OP<br>S |
| **Lure Resort** 530-289-3465<br>100 Lure Bridge Lane  800-671-4084<br>www.lureresort.com  each pet $20/day<br>modern cottages/rustic wooden "camping cabins"<br>with public bathhouse, wooded walking area along<br>river | (19)<br>$55–<br>$220 | C<br>K | |
| **Riverside Inn** 530-289-1000<br>206 Commercial St  888-883-5100<br>www.downiville.com  pet fee $10/stay<br>knotty pine rooms, balconies overlooking river,<br>riverside walking area, surrounded by national forest | (11)<br>$70–<br>$86 | CB<br>K<br>M/F | |

## Doyle

| | | | |
|---|---|---|---|
| **J Motel** 530-827-3210<br>436-760 Hwy 395<br>lawn walking area | (6)<br>$30–<br>$35 | M/F | |

## Drytown

| | | | |
|---|---|---|---|
| **Old Well Motel & Grill** 209-245-6467<br>15947 Hwy 49  pet fee $5/day<br>www.route49.com<br>large yard with seasonal creek, short drive to park | (12)<br>$49 | R | OP |

| C = coffee<br>CB = continental<br>  breakfast<br>F = refrigerator<br>FB = full breakfast<br>FR = fitness room | GP = guest pass to<br>  fitness center<br>IP = indoor pool<br>IS = in-room spa<br>K = full kitchen<br>(k) = kitchenette | L = lounge<br>M = microwave<br>OP = outdoor pool<br>R = restaurant<br>S = sauna/steam<br>T = spa or hot tub | (# of units)<br>& rates | food<br>& drink | pool, sauna<br>& hot tub |
|---|---|---|---|---|---|

## Dublin

| | | | | |
|---|---|---|---|---|
| **AmeriSuites**<br>4950 Hacienda Dr<br>www.amerisuites.com<br>1 bdrm suites sleep 6, dogs must be in travel kennel<br>while in room, small grassy areas, 4 blocks to park | 925-828-9006<br>800-833-1516 | (128)<br>$69–<br>$159 | CB<br>M/F<br>(k) | OP<br>FR |
| **Radisson Dublin Inn**<br>6680 Regional St<br>www.radisson.com<br>courtyard and lawn walking area | 925-828-7750<br>800-422-4656<br>pet fee $35/stay | (234)<br>$89–<br>$129 | R | IP<br>S<br>T |

## Duncans Mills

| | | | | |
|---|---|---|---|---|
| **Inn at Duncans Mills**<br>25233 Steelhead Blvd<br>www.sonic.net/~theinndm<br>rooms/3 bdrm suite that sleeps 8, weekend social<br>hour with beer/wine/hot appetizers, country road<br>and riverfront walking area | 707-865-1855 | (5)<br>$125 | FB | |
| **Superintendent's House**<br>24951 Hwy 116<br>www.sterba.com/river/super<br>dogs by advance reservation only, fenced yard along<br>river, 4 miles to dog-friendly beaches | 707-865-1572<br>pet fee $10/day | (5)<br>$85–<br>$120 | FB | |

## Dunnigan

| | | | | |
|---|---|---|---|---|
| **Best Value Inn**<br>3930 Country Road 89<br>small lawn walking area | 530-724-3333<br>pet fee $10/day | (45)<br>$64–<br>$68 | CB<br>F | OP |
| **Best Western Country Inn**<br>3930 Country Road 89<br>www.bestwesterncalifornia.com<br>lawn walking area | 530-724-3471<br>800-937-8376<br>pet fee $10/day | (50)<br>$64–<br>$78 | CB<br>M/F | OP |

## Dunsmuir

| | | | | |
|---|---|---|---|---|
| **Acorn Inn**  530-235-4805<br>4310 Dunsmuir Ave<br>large lawn, walking distance to several parks | (15)<br>$35–<br>$45 | | | OP |
| **Bavaria Lodge**  530-235-4707<br>4601 Dunsmuir Ave<br>www.bavarialodge.net<br>cabins sleep 5, meadow, close to parks | (8)<br>$50 | C<br>K | | |
| **Cave Springs Motel & Resort**  530-235-2721<br>4727 Dunsmuir Ave  pet fee $4/day<br>www.cavesprings.com<br>rooms/cabins/vacation homes, field, wooded area | (35)<br>$39 | C<br>M/F | OP<br>T | |
| **Cedar Lodge Motel**  530-235-4331<br>4201 Dunsmuir Ave  each pet $5/day<br>www.cedarlodgedunsmuir.com<br>dogs under 50 lbs only, open field | (14)<br>$42–<br>$125 | C<br>K<br>M/F | | |
| **Dunsmuir Inn**  530-235-4543<br>5423 Dunsmuir Ave  each pet $25/stay<br>lawn walking area | (5)<br>$50–<br>$85 | FB | | |
| **Oak Tree Inn**  530-235-2884<br>6604 Dunsmuir Ave  877-235-2884<br>www.oaktreeinn.com<br>small dogs by advance reservation only, lawn area | (18)<br>$48–<br>$62 | C | | |
| **Railroad Park Resort & Caboose Motel**  (27)<br>100 Railroad Park Rd  530-235-4440<br>www.rrpark.com  each pet $10/day<br>cabins and cabooses outfitted as sleeping units, sleep<br>up to 5, park-like grounds to walk dogs, near lakes | (27)<br>$95–<br>$119 | C<br>R/L | OP<br>T | |

## El Cajon

| | | | | |
|---|---|---|---|---|
| **Belair Motel**  619-442-5415<br>638 El Cajon Blvd  pet fee $20/stay<br>open walking area | (10)<br>$45 | C<br>M/F | | |
| **Best Western Courtesy Inn**  619-440-7378<br>1355 E Main St  800-528-1234<br>www.bestwesterncalifornia.com  each pet $6/day<br>dogs allowed in smoking rooms only, 1 mile to park | (47)<br>$72–<br>$76 | CB | T | |

| C = coffee<br>CB = continental<br>    breakfast<br>F = refrigerator<br>FB = full breakfast<br>FR = fitness room | GP = guest pass to<br>    fitness center<br>IP = indoor pool<br>IS = in-room spa<br>K = full kitchen<br>(k) = kitchenette | L = lounge<br>M = microwave<br>OP = outdoor pool<br>R = restaurant<br>S = sauna/steam<br>T = spa or hot tub | (# of units)<br>& rates | food<br>& drink | pool, sauna<br>& hot tub |
|---|---|---|---|---|---|

## El Cajon (continued)

| | | | |
|---|---|---|---|
| **Budget Inn Motel**<br>1538 E Main St<br>dogs allowed in smoking rooms only, pet relief area,<br>4 blocks to park | 619-440-4343<br>each pet $5/day | (55)<br>$47–<br>$54 | | OP |
| **Motel 6**<br>550 Montrose Ct<br>www.motel6.com<br>1 small dog only, grassy areas, short drive to park | 619-588-6100<br>800-466-8356 | (183)<br>$46–<br>$56 | C | OP |
| **Quality Inn & Suites**<br>1250 El Cajon Blvd<br>www.qualityinnsandiegoeast.com<br>dogs under 20 lbs, open walking area, cleanup bags | 619-588-8808<br>800-588-1775<br>pet fee $10/stay | (96)<br>$68–<br>$75 | CB | OP<br>T |
| **Relax Inn & Suites**<br>1220 W Main St<br>www.relaxinnsd.com<br>grassy walking area | 619-442-2576<br>pet fee $10/day | (38)<br>$45–<br>$60 | M/F<br>R | OP |
| **Travelodge**<br>471 N Magnolia Ave<br>www.travelodge.com<br>dogs allowed in smoking rooms only, ½ mile to park | 619-447-3999<br>pet fee $15/day | (47)<br>$69–<br>$99 | CB<br>M/F | OP |

## El Centro

| | | | |
|---|---|---|---|
| **Brunner's Inn & Suites**<br>215 N Imperial Ave<br>dogs under 25 lbs only, lawn area, next to park | 760-352-6431 | (90)<br>$60–<br>$140 | FB<br>M/F<br>R/L | OP<br>T<br>FR |
| **Budget Inn & Suites**<br>1212 Adams Ave<br>lawn walking area, ½ mile to park | 760-353-9600<br>pet fee $10/day | (29)<br>$38 | M/F | OP |
| **Crown Motel**<br>330 N Imperial Ave<br>dogs allowed in smoking rooms only, grassy areas | 760-353-0030<br>pet fee $10/day | (50)<br>$45 | M/F | OP |

| | | | | |
|---|---|---|---|---|
| **Desert Star Motel** 850 Adams Ave grassy areas for walking dogs | 760-353-7900 pet fee $20/stay | (18) $30–$40 | K M/F | |
| **El Dorado Motel** 1464 Adams Ave pet relief area, next to park | 760-352-7333 pet fee $10/day | (75) $33–$37 | CB M/F | OP |
| **El Patio Motel** 670 Adams Ave dogs in smoking rooms only, lawn area, next to park | 760-353-1028 | (19) $30 | M/F | |
| **Golden West Motel** 1080 Adams Ave 3 blocks to park | 760-337-8956 | (22) $30–$35 | | |
| **Kon Tiki Motel** 1226 Adams Ave quiet well-behaved dogs only, ½ mile to park | 760-352-8631 pet fee $5/day | (22) $30–$33 | M/F | |
| **Laguna Inn** 2030 Cottonwood Cir dogs allowed in smoking rooms only | 760-353-7750 800-291-4466 | (27) $45–$55 | C M/F | OP |
| **Motel 6** 395 Smoketree Dr www.motel6.com | 760-353-6766 800-466-8356 gravel walking area | (110) $46 | C | OP |
| **Ramada Inn** 1455 Ocotillo Dr www.ramada.com large lawn, 3 blocks to park | 760-352-5152 800-805-4000 pet fee $10/day | (140) $97 | C M/F | OP T FR |
| **Ranch House Motel** 808 Adams Ave small dogs only, residential street for walking dogs, close to public swimming pool, 1 block to park | 760-352-5571 | (16) $30 | C M/F | |
| **Vacation Inn** 2015 Cottonwood Cir www.vacationinnelcentro.com well-mannered dogs under 50 lbs only, large lawn, ½ mile to small park, 2 miles to larger park | 760-352-9700 800-328-6289 | (189) $49–$55 | CB M/F R | OP T FR |
| **Value Inn & Suites** 455 4th St | 760-352-6620 each pet $5/day | (50) $42–$45 | CB M/F | OP |

| C = coffee<br>CB = continental<br>   breakfast<br>F = refrigerator<br>FB = full breakfast<br>FR = fitness room | GP = guest pass to<br>   fitness center<br>IP = indoor pool<br>IS = in-room spa<br>K = full kitchen<br>(k) = kitchenette | L = lounge<br>M = microwave<br>OP = outdoor pool<br>R = restaurant<br>S = sauna/steam<br>T = spa or hot tub | (# of units)<br>& rates | food<br>& drink | pool, sauna<br>& hot tub |
|---|---|---|---|---|---|
| **El Monte** | | | | | |
| **Budget Inn**<br>10038 Valley Blvd<br>small dogs only, 2 blocks to open walking area | 626-575-7997<br>pet fee $10/day | | (39)<br>$40–<br>$65 | | IS |
| **Motel 6**<br>3429 Peck Rd<br>www.motel6.com open walking area, 3 miles to park | 626-448-6660<br>800-466-8356 | | (68)<br>$51–<br>$62 | C | OP |
| **El Portal** | | | | | |
| **Yosemite View Lodge**<br>11156 Hwy 140<br>www.yosemite-motels.com<br>riverside natural walking area, close to trails | 209-379-2681<br>800-321-5261<br>each pet $10/day | | (335)<br>$99–<br>$250 | (k)<br>R | IP<br>OP<br>T<br>IS |
| **El Segundo** | | | | | |
| **Embassy Suites Hotel**<br>1440 E Imperial Ave<br>www.embassysuites.com<br>up to 3 dogs under 25 lbs only, evening beverages<br>and appetizers, short walk to dog park | 310-640-3600<br>800-362-2779<br>each pet $25/day | | (350)<br>$139–<br>$169 | FB<br>M/F<br>R | IP |
| **Homestead Studio Suites**<br>1910 E Mariposa Ave<br>www.homesteadhotels.com<br>open field, 5 minute drive to park | 310-607-4000<br>888-782-9473<br>pet fee $75/stay | | (151)<br>$63–<br>$99 | (k) | |
| **Residence Inn–LAX**<br>2135 E El Segundo Blvd<br>www.ri-elsegundo.com<br>Mon–Thur evening beverages and light dinner,<br>pet relief area, close to park | 310-333-0888<br>800-331-3131<br>pet fee $75/stay | | (150)<br>$159–<br>$199 | CB<br>K | OP<br>T<br>FR |
| **Summerfield Suites**<br>810 S Douglas St<br>www.wyndham.com<br>1–2 bdrm suites, gravel walking trail, 1 mile to park | 310-725-0100<br>800-946-3426<br>pet fee $150/stay | | (122)<br>$99–<br>$159 | FB<br>K | OP<br>T<br>FR |

## Elk

| | | | | |
|---|---|---|---|---|
| **Greenwood Pier Inn** 707-877-9997<br>5926 S Hwy 1 800-807-3423<br>www.greenwoodpierinn.com pet fee $15/day<br>private hot tubs, lawn walking area, 5 minute walk<br>to beach | (14)<br>$165–<br>$185 | CB<br>M/F | T |
| **Griffin House** 707-877-3422<br>5910 S Hwy 1 pet fee $20/stay<br>www.griffinn.com<br>dog-friendly cottage sleeps 2, backyard and deck,<br>5 minute walk to state park and dog-friendly beach | (7)<br>$98–<br>$148 | FB<br>R/L | |

## Emeryville

| | | | | |
|---|---|---|---|---|
| **Woodfin Suite Hotel** 510-601-5880<br>5800 Shellmound St 888-433-9042<br>www.woodfinsuites.com pet fee $5/day<br>1–2 bdrm suites, small grassy walking areas, 1 mile<br>to hiking trails, 2 miles to off-leash dog park | (202)<br>$129–<br>$169 | FB<br>(k)<br>M/F | OP<br>FR<br>T |

## Encinitas

| | | | | |
|---|---|---|---|---|
| **Best Western Encinitas Inn** 760-942-7455<br>85 Encinitas Blvd 800-362-4648<br>www.bwencinitas.com pet fee $50/stay<br>across street to park, 2 miles to dog-friendly beach | (94)<br>$109–<br>$139 | CB<br>M/F | OP<br>T |
| **Econo Lodge** 760-436-4999<br>410 N Coast Hwy 101 800-553-2666<br>www.choicehotels.com pet fee $5/day<br>dogs under 10 lbs only, 2 blocks to beach | (30)<br>$65–<br>$89 | CB<br>F | OP |
| **Holiday Inn Express** 760-944-3800<br>607 Leucadia Blvd 800-992-9330<br>www.holiday-inn.com pet fee $20/day<br>residential streets for walking dogs, ½ mile to park | (101)<br>$69–<br>$129 | CB<br>M/F | OP<br>T |
| **Leucadia Beach Motel** 760-943-7461<br>1322 N Coast Hwy 101 800-706-7461<br>www.leucadiabeachmotel.com<br>roadside walking area, 1 block to dog-friendly beach | (21)<br>$50–<br>$65 | C<br>(k) | |

| C = coffee<br>CB = continental<br>　breakfast<br>F = refrigerator<br>FB = full breakfast<br>FR = fitness room | GP = guest pass to<br>　fitness center<br>IP = indoor pool<br>IS = in-room spa<br>K = full kitchen<br>(k) = kitchenette | L = lounge<br>M = microwave<br>OP = outdoor pool<br>R = restaurant<br>S = sauna/steam<br>T = spa or hot tub | (# of units)<br>& rates | food<br>& drink | pool, sauna<br>& hot tub |
|---|---|---|---|---|---|

## Encinitas (continued)

| | | | | |
|---|---|---|---|---|
| **Portofino Beach Inn**<br>186 N Coast Hwy 101<br>www.portofinobeachinn.com　　pet fee $20–$50/day<br>5 minute walk to dog-friendly beach | 760-944-0301<br>800-566-6654 | (45)<br>$60–<br>$130 | CB<br>M/F | T |

## Encino

| | | | | |
|---|---|---|---|---|
| **Tokyo Princess Inn**<br>17448 Ventura Blvd<br>small dogs by advance approval only, 1¼ mile to park | 818-788-3820 | (26)<br>$70 | CB<br>M/F | T |

## Escondido

| | | | | |
|---|---|---|---|---|
| **Best Value Inn & Suites**<br>555 N Centre City Pkwy<br>www.bestvalueinnesc.com<br>small dogs only, 3 blocks to park | 760-743-3700<br>pet fee $5/day | (82)<br>$55–<br>$65 | CB<br>M/F<br>R | OP |
| **Best Western Escondido Hotel**<br>1700 Seven Oakes Rd<br>www.bestwestern.com/escondido　　pet fee $25/stay<br>dogs under 15 lbs only, 2 blocks to park | 760-740-1700<br>800-752-1710 | (100)<br>$80–<br>$120 | CB<br>M/F | OP<br>T<br>GP |
| **Castle Creek Inn Resort & Spa**<br>29850 Circle R Way<br>www.castlecreekinn.com　　each pet $35/day<br>hillside walkway, 10 minute drive to national park | 760-751-8800<br>800-253-5341 | (31)<br>$99–<br>$189 | C<br>M/F<br>R | OP<br>S<br>T<br>FR |
| **Comfort Inn**<br>1290 W Valley Pkwy<br>www.choicehotels.com　　pet fee $15/day<br>close to walking trail | 760-489-1010<br>800-541-6012 | (93)<br>$59–<br>$99 | CB<br>M/F | OP<br>T<br>FR |
| **Howard Johnson**<br>515 W Washington Ave<br>www.howardjohnson.com　　pet fee $10/day<br>small dogs allowed in smoking rooms only, grassy<br>walking areas | 760-743-1443<br>800-446-4656 | (70)<br>$74 | CB<br>M/F<br>R | OP<br>T |

| | | | | |
|---|---|---|---|---|
| Motel 6 | 760-745-9252 | (130) | C | OP |
| 900 N Quince St | 800-466-8356 | $48– | | |
| www.motel6.com | lawn, 2 miles to park | $60 | | |
| **Palm Tree Lodge** | 760-745-7613 | (38) | C | OP |
| 425 W Mission Ave | 800-745-1062 | $54– | M/F | |
| www.palmtreelodge.com | pet fee $10/day | $64 | | |
| garden, short drive to park | | | | |
| **Rodeway Inn** | 760-746-0441 | (25) | CB | IS |
| 250 W El Norte Pkwy | pet fee $15/day | $60– | M/F | |
| www.choicehotels.com | | $100 | | |
| dogs by manager's approval only, pet walking area in parking lot, 2 miles to park | | | | |

## Etna

| | | | | |
|---|---|---|---|---|
| Motel Etna | 530-467-5338 | (10) | M/F | |
| 317 Collier Way | pet fee $5/day | $43 | | |
| open walking area, ¼ mile to park and trails | | | | |

## Eureka

| | | | | |
|---|---|---|---|---|
| **Bayview Motel** | 707-442-1673 | (17) | C | |
| 2844 Fairfield St | 866-725-6813 | $70– | F | |
| www.bayviewmotel.com | pet fee $5/day | $150 | | |
| small dogs only, rooms/suites sleep up to 6, private patios, yard, 1 mile to hiking trails | | | | |
| **Best Western Bayshore Inn** | 707-268-8005 | (81) | FB | S/T |
| 3500 Broadway St | 888-268-8005 | $79– | M/F | IP |
| www.bwbayshoreinn.com | pet fee $20/stay | $161 | R/L | FR |
| landscaped walking area, 2 blocks to park | | | | IS |
| **Broadway Motel** | 707-443-3156 | (29) | C | |
| 1921 Broadway St | | $39– | | |
| dogs allowed by manager's approval only, open field, ½ mile to bayfront walking area | | $69 | | |
| **Budget Motel** | 707-443-7321 | (44) | C | |
| 1140 4th St | | $44 | M/F | |
| grassy walking area, 3 blocks to waterfront | | | | |
| **Econo Lodge** | 707-443-8041 | (41) | CB | IP |
| 1630 4th St | pet fee $5/day | $49– | M/F | |
| small grassy walking area, 5 minute walk to ocean | | $61 | | |

| C = coffee   GP = guest pass to   L = lounge<br>CB = continental     fitness center   M = microwave<br>    breakfast    IP = indoor pool   OP = outdoor pool<br>F = refrigerator   IS = in-room spa   R = restaurant<br>FB = full breakfast   K = full kitchen   S = sauna/steam<br>FR = fitness room   (k) = kitchenette   T = spa or hot tub | (# of units)<br>& rates | food<br>& drink | pool, sauna<br>& hot tub |
|---|---|---|---|
| **Eureka (continued)** | | | |
| **Halcyon Inn**    707-444-1310<br>1420 C St    888-882-1310<br>www.halcyoninn.com    pet fee $20/day<br>dogs allowed in first floor room only, afternoon tea,<br>back yard and alley to walk dogs, 3 blocks to park | (3)<br>$125–<br>$135 | FB<br>F | |
| **Lamplighter Motel**    707-443-5001<br>4033 Broadway St    pet fee $5/day<br>small dogs allowed by manager's approval only,<br>large yard, short drive to waterfront | (20)<br>$45–<br>$60 | C | |
| **Motel 6**    707-445-9631<br>1934 Broadway St    800-466-8356<br>www.motel6.com<br>1 dog only, lawn area, 5 blocks to bayfront trail and<br>fishing pier | (98)<br>$46–<br>$62 | C | |
| **Old Town B & B**    707-443-5235<br>1521 3rd St    888-508-5235<br>www.oldtownbnb.com    pet fee $15/stay<br>small fenced yard and residential neighborhood | (4)<br>$110–<br>$140 | FB | |
| **Quality Inn**    707-443-1601<br>1209 4th St    800-722-1622<br>www.qualityinneureka.com<br>2 blocks to small walking area beside the bay | (60)<br>$60–<br>$135 | CB<br>M/F | OP<br>T<br>IS |
| **Ramada Ltd**    707-443-2206<br>270 5th St    800-233-3782<br>www.ramada.com    pet fee $8/day<br>dogs under 50 lbs, very small shrubby area for<br>walking dogs, 3 miles to peninsula and public parks | (39)<br>$69–<br>$76 | CB<br>M/F | T |
| **Red Lion Hotel**    707-445-0844<br>1929 4th St    800-733-5466<br>www.redlion.com    pet fee $15/stay<br>small grassy area, close to bayfront boardwalk | (175)<br>$99–<br>$149 | C<br>R/L | OP<br>T<br>FR |

| | | | | |
|---|---|---|---|---|
| **Royal Inn**<br>1137 5th St<br>dogs by manager's approval, 2 blocks to waterfront | 707-442-2114<br>pet fee $7/day | (29)<br>$45–<br>$49 | C | |
| **Sunrise Inn & Suites**<br>129 4th St<br>3 blocks to waterfront walking area | 707-443-9751<br>800-444-9751<br>pet fee $8/day | (25)<br>$50–<br>$70 | CB<br>M/F | IS |
| **Town House Motel**<br>933 4th St<br>www.eurekatownhousemotel.com<br>small to medium dog only, 4 blocks to bayfront | 707-443-4536<br>800-445-6888<br>pet fee $6/day | (20)<br>$48–<br>$95 | C<br>M/F | |
| **Travelodge**<br>4 Fourth St<br>www.travelodge.com<br>grassy walking area | 707-443-6345,<br>800-578-7878<br>each pet $10/day | (46)<br>$54–<br>$62 | CB<br>M/F | OP |

## Fairfield

| | | | | |
|---|---|---|---|---|
| **E-Z8 Motel**<br>3331 N Texas St<br>www.ez8motels.com<br>dogs under 25 lbs only, open field, ½ mile to park | 707-426-6161 | (101)<br>$45–<br>$55 | C<br>F | OP<br>T |
| **Econo Lodge Inn & Suites**<br>4625 Central Way<br>www.choicehotels.com<br>dogs under 50 lbs only, large lawn | 707-864-2426 | (110)<br>$49–<br>$79 | CB<br>M/F | |
| **Inns of America**<br>4376 Central Pl<br>www.innsofamerica.com<br>open field to walk dogs | 707-864-1728<br>800-826-0778 | (101)<br>$62–<br>$80 | C<br>M/F | OP |
| **Motel 6**<br>1473 Holiday Lane<br>www.motel6.com<br>open field, short drive to park | 707-425-4565<br>800-466-8356 | (89)<br>$50–<br>$72 | C | OP |

## Fall River Mills

| | | | | |
|---|---|---|---|---|
| **Fall River Hotel**<br>24860 Main St<br>www.fallriverhotel.com<br>rooms/suites sleep up to 5, field and woods | 530-336-5550<br>pet fee $5/day | (18)<br>$55–<br>$85 | C<br>M/F<br>R | |

| C = coffee  GP = guest pass to  L = lounge<br>CB = continental  fitness center  M = microwave<br>  breakfast  IP = indoor pool  OP = outdoor pool<br>F = refrigerator  IS = in-room spa  R = restaurant<br>FB = full breakfast  K = full kitchen  S = sauna/steam<br>FR = fitness room  (k) = kitchenette  T = spa or hot tub | (# of units)<br>& rates | food<br>& drink | pool, sauna<br>& hot tub |
|---|---|---|---|

### Fall River Mills (continued)

| | | | |
|---|---|---|---|
| **Fall River Lodge**  530-336-5678<br>43288 Hwy 299 East<br>lawn and field, close to lake, 15 miles to state park | (18)<br>$48–<br>$71 | C<br>(k)<br>M/F | |
| **Hi-Mont Motel**  530-336-5541<br>Hwy 299 East  pet fee $5–$10/day<br>wooded walking area | (30)<br>$54–<br>$85 | CB<br>M/F | |
| **Pit River Lodge**  530-336-5005<br>24500 Pit 1 Powerhouse Rd<br>www.pitriverlodge.com<br>2–3 bdrm cottages sleep up to 7, open April–Nov and<br>by special arrangement in winter, riverside walking<br>trails, very secluded wooded setting | (14)<br>$125–<br>$330 | K<br>R | |

### Fallbrook

| | | | |
|---|---|---|---|
| **Best Western Franciscan Inn**  760-728-6174<br>1635 S Mission Rd  800-937-8376<br>www.bestwestern.com/franciscaninn  pets $10/stay<br>lawn walking area, across street to park | (50)<br>$68–<br>$75 | CB<br>M/F | OP<br>T |
| **Fallbrook Country Inn**  760-728-1114<br>1425 S Mission Rd  800-567-5496<br>www.pinnaclehotelsusa.com  pet fee $10/day<br>large field, ½ mile to off-leash dog park | (28)<br>$75–<br>$85 | CB<br>(k) | OP<br>T |
| **Fallbrook Lodge**  760-723-1127<br>1608 S Mission Rd  pet fee $5/stay<br>dogs by manager's approval only, lawn walking area | (26)<br>$57–<br>$69 | CB<br>M/F | |
| **Pala Mesa Resort**  760-728-5881<br>2001 Old Hwy 395  800-722-4700<br>www.palamesa.com  pet fee $75/stay<br>lawn walking area, golf, tennis, 2 miles of walking<br>trails | (133)<br>$139–<br>$309 | C<br>F<br>R/L | OP<br>T<br>FR |

## Fawnskin

| | | | | |
|---|---|---|---|---|
| **Inn At Fawnskin Resort Rentals** 880 Canyon Rd www.fawnskininn.com 2 bdrm cabins, woods, trails | 909-866-3200 888-329-6754 | (2) $175–$225 | K | T |
| **North Shore Cabins** 39544 North Shore Dr www.northshorecabins.net cabins sleep 10, walking area, ½ mile to lakeside trail | 909-866-0874 each pet $10/day | (11) $95 | C K M/F | |
| **Quail Cove** 39117 North Shore Dr www.quailcove.com cabins, woods, grassy and sandy walking areas | 909-866-5957 800-595-2683 each pet $15/day | (6) $99–$119 | K | T |

## Ferndale

| | | | | |
|---|---|---|---|---|
| **Collingwood B & B** 831 Main St www.collingwoodinn.com dog treats/bowls/blankets, dogsitting service, large garden, next to park, 4 miles to off-leash dog beach | 707-786-9219 800-469-1632 pet fee $25/day | (5) $99–$203 | FB | |
| **Ferndale Motel** 632 Main St 2-room units sleep 6, dogwashing facility, 1 block to grassy area and park, 1 mile to dog-friendly beach | 707-496-3712 pet fee $10/day | (2) $49–$125 | (k) | |
| **Shaw House B & B** 703 Main St www.shawhouse.com dogs by advance approval only, rooms with outside entrances, on 1 acre private park, near walking trails | 707-786-9958 800-557-7429 pet fee $50/stay | (8) $85–$245 | FB | |

## Firebaugh

| | | | | |
|---|---|---|---|---|
| **Best Western Apricot Inn** 46290 W Panoche Rd large open field | 559-659-1444 800-937-8376 pet fee $5/day | (74) $70–$80 | CB M/F | OP |
| **Mercey Hot Springs** 62964 Little Panoche Rd www.merceyhotsprings.com rustic cabins, bathhouse and kitchen, desert area | 209-826-3388 each pet $10/day | (5) $60–$90 | K (k) | |

| | | | (# of units) & rates | food & drink | pool, sauna & hot tub |
|---|---|---|---|---|---|

C = coffee  GP = guest pass to  L = lounge
CB = continental  fitness center  M = microwave
  breakfast  IP = indoor pool  OP = outdoor pool
F = refrigerator  IS = in-room spa  R = restaurant
FB = full breakfast  K = full kitchen  S = sauna/steam
FR = fitness room  (k) = kitchenette  T = spa or hot tub

### Fish Camp

**Apple Tree Inn** — 559-683-5111 — (53) $79–$199 — CB M — IP T
1110 Hwy 41 — 888-683-5111
www.moonstonehotels.com — each pet $25/day
on 10 wooded acres for walking dogs

**Narrow Gauge Inn** — 559-683-7720 — (26) $79–$129 — CB R/L — OP T
48571 Hwy 41 — 888-644-9050
www.narrowgaugeinn.com — each pet $25/stay
treats/bowls/scoopers, next to historic steam train that allows dogs to ride with their owners, creekside nature trail, list of pet-friendly trails and pet rules in Yosemite

### Folsom

**Lake Natoma Inn** — 916-351-1500 — (138) $89–$109 — R/L — OP S T FR
702 Gold Lake Dr — 800-808-5253
www.lakenatomainn.com
next to riverfront state park, hiking trails, outdoor patio dining, 3 miles to boat rentals

**Residence Inn** — 916-983-7289 — (107) $99–$145 — CB K — IP T FR
2555 Iron Point Rd — 800-331-3131
www.marriott.com — pet fee $10/day plus $100 cleaning fee
Mon–Thur beverages and light dinner, open field

### Fontana

**Amerihost Inn & Suites** — 909-463-5900 — (80) $89–$141 — CB M/F — IP T FR
13500 Baseline Ave — 800-434-5800
www.amerihostinn.com — pet fee $50/stay
large grassy area, residential streets to walk dogs

**Circle Inn Motel** — 909-822-9400 — (58) $49–$54 — CB M/F — OP
10227 Cherry Ave — pet fee $5/day
small dogs only

| Motel 6 | 909-823-8686 | (101) | |
|---|---|---|---|
| 10195 Sierra Ave | 800-466-8356 | $50– | |
| www.motel6.com | | $62 | |
| small grassy area, 1 mile to park | | | |

### Forest Ranch

| Bambi Inn | 530-873-4125 | (4) | F |
|---|---|---|---|
| 7436 Humboldt Rd | | $65 | R |
| cabins sleep up to 4, woods and logging roads | | | |

### Fort Bragg

| **Atrium–a Garden Inn by the Sea** | | (10) | FB | |
|---|---|---|---|---|
| 700 N Main St | 707-964-9440 | $99– | | |
| www.atriumbnb.com | pet fee $10/day | $145 | | |
| enclosed garden, dirt walking area, 3 blocks to beach | | | | |
| **Beach House Inn** | 707-961-1700 | (30) | C | |
| 100 Pudding Creek Rd | 888-559-9992 | $79– | M/F | |
| www.beachinn.com | | $150 | | |
| pet fee $10/day up to 30 lbs, $25/day over 30 lbs | | | | |
| creekside logging road for walking dogs | | | | |
| **Beachcomber Motel** | 707-964-2402 | (72) | CB | IS |
| 1111 N Main St | 800-400-7873 | $49– | M/F | |
| www.thebeachcombermotel.com | | $260 | | |
| pet fee $20/day for 1 dog, $30/day for 2 dogs | | | | |
| beachfront walking area, close to state park | | | | |
| **Cleone Gardens Inn** | 707-964-2788 | (12) | CB | T |
| 24600 N Hwy 1 | pet fee $6/day | $86– | FB | |
| www.cleonegardensinn.com | | $140 | K | |
| rooms/2 bdrm cottage sleeps 6, on 6 acres with | | | | |
| open field for walking dogs, short walk to beach | | | | |
| **Coast Motel** | 707-964-2852 | (28) | C | OP |
| 18661 N Hwy 1 | pet fee $10/day | $39– | F | |
| large grassy walking area, 5 minute walk to beach | | $109 | | |
| **Colonial Inn** | 707-964-1384 | (10) | CB | GP |
| 533 E Fir St | 877-964-1384 | $100– | | |
| www.colonialinnfortbragg.com | pet fee $20/day | $175 | | |
| dogs allowed by advance approval only, quiet garden, | | | | |
| lawn and residential streets for walking dogs | | | | |

| C = coffee<br>CB = continental<br>   breakfast<br>F = refrigerator<br>FB = full breakfast<br>FR = fitness room | GP = guest pass to<br>   fitness center<br>IP = indoor pool<br>IS = in-room spa<br>K = full kitchen<br>(k) = kitchenette | L = lounge<br>M = microwave<br>OP = outdoor pool<br>R = restaurant<br>S = sauna/steam<br>T = spa or hot tub | (# of units)<br>& rates | food<br>& drink | pool, sauna<br>& hot tub |
|---|---|---|---|---|---|

### Fort Bragg (continued)

| | | | (# of units)<br>& rates | food<br>& drink | pool, sauna<br>& hot tub |
|---|---|---|---|---|---|
| **Emerald Dolphin Inn**<br>1211 S Main St<br>www.emeralddolphin.com<br>large field for walking dogs, walking trail along<br>ocean bluff, ¾ mile to beach | 707-964-6699<br>866-964-6699<br>pet fee $10/day | | (43)<br>$70–<br>$106 | CB<br>F | |
| **Glass Beach B & B Inn**<br>726 N Main St<br>www.glassbeachinn.com<br>walking trail, 1½ blocks to parks, 2½ blocks to beach | 707-964-6774<br>pet fee $20/stay | | (8)<br>$70–<br>$105 | FB | T |
| **Hi-Seas Inn**<br>1201 N Main St<br>small dogs only, lawn walking area, close to bike trail<br>and dog-friendly beach | 707-964-5929<br>800-990-7327 | | (14)<br>$59–<br>$109 | C | |
| **Old Stewart House Inn**<br>511 Stewart St<br>www.oldstewarthouseinn.com   each pet $10/day<br>beach house sleeps 4, fenced yard and gardens | 707-961-0775<br>800-287-8392 | | (5)<br>$130–<br>$145 | FB<br>(k) | |
| **Pine Beach Inn**<br>16801 N Hwy 1<br>www.pinebeachinn.com<br>walking trail to beach | 707-964-5603<br>888-987-8388<br>pet fee $10/day | | (50)<br>$70–<br>$120 | C<br>M/F | |
| **Seabird Lodge**<br>191 South St<br>www.seabirdlodge.com<br>open field, 4 blocks to beach | 707-964-4731<br>800-345-0022<br>pet fee $8/day | | (65)<br>$75–<br>$110 | C<br>M/F | IP<br>T |
| **Shoreline Cottages**<br>18725 N Hwy 1<br>www.shoreline-cottage.com   each pet $10/stay<br>rooms/cottages sleep 2, lawn and undeveloped<br>areas, 9 minute walk to off-leash dog beach | 707-964-2977<br>800-930-2977 | | (11)<br>$55–<br>$85 | K | |

| | | | | |
|---|---|---|---|---|
| **Surf Motel Fort Bragg** 1220 S Main St www.surfmotelfortbragg.com oceanview rooms and apartments sleep up to 6, grassy field, ½ mile to bluff viewpoint, close to beach | 707-964-5361 800-339-5361 | (54) $43– $160 | CB M/F | |
| **Tradewinds Lodge** 400 S Main St www.fortbragg.org 10 blocks to park, 1 mile to dog-friendly beach | 707-964-4761 800-524-2244 pet fee $10/day | (92) $59– $140 | C M/F R/L | IP T |

## Fort Jones

| | | | | |
|---|---|---|---|---|
| **Marble View Motel** 12425 Main St (Hwy 3) | 530-468-2394 on 2 acres lawn and field | (6) $40 | | |

## Fortuna

| | | | | |
|---|---|---|---|---|
| **Best Western Country Inn** 2025 Riverwalk Dr www.bwcountryinnfortuna.com grassy area behind building, riverside walking trail | 707-725-6822 800-679-7511 pet fee $10/stay | (66) $80– $115 | FB M/F | IP S GP |
| **Holiday Inn Express Fortuna** 1859 Alamar Way www.hiexpress.com/fortunaca dogs under 40 lbs only, lawn, riverside walking trails | 707-725-5500 800-483-9446 pet fee $10/day | (46) $73– $114 | FB M/F | IP T IS GP |
| **Super 8 Motel** 1805 Alamar Way www.super8.com small dogs only, vacant lot, riverside walking trail | 707-725-2888 800-800-8000 each pet $10/day | (46) $55– $84 | CB M/F | |

## Fountain Valley

| | | | | |
|---|---|---|---|---|
| **Ramada Inn** 9125 Recreation Cir www.ramadahb.com dogs in smoking rooms only, grassy walking area, 1 mile to park | 714-847-3388 800-826-1964 each pet $25/day | (64) $89– $99 | CB M/F | OP T |
| **Residence Inn** 9930 Slater Ave www.residenceinn.com Mon–Thur beverages and light dinner, lawn walking areas, ½ mile to park | 714-965-8000 800-331-3131 pet fee $75/stay | (122) $139– $149 | FB K | OP T FR |

| C = coffee<br>CB = continental<br>   breakfast<br>F = refrigerator<br>FB = full breakfast<br>FR = fitness room | GP = guest pass to<br>   fitness center<br>IP = indoor pool<br>IS = in-room spa<br>K = full kitchen<br>(k) = kitchenette | L = lounge<br>M = microwave<br>OP = outdoor pool<br>R = restaurant<br>S = sauna/steam<br>T = spa or hot tub | # of units<br>& rates | food<br>& drink | pool, sauna<br>& hot tub |
|---|---|---|---|---|---|

## Frazier Park

| | | | | |
|---|---|---|---|---|
| **Mountain Properties**      661-242-2500<br>16229 Pine Valley Ln<br>www.mountainproperties.org<br>modern cabins sleep 4 to 20, decks, near golf course,<br>surrounded by national forest to walk dogs | | (3)<br>$90–<br>$300 | K | T<br>IS |
| **Pine Mountain Inn**      661-242-0144<br>16231 Askin Dr<br>1–2 dogs only, community clubhouse, golf course,<br>walking trails | | (8)<br>$79–<br>$99 | C<br>L | OP |

## Freedom

| | | | | |
|---|---|---|---|---|
| **Comfort Inn**      831-728-2300<br>112 Airport Blvd      pet fee $30–$50/stay<br>www.choicehotels.com<br>dogs in smoking rooms only, 5 miles to beach | | (41)<br>$80–<br>$120 | CB<br>M/F | |

## Fremont

| | | | | |
|---|---|---|---|---|
| **AmeriSuites**      510-623-6000<br>3101 W Warren Ave      800-833-1516<br>www.amerisuites.com      lawn areas, walking trail | | (151)<br>$59–<br>$89 | CB<br>(k) | OP<br>GP |
| **Best Western Garden Court Inn**   510-792-4300<br>5400 Mowry Ave      800-541-4909<br>www.gardencourtinn.com      pet fee $10/day<br>grassy walking area, 2 miles to park | | (125)<br>$59–<br>$69 | CB | OP<br>T<br>GP |
| **Fremont Marriott**      510-413-3700<br>46100 Landing Pkwy      800-228-9290<br>www.marriott.com<br>dogs under 25 lbs only, lawn walking area | | (357)<br>$75–<br>$130 | C<br>M/F<br>R/L | IP<br>T<br>FR |
| **Homestead Studio Suites**      510-353-1664<br>46080 Fremont Blvd      888-782-9473<br>www.homesteadhotels.com      pet fee $75/stay<br>walking area in parking lot, 1 mile to park | | (200)<br>$59–<br>$69 | K | GP |

| | | | |
|---|---|---|---|
| **Howard Johnson** 510-656-2366 43643 Mission Blvd 800-446-4656 www.hojo.com pet fee $15/day close to walking trail and college campus | (36) $55 | CB K M/F | |
| **La Quinta Inn** 510-445-0808 46200 Landing Pkwy 800-531-5900 www.lq.com lawn, enclosed dog run, 5 miles to off-leash dog park | (144) $69– $109 | FB M/F | OP T FR |
| **Motel 6 North** 510-793-4848 34047 Fremont Blvd 800-466-8356 www.motel6.com small dogs only, lawn and gravel walking areas, 2 blocks to park | (211) $50 | C | OP |
| **Motel 6 South** 510-490-4528 46101 Research Ave 800-466-8356 www.motel6.com grassy areas, close to park | (159) $35– $46 | C | OP |
| **Residence Inn** 510-794-5900 5400 Farwell Pl 800-331-3131 www.marriott.com pet fee $75/stay Mon–Thur light dinner and beverages, lawn walking area, short drive to park | (80) $74– $109 | CB K | OP T FR |
| **Fresno** | | | |
| **Best Western Garden Court Inn** 559-237-1881 2141 N Parkway Dr 800-437-3766 www.bestwesterncalifornia.com pet fee $10/day lawn and open field, 2 miles to park and zoo | (106) $79– $88 | FB M/F | OP T |
| **Comfort Inn** 559-275-2374 5455 W Shaw Ave 800-228-5150 www.choicehotels.com each pet $25/stay dogs allowed in smoking rooms only, grassy sidewalk strip, 4 miles to park | (69) $70– $90 | CB M/F | OP T FR |
| **Days Inn** 559-268-62116 1101 N Parkway Dr 800-329-746 www.daysinn.com pet fee $5/day open field, close to park | (98) $52– $59 | CB F | OP |

| C = coffee   GP = guest pass to   L = lounge<br>CB = continental     fitness center   M = microwave<br>    breakfast    IP = indoor pool   OP = outdoor pool<br>F = refrigerator   IS = in-room spa   R = restaurant<br>FB = full breakfast   K = full kitchen   S = sauna/steam<br>FR = fitness room   (k) = kitchenette   T = spa or hot tub | # of units)<br>& rates | food<br>& drink | pool, sauna<br>& hot tub |
|---|---|---|---|
| **Fresno (continued)** | | | |
| **Days Inn–Fresno South**    559-237-6644<br>2640 S 2nd St      800-329-7466<br>www.daysinn.com    each pet $10/day<br>small dogs by advance reservation only, petwalking<br>area in paved parking lot, short drive to park | (148)<br>$70–<br>$90 | CB<br>M/F | OP<br>T<br>FR |
| **Econo Lodge**    559-485-5019<br>445 N Parkway Dr    pet fee $30/stay<br>lawn and open field, ½ block to park | (60)<br>$40–<br>$52 | CB<br>M/F | OP |
| **Holiday Inn Express**    559-277-5700<br>5046 N Barcus Ave    800-465-4329<br>www.holidayinnexpress.com   pet fee $20/stay<br>next to park | (50)<br>$100 | CB<br>M/F | OP |
| **La Quinta Inn Fresno**    559-442-1110<br>2926 Tulare St    800-531-5900<br>www.lq.com<br>across street to grassy area for walking dogs | (129)<br>$82–<br>$86 | CB<br>M/F | OP |
| **Motel 6 Blackstone North**    559-221-0800<br>4245 N Blackstone Ave    800-466-8356<br>www.motel6.com<br>small lawn walking area | (82)<br>$54 | C<br>M/F | OP |
| **Motel 6 Blackstone South**    559-222-2431<br>4080 N Blackstone Ave    800-466-8356<br>www.motel6.com<br>small grassy area, close to park | (139)<br>$43–<br>$46 | C<br>M/F | OP |
| **Motel 6 Hwy 99**    559-237-0855<br>1240 N Crystal Ave    800-466-8356<br>www.motel6.com<br>lawn walking area, 1 mile to park | (98)<br>$52 | C<br>F<br>R | OP |

| | | | | |
|---|---|---|---|---|
| **Radisson Hotel**<br>2233 Ventura St<br>www.radisson.com<br>dogs allowed only in first floor smoking rooms with<br>outside entrances, lawn area, 3 blocks to park | 559-268-1000<br>pet fee $50/stay | (321)<br>$154 | C<br>R/L | OP<br>S<br>T<br>FR |
| **Red Roof Inn**<br>6730 N Blackstone Ave<br>www.redroof.com<br>small grassy walking areas, short drive to park | 559-431-3557<br>800-733-7663 | (138)<br>$65–<br>$70 | CB<br>M/F | OP<br>T |
| **Residence Inn**<br>5322 N Diana St<br>www.marriott.com<br>studios/1–2 bdrm suites sleep up to 5, Mon–Thur<br>beverages and light dinner, lawn walking area | 559-222-8900<br>800-331-3131 | (120)<br>$89–<br>$159 | FB<br>K | OP<br>T<br>FR |
| **Sahara Motel**<br>530 N Weber Ave<br>dogs allowed in smoking rooms by advance approval<br>only, gravel walking areas, 5 minute walk to park | 559-498-6156<br>pet fee $5/day | (60)<br>$45 | C<br>K | |
| **Super 8 Motel**<br>1087 N Parkway Dr<br>www.super8.com<br>lawn area, 3 blocks to park | 559-268-0741<br>pet fee $10/day | (48)<br>$62–<br>$67 | CB<br>M/F | OP |
| **Towneplace Suites by Marriott**<br>7127 N Fresno St<br>www.towneplacesuites.com<br>lawn and vacant lot, ½ block to park | 559-435-4600<br>800-257-3000 | (92)<br>$99–<br>$120 | CB<br>K | OP<br>T<br>FR |
| **Travelodge**<br>3876 N Blackstone Ave<br>www.travelodge.com<br>small lawn area, close to canal and jogging trail | 559-229-9840<br>pet fee $5/stay | (44)<br>$40–<br>$60 | CB<br>M/F | OP |
| **University Inn**<br>2655 E Shaw Ave<br>www.cmpm.net          dog treats, lawn walking area | 559-294-0224 | (108)<br>$45–<br>$66 | CB<br>M/F | OP<br>T |
| **Vagabond Inn**<br>2570 S East Ave<br>www.vagabondinn.com<br>grassy walking area | 559-486-1188<br>800-826-0778<br>pet fee $5/day | (120)<br>$50–<br>$55 | CB<br>M/F | OP |

| C = coffee<br>CB = continental<br>    breakfast<br>F = refrigerator<br>FB = full breakfast<br>FR = fitness room | GP = guest pass to<br>    fitness center<br>IP = indoor pool<br>IS = in-room spa<br>K = full kitchen<br>(k) = kitchenette | L = lounge<br>M = microwave<br>OP = outdoor pool<br>R = restaurant<br>S = sauna/steam<br>T = spa or hot tub | # of units)<br>& rates | food<br>& drink | pool, sauna<br>& hot tub |
|---|---|---|---|---|---|
| **Fullerton** | | | | | |
| **Fullerton Inn**    714-773-4900<br>2601 W Orangethorpe Ave    pet fee $10/day<br>small dog in smoking rooms only, small walking area | | | (50)<br>$55 | C | OP |
| **Fullerton Marriott Cal St Univ**    714-738-7800<br>2701 Nutwood Ave    800-228-9290<br>www.marriott.com    pet fee $35/stay<br>small grassy walking area, 4 blocks to park | | | (224)<br>$99–<br>$149 | C<br>M/F | OP<br>T<br>FR |
| **Galt** | | | | | |
| **Royal Delta Inn**    209-745-9181<br>1040 N Lincoln Way<br>dogs under 30 lbs allowed by advance approval only,<br>large grass and dirt walking areas | | | (104)<br>$49 | C | OP |
| **Garberville** | | | | | |
| **Best Western Humboldt House Inn**<br>701 Redwood Dr    707-923-2771<br>   800-862-7756<br>www.bestwestern.com/humboldthouseinn<br>dogs allowed in smoking rooms only, garden<br>walking area, close to parks and trails | | | (76)<br>$105–<br>$112 | CB<br>F | OP<br>T |
| **Johnston's Motel**    707-923-3327<br>839 Redwood Dr<br>dogs allowed in smoking rooms only, paved walking<br>area, ½ mile to park | | | (14)<br>$30–<br>$55 | C | |
| **Lone Pine Motel**    707-923-3520<br>912 Redwood Dr<br>dogs in smoking rooms only, grassy walking area | | | (17)<br>$36–<br>$58 | C<br>M/F | OP |
| **Sherwood Forest Motel**    707-923-2721<br>814 Redwood Dr<br>www.sherwoodforestmotel.com<br>on 3½ acres with lawn and gardens | | | (32)<br>$54–<br>$92 | C<br>M/F | OP<br>T |

## Garden Grove

| Anaheim Marriott Suites<br>12015 Harbor Blvd<br>www.marriott.com<br>pet relief area | 714-750-1000<br>pet fee $15/day | (371)<br>$99–<br>$169 | C<br>M/F<br>R | T<br>FR |
|---|---|---|---|---|
| Candlewood Suites–Anaheim<br>12901 Garden Grove Blvd<br>www.candlewoodsuites.com<br>studios/1 bdrm suites sleep up to 4, 1 block to park | 714-539-4200<br>888-226-3539<br>pet fee $75/stay | (133)<br>$79–<br>$118 | C<br>K<br>M/F | FR |
| Hospitality Inn<br>7900 Garden Grove Blvd<br>well-behaved dog allowed in smoking rooms only,<br>large lawn walking area, short drive to park | 714-898-1306 | (53)<br>$36–<br>$39 | M/F | |
| Residence Inn–Anaheim Resort<br>11931 Harbor Blvd<br>www.residenceinnanaheim.com<br>pet fee $10/day plus $150 cleaning fee<br>lawn walking area, 5 minute walk to park | 714-591-4000<br>800-532-7202 | (200)<br>$89–<br>$129 | FB<br>K<br>M/F | OP<br>T<br>FR |

## Gardena

| Crossland Economy Studios<br>18602 S Vermont Ave<br>www.extendedstay.com<br>studios sleep 4, lawn walking area, 2 miles to park | 310-515-5139<br>800-398-7829 | (130)<br>$70–<br>$75 | C<br>M/F | |
|---|---|---|---|---|
| Redondo Beach Inn<br>1912 W Redondo Beach Blvd<br>small dogs only, 1 mile to park | 310-538-1488<br>pet fee $10/day | (25)<br>$55–<br>$60 | C<br>F | |

## Georgetown

| American River Inn<br>6600 Orleans St<br>www.americanriverinn.com    1 small dog $10/day<br>rooms/suites with outside entrances sleep up to 4,<br>evening wine and appetizers, walking trails | 530-333-4499<br>800-245-6566 | (13)<br>$85–<br>$115 | FB | |
|---|---|---|---|---|
| Hilltop Motel<br>6350 Hwy 193 S<br>dogs by manager's approval, over an acre of lawn | 530-333-4141 | (10)<br>$58 | C<br>M/F | |

| C = coffee | GP = guest pass to | L = lounge |
|---|---|---|
| CB = continental | fitness center | M = microwave |
| breakfast | IP = indoor pool | OP = outdoor pool |
| F = refrigerator | IS = in-room spa | R = restaurant |
| FB = full breakfast | K = full kitchen | S = sauna/steam |
| FR = fitness room | (k) = kitchenette | T = spa or hot tub |

## Gilroy

| | | # of units & rates | food & drink | pool, sauna & hot tub |
|---|---|---|---|---|
| **Budget Motel** 8897 Monterey Rd dogs in smoking rooms, yard, short walk to park | 408-842-4138 | (17) $59–$79 | M/F | |
| **Comfort Inn** 8292 Murray Ave www.choicehotels.com walking area in parking lot | 408-848-3500 800-424-6423 pet fee $10/day | (65) $69–$79 | CB M/F | OP T FR |
| **Leavesley Inn** 8430 Murray Ave large lawn, short drive to park | 408-847-5500 800-624-8225 pet fee $20/stay | (48) $68 | CB M/F | OP T |
| **Motel 6** 6110 Monterey Hwy www.motel6.com         no pet fee for 1 dog, $25/day for 2 dogs lawn area, ½ mile to park | 408-842-6061 800-466-8356 | (127) $56–$66 | C (k) | |
| **National 9 Inn** 5530 Monterey Rd lawn walking area | 408-842-6464 | (24) $55–$65 | C M/F | |

## Glen Ellen

| | | # of units & rates | food & drink | pool, sauna & hot tub |
|---|---|---|---|---|
| **Glenelly Inn** 5131 Warm Springs Rd www.glenellyinn.com dogs by advance approval only, walking trails | 707-996-6720 | (10) $150–$250 | FB | T |
| **Relais Du Soleil** 1210 Nuns Canyon Rd www.relaisdusoleil.com cottage sleeps 6, 120 acre ranch with livestock, creek and swimming hole, across road to state park, trails | 707-833-6264 | (3) $195–$250 | FB K | T |

## Glendale

**Days Inn** 818-956-0202 (700) C OP
600 N Pacific Ave 800-329-7466 $104– F T
www.daysinn.com $114 R
dogs in smoking rooms only, lawn, 2 blocks to park

**Homestead Studio Suites** 818-956-6665, (86) C
1377 W Glenoaks Blvd 888-782-9473 $90– K
www.homesteadhotels.com $110 M/F
pet fee $25/day, up to maximum of $75
dogs under 30 lbs, small lawn area, 2 blocks to park

**Vagabond Inn** 818-240-1700 (52) CB OP
120 W Colorado St pet fee $10/day $79– M/F
www.vagabondinns.com $89
dogs allowed in first floor rooms with outside
entrances, 10 minute drive to park

## Glenhaven

**Indian Beach Resort** 707-998-3760 (10) C
9945 E Hwy 20 pet fee $7/day $68– K
lakefront cabins, open February–November only, $125 M/F
park-like walking area

**Lake Place Resort** 707-998-3331 (10) C
9515 Harbor Dr $60– (k)
www.lakeplaceresort.com $105
rooms/cabins sleep up to 8, lawn walking area

## Glennville

**Bunkhouse Motel** 661-536-9100 (8) CB
12036 Hwy 155 $54– F
large open field $59

## Gold River

**Wingate Inn** 916-858-8680 (101) CB OP
10745 Gold Center Dr 800-228-1000 $69– M/F T
www.wingateinns.com $89 FR
lawn walking area, ½ mile to park, trails and pond

| C = coffee<br>CB = continental<br>   breakfast<br>F = refrigerator<br>FB = full breakfast<br>FR = fitness room | GP = guest pass to<br>   fitness center<br>IP = indoor pool<br>IS = in-room spa<br>K = full kitchen<br>(k) = kitchenette | L = lounge<br>M = microwave<br>OP = outdoor pool<br>R = restaurant<br>S = sauna/steam<br>T = spa or hot tub | (# of units)<br>& rates | food<br>& drink | pool, sauna<br>& hot tub |
|---|---|---|---|---|---|
| **Goleta** | | | | | |
| **Bacara Resort & Spa**<br>8301 Hollister Ave<br>www.bacararesort.com<br>dogs under 35 lbs only, rooms/suites, 78 beachfront<br>acres, nature hikes | 805-968-0100<br>877-422-4245<br>pet fee $125/stay | | (360)<br>$425–<br>$1000 | R | OP |
| **Motel 6 Santa Barbara/Goleta**<br>5897 Calle Real<br>www.motel6.com<br>lawn areas, short drive to park | 805-964-3596<br>800-466-8356 | | (87)<br>$62–<br>$76 | C<br>M/F | OP |
| **Graeagle** | | | | | |
| **Gray Eagle Lodge**<br>5000 Gold Lake Rd<br>www.grayeaglelodge.com<br>room rate includes gourmet dinner, creek and trails | 530-836-2511<br>800-635-8778<br>each pet $20/day | | (20)<br>$195–<br>$235 | FB | |
| **River Pines Resort**<br>8296 Hwy 89<br>www.riverpines.com/rentals1.htm   pet fee $10/stay<br>rooms/suites/2–4 bdrm townhomes, open walking<br>areas, residential streets and hiking trails | 530-836-2552<br>800-696-2551 | | (45)<br>$70–<br>$135 | CB<br>K<br>R | OP<br>T |
| **Grass Valley** | | | | | |
| **Alta Sierra Village Inn**<br>11858 Tammy Way<br>2 acres for walking dogs | 530-273-9102<br>800-992-5300<br>pet fee $10/stay | | (15)<br>$59–<br>$175 | C<br>M/F | |
| **Annie Horan's B & B**<br>415 W Main St<br>www.anniehoran.com<br>large yard, less than 1 mile to park and walking trails | 530-272-1516<br>800-771-4676 | | (4)<br>$89 | FB | |
| **Best Western Gold Country Inn**<br>11972 Sutton Way<br>pet relief area | 530-273-1393<br>800-937-8376<br>pet fee $10/stay | | (84)<br>$89–<br>$113 | CB | OP<br>T |

| | | | | |
|---|---|---|---|---|
| **Coach 'n' Four Motel** | 530-273-8009 | (19) | CB | |
| 628 S Auburn St | pet fee $10/day | $57 | M/F | |
| open field, close to hiking trails at Empire Mine | | | | |
| **Golden Chain Resort Motel** | 530-273-7279 | (21) | CB | OP |
| 13413 State Hwy 49 | pet fee $10/stay | $49– | M/F | |
| small dogs only, wooded walking area | | $80 | | |
| **Grass Valley Courtyard Suites** | 530-272-7696 | (33) | CB | OP |
| 210 N Auburn St | each pet $25/stay | $120– | K | S |
| www.gvcourtyardsuites.com | | $240 | F | T |
| pet relief area, 1 mile to trails at Empire Park | | | | FR |
| **Holiday Lodge** | 530-273-4406 | (34) | CB | OP |
| 1221 E Main St | 800-742-7125 | $72– | M/F | S |
| www.holidaylodge.biz pet relief area, open field | | $77 | | |
| **Sierra Motel** | 530-273-8133 | (13) | CB | |
| 816 W Main St | pet fee $20/stay | $85– | K | |
| rooms/2 bdrm suite/1 bdrm cottage, residential | | $140 | M/F | |
| walking area, near fairground and riverside trails | | | | |
| **Stage Coach Motel** | 530-272-3701 | (17) | CB | |
| 405 S Auburn St | each pet $10/day | $70– | M/F | |
| 1 block to park | | $90 | | |
| **Swan Levine House** | 530-272-1873 | (4) | FB | OP |
| 328 S Church St | pet fee $15/day | $100 | M/F | |
| www.swanlevinehouse.com | | | | |
| room with outside entry, large yard, 1 mile to park | | | | |

### Greenfield

| | | | | |
|---|---|---|---|---|
| **Travel Inn** | 831-674-5816 | (17) | C | |
| 120 El Camino Real | pet fee $7/stay | $39– | M/F | |
| lawn walking area | | $49 | | |

### Greenville

| | | | | |
|---|---|---|---|---|
| **Hideaway Resort Motel** | 530-284-7915 | (13) | C | |
| 761 Hideaway Rd | pet fee $5/day | $53 | K | |
| www.indianvalleychamber.com | | | M/F | |
| dogs by advance approval only, field and woods | | | | |
| **Oak Grove Motor Lodge** | 530-284-6671 | (8) | C | |
| 700 Hwy 89 | | $60– | K | |
| wooded walking area, hillside trails and logging road | | $85 | | |

| C = coffee          GP = guest pass to   L = lounge<br>CB = continental         fitness center   M = microwave<br>  breakfast          IP = indoor pool   OP = outdoor pool<br>F = refrigerator     IS = in-room spa    R = restaurant<br>FB = full breakfast   K = full kitchen   S = sauna/steam<br>FR = fitness room    (k) = kitchenette    T = spa or hot tub | # of units) & rates | food & drink | pool, sauna & hot tub |
|---|---|---|---|

### Greenville (continued)

| | | | |
|---|---|---|---|
| **Sierra Lodge Hotel**            530-284-6154<br>303 Main St                       small dogs only<br>historic 1872 hotel, lawn, 10 minute drive to park | (25)<br>$45 | C<br>M/F | |
| **Spring Meadow Resort Motel**    530-284-6768<br>18964 Hwy 89                     each pet $5/day<br>lawn, gravel area and open field, 1 mile to park | (6)<br>$45 | K<br>F | |

### Gridley

| | | | |
|---|---|---|---|
| **Pacific Motel**                 530-846-4580<br>1308 Hwy 99                      each pet $3/day<br>lawn and field, short drive to park | (15)<br>$55–<br>$60 | C<br>M/F | OP |

### Groveland

| | | | |
|---|---|---|---|
| **Groveland Hotel**               209-962-4000<br>18767 Main St                    800-273-3314<br>www.groveland.com                pet fee $10/day<br>large shady parking area, across street to park  - | (17)<br>$135–<br>$275 | FB<br>R/L | IS |
| **Hotel Charlotte**               209-962-6455<br>18736 Main St                    800-961-7799<br>www.hotelcharlotte.com           pet fee $10/stay<br>old railroad bed for walking dogs, 1 block to park | (10)<br>$89 | CB | |
| **Sunset Inn**                    209-962-4360<br>33569 Hardin Flat Rd             pet fee $20/day<br>www.sunsetinnusa.com<br>cabins sleep 5, dirt roads and trails, 2 miles to river | (3)<br>$100–<br>$200 | C<br>K | |
| **Yosemite Gatehouse Lodge**      209-379-2260<br>34001 Hwy 120                    pet fee $25/stay<br>www.yosemitecabins.com<br>suites/1 bdrm cabins, wooded walking area | (7)<br>$68–<br>$106 | C<br>K<br>M/F | |

| | | | | |
|---|---|---|---|---|
| **Yosemite Rose B & B** 22830 Ferretti Rd www.yosemiterose.com dogs allowed in 1 bdrm cottage that sleeps 4, on 210 acres, hiking trails, dogs can swim in the bass pond | 209-962-6548 866-962-6548 | (7) $160– $235 | K | |
| **Yosemite Westgate Lodge** 7633 Hwy 120 www.innsight.com lawn and dirt roads for walking dogs | 209-962-5281 800-253-9673 pet fee $10/day | (55) $79– $119 | C M/F | OP |

## Gualala

| | | | | |
|---|---|---|---|---|
| **Beach Rentals–The Sea Ranch** 39200 S Hwy 1 www.searanchrentals.com 1–3 bdrm homes, off-leash dog park, walking trails | 707-884-4235 pet fee $10/stay | (50) $115– $300 | K | T OP |
| **Gualala Country Inn** 47955 Center St www.gualala.com vacant lot and dirt road for walking dogs | 707-884-4343 800-564-4466 each pet $10/stay | (20) $110– $165 | CB M/F | IS |
| **Mar Vista Cottages** 35101 S Hwy 1 www.marvistamendocino.com         $25/stay for 1 dog, $35/stay for 2 dogs 1–2 bdrm cottages sleep up to 5, semi-private dog-friendly beach, on 9 open acres, walking trails | 707-884-3522 877-855-3522 | (12) $140– $200 | K | T |
| **North Coast Country Inn** 34591 South Hwy 1 www.northcoastcountryinn.com all rooms have fireplaces and decks, meadow for walking dogs, 2 minute walk to beach | 707-884-4537 800-959-4537 | (6) $185– $225 | FB C M/F (k) | T |
| **Old Milano Hotel** 38300 S Hwy 1 www.oldmilanohotel.com cottages sleep 2, lawn walking area, 1 mile to park | 707-884-3256 | (6) $105– $210 | F | T |
| **Serenisea Ocean Cabins** 36100 S Hwy 1 www.serenisea.com cabins/homes sleep up to 6, lawn, trail to tidepools | 707-884-3836 800-331-3836 | (10) $95– $210 | K | T |

| C = coffee  GP = guest pass to  L = lounge<br>CB = continental  fitness center  M = microwave<br>breakfast  IP = indoor pool  OP = outdoor pool<br>F = refrigerator  IS = in-room spa  R = restaurant<br>FB = full breakfast  K = full kitchen  S = sauna/steam<br>FR = fitness room  (k) = kitchenette  T = spa or hot tub | (# of units)<br>& rates | food<br>& drink | pool, sauna<br>& hot tub |
|---|---|---|---|

## Gualala (continued)

| **Surf Motel at Gualala**<br>39170 S Hwy 1<br>www.gualala.com<br>walking trails through gardens and naturalized areas | 707-884-3571<br>888-451-7873<br>each pet $10/stay | (20)<br>$95–<br>$179 | C<br>M/F | |
|---|---|---|---|---|

## Guerneville

| **Creekside Inn & Resort**<br>16180 Neeley Rd<br>www.creeksideinn.com<br>studios/cottages/2 bdrm riverside home sleep up<br>to 6, open walking areas, close to hiking trails | 707-869-3623<br>800-776-6586 | (17)<br>$84–<br>$255 | C<br>K<br>(k) | T |
|---|---|---|---|---|
| **Fern Grove Cottages**<br>16650 River Rd<br>www.ferngrove.com<br>dogs by owner's approval only, wooded walking area,<br>close to public park, 30 minute drive to beach | 707-869-8105<br>each pet $15/day | (21)<br>$89–<br>$219 | CB<br>K | OP<br>IS |
| **Fife's Guest Ranch**<br>16467 River Rd<br>www.fifes.com<br>1-room cabins/1–2 bdrm cottages sleep up to 6,<br>15 acres with meadow and riverbank walking areas | 707-869-0656<br>800-734-3371<br>each pet $25/day | (50)<br>$65–<br>$175 | R/L | OP |
| **Inn at the Willows**<br>15905 River Rd<br>www.innatthewillows.com<br>riverside area for walking dogs, 2 miles to park | 707-869-2824<br>800-953-2828 | (14)<br>$119 | CB | T |
| **New Dynamic Inn**<br>14030 Mill St<br>www.newdynamicinn.com<br>open field for walking dogs, close to river, 2 miles<br>to park | 707-869-5082<br>800-639-3962<br>pet fee $10/stay | (10)<br>$69–<br>$165 | M/F | |

| | | | | |
|---|---|---|---|---|
| **Ridenhour Ranch House Inn**  707-887-1033<br>12850 River Rd  888-877-4466<br>www.ridenhourinn.com  pet fee $20/day<br>2 dog-friendly cottages, dog bowls/treats, guest use<br>of kitchen in main house | (8)<br>$185 | FB<br>K | T |
| **Rio Inn**  707-869-4444<br>4444 Wood Rd  800-344-7018<br>www.rioinn.com  pet fee $20/day<br>public swimming pool across street, lawn and<br>wooded walking areas | (10)<br>$89–<br>$169 | CB | |
| **River Village Resort**  707-869-8139<br>14880 River Rd  each pet $10/day<br>www.rivervillageresort.com<br>studios/2 bdrm cabins/apartments sleep up to 4,<br>lawn and garden walking area, 2 miles to state park | (19)<br>$79–<br>$174 | FB<br>(k) | OP |
| **Russian River Getaways**  707-869-4560<br>14075 Mill St  800-433-6673<br>www.rrgetaways.com<br>vacation homes sleep 2 to 20, hot tubs or riverfront<br>locations, close to dog-friendly trails and beaches | (52)<br>$175–<br>$950 | K | T |
| **Russian River Resort**  707-869-0691<br>16390 4th St  800-417-3767<br>www.russianriverresort.com<br>dogs in smoking rooms only, open walking areas | (24)<br>$55–<br>$180 | C<br>M/F<br>R | OP<br>T |
| **Russian River Vacation Homes**  707-869-9030<br>14080 Mill St  800-997-3312 or<br>www.riverhomes.com  800-310-0804<br>1–4 bdrm vacation homes, close to dog-friendly<br>park and off-leash dog beach | (52)<br>$175–<br>$535 | | OP<br>T |

### Hacienda Heights

| | | | | |
|---|---|---|---|---|
| **Motel 6 Los Angeles/Hacienda Heights**<br>1154 S Seventh Ave  626-968-9462<br>www.motel6.com  800-466-8356<br>1 small dog only, lawn walking area, 2 blocks to park | (154)<br>$48–<br>$60 | C | OP |

| C = coffee, CB = continental breakfast, F = refrigerator, FB = full breakfast, FR = fitness room; GP = guest pass to fitness center, IP = indoor pool, IS = in-room spa, K = full kitchen, (k) = kitchenette; L = lounge, M = microwave, OP = outdoor pool, R = restaurant, S = sauna/steam, T = spa or hot tub | (# of units) & rates | food & drink | pool, sauna & hot tub |
|---|---|---|---|
| **Half Moon Bay** | | | |
| **Harbor View Inn** 650-726-2329 51 Avenue Alhambra 800-886-6997 www.harbor-view-inn.com vacant lot, short drive to beach trail | (17) $76–$144 | CB M/F | |
| **Holiday Inn Express** 650-726-3400 230 Cabrillo Hwy S 800-465-4329 www.hiexpress.com/halfmoonbay  pet fee $10/day open lot for walking dogs, 2 blocks to beach | (52) $99–$109 | CB M/F | |
| **Miramar Lodge & Conference Ctr** 650-712-1999 2930 Cabrillo Hwy N 800-733-5269 www.miramarlodge.com  pet fee $20/stay 10 minute walk to beach and trails | (53) $79–$160 | CB M/F | FR |
| **Ramada Ltd** 650-726-9700 3020 Cabrillo Hwy N  each pet $15/day www.ramada.com 5 minutes to dog-friendly beach | (27) $79–$125 | CB M/F | |
| **Ritz-Carlton Half Moon Bay** 650-712-7000 1 Miramontes Point Rd  pet fee varies www.ritzcarlton.com | (261) $295–$325 | F R/L | |
| **Zaballa House** 650-726-9123 324 Main St www.zaballahouse.net Victorian rooms/suites, ¼ mile to beach | (22) $129–$275 | CB M/F | IS |
| **Hanford** | | | |
| **Irwin Street Inn** 559-583-8000 522 N Irwin St 866-583-7378 www.irwinstreetinn.com  pet fee $25/stay Victorian hotel, rooms/1 bdrm suites sleep up to 4, private balconies and porches, lawn walking area | (27) $79–$145 | FB M/F R | OP |

| | | | | |
|---|---|---|---|---|
| **Sequoia Inn** 1655 Mall Dr lawn walking area, 3 miles to park | 559-582-0338 800-626-1900 | (58) $60– $65 | CB M/F | OP FR S/T |
| **Travel Haven Motel** 750 E Lacey Blvd dogs allowed by manager's approval only, 4 blocks to park | 559-584-4462 | ·(27) $42 | M/F | OP |

### Happy Camp

| | | | | |
|---|---|---|---|---|
| **Bear Cove Cabins** 64727 Hwy 96 lawn and field, near riverbank and trails | 530-493-2677 | (9) $30– $45 | K | |
| **Forest Lodge Motel** 63712 Hwy 96 www.forestlodgemotel.com dogs by manager's approval only, lawn walking area, ¼ mile to riverside park | 530-493-5296 pet fee $5/day | (15) $55– $60 | C M/F | |
| **Klamath River Resort Inn** 61700 Hwy 96 www.klamathriverresortinn.com on 4 landscaped riverside acres for walking dogs | 530-493-2735 | (8) $59– $89 | C K M/F | T |

### Harbor City

| | | | | |
|---|---|---|---|---|
| **Motel 6** 820 Sepulveda Blvd www.motel6.com small grassy areas | 310-549-9560 800-466-8356 | (56) $54– $60 | C | OP |

### Hayfork

| | | | | |
|---|---|---|---|---|
| **Big Creek Lodge & Motel** Big Creek Road off Hwy 3 rural setting, horse stalls and corral | 530-628-5521 866-628-5521 | (12) $47– $57 | C M/F | |

### Hayward

| | | | | |
|---|---|---|---|---|
| **All Suites Islander Motel** 29083 Mission Blvd rooms/1 bdrm suites, pet relief area, hillside trails, 1½ blocks to park | 510-538-8700 each pet $50/stay | (68) $43– $45 | K M/F | OP |

| C = coffee  GP = guest pass to  L = lounge<br>CB = continental  fitness center  M = microwave<br>  breakfast  IP = indoor pool  OP = outdoor pool<br>F = refrigerator  IS = in-room spa  R = restaurant<br>FB = full breakfast  K = full kitchen  S = sauna/steam<br>FR = fitness room  (k) = kitchenette  T = spa or hot tub | (# of units)<br>& rates | food<br>& drink | pool, sauna<br>& hot tub |
|---|---|---|---|

### Hayward (continued)

| | | | |
|---|---|---|---|
| **Comfort Inn**  510-538-4466<br>24997 Mission Blvd  800-835-6159<br>www.comfortinnhayward.com  pet fee $15/day<br>vacant lot, 3 blocks to trails, 6 blocks to dog park | (62)<br>$69–<br>$79 | CB<br>M/F | S |
| **Heritage Inn**  510-785-0260<br>410 West A St  2 blocks to off-leash park | (55)<br>$50 | CB<br>M/F | OP<br>T |
| **La Quinta Inn**  510-732-6300<br>20777 Hesperian Blvd  800-553-5083<br>www.lq.com<br>evening beverages and snacks, 1 block to park | (141)<br>$89 | CB<br>M/F | OP<br>T<br>FR |
| **Mainstay Suites**  510-731-3571<br>835 W A St  866-624-6789<br>www.mainstaysuites.com/hotel/ca564<br>3 blocks to park  pet fee $15/day | (47)<br>$70–<br>$90 | CB<br>M/F | OP<br>FR |
| **Motel 6**  510-489-8333<br>30155 Industrial Pkwy SW  800-466-8356<br>www.motel6.com  lawn walking area | (177)<br>$46 | C | |
| **Super 8 Motel**  510-489-3888<br>2460 Whipple Rd  800-800-8000<br>www.super8.com  pet fee $10/stay<br>large gravel and grass walking area, 1½ miles to park | (76)<br>$59–<br>$65 | CB<br>M/F | |
| **Vagabond Inn**  510-785-5480<br>20455 Hesperian Blvd  800-522-1555<br>www.vagabondinns.com  each pet $10/day<br>grassy walking area, 1 block to park | (99)<br>$59–<br>$79 | CB | OP<br>T |

### Healdsburg

| | | | |
|---|---|---|---|
| **Best Western Dry Creek Inn**  707-433-0300<br>198 Dry Creek Rd  800-222-5784<br>www.drycreekinn.com  pet fee $20/day<br>rural area and country road, 1 mile to dog park | (103)<br>$79–<br>$199 | CB<br>F | OP<br>T<br>FR |

| | | | | |
|---|---|---|---|---|
| **Duchamp Hotel** | 707-431-1300 | (10) | CB | OP |
| 421 Foss St | 800-431-9341 | $350– | F | T |
| www.duchamphotel.com | | $390 | | |
| 1 bdrm cottage sleeps 4, field, close to 3 dog parks | | | | |
| **Fairview Motel** | 707-433-5548 | (18) | CB | T |
| 74 Healdsburg Ave | pet fee $10/day | $79– | M/F | |
| www.fairviewmotel.com | | $128 | | |
| garden walking area | | | | |
| **Hotel Healdsburg** | 707-431-2800 | (55) | CB | OP |
| 25 Matheson St | 800-889-7188 | $295– | F | T |
| www.hotelHealdsburg.com | pet fee $150/stay | $345 | R/L | |
| dogs under 16 lbs only, lawn, 3 blocks to dog park | | | | |
| **The Irish Rose Inn B & B** | 707-431-2801 | (2) | FB | IS |
| 3232 Dry Creek Rd | | $135– | | |
| www.theirishroseinn.com | | $150 | | |
| dogs by advance approval only, vineyard | | | | |
| **Piper Street Inn** | 707-433-8721 | (2) | CB | T |
| 402 Piper St | 877-703-0570 | $95– | K | |
| www.piperstreetinn.com | | $195 | R | |
| Victorian inn, garden, short drive to dog park | | | | |
| **Villa Messina** | 707-433-6655 | (5) | FB | T |
| 316 Burgundy Rd | | $200– | | IS |
| www.villamessina.com | | $350 | | |
| small dogs by advance approval only, lawn and country road for walking dogs | | | | |

## Hemet

| | | | | |
|---|---|---|---|---|
| **Best Value Western Inn** | 909-929-6366 | (65) | CB | OP |
| 800 W Florida Ave | pet fee $10/day | $57– | M/F | T |
| www.westerninn.us | | $99 | | |
| dogs under 15 lbs only, sun deck, 1 mile to park | | | | |
| **Best Western Inn** | 951-925-6605 | (68) | FB | OP |
| 2625 W Florida Ave | 800-605-0001 | $75– | F | T |
| www.bestwesterncalifornia.com | pet fee $10/day | $100 | | GP |
| small dogs by manager's approval only | | | | |
| **Coach Light Motel** | 909-658-3237 | (32) | C | OP |
| 1640 W Florida Ave | 800-678-0124 | $50– | M/F | |
| vacant lot, ½ block to park | each pet $5/day | $60 | | |

| C = coffee          GP = guest pass to    L = lounge<br>CB = continental              fitness center    M = microwave<br>     breakfast       IP = indoor pool      OP = outdoor pool<br>F  = refrigerator    IS = in-room spa      R = restaurant<br>FB = full breakfast  K = full kitchen      S = sauna/steam<br>FR = fitness room    (k) = kitchenette     T = spa or hot tub | (# of units) & rates | food & drink | pool, sauna & hot tub |
|---|---|---|---|

## Hemet (continued)

| **Motel 6**<br>3885 W Florida Ave<br>www.motel6.com<br>grassy walking areas | 909-929-8900<br>800-466-8356 | (100)<br>$50–<br>$59 | C<br>(k)<br>F | OP<br>T |
| **Super 8 Motel**<br>3510 W Florida Ave<br>www.super8.com<br>lawn walking area, 4 blocks to park | 909-658-2281<br>pet fee $5–$10/day | (68)<br>$52–<br>$70 | CB<br>M/F | OP<br>T |
| **Twin Palms Ranch B & B**<br>1270 S Santa Fe St<br>www.twinpalmsranch.com<br>rooms/cottage sleeps 2, lawn walking area, close to<br>hiking trails, 2 miles to lake | 909-929-9933<br>pet fee $10/day | (2)<br>$99–<br>$150 | FB | |

## Hesperia

| **Days Inn**<br>14865 Bear Valley Rd<br>www.daysinn.com<br>open field, 2 miles to park | 760-948-0600<br>800-329-7466<br>pet fee $7/day | (29)<br>$59–<br>$89 | CB<br>M/F | T |
| **Holiday Inn Express**<br>9750 Keypoint Ave<br>www.hiexpress.com/hesperiaca<br>dogs under 25 lbs, pet relief area, 1½ miles to park | 760-244-7674<br>800-465-4329<br>pet fee $25/stay | (100)<br>$79–<br>$89 | CB<br>M/F | IP<br>T<br>FR |
| **La Quinta Inn & Suites**<br>12000 Mariposa Rd<br>www.lq.com<br>dogs under 10 lbs only, grassy areas, 1 mile to park | 760-949-9900<br>800-531-59900 | (53)<br>$90 | CB<br>M/F | OP<br>T<br>FR |
| **Super 8 Motel**<br>12033 Oakwood Ave<br>www.super8.com<br>grassy walking area | 760-949-3231<br>800-800-8000<br>pet fee $10/day | (71)<br>$49–<br>$80 | CB<br>M/F | OP<br>T |

| | | | |
|---|---|---|---|
| **Thrifty Motel**  760-244-4119 | (25) | M/F | |
| 14320 Main St  pet fee $5/day | $50 | | |
| lawn and open field for walking dogs | | | |

## Holtville

| | | | |
|---|---|---|---|
| **Barbara Worth Country Club & Hotel** | (108) | C | OP |
| 2050 Country Club Dr  760-356-2806 | $80– | M/F | T |
| www.bwresort.com  800-356-3806 | $100 | R/L | FR |
| dogs under 20 lbs only, open field | | | |

## Honeydew

| | | | |
|---|---|---|---|
| **Mattole River Resort**  707-629-3445 | (5) | K | |
| 42354 Mattole Rd  800-845-4607 | $65– | | |
| cabins sleep 5, on 26 acre farm, riverside walking | $100 | | |
| areas, 12 miles to dog-friendly beach | | | |

## Hope Valley

| | | | |
|---|---|---|---|
| **Sorensen's Resort**  530-694-2203 | (33) | C | S |
| 14255 State Route 88  800-423-9949 | $135– | K | |
| www.sorensensresort.com | $200 | R | |
| cabins/house sleep up to 8, forest and meadows | | | |

## Huntington Beach

| | | | |
|---|---|---|---|
| **Hilton Waterfront**  714-960-7873 | (290) | C | OP |
| 21100 Pacific Coast Hwy  800-822-7873 | $194– | F | T |
| www.waterfrontbeachresort.hilton.com | $350 | R/L | FR |
| dogs under 10 lbs only, 1 mile to dog-friendly beach | | | |

## Idyllwild

| | | | |
|---|---|---|---|
| **Bluebird Cottage Inn**  909-659-2696 | (25) | C | IS |
| 26905 Hwy 243  866-439-5594 | $65– | K | |
| www.bluebirdcottageinn.com  pet fee $20/stay | $195 | M/F | |
| rooms/duplexes/cottages, 3 wooded acres, trails | | | |
| **Fern Valley Inn & Cabins**  909-659-2205 | (4) | C | |
| 25240 Fern Valley Rd  800-659-7775 | $140– | K | |
| www.fernvalleyinn.com  wooded walking area | $195 | | |
| **Fern Village Chalets & Motel**  909-659-2869 | (9) | (k) | |
| 54821 N Circle Dr  pet fee $5/stay | $60– | | |
| www.fernvillage.com  creekside woods and trails | $90 | | |

| C = coffee        GP = guest pass to  L = lounge<br>CB = continental          fitness center  M = microwave<br>     breakfast   IP = indoor pool   OP = outdoor pool<br>F = refrigerator  IS = in-room spa   R = restaurant<br>FB = full breakfast K = full kitchen   S = sauna/steam<br>FR = fitness room (k) = kitchenette   T = spa or hot tub | (# of units)<br>& rates | food<br>& drink | pool, sauna<br>& hot tub |
|---|---|---|---|

## Idyllwild (continued)

| | | | |
|---|---|---|---|
| **Fireside Inn**                909-659-2966<br>54540 N Circle Dr              pet fee $20/stay<br>www.thefireside-inn.com<br>rooms/cabins sleep 6, yard, 1 mile to creek and trails | (16)<br>$78–<br>$130 | K | |
| **Idyllwild Inn**               909-659-2552<br>54300 Village Center Dr        888-659-2552<br>www.idyllwildinn.com<br>studio to 3 bdrm cabins sleep up to 9, on 5½ acres<br>of woods and meadows for walking dogs | (20)<br>$66–<br>$162 | K | |
| **Idyllwild Mountain Rentals**  909-659-5349<br>54240 N Circle Dr<br>www.sparkyscabins.com<br>cabins sleep up to 10, pools or jacuzzis, trails | (50)<br>$110–<br>$300 | K | OP<br>T |
| **Idyllwild Vacation Rentals**  909-659-5015<br>54085 S Circle Dr              800-297-1410<br>www.idyllvacationrentals.com   each pet $50/stay<br>1–5 bdrm homes sleep up to 12, woods, hiking trails | (50)<br>$100–<br>$375 | K | T |
| **Knotty Pine Cabins**          909-659-2933<br>54340 Pine Crest Ave           each pet $20/stay<br>studio/1–3 bdrm cabins, wooded walking area,<br>trails, across street to state park | (3)<br>$59–<br>$135 | K | |
| **Muir's Mountain Vacation Rentals** 909-659-4145<br>54440 North Circle Dr         877-270-3285<br>www.idyllwildcabins.com<br>cabins/vacation homes sleep up to 18, wooded<br>areas and dog-friendly hiking trails nearby | (30)<br>$150–<br>$400 | K | S<br>T<br>FR |
| **Tahquitz Inn**                909-659-4554<br>25840 Hwy 243                  877-659-4554<br>www.tahquitzinn.com            pet fee $10/day<br>1–2 bdrm units sleep up to 6, surrounded by state/<br>county/federal forestland for walking dogs | (16)<br>$85–<br>$110 | C<br>K | OP<br>T |

| Wilder Cabins 909-659-2926<br>54550 S Circle Dr pet fee $8/day<br>www.wildercabins.com<br>studio cabins sleep 2–3, open May–September only,<br>woodland garden, creekside fenced area | (3)<br>$75–<br>$80 | K | |
|---|---|---|---|
| Woodland Park Manor 909-659-2657<br>55350 S Circle Dr 877-659-2657<br>www.woodlandparkmanor.com<br>1–2 bdrm cabins, wooded walking areas, near trails | (5)<br>$125–<br>$180 | K | T |

## Igo

| Brigadoon Castle 530-396-2785<br>9036 Zogg Mine Rd 888-343-2836<br>www.brigadooncastle.com<br>dogs allowed in 1 bdrm cottage by owner's advance<br>approval only, on 86 wooded acres, hiking trails | (4)<br>$298–<br>$350 | FB<br>K | T |
|---|---|---|---|

## Imperial

| Imperial Valley Inn 760-355-4500<br>1093 Airport Rd 800-232-2378<br>pet fee $5–$10/stay<br>large lawn walking area | (92)<br>$39 | C<br>M/F | OP<br>S<br>T |
|---|---|---|---|

## Imperial Beach

| Hawaiian Gardens Suite Hotel 619-429-5303<br>1031 Imperial Beach Blvd # 1 800-334-3071<br>www.hawaiian-gardens.com pet fee $50/stay<br>studios/1 bdrm suites, small grass walking area,<br>2 blocks to park, 9 blocks to dog-friendly beach | (63)<br>$119–<br>$155 | CB<br>K | OP<br>S |
|---|---|---|---|

## Independence

| Independence Courthouse Motel 760-878-2732<br>157 N Edwards St 800-801-0703<br>open desert area, close to parks pet fee $6/day | (10)<br>$47–<br>$72 | C<br>M/F | |
|---|---|---|---|
| Mt Williamson Motel 760-878-2121<br>515 S Edwards St pet fee $5/day<br>small well-groomed dogs only, modernized historic<br>cabins, vacant lot, park, surrounded by open desert | (10)<br>$53–<br>$62 | FB<br>M/F | |

| C = coffee GP = guest pass to L = lounge<br>CB = continental fitness center M = microwave<br>  breakfast IP = indoor pool OP = outdoor pool<br>F = refrigerator IS = in-room spa R = restaurant<br>FB = full breakfast K = full kitchen S = sauna/steam<br>FR = fitness room (k) = kitchenette T = spa or hot tub | (# of units) & rates | food & drink | pool, sauna & hot tub |
|---|---|---|---|

## Independence (continued)

| Ray's Den Motel 760-878-2122<br>405 N Edwards St   pet fee $6/day<br>open desert area, 1 block to park and creek | (8)<br>$57–<br>$72 | C<br>M/F | |
| Winnedumah B & B Hotel 760-878-2040<br>211 N Edwards St   pet fee $10/day<br>www.winnedumah.com<br>patio and back yard, close to parks and hiking trails | (24)<br>$55–<br>$65 | CB<br>K | |

## Indian Wells

| Miramonte Resort 760-341-2200<br>45000 Indian Wells Lane   800-237-2926<br>dogs under 30 lbs only   pet fee $75/stay | (215)<br>$99–<br>$299 | C<br>R | OP<br>FR<br>S/T |

## Indio

| Best Western Date Tree Hotel 760-347-3421<br>81909 Indio Blvd   800-292-5599<br>www.datetree.com   each pet $10/day<br>dogs in smoking rooms only, beds/bowls/treats,<br>5½ acres of lawn for walking, 5 minute drive to park | (119)<br>$55–<br>$189 | CB<br>K<br>M/F | OP<br>FR<br>T<br>IS |
| Holiday Inn Express 760-342-6344<br>84096 Indio Springs Dr   800-345-2008<br>www.hiexpress.com/indioca   pet fee $25/stay<br>lawn walking area, 2 miles to park | (125)<br>$99 | CB<br>F | OP<br>T |
| Motel 6 760-342-6311<br>82195 Indio Blvd   800-466-8356<br>www.motel6.com<br>lawn, 5 minute walk to park | (138)<br>$46 | C | OP |
| Palm Shadow Inn 760-347-3476<br>80761 Hwy 111   pet fee $5/day<br>www.palmshadowinn.com<br>large lawn to walk dogs | (18)<br>$49–<br>$144 | C<br>(k)<br>F | OP<br>T |

| | | | | |
|---|---|---|---|---|
| **Palm Tree Inn** | 760-342-4747 | (70) | C | OP |
| 84115 Indio Blvd | pet fee $10/day | $42– | | |
| surrounded by park-like walking area | | $80 | | |
| **Quality Inn** | 760-347-4045 | (62) | FB | OP |
| 43505 Monroe St | 800-228-5151 | $75 | M/F | T |
| www.qualityinn-indio.com | | | | |
| dogs under 35 lbs only, grass and gravel walking | | | | |
| areas, 5 minutes to park | | | | |
| **Royal Plaza Inn** | 760-347-0911 | (99) | C | OP |
| 82347 Hwy 111 | 800-228-9559 | $59– | M/F | T |
| www.royalplazainn.com | pet fee $5/day | $129 | R | |
| pet relief area, 2 miles to park | | | | |

## Inverness

| | | | | |
|---|---|---|---|---|
| **Bayshore Cottage** | 415-669-1148 | (1) | C | |
| 12732 Sir Francis Drake Blvd | | $150 | K | |
| www.innformation.com/ca/bayshore | | | | |
| dogs by advance approval only, breakfast supplies, | | | | |
| fenced lawn, short drive to park and off-leash beach | | | | |
| **Dancing Coyote Beach** | 415-669-7200 | (3) | K | |
| 12794 Sir Francis Drake Blvd | pet fee $50/stay | $120– | | |
| 1 bdrm cottages, breakfast supplies, bayside beach | | $195 | | |
| **Inns of Marin** | 415-663-2000 | (25) | K | T |
| 105 Vision Rd | 800-887-2880 | $140– | | |
| www.innsofmarin.com | | $250 | | |
| cottages sleep 2 to 6, dog-friendly beaches and trails | | | | |
| **Manka's Inverness Lodge** | 415-669-1034 | (14) | R | IS |
| Argyle Way | each pet $50/stay | $215– | | |
| www.mankas.com | 1 dog only, near forest trails | $565 | | |
| **Rosemary Cottages** | 415-663-9338 | (3) | C | T |
| 75 Balboa Ave | pet fee $25/stay for 1 dog | $195– | K | |
| www.rosemarybb.com | $35/stay for 2 dogs | $265 | | |
| cottages sleep up to 6, wooded walking area | | | | |
| **The Tree House** | 415-663-8720 | (1) | K | |
| 73 Drake Summit Rd | 800-977-8720 | $155 | | |
| www.www.treehousebnb.com | | | | |
| breakfast supplies, on 2½ wooded acres, near trails | | | | |

| C = coffee<br>CB = continental<br>  breakfast<br>F = refrigerator<br>FB = full breakfast<br>FR = fitness room | GP = guest pass to<br>  fitness center<br>IP = indoor pool<br>IS = in-room spa<br>K = full kitchen<br>(k) = kitchenette | L = lounge<br>M = microwave<br>OP = outdoor pool<br>R = restaurant<br>S = sauna/steam<br>T = spa or hot tub | (# of units)<br>& rates | food<br>& drink | pool, sauna<br>& hot tub |
|---|---|---|---|---|---|

### Inyokern

| **Mayfair Motel**<br>1352 N 2nd St (2nd St & Hwy 178)<br>open desert area, ½ block to park | 760-377-4321 | (21)<br>$33–<br>$40 | C<br>M/F | |
|---|---|---|---|---|

### Irvine

| **Candlewood Suites**<br>16150 Sand Canyon Ave<br>www.candlewoodsuites.com<br>dogs under 50 lbs, studios/1 bdrm suites, bike trail | 949-788-0500<br>888-226-3539<br>pet fee $75/stay | (122)<br>$94–<br>$119 | K | FR |
|---|---|---|---|---|
| **Hilton Orange County Airport**<br>18800 MacArthur Blvd<br>www.irvineorangecountyairport.hilton.com<br>pet fee $50/day<br>dogs allowed in smoking rooms only, pet relief area | 949-833-9999<br>800-498-7391 | (289)<br>$159–<br>$189 | C<br>R | OP<br>T<br>FR |
| **Homestead Studio Suites**<br>30 Technology Dr<br>www.homesteadhotels.com<br>pet relief area, 7 miles to off-leash dog park | 949-727-4228<br>888-782-9473<br>pet fee $25/day | (149)<br>$100–<br>$110 | K | GP |
| **La Quinta Inn**<br>14972 Sand Canyon Ave<br>www.lq.com          grassy area, 2 blocks to dog park | 949-551-0909<br>800-531-5900 | (147)<br>$89–<br>$99 | CB<br>M/F | OP<br>T<br>FR |
| **Residence Inn–Irvine Spectrum**<br>10 Morgan<br>www.marriott.com          $$75/stay<br>studios/1–2 bdrm suites, Mon–Thur beverages and<br>light dinner, grassy walking areas | 949-380-3000<br>800-331-3131 | (112)<br>$89–<br>$189 | FB<br>K | OP<br>T<br>FR |
| **Residence Inn–Airport**<br>2855 Main St<br>www.marriott.com/snaiv<br>pet fee $10/day plus $100 cleaning fee<br>Mon–Thur beverages and dinner, 4 blocks to park | 949-261-2020<br>800-331-3131 | (174)<br>$179–<br>$199 | FB<br>(k) | OP<br>T |

### Isleton

| | | | | |
|---|---|---|---|---|
| **Delta Daze Inn** <br> 20 Main St <br> www.deltadazeinn.com <br> dogs by advance approval only, lawn, ½ block to park | 916-777-7777 | (10) <br> $49– <br> $99 | FB | |

### Jackson

| | | | | |
|---|---|---|---|---|
| **Amador Motel** <br> 12408 Kennedy Flat Rd <br> gardens, lawn walking area, 1½ miles to park | 209-223-0970 | (10) <br> $53– <br> $58 | C <br> M/F | OP |
| **Best Western Amador Inn** <br> 200 S Hwy 49 <br> www.bestwesterncalifornia.com <br> small dogs only, small grassy area, ¼ mile to park | 209-223-0211 <br> 800-543-5221 <br> pet fee $10/day | (119) <br> $65– <br> $80 | C <br> M/F | OP |
| **Country Squire Motel** <br> 1105 N Main St <br> www.caohwy.com/c/countrsm.htm <br> dogs by manager's approval only, large lawn, creek | 209-223-1657 | (12) <br> $65– <br> $95 | CB | |
| **Jackson Gold Lodge** <br> 850 N Hwy 49 & 88 <br> grassy walking area, 1 block to park | 209-223-0486 <br> pet fee $10/day | (36) <br> $60– <br> $110 | CB <br> M/F | OP |
| **Linda Vista Motel** <br> 10708 State Hwy 49 & 88 <br> 1 dog allowed by manager's approval only, open field | 209-223-1096 <br> pet fee varies | (21) <br> $60– <br> $68 | CB <br> M/F | OP |

### Jacumba

| | | | | |
|---|---|---|---|---|
| **Jacumba Hot Springs Spa** <br> 44500 Old Hwy 80 <br> www.jacumbaspa.com <br> dogs by advance reservation only, open desert area | 619-766-4333 <br> each pet $5/day | (17) <br> $75 | C <br> F <br> R | OP <br> T |

### Jamestown

| | | | | |
|---|---|---|---|---|
| **Country Inn Sonora** <br> 18730 Hwy 108 <br> www.countryinnsonora.com <br> undeveloped walking area, 15 minutes to park | 209-984-0315 <br> each pet $10/day | (61) <br> $59– <br> $109 | CB <br> M/F | OP |

| C = coffee  GP = guest pass to  L = lounge<br>CB = continental  fitness center  M = microwave<br>breakfast  IP = indoor pool  OP = outdoor pool<br>F = refrigerator  IS = in-room spa  R = restaurant<br>FB = full breakfast  K = full kitchen  S = sauna/steam<br>FR = fitness room  (k) = kitchenette  T = spa or hot tub | (# of units)<br>& rates | food<br>& drink | pool, sauna<br>& hot tub |
|---|---|---|---|

## Jamestown (continued)

| | | | |
|---|---|---|---|
| **Historic National Hotel**  209-984-3446<br>18183 Main St  800-894-3446<br>www.www.national-hotel.com  each pet $10/day<br>one of California's oldest hotels, 1 block to park | (9)<br>$120 | CB<br>R | |
| **Miners Motel**  209-532-7850<br>18740 Hwy 108  each pet $10/day<br>small dogs only, lawn walking area, 2 miles to park | (18)<br>$60 | CB<br>M/F | OP |
| **Royal Carriage Inn**  209-984-5271<br>18239 Main St<br>www.royalcarriageinn.com<br>across street to park | (13)<br>$95–<br>$150 | CB<br>K | |

## Jenner

| | | | |
|---|---|---|---|
| **Jenner Inn by the Sea**  707-865-2377<br>10400 Hwy 1  800-732-2377<br>www.jennerinn.com  pet fee $35/stay<br>rooms/2 bdrm home/100-year old cottage sleep up<br>to 6, patios, field, grotto with walk-behind waterfall | (4)<br>$138–<br>$288 | K<br>R | |
| **Stillwater Cove Ranch**  707-847-3227<br>22555 Hwy 1  each pet $10/day<br>www.media.malamud.com<br>bunkhouse rooms/cottages, decks, working farm | (6)<br>$55–<br>$95 | (k) | |
| **Timber Cove Inn**  707-847-3231<br>21780 Hwy 1  800-987-8319<br>www.timbercoveinn.com  pet fee $7/day<br>dogs by manager's approval, country setting, trails | (52)<br>$88–<br>$490 | R/L | IS |

## Joshua Tree

| | | | |
|---|---|---|---|
| **Joshua Tree Inn**  760-366-1188<br>61259 29 Palms Hwy  pet fee $15/day<br>www.joshuatreeinn.com<br>enclosed patios, weekend breakfast, open desert | (10)<br>$70–<br>$145 | CB<br>K | OP |

## Julian

| | | | |
|---|---|---|---|
| **Angel's Landing Country Inn**    760-765-2578<br>2323 Farmer Rd    888-253-7747<br>www.angelresort.com    pet fee $10/stay<br>2 bdrm suites, on 53 secluded acres, meadows, trails | (10)<br>$50–<br>$190 | K<br>R | |
| **Apple Tree Inn**    760-765-0222<br>4360 Hwy 78    800-410-8683<br>www.julianappletreeinn.com    pet fee $10/day<br>lawn and wooded walking areas | (17)<br>$69–<br>$114 | C<br>R | OP |
| **Eaglenest B & B**    760-765-1252<br>2609 D St    888-345-6378<br>www.eaglenestbandb.com    1 small pet $25/stay<br>Victorian home, bedroom suites, fenced yard, trail | (4)<br>$145–<br>$185 | FB | OP<br>T |
| **Pine Hills Lodge**    760-765-1100<br>2960 La Posada Way<br>www.pinehillslodge.com<br>1–2 bdrm cabins sleep up to 6, wooded walking area | (16)<br>$123–<br>$180 | CB | OP |
| **Wikiup B & B**    760-765-1890<br>1645 Whispering Pines Dr    800-526-2725<br>www.wikiupbnb.com<br>small pets welcome, on 4 fenced acres | (4)<br>$175 | FB | T<br>IS |

## June Lake

| | | | |
|---|---|---|---|
| **Double Eagle Resort & Spa**    760-648-7004<br>5587 Hwy 158    pet fee $15/day<br>www.doubleeagleresort.com<br>2 bdrm cabins sleep 6, forested trails and streams | (16)<br>$287–<br>$319 | K<br>R/L | IP<br>FR |
| **Gull Lake Lodge**    760-648-7516<br>132 Leonard Ave    800-631-9081<br>www.gulllakelodge.com<br>1 bdrm suites, lawn, near hiking trails and lakes | (15)<br>$89–<br>$129 | K | |
| **June Lake Pines Cottages**    760-648-7522<br>2733 Hwy 158    800-481-3637<br>www.junelakepines.com<br>     each pet $10/1st day, $5/each additional day<br>1–5 bdrm cottages, lawn and woods, ¼ mile to lake | (11)<br>$75–<br>$200 | K | |

| C = coffee<br>CB = continental<br>    breakfast<br>F = refrigerator<br>FB = full breakfast<br>FR = fitness room | GP = guest pass to<br>    fitness center<br>IP = indoor pool<br>IS = in-room spa<br>K = full kitchen<br>(k) = kitchenette | L = lounge<br>M = microwave<br>OP = outdoor pool<br>R = restaurant<br>S = sauna/steam<br>T = spa or hot tub | (# of units)<br>& rates | food<br>& drink | pool, sauna<br>& hot tub |
|---|---|---|---|---|---|

## June Lake (continued)

| | | | |
|---|---|---|---|
| **June Lake Villager Motel**<br>2640 Hwy 158<br>www.junelakevillager.com<br>lawn and trails | 760-648-8519<br>800-655-6545 | (24)<br>$50–<br>$125 | C<br>K | T |
| **Knoll Haus**<br>68 Knoll Ave<br>www.knollhaus.com<br>1 bdrm cabin near lake, trails | 760-648-7294<br>pet fee $10/day | (1)<br>$99–<br>$125 | K | |

## Kelseyville

| | | | |
|---|---|---|---|
| **Creekside Lodge**<br>7990 Hwy 29<br>www.kitscorner.com<br>small dogs in smoking rooms only, walking area | 707-279-9258<br>each pet $10/day | (14)<br>$52–<br>$62 | C | |
| **Edgewater Resort & RV Park**<br>6420 Soda Bay Rd<br>www.edgewaterresort.net<br>cabins/house sleep up to 12, pet treats/ID tags,<br>shady "OK-9 Corral," lakefront off-leash area | 707-279-0208<br>800-396-6224<br>pet fee $10/day | (9)<br>$125–<br>$175 | K | OP |
| **Kelseyville Motel**<br>5575 7th St<br>www.kvmotel.com<br>dogs in smoking rooms only, short walk to vacant lot | 707-279-1874<br>800-586-6835<br>pet fee $10/stay | (16)<br>$56–<br>$60 | M/F | |
| **Lakeside Inn Pub and B & B**<br>6330 Soda Bay Rd<br>www.clear-lake.com          lakeside walking area | 707-279-1620 | (2)<br>$99 | CB<br>R/L | |

## Kenwood

| | | | |
|---|---|---|---|
| **Kenwood Oaks Guest House**<br>Warm Springs Rd<br>www.kenwoodoaksguesthouse.com<br>1 bdrm house sleeps 4, shaded dog run, open field | 707-833-1221 | (1)<br>$175–<br>$225 | K<br>CB | |

## Kernville

| | | | | |
|---|---|---|---|---|
| **River View Lodge** | 760-376-6019 | (11) | CB | T |
| 2 Sirretta St | 877-885-6333 | $79– | M/F | |
| www.riverviewlodge.net | pet fee $20/day | $119 | | |
| large riverside yard, next to park and private beach | | | | |

## Kettleman City

| | | | | |
|---|---|---|---|---|
| **Best Western Kettleman City Inn** | 559-386-0804 | (73) | CB | OP |
| 33410 Powers Dr | 800-937-8376 | $84 | M/F | T |
| www.bestwesterncalifornia.com | each pet $7/day | | | |
| pet treats, small lawn and open desert area | | | | |

## King City

| | | | | |
|---|---|---|---|---|
| **Ciudad Del Rey Motel & Trailer Park** | | (10) | M/F | OP |
| 50620 Mesa Verde | 831-385-4828 | $46 | | |
| grassy area and country roads for walking dogs | | | | |
| **Courtesy Inn** | 831-385-4646 | (63) | CB | OP |
| 4 Broadway Cir | 800-350-5616 | $54– | M/F | IS |
| www.kingcitycourtesyinn.com | pet fee $10/stay | $89 | | |
| lawn and open field, 2 blocks to park | | | | |
| **Days Inn** | 831-385-5921 | (30) | CB | |
| 1130 Broadway St | 800-329-7466 | $45– | M/F | |
| www.daysinn.com | pet fee $5/day | $99 | | |
| across street to park | | | | |
| **Motel 6** | 831-385-5000 | (100) | C | OP |
| 3 Broadway Cir | 800-466-8356 | $42– | | |
| www.motel6.com | lawn, small park | $52 | | |

## Kings Beach

| | | | | |
|---|---|---|---|---|
| **North Lake Lodge** | 530-546-2731 | (21) | FB | |
| 8716 N Lake Blvd | 888-923-5253 | $45– | M/F | |
| www.northlakelodge.com | pet fee $7/day | $110 | | |
| pet towels/blankets, lawn, 3 minute walk to | | | | |
| dog-friendly beach, close to hiking trails | | | | |
| **North Shore Lodge** | 530-546-4833 or | (11) | K | OP |
| 8755 N Lake Blvd | 530-412-0199 | $50– | M/F | |
| | pet fee $10/stay | $65 | | |
| ½ acre for walking dogs, ½ mile to dog-friendly beach | | | | |

| | | | # of units) & rates | food & drink | pool, sauna & hot tub |
|---|---|---|---|---|---|
| C = coffee<br>CB = continental<br>breakfast<br>F = refrigerator<br>FB = full breakfast<br>FR = fitness room | GP = guest pass to<br>fitness center<br>IP = indoor pool<br>IS = in-room spa<br>K = full kitchen<br>(k) = kitchenette | L = lounge<br>M = microwave<br>OP = outdoor pool<br>R = restaurant<br>S = sauna/steam<br>T = spa or hot tub | | | |

## Kings Beach (continued)

| | | | | | |
|---|---|---|---|---|---|
| **Stevenson's Holliday Inn**<br>8742 N Lake Blvd<br>www.stevensonshollidayinn.com<br>small back yard, 1 block to dog-friendly beach | 530-546-2269<br>800-634-9141<br>pet fee $5/day | (22)<br>$69–<br>$129 | CB<br>M/F | OP<br>T |

## Kingsburg

| | | | | | |
|---|---|---|---|---|---|
| **Kingsburg's Swedish Inn**<br>401 Sierra St<br>www.swedishinn.com<br>gardens, lawn walking area | 559-897-1022<br>800-834-1022 | (47)<br>$58–<br>$64 | C<br>M/F | OP<br>T |

## Kirkwood

| | | | | | |
|---|---|---|---|---|---|
| **Kirkwood Accommodations**<br>www.kirkwoodaccommodations.com<br>1–2 bdrm condominiums<br>woods, hiking trails, dog-friendly x-country ski trails | 209-258-8575<br>866-471-3932<br>pet fee $35/stay | (35)<br>$130–<br>$279 | K | |

## Klamath

| | | | | | |
|---|---|---|---|---|---|
| **Camp Marigold Garden Cottages**<br>16101 Hwy 101 South<br>1-room cabins, close to walking trails | 707-482-3585 | (16)<br>$58 | F | |
| **Terwer Park Resort**<br>641 Terwer Riffle Rd<br>1 bdrm cabins, open May–November, walking area | 707-482-3855<br>866-662-1249 | (8)<br>$40 | K | |
| **Woodland Villa Cabins**<br>15870 Hwy 101 North<br>www.klamathusa.com<br>cabins sleep 8, on 8 wooded acres, hillside trail | 707-482-2081<br>888-866-2466<br>pet fee $20/stay | (9)<br>$60–<br>$130 | K | |

## Klamath River

| | | | | | |
|---|---|---|---|---|---|
| **Sportsman's Lodge**<br>20502 Hwy 96<br>cabins sleep 4, lawn walking area, 1 mile to bike trail | 530-465-2366 | (11)<br>$50–<br>$60 | C<br>(k) | |

## Knights Landing

| | | | |
|---|---|---|---|
| **Snowball Mansion Inn**       530-735-1122 | (4) | FB | |
| 42485 Front St | $145– | | |
| www.snowballmansioninn.com | $295 | | |
| on 7½ riverside acres for walking dogs, pond | | | |

## Kyburz

| | | | |
|---|---|---|---|
| **Kyburz Resort Motel**       530-293-3382 | (20) | C | |
| 13666 Hwy 50       pet fee $10/day | $49– | M/F | |
| riverside grassy and sandy areas, swimming hole | $79 | | |

## La Jolla

| | | | |
|---|---|---|---|
| **La Jolla Cove Suites, Shell Beach Motel** | (150) | CB | OP |
| 1155 Coast Blvd       858-459-4306 | $139– | K | T |
| www.lajollacove.com       888-525-6552 | $324 | | GP |
| pet fee $15/day | | | |
| rooms/studios/minisuites/beach bungalows, pet | | | |
| supplies, across street to park, beach access | | | |
| **La Jolla Village Lodge**       858-551-2001 | (30) | CB | |
| 1141 Silverado St       877-551-2001 | $69– | M/F | |
| www.lajollavillagelodge.com       pet fee $20/stay | $179 | | |
| lawn, 3 blocks to park, near pet-friendly restaurants | | | |
| **La Valencia Hotel**       858-454-0771 | (107) | C | OP |
| 1132 Prospect St       800-451-0772 | $275– | F | T |
| www.lavalencia.com       pet fee $75/stay | $550 | R | FR |
| 1920s hotel, dogs by advance reservation, large park | | | |
| **Redwood Hollow Cottages**       858-459-8747 | (7) | K | |
| 256 Prospect St       pet fee $50–$100/stay | $125– | | |
| www.redwoodhollow-lajolla.com | $299 | | |
| dogs under 25 lbs by advance approval only, cottages | | | |
| sleep 6, enclosed patios, 100 ft to dog-friendly beach | | | |
| **Residence Inn**       858-587-1770 | (288) | FB | OP |
| 8901 Gilman Dr       800-876-1778 | $149– | (k) | T |
| www.residenceinncom       pet fee $75/stay | $189 | | FR |
| studios/1 bdrm suites, small park | | | |

| C = coffee<br>CB = continental<br>    breakfast<br>F = refrigerator<br>FB = full breakfast<br>FR = fitness room | GP = guest pass to<br>    fitness center<br>IP = indoor pool<br>IS = in-room spa<br>K = full kitchen<br>(k) = kitchenette | L = lounge<br>M = microwave<br>OP = outdoor pool<br>R = restaurant<br>S = sauna/steam<br>T = spa or hot tub | (# of units)<br>& rates | food<br>& drink | pool, sauna<br>& hot tub |
|---|---|---|---|---|---|

## La Jolla (continued)

| | | | | | |
|---|---|---|---|---|---|
| **San Diego Marriott La Jolla**<br>4240 La Jolla Village Dr<br>www.marriott.com/sanlj<br>3 blocks to enclosed off-leash dog park | 858-587-1414<br>800-228-9290<br>pet fee $50/stay | | (360)<br>$139–<br>$229 | R/L | IP<br>OP<br>S/T<br>FR |

## La Mesa

| | | | | | |
|---|---|---|---|---|---|
| **E-Z8 Motel**<br>7851 Fletcher Pkwy<br>www.ez8motels.com<br>dogs under 20 lbs only, close to lakeside hiking trail | 619-698-9444 | | (105)<br>$32–<br>$80 | C<br>F | OP<br>T |
| **Motel 6 San Diego/La Mesa**<br>7621 Alvarado Rd<br>www.motel6.com<br>grassy area, 1 mile to park | 619-464-7151<br>800-466-8356 | | (50)<br>$50–<br>$66 | C | |

## La Mirada

| | | | | | |
|---|---|---|---|---|---|
| **Residence Inn**<br>14419 Firestone Blvd<br>www.marriott.com<br>dogs under 25 lbs only, lawn, short drive to park | 714-523-2800<br>800-331-3131<br>pet fee $75/stay | | (147)<br>$119–<br>$149 | FB<br>K | OP<br>T<br>FR |

## La Palma

| | | | | | |
|---|---|---|---|---|---|
| **La Quinta Inn–Buena Park**<br>3 Centerpointe Dr<br>www.lq.com<br>2 miles to park | 714-670-1400<br>800-531-5900 | | (156)<br>$110 | CB<br>M/F | OP<br>T<br>FR |

## La Porte

| | | | | | |
|---|---|---|---|---|---|
| **Gold Country B & B**<br>2140 Main St<br>dogs allowed in smoking rooms only, rooms/suites,<br>lawn, open field, 1 block to trails, 3 miles to lake | 530-675-2322 | | (8)<br>$85–<br>$125 | CB<br>K<br>M/F<br>L | T<br>IS |

## La Quinta

| | | | | |
|---|---|---|---|---|
| **La Quinta Resort & Club** 760-564-4111 <br> 49-499 Eisenhower Dr 800-598-3828 <br> www.laquintaresort.com each pet $100/stay <br> dogs under 30 lbs allowed in rooms with enclosed <br> patios, on 45 acres with lawn and walking trails | (920) <br> $89– <br> $295 | C <br> F <br> R/L | OP <br> T |

## Lafayette

| | | | | |
|---|---|---|---|---|
| **Hillside Inn & Suites** 925-283-8200 <br> 3748 Mt Diablo Blvd <br> www.bayareainns.com <br> across street to park | (65) <br> $65– <br> $75 | CB <br> M/F | OP <br> T |

## Laguna Beach

| | | | | |
|---|---|---|---|---|
| **Aliso Creek Inn** 949-499-2271 <br> 31106 Coast Hwy 800-223-3309 <br> www.alisocreekinn.com pet fee $50/stay <br> dogs under 35 lbs only, small grassy walking areas, <br> across street to dog-friendly beach | (61) <br> $114– <br> $172 | C <br> K | OP <br> T <br> FR |
| **Carriage House** 949-494-8945 <br> 1322 Catalina 888-335-8945 <br> www.carriagehouse.com pet fee $10/day <br> 1–2 bdrm suites, residential walking area, 2½ blocks <br> to dog-friendly beach (limited summer hrs) | (6) <br> $140– <br> $175 | FB <br> K | |
| **Casa Laguna Inn** 949-494-2996 <br> 2510 S Coast Hwy 800-233-0449 <br> www.casalaguna.com pet fee $25/day <br> suites/cottage sleep 4, across from dog-friendly <br> beach (limited summer hrs), 5 miles to dog park | (23) <br> $130– <br> $420 | CB <br> M/F | OP <br> IS |
| **La Casa Del Camino** 949-497-2446 <br> 1289 S Coast Hwy 888-436-7523 <br> www.casacamino.com pet fee $35/day <br> dogs under 35 lbs only, lawn area, dog-friendly beach <br> (limited summer hrs), 2 miles to off-leash dog park | (41) <br> $119– <br> $359 | CB <br> M/F | |
| **Laguna Brisas Spa Hotel** 949-497-7272 <br> 1600 S Coast Hwy 888-296-6834 <br> www.lagunabrisas.com pet fee $50/day <br> dogs under 15 lbs only, dog-friendly beach | (66) <br> $89– <br> $296 | CB <br> F | OP <br> T <br> IS |

| C = coffee<br>CB = continental<br>  breakfast<br>F = refrigerator<br>FB = full breakfast<br>FR = fitness room | GP = guest pass to<br>  fitness center<br>IP = indoor pool<br>IS = in-room spa<br>K = full kitchen<br>(k) = kitchenette | L = lounge<br>M = microwave<br>OP = outdoor pool<br>R = restaurant<br>S = sauna/steam<br>T = spa or hot tub | (# of units)<br>& rates | food<br>& drink | pool, sauna<br>& hot tub |
|---|---|---|---|---|---|
| **Laguna Beach (continued)** | | | | | |
| **Montage Resort & Spa**<br>30801 Southcoast Hwy<br>www.montagelagunabeach.com     pet fee $100/stay<br>dogs under 25 lbs only, dogsitting service, trails | 949-499-4554<br>888-715-6700 | | (262)<br>$475–<br>$5,500 | R | IP<br>S<br>T |
| **Tides Motor Inn**<br>460 N Coast Hwy<br>www.tideslaguna.com     pet fee $50/stay<br>dogs under 50 lbs only, next to dog-friendly beach | 949-494-2494<br>888-777-2107 | | (21)<br>$79–<br>$225 | C<br>K | OP |
| **Vacation Village**<br>647 S Coast Hwy<br>www.vacationvillage.com     pet fee $10/stay<br>1 dog allowed September–May only, on 4 acres,<br>next to dog-friendly beach (limited summer hrs) | 949-494-8566<br>800-843-6895 | | (24)<br>$85–<br>$360 | C<br>K | OP<br>T |
| **Lake Almanor** | | | | | |
| **Big Springs Resort**<br>2655 Big Springs Rd<br>www.bigspringsresort.com<br>cabins/guesthouse/chalet, lake, walking trails | 530-596-3390 | | (5)<br>$60–<br>$85 | (k) | |
| **Knotty Pine Resort & Marina**<br>430 Peninsula Dr<br>www.knottypine.net<br>2 bdrm waterfront cabins/guesthouse sleep 6,<br>small fenced area, lakefront walking area | 530-596-3348<br>pet fee varies | | (6)<br>$96–<br>$140 | K | OP<br>T |
| **Lake Almanor Resort**<br>2706 Big Springs Rd<br>www.lakealmanorresort.com<br>dogs by advance approval only, 1–3 bdrm cabins,<br>on 3 wooded acres and walking trails | 530-596-3337<br>pet fee $9/day | | (7)<br>$80–<br>$93 | K | |

| | | | | |
|---|---|---|---|---|
| **Lake Haven Resort** 530-596-3249<br>7329 Hwy 147 Eastshore            pet fee varies<br>www.lakehavenresort.com<br>rooms/1 bdrm cabins, lawn, dog-friendly beach | (8)<br>$60–<br>$85 | K | | |
| **Little Norway Resort** 530-596-3225<br>432 Peninsula Dr            pet fee $10/day<br>www.littlenorway.net<br>1–4 bdrm cabins, lawn, woods, lakeside walking area | (14)<br>$80–<br>$150 | K | | |
| **Vagabond Resort** 530-596-3240<br>7371 Hwy 147<br>www.lakealmanorvagabondrvresort.com<br>1 dog only, 1 bdrm cabin/mobile home sleep up to 4,<br>open midMay–midOctober, lakeside areas, close to<br>hiking trails | (2)<br>$90–<br>$95 | K | | |
| **Lake Arrowhead** | | | | |
| **ABC Mountain Accommodations** 909-337-1003<br>26705 Modac Ln            800-550-5253<br>www.lakearrowheadabc.com            pet fee varies<br>hotels/B & Bs/cabins, lawn and woods, close to<br>hiking trails | (25)<br>$79 | | | |
| **Arrowhead Holiday Cabin Rental** 909-337-2411<br>291 S Hwy 173<br>dogs by advance approval only, 1–4 bdrm cabins<br>sleep up to 20, wooded walking area | (7)<br>$79–<br>$450 | K | | |
| **Arrowhead Tree Top Lodge** 909-337-2311<br>27992 Rainbow Dr            800-358-8733<br>www.arrowheadtreetop.com            pet fee $8/day<br>nature walk, ¾ mile to lakefront walking area | (21)<br>$69–<br>$128 | CB<br>K<br>F | OP |
| **Broken Arrow B & B** 909-337-0125<br>1168 N Hwy 173            866-262-7769<br>www.brokenarrowbb.com<br>dogs under 45 lbs only, fenced yard, trails | (5)<br>$125–<br>$185 | FB | T<br>IS |
| **Gray Squirrel Inn** 909-336-3602<br>326 State Hwy 173            888-719-3563<br>www.graysquirrelinn.com<br>close to creek and wilderness area for walking dogs | (10)<br>$79–<br>$210 | CB<br>M/F | |

| C = coffee<br>CB = continental breakfast<br>F = refrigerator<br>FB = full breakfast<br>FR = fitness room    GP = guest pass to fitness center<br>IP = indoor pool<br>IS = in-room spa<br>K = full kitchen<br>(k) = kitchenette    L = lounge<br>M = microwave<br>OP = outdoor pool<br>R = restaurant<br>S = sauna/steam<br>T = spa or hot tub | # of units) & rates | food & drink | pool, sauna & hot tub |
|---|---|---|---|
| ## Lake Arrowhead (continued) | | | |
| **Lake Arrowhead Resort**    909-336-1511<br>27984 Hwy 189    800-800-6792<br>www.laresort.com<br>lawn and private beach | (177)<br>$99–<br>$199 | C<br>F<br>R | OP<br>S/T<br>FR |
| **Little Bear B & B**    909-336-4997<br>191 Hwy 173<br>www.bedandbreakfast.com<br>dogs by owner's approval, patio, yard, lakeside trails | (3)<br>$85–<br>$135 | FB<br>M/F | |
| **Prophets Paradise B & B**    909-336-1969<br>26845 Modoc Lane    800-987-2231<br>www.prophetsparadise.com<br>private decks, hillside paths, close to lakeside park | (3)<br>$120–<br>$185 | FB | IS<br>T |
| **Saddleback Inn**    909-336-3571<br>300 S Hwy 173    800-858-3334<br>www.saddlebackinn.com    each pet $8/day<br>dogs in smoking units only, 1–3 bdrm cottages, pool<br>at nearby lodge, park-like walking area, close to lake | (34)<br>$98–<br>$250 | CB<br>R | IS<br>OP |
| **Unique Mountain Rentals**    909-337-6155<br>28200 Hwy 189<br>www.mountaininfo.com see reference name "Judy,"<br>3 bdrm cabin sleeps 8, deck, residential area, trails | (22)<br>$240 | | |
| ## Lake Elsinore | | | |
| **Travel Inn**    909-245-8998<br>31610 Auto Center Dr    pet fee $8/day<br>dogs under 50 lbs only, grassy area, open field | (60)<br>$45–<br>$55 | C<br>M/F | OP |
| ## Lake Forest | | | |
| **Best Western Laguna El Toro Inn**<br>23702 Rockfield Blvd    949-458-1900<br>www.bestwesterncalifornia.com    800-937-8376<br>small lawn area behind building    pet fee $50/stay | (110)<br>$90–<br>$200 | CB<br>F<br>R/L | OP<br>T<br>FR |

| | | | | |
|---|---|---|---|---|
| **Candlewood Suites** | 949-598-9105 | (122) | C | FR |
| 3 S Pointe Dr | 888-226-3539 | $99– | K | |
| www.candlewoodsuites.com | pet fee $75/stay | $139 | | |
| dogs under 50 lbs only, small grassy area, near park | | | | |

### Lake San Marcos

| | | | | |
|---|---|---|---|---|
| **Quails Inn Hotel** | 760-744-0120 | (140) | C | OP |
| 1025 La Bonita Dr | 800-447-6556 | $107– | K | T |
| www.quailsinn.com | pet fee $10/day | $179 | F | FR |
| lawn walking areas | | | | |

### Lakehead

| | | | | |
|---|---|---|---|---|
| **Lakeshore Inn** | 530-238-2003 | (11) | (k) | OP |
| 20483 Lakeshore Dr | each pet $1/day | $85– | | |
| www.shastacamping.com | | $195 | | |
| rooms/cabins/travel trailers/house, field and trails | | | | |
| **Neu Lodge Motel** | 530-238-2698 | (15) | C | OP |
| 20821 Antlers Rd | | $68– | M/F | |
| www.redding-online.com | | $75 | | |
| on 2 acres for walking dogs, 3 blocks to lake, trails | | | | |
| **Shasta Lake Motel** | 530-238-2545 | (10) | C | OP |
| 20714 Lakeshore Dr | 866-355-8189 | $44– | M/F | |
| www.shastalakemotel.com | pet fee $10/day | $77 | | |
| open field, surrounded by national forest | | | | |
| **Sugarloaf Cottages Resort** | 530-238-2448 | (15) | C | OP |
| 19667 Lakeshore Dr | 800-953-4432 | $88– | K | |
| www.shastacabins.com | pet fee $5/day | $143 | M/F | |
| 1–3 bdrm cabins sleep up 12, lakeside walking area | | | | |
| **Tsasdi Resort** | 530-238-2575 | (20) | K | OP |
| 19990 Lakeshore Dr | 800-995-0291 | $85– | | |
| www.tsasdiresort.com | pet fee $12/day | $130 | | |
| 1 bdrm cabins up to modular home that sleeps 12, | | | | |
| on 20 wooded lakefront acres for walking dogs | | | | |

### Lakeport

| | | | | |
|---|---|---|---|---|
| **Forbestown Inn** | 707-263-7858 | (4) | FB | OP |
| 825 N Forbes St | 866-268-7858 | $105– | | |
| www.forbestowninn.com | pet fee $10/day | $125 | | |
| dog by advance approval, vacant lot, 2 blocks to park | | | | |

| C = coffee    GP = guest pass to   L = lounge<br>CB = continental      fitness center   M = microwave<br>    breakfast    IP = indoor pool    OP = outdoor pool<br>F = refrigerator    IS = in-room spa    R = restaurant<br>FB = full breakfast   K = full kitchen    S = sauna/steam<br>FR = fitness room    (k) = kitchenette    T = spa or hot tub | (# of units)<br>& rates | food<br>& drink | pool, sauna<br>& hot tub |
|---|---|---|---|
| **Lakeport (continued)** | | | |
| **Rainbow Lodge**       707-263-4309<br>2569 Lakeshore Blvd      pet fee $5/day<br>log cabin-style studios/1 bdrm suites, patios,<br>lakefront walking area, ½ mile to park | (12)<br>$55–<br>$85 | C<br>M/F | |
| **Lakeshore** | | | |
| **Cedar Crest Resort**      559-893-3233<br>61011 Cedar Crest Ln     pet fee $10/day<br>www.cedarcrestresort.com<br>1–2 bdrm cabins sleep up to 9, tent cabins and public<br>bathhouse, 200 ft above lake in national forest land | (14)<br>$95–<br>$150 | K | |
| **Huntington Lake Resort**    559-893-6750<br>58910 Huntington Lake Rd    each pet $15/day<br>cabins, boat rentals, lakefront wooded walking area | (8)<br>$65–<br>$75 | K<br>R | |
| **Lakeshore Resort**      559-893-3193<br>61953 Huntington Lake Rd    pet fee $15/day<br>www.lakeshoreresort.com<br>1–2 dogs only, cabins sleep 6, lakefront areas, trails | (27)<br>$77–<br>$150 | C<br>F | |
| **Lakeview Cottages**      559-893-2330<br>Huntington Lodge Rd     pet fee $12/day<br>www.lakeviewcottages.net<br>small dogs, 1–2 bdrm rustic cottages, walking areas | (11)<br>$400 | K | |
| **Tamarack Motor Lodge**    559-893-3244<br>55380 Flintridge Rd      888-268-0274<br>www.tamarackmotorlodge.com   pet fee $25/day<br>dogs by manager's approval only, studios sleep 4,<br>on private road with lawn and woods | (9)<br>$75–<br>$125 | C<br>K<br>M/F | |
| **Lancaster** | | | |
| **Best Western Antelope Valley Inn**   661-948-4651<br>44055 Sierra Hwy       800-810-9430<br>lawn walking area, 3 miles to park   pet fee $35/stay | (142)<br>$84–<br>$130 | CB<br>F<br>L | OP<br>T |

| | | | | |
|---|---|---|---|---|
| **E-Z8 Motel**<br>43530 17th St W<br>www.ez8motels.com<br>dogs under 20 lbs only | 661-945-9477 | (102)<br>$53 | C<br>F | OP<br>T |
| **Motel 6**<br>43540 17th St W<br>www.motel6.com<br>small grass area, 1 mile to park | 661-948-0435<br>800-466-8356 | (72)<br>$50–<br>$56 | | OP |
| **Oxford Suites**<br>1651 W Avenue K<br>www.oxfordsuites.com<br>pet fee $25/stay up to 50 lbs, $50/stay over 50 lbs<br>dirt area for walking dogs, 1½ miles to park | 661-949-3423<br>800-522-3050 | (172)<br>$85–<br>$115 | FB<br>(k) | OP<br>T<br>GP |

### Landers

| | | | | |
|---|---|---|---|---|
| **Lonesome Dove Motel**<br>1473 Wamego Trail<br>dogs by manager's approval only, open desert area | 760-364-2331 | (8)<br>$35–<br>$47 | (k)<br>F | |

### Lathrop

| | | | | |
|---|---|---|---|---|
| **Days Inn**<br>14750 S Harlan Rd<br>www.daysinn.com<br>undeveloped walking area, 2 blocks to park | 209-982-1959<br>800-329-7466<br>pet fee $10/day | (40)<br>$71 | C<br>M/F | OP<br>T |

### Lawndale

| | | | | |
|---|---|---|---|---|
| **Best Western South Bay Hotel**<br>15000 Hawthorne Blvd<br>2 blocks to park | 310-973-0998<br>800-660-9962<br>pet fee $50/stay | (95)<br>$71–<br>$81 | CB<br>M/F<br>R | OP<br>FR<br>S/T |

### Laytonville

| | | | | |
|---|---|---|---|---|
| **Express Inn**<br>44761 N Hwy 101<br>undeveloped walking area, 5 minute walk to park | 707-984-8456<br>pet fee $5/day | (14)<br>$49 | C<br>F | |

### Lebec

| | | | | |
|---|---|---|---|---|
| **Econo Lodge**<br>49713 Gorman Post Rd<br>www.econolodge.com<br>open walking area behind building, 5 miles to park | 661-248-6411<br>pet fee $10/stay | (60)<br>$59–<br>$69 | CB | OP |

| C = coffee   GP = guest pass to   L = lounge<br>CB = continental     fitness center   M = microwave<br>    breakfast   IP = indoor pool   OP = outdoor pool<br>F = refrigerator   IS = in-room spa   R = restaurant<br>FB = full breakfast   K = full kitchen   S = sauna/steam<br>FR = fitness room   (k) = kitchenette   T = spa or hot tub | # of units)<br>& rates | food<br>& drink | pool, sauna<br>& hot tub |
|---|---|---|---|
| **Lebec (continued)** | | | |
| **Ramada Ltd**    661-248-1530<br>9000 Country Side Ct    pet fee $5/day<br>www.ramada.com<br>lawn, field, walking trail | (71)<br>$72–<br>$125 | CB<br>F | OP<br>T |
| **Lee Vining** | | | |
| **El Mono Motel**    760-647-6310<br>51 Hwy 395 & 3rd St<br>small dogs only, newly remodeled 1920s motel,<br>streamfront walking area, ¼ mile to park and trails | (11)<br>$52–<br>$89 | | |
| **Murphey's Motel**    760-647-6316<br>51493 Hwy 395    800-334-6316<br>www.murpheysyosemite.com    pet fee $5/day<br>dogs by manager's approval only, small lawn area | (44)<br>$58–<br>$98 | C<br>F | |
| **Leggett** | | | |
| **River's Run Lodge**    707-984-6321<br>63250 Drive Thru Tree Rd    800-326-9469<br>www.riversrunlodge.com    each pet $10/day<br>duplex cottages, on 16 riverfront acres with dog run,<br>2 private beaches, swimming hole | (9)<br>$75–<br>$120 | K | |
| **Lemoore** | | | |
| **Best Western Vineyard Inn**    559-924-1261<br>877 East D St    888-924-7384<br>www.bestwesterncalifornia.com<br>2 acres with grassy walking area, ½ mile to park | (66)<br>$71–<br>$77 | CB<br>M/F | OP |
| **Lewiston** | | | |
| **Lakeview Terrace Resort**    530-778-3803<br>HC 01 Box 250    pet fee $10/day<br>www.lakeviewterraceresort.com<br>1–5 bdrm cabins, lawn, lakeside trails | (12)<br>$72–<br>$173 | K | OP |

## Likely

| | | | | |
|---|---|---|---|---|
| **Mahogany Ridge Guest Ranch** 300 County Road 64D www.mahoganyridgeranch.com adult dogs only, 3 bdrm home, lawn, walking areas | 530-233-4996 | (1) $115– $125 | K | T |

## Lincoln

| | | | | |
|---|---|---|---|---|
| **Lincoln Oaks B & B** 2819 McCourtney Rd www.lincolnoaks.com 5 acre ranch, open fields | 916-645-1965 pet fee $15/stay | (3) $95– $125 | FB K. | |

## Lindsay

| | | | | |
|---|---|---|---|---|
| **Super 8 Motel** 390 N Hwy 65 www.super8.com lawn walking area, 1 mile to park | 559-562-5188 800-800-8000 pet fee $10/day | (50) $59– $75 | CB F | OP T |

## Little River

| | | | | |
|---|---|---|---|---|
| **Inn at School House Creek** 7051 N Hwy 1 www.schoolhousecreek.com    pet fee $25–$75/stay rooms/cottages sleep up to 7, dogwashing facility, pet supplies, meadow, private off-leash beach | 707-937-5525 800-731-5525 | (15) $89– $275 | FB | T |
| **Little River Inn** 7901 N Hwy 1 www.littleriverinn.com    each pet $25/day 1–2 dogs only, rooms/cottage sleep up to 4, lawn walking area, next to state park | 707-937-5942 888-466-5683 | (66) $135– $265 | C F R/L | IS |
| **Seafoam Lodge** 6751 N Hwy 1 www.seafoamlodge.com    pet fee $10/stay large lawn for walking dogs, 1 mile to state park | 707-937-1827 800-606-1827 | (24) $110– $225 | CB F | T |

## Livermore

| | | | | |
|---|---|---|---|---|
| **Motel 6** 4673 Lassen Rd www.motel6.com grassy walking area | 925-443-5300 800-466-8356 | (102) $46– $56 | C | OP |

| C = coffee<br>CB = continental<br>breakfast<br>F = refrigerator<br>FB = full breakfast<br>FR = fitness room | GP = guest pass to<br>fitness center<br>IP = indoor pool<br>IS = in-room spa<br>K = full kitchen<br>(k) = kitchenette | L = lounge<br>M = microwave<br>OP = outdoor pool<br>R = restaurant<br>S = sauna/steam<br>T = spa or hot tub | (# of units)<br>& rates | food<br>& drink | pool, sauna<br>& hot tub |
|---|---|---|---|---|---|

### Livermore (continued)

| **Ramada Inn**<br>7600 Southfront Rd<br>www.ramada.com<br>large open field, 1 mile to parks | 925-456-5422<br>800-272-6232<br>pet fee $50/stay | (66)<br>$89–<br>$119 | CB<br>M/F | OP<br>FR<br>IS |
|---|---|---|---|---|
| **Residence Inn**<br>1000 Airway Blvd<br>each pet $6/day, plus $75 cleaning fee<br>www.marriott.com<br>lawn area, 5 miles to park | 925-373-1800<br>800-331-3131 | (96)<br>$89–<br>$139 | FB<br>K | OP<br>T<br>FR |
| **Springtown Inn**<br>933 Bluebell Dr<br>www.springtowninn.com<br>lawn and open field to walk dogs, 4 blocks to park | 925-449-2211<br>pet fee $10/stay | (125)<br>$47 | C<br>M/F | OP |
| **Vineyard Inn at Crane Ridge**<br>5405 Greenville Rd<br>www.whitecranewinery.com<br>dogs by manager's advance approval only, private<br>balconies, lawn and field, vineyard, 6 miles to lake | 925-455-8085 | (2)<br>$195–<br>$225 | CB | |

### Loch Lomond

| **Edie's Resort**<br>10545 Loch Lomond Rd<br>www.ediesresort.com<br>1–2 bdrm cottages, private decks, lawn and woods | 707-928-9804 | (2)<br>$55–<br>$93 | K | OP |
|---|---|---|---|---|

### Lodi

| **Amoroso Inn & Gardens**<br>7889 E Harney Ln<br>www.amorosainn.com<br>well-trained dogs by advance reservation only, patio,<br>3 acre garden, on 22 acre vineyard | 209-368-5658<br>866-368-5658 | (4)<br>$149–<br>$179 | FB | |
|---|---|---|---|---|

| | | | | |
|---|---|---|---|---|
| **Microtel Inns & Suites** 209-367-9700 | (51) | CB | OP |
| 6428 W Banner Rd (I-5 and Hwy 12) 888-771-7171 | $69 | M/F | |
| www.microtelinn.com pet fee $10/day | | | |
| small grassy walking area, 2 miles to park | | | |

| | | | |
|---|---|---|---|
| **Wine & Roses Hotel** 209-334-6988 | (36) | CB | |
| 2505 W Turner Rd 877-310-3358 | $139– | F | |
| dogs under 25 lbs only each pet $25/day | $365 | R | |
| dog-friendly rooms have outside entrances to patios, next to park, short walk to lake and nature trail | | | |

## Lompoc

| | | | |
|---|---|---|---|
| **Budget Inn Motel** 805-736-1241 | (25) | M/F | |
| 817 North H St pet fee $10/day | $46 | | |
| ½ block to school field, 1 mile to park | | | |

| | | | |
|---|---|---|---|
| **Days Inn** 805-733-5000 | (63) | CB | OP |
| 3955 Apollo Way 866-221-2208 | $79– | M/F | T |
| www.daysinnlompoc.com pet fee $25/stay | $85 | | GP |
| on 7 acres with lawn and walking paths | | | |

| | | | |
|---|---|---|---|
| **First Value Inn** 805-736-6514 | (46) | C | OP |
| 1415 E Ocean Ave each pet $10/day | $34– | M/F | |
| sidewalks for walking dogs, 2–3 miles to parks | $109 | | |

| | | | |
|---|---|---|---|
| **Motel 6** 805-735-7631 | (134) | C | OP |
| 1521 North H St 800-466-8356 | $44– | | |
| www.motel6.com | $53 | | |
| grassy walking area | | | |

| | | | |
|---|---|---|---|
| **Quality Inn** 805-735-8555 | (200) | CB | OP |
| 1621 N H St 800-224-6530 | $91– | M/F | T |
| www.qualitysuiteslompoc.com pet fee $25/stay | $99 | | GP |
| small grassy walking area, 5–10 minute drive to park | | | |

| | | | |
|---|---|---|---|
| **Super 8 Motel** 805-735-6444 | (54) | CB | S |
| 1020 E Ocean Ave 800-800-8000 | $55– | K | T |
| www.super8.com pet fee $10/day | $109 | | |
| grassy walking area | | | |

| | | | |
|---|---|---|---|
| **Vagabond Inn** 805-735-7744 | (90) | CB | IP |
| 1122 North H St 800-548-8231 | $70– | M/F | T |
| www.vagabondinn.com pet fee $25/stay | $90 | | FR |
| small grassy walking area, 7 blocks to park | | | |

| C = coffee<br>CB = continental<br>   breakfast<br>F = refrigerator<br>FB = full breakfast<br>FR = fitness room | GP = guest pass to<br>   fitness center<br>IP = indoor pool<br>IS = in-room spa<br>K = full kitchen<br>(k) = kitchenette | L = lounge<br>M = microwave<br>OP = outdoor pool<br>R = restaurant<br>S = sauna/steam<br>T = spa or hot tub | (# of units)<br>& rates | food<br>& drink | pool, sauna<br>& hot tub |
|---|---|---|---|---|---|
| **Lone Pine** | | | | | |
| **Best Western Frontier Motel**<br>1008 S Main St<br>www.bestwesterncalifornia.com<br>dirt walking area, ¾ mile to park | | 760-876-5571<br>800-231-4071 | (74)<br>$79–<br>$103 | CB<br>F | OP<br>IS |
| **Dow Hotel & Motel**<br>310 S Main St<br>www.dowvillamotel.com<br>1 block to vacant lot for walking dogs | | 760-876-5521<br>800-824-9317 | (9)<br>$82–<br>$115 | M/F | OP<br>T |
| **Portal Motel**<br>425 S Main St<br>gravel area, 5 blocks to park | | 760-876-5930<br>800-531-7054<br>pet fee $7/day | (17)<br>$42–<br>$99 | C<br>M/F | |
| **Trails Motel**<br>633 S Main St<br><br>small dogs allowed in smoking rooms only, field | | 760-876-5555<br>800-862-7020<br>each pet $10/day | (17)<br>$49–<br>$99 | CB<br>M/F | OP |
| **Long Barn** | | | | | |
| **Long Barn Lodge**<br>25957 Long Barn Rd<br>www.longbarn.com<br>well-behaved dogs only, rooms/cabins sleep up to 4,<br>large grassy walking area and residential road | | 209-586-3533<br>800-310-3533 | (24)<br>$79–<br>$99 | C<br>K | OP |
| **Slide Inn Lodge**<br>26161 Long Barn Rd<br>sleeping cabins/studios/2 bdrm apartments, use of<br>swimming pool nearby, lawn, wooded walking areas | | 209-586-5257 | (5)<br>$60–<br>$95 | K<br>M/F | OP |
| **Long Beach** | | | | | |
| **Beach Plaza Hotel**<br>2010 E Ocean Blvd<br>dogs under 25 lbs only, beachfront, park | | 562-437-0771<br>pet fee $25/stay | (40)<br>$70–<br>$150 | C | OP<br>T |

| | | | | |
|---|---|---|---|---|
| **Coast Long Beach Hotel** 700 Queensway Dr www.coasthotels.com bayfront walkway, beach trail | 562-435-7676 800-663-1144 | (200) $115 | R | OP FR |
| **Days Inn–City Center** 1500 E Pacific Coast Hwy www.daysinnlongbeach.com 4 dog-friendly rooms, open walking area | 562-591-0088 800-329-7466 each pet $10/day | (44) $59– $89 | CB M/F | |
| **GuestHouse International Hotel** 5325 E Pacific Coast Hwy www.guesthouselb.com | 562-597-1341 800-990-9991 next to park | (143) $79– $129 | CB K | OP IS |
| **Hilton Long Beach** 701 W Ocean Blvd www.longbeach.hilton.com dogs under 25 lbs by advance reservation, near park | 562-983-3400 800-445-8667 | (393) $100– $180 | C R/L | OP T FR |
| **Holiday Inn Long Beach Airport** 2640 N Lakewood Blvd www.hilongbeach.com pet relief area, 5 blocks to park, 5 miles to trails | 562-597-4401 800-465-4329 each pet $25/stay | (234) $89– $149 | R/L | OP FR |
| **Motel 6 Los Angeles/Long Beach** 5665 E 7th St www.motel6.com | 562-597-1311 800-466-8356 short drive to park | (42) $60– $73 | C | |
| **Palms Motel** 1059 Pacific Ave beachfront walking area, 6 blocks to park | 562-432-4366 | (19) $50– $60 | | |
| **Residence Inn** 4111 E Willow St www.marriott.com/laxbh pet fee $10/day plus $75 cleaning fee Mon–Thur beverages and light dinner, lawn area | 562-595-0909 800-331-3131 | (268) $139– $175 | FB | OP T FR |
| **Vagabond Inn** 150 Alamitos Ave www.vagabondinn.com each pet $10/day lawn walking area, 10 to 15 minute walk to park | 562-435-7621 800-522-1555 | (61) $71– $95 | CB | OP IS |
| **Westin Hotel** 333 E Ocean Blvd www.westin.com/longbeach 3 blocks to park | 562-436-3000 800-937-8461 | (460) $169 | R/L | OP S/T FR |

| C = coffee | GP = guest pass to | L = lounge |
|---|---|---|
| CB = continental | fitness center | M = microwave |
| breakfast | IP = indoor pool | OP = outdoor pool |
| F = refrigerator | IS = in-room spa | R = restaurant |
| FB = full breakfast | K = full kitchen | S = sauna/steam |
| FR = fitness room | (k) = kitchenette | T = spa or hot tub |

| | | | (# of units) & rates | food & drink | pool, sauna & hot tub |
|---|---|---|---|---|---|
| **Los Alamos** | | | | | |
| **Alamo Motel** | | 805-344-2852 | (15) | C | |
| 425 Bell St | | | $65– | M/F | |
| grassy walking area, short drive to park | | | $75 | | |
| **Skyview Motel** | | 805-344-3770 | (32) | CB | OP |
| 9150 Hwy 101 | | pet fee $25/stay | $55– | F | |
| www.theskyviewmotel.com | | | $75 | | |
| 1950s western-style motel, on 5 acres to walk dogs | | | | | |
| **Los Angeles** | | | | | |
| **Argyle Hotel** | | 323-654-7100 | (64) | F | OP |
| 8358 W Sunset Blvd | | 800-225-2637 | $199 | R | T |
| www.argylehotel.com | | | | | FR |
| next to dog-friendly park | | | | | |
| **Best Value Inn & Suites** | | 323-728-5165 | (70) | CB | |
| 7701 E Slauson Ave | | pet fee $10/day | $64– | M/F | |
| small dogs only, small lawn, 2 blocks to public park | | | $69 | | |
| **Best Western Dragon Gate Inn** | | 213-617-3077 | (52) | CB | FR |
| 818 N Hill St | | 800-282-9999 | $99– | F | |
| www.dragongateinn.com | | | $179 | R | |
| small dogs only, across street from park | | | | | |
| **Best Western Hollywood Hills** | | 323-464-5181 | (86) | C | OP |
| 6141 Franklin Ave | | 800-287-1700 | $119– | M/F | |
| www.bestwesterncalifornia.com | | pet fee $25/day | $159 | R | |
| 5 minute drive to park | | | | | |
| **Beverly Hills Plaza Hotel** | | 310-275-5575 | (116) | C | OP |
| 10300 Wilshire Blvd | | 800-800-1234 | $145– | K | T |
| www.beverlyhillsplazahotel.com | | pet fee $200/stay | $255 | R/L | FR |
| small dogs only, across street to park | | | | | |
| **Beverly Laurel Motor Hotel** | | 323-651-2441, | (52) | K | OP |
| 8018 Beverly Blvd | | 800-962-3824 | $94– | M/F | |
| 1–2 dogs only, 3 miles to park | | each pet $25/day | $109 | R | |

| | | | | |
|---|---|---|---|---|
| **Century Plaza Hotel & Tower** | 310-277-2000 | (727) | C | OP |
| 2025 Avenue of the Stars | 800-228-3000 | $190 | F | T |
| www.centuryplazala.com | pet fee $30/day | | R/L | FR |
| dogs under 40 lbs only, pet bowls/beds, grassy | | | | |
| walking area, 2 blocks to large park | | | | |
| **Farmer's Daughter Hotel** | 323-937-3930 | (66) | C | OP |
| 115 S Fairfax Ave | 800-334-1658 | $115– | F | |
| www.farmersdaughterhotel.com | pet fee $50/stay | $125 | | |
| dogs allowed in 2 rooms, 1 block to park | | | | |
| **Four Points Sheraton Hotel** | 310-645-4600 | (900) | M/F | OP |
| 9750 Airport Blvd | 800-529-4683 | $79– | R | FR |
| www.fourpointslax.com | pet fee $10/day | $150 | | |
| short drive to park | | | | |
| **Four Seasons Hotel** | 310-273-2222 | (285) | C | IP |
| 300 S Doheny Dr | 800-332-3442 | $350– | R/L | T |
| www.fourseasons.com/losangeles | | $500 | | FR |
| dogs under 15 lbs only, pet bowls/beds, petwalking/ | | | | |
| petsitting service, garden setting, residential street | | | | |
| **Furama Hotel** | 310-670-8111 | (663) | R | OP |
| 8601 Lincoln Blvd | 800-225-8126 | $67– | | T |
| www.furamalax.com | pet fee $10/day | $75 | | |
| across street to park | | | | |
| **Grafton on Sunset** | 323-654-4600 | (113) | R/L | OP |
| 8462 W Sunset Blvd | 800-821-3660 | $149– | | |
| www.graftononsunset.com | pet fee $100/stay | $300 | | |
| small dogs only, 1 block to small park | | | | |
| **Highland Gardens Hotel** | 323-850-0536 | (72) | CB | OP |
| 7047 Franklin Ave | 800-404-5472 | $69– | K | |
| www.highlandgardenshotel.com | pet fee $25/day | $239 | M/F | |
| rooms/1–3 bdrm suites, garden, near off-leash trails | | | | |
| **Hilton Los Angeles Airport** | 310-410-4000 | (1,234) | R/L | OP |
| 5711 W Century Blvd | 800-445-8667 | $99– | | T |
| www.losangelesairport.hilton.com | | $189 | | FR |
| | each pet $15/day | | | |
| garden walking areas, short drive to beach and park | | | | |

| C = coffee  GP = guest pass to  L = lounge  CB = continental fitness center  M = microwave  breakfast  IP = indoor pool  OP = outdoor pool  F = refrigerator  IS = in-room spa  R = restaurant  FB = full breakfast  K = full kitchen  S = sauna/steam  FR = fitness room  (k) = kitchenette  T = spa or hot tub | (# of units) & rates | food & drink | pool, sauna & hot tub |
|---|---|---|---|
| **Los Angeles (continued)** | | | |
| **Holiday Inn Brentwood/Bel Air**   310-476-6411 <br> 170 N Church Lande    800-465-4329 <br> www.hibrentwood.com    pet fee $50/stay <br> dogs under 30 lbs only, 10 minute drive to park | (211) <br> $100– <br> $120 | C <br> R/L | OP <br> T <br> FR |
| **Hollywood Roosevelt Hotel**   323-466-7000 <br> 7000 Hollywood Blvd    pet fee $100/stay <br> www.hollywoodroosevelt.com <br> dogs under 20 lbs only, 7 blocks to park | (237) <br> $199 | C <br> F <br> R | IP <br> FR |
| **Hotel Bel Air**   310-472-1211 <br> 701 Stone Canyon Rd    800-648-4097 <br> www.hotelbelair.com    pet fee $300/stay <br> dogs under 30 lbs only, rooms/suites, 12 acres with <br> landscaped garden, residential street to walk dogs | (92) <br> $385– <br> $3,500 | F <br> R | OP <br> T <br> FR |
| **Hotel Sofitel**   310-278-5444 <br> 8555 Beverly Blvd    800-763-4835 <br> www.sofitel.com <br> ¼ mile to park | (311) <br> $179– <br> $199 | M/F <br> R/L | OP <br> S <br> FR |
| **Le Meridien at Beverly Hills**   310-247-0400 <br> 465 S La Cienega Blvd    800-645-5624 <br> www.lemeridien.com    pet fee $100/stay <br> residential walking area, next to small park | (297) <br> $289– <br> $489 | C <br> F <br> R/L | OP <br> T <br> FR |
| **Los Angeles Airport Marriott**   310-641-5700 <br> 5855 W Century Blvd    800-228-9290 <br> www.marriott.com <br> dogs allowed in first floor rooms with outside access, <br> lawn walking area | (1,004) <br> $89– <br> $205 | R/L | OP <br> T <br> FR |
| **Los Feliz Motel**   323-667-2567 <br> 3101 Los Feliz Blvd    pet fee $10/day <br> dogs allowed in smoking rooms only, 5 blocks to <br> park | (12) <br> $79 | C <br> M/F | |

| | | | | |
|---|---|---|---|---|
| **Luxe Summit Hotel Bel-Air** 11461 W Sunset Blvd www.luxehotels.com dogs under 50 lbs only, pet-friendly garden on upper floor, 7 acre landscaped grounds | 310-476-6571 pet fee $10 per day plus $200 cleaning fee | (160) $149– $289 | C M/F R | OP T FR |
| **Magic Castle Hotel** 7025 Franklin Ave www.magiccastlehotel.com dogs under 10 lbs only, small park across street, close to hillside hiking trail | 323-851-0800 800-741-4915 pet fee $35/stay | (63) $99– $239 | CB K F | OP |
| **Motel 6 Hollywood** 1738 N Whitley Ave www.motel6.com 1 dog under 50 lbs, close to park | 323-464-6006 800-466-8356 | (125) $66– $76 | C | |
| **Motel 6 Los Angeles/Rosemead** 1001 S San Gabriel Blvd 1 small dog only, grassy walking area, ½ mile to park | 626-572-6076 | (130) $52– $62 | C | OP |
| **Ocean Park Hotel** 2680 32nd St walking area behind building | 323-466-0524 or 310-395-7368 pet fee $10/day | (40) $67 | C M/F | |
| **Omni Los Angeles Hotel** 251 S Olive St www.omnilosangeles.com 1 block to small grassy area, 7 miles to park | 213-617-3300 800-843-6664 pet fee $50/stay | (439) $189– $249 | CB F R/L | OP T FR |
| **Park Plaza Lodge** 6001 W 3rd St small dogs by manager's approval only, lawn walking area, 2 blocks to park | 323-931-1501 pet fee $25/day | (47) $89– $99 | C F | OP |
| **Ramada Inn** 7272 E Gage Ave www.ramada.com small well-behaved dogs in smoking rooms only, grassy areas in parking lot, ½ block to riverside trail | 562-806-4777 800-547-4777 | (156) $59– $64 | C R | OP FR |
| **Ramada Plaza Hotel & Suites** 8585 Santa Monica Blvd www.ramadaweho.com suites sleep 2–6, paved walking area, 1 mile to park | 310-652-6400 800-845-8585 | (176) $149– $199 | C M/F R | OP FR |

| C = coffee | GP = guest pass to | L = lounge | (# of units) & rates | food & drink | pool, sauna & hot tub |
|---|---|---|---|---|---|
| CB = continental breakfast | fitness center | M = microwave | | | |
| | IP = indoor pool | OP = outdoor pool | | | |
| F = refrigerator | IS = in-room spa | R = restaurant | | | |
| FB = full breakfast | K = full kitchen | S = sauna/steam | | | |
| FR = fitness room | (k) = kitchenette | T = spa or hot tub | | | |

## Los Angeles (continued)

| | | | | |
|---|---|---|---|---|
| **Residence Inn Beverly Hills** 1177 S Beverly Dr www.residenceinn.com pet fee $10/day plus $80 cleaning fee dogs under 50 lbs only, studios/1–2 bdrm suites, Mon–Thur beverages and appetizers, 5 minute walk to park | 310-277-2357 800-331-3131 | (186) $139– $179 | FB (k) | T FR |
| **St. Regis Los Angeles Hotel & Spa** 2055 Avenue of the Stars www.stregis.com pet supplies, grassy area, 10 minute walk to park | 310-277-6111 | (297) $485 | C F R | OP FR |
| **Standard Hotel–Downtown** 550 S Flower St www.standardhotel.com rooftop swimming pool, 1 block to park | 213-892-8080 pet fee $100/stay | (207) $135– $165 | F R | OP |
| **Standard Hotel–Hollywood** 8300 W Sunset Blvd www.standardhotel.com dogs under 20 lbs, next to dog park | 323-650-9090 pet fee $100/stay | (139) $99– $450 | F R | OP GP |
| **Super 8 Motel** 5350 Huntington Dr S www.super8.com lawn walking area, ½ mile to park | 323-225-2310 800-800-8000 each pet $10/day | (52) $54 | CB M/F | |
| **Travelodge Hotel–LAX** 5547 W Century Blvd www.travelodgelax.com pet relief area, open field, 3 miles to park | 310-649-4000 800-421-3939 each pet $10/day | (147) $63– $70 | CB R/L | OP FR |
| **Vagabond Inn** 3101 S Figueroa St www.vagabondinn.com 3 blocks to park | 213-746-1531 800-522-1555 pet fee $10/day | (72) $69– $109 | CB M/F | OP |

| | | | | |
|---|---|---|---|---|
| **Villa Brasil Motel** | 310-636-0141 | (19) | C | |
| 11740 W Washington Blvd | 310-350-1171 | $50– | M/F | |
| www.villabrasilmotel.com | pet fee $10/day | $60 | | |
| small dogs only, short drive to park | | | | |
| **W Hotel Los Angeles Westwood** | 310-208-8765 | (258) | C | OP |
| 930 Hilgard Ave | 877-946-8357 | $199– | F | FR |
| www.whotels.com | each pet $75/stay | $1,199 | R/L | |
| dogsitting/dogwalking services, next to college | | | | |
| campus, pet supplies, list of local pet-friendly parks | | | | |

## Los Banos

| | | | | |
|---|---|---|---|---|
| **Best Western Executive Inn** | 209-827-0954 | (56) | CB | OP |
| 301 W Pacheco Blvd | 800-528-1234 | $65 | M/F | S |
| www.bestwesterncalifornia.com each pet $10/day | | | | T |
| small dogs only, grassy areas, 1 mile to park | | | | FR |
| **Days Inn** | 209-826-9690 | (60) | CB | OP |
| 2169 E Pacheco Blvd | 800-329-7466 | $49– | M/F | IS |
| www.daysinn.com | pet fee $10/day | $89 | | |
| large grassy walking area | | | | |
| **Sun Star Inn** | 209-826-3805 | (40) | C | OP |
| 839 W Pacheco Blvd | pet fee $5/day | $45 | M/F | |
| large grassy walking area | | | | |

## Los Gatos

| | | | | |
|---|---|---|---|---|
| **Hotel Los Gatos** | 408-335-1701 | (72) | F | OP |
| 210 E Main St | 866-335-1700 | $169– | R | T |
| www.hotellosgatos.com | pet fee $50/stay | $479 | | FR |
| dogs under 50 lbs only, lawn and creekside trail | | | | |
| **Los Gatos Lodge** | 408-354-3300 | (128) | FB | OP |
| 50 Los Gatos Saratoga Rd | 800-231-8676 | $79– | CB | T |
| www.losgatoslodge.com | | $169 | M/F | FR |
| dogs under 50 lbs, rooms/suites, 11 garden acres | | | R/L | |

## Los Olivos

| | | | | |
|---|---|---|---|---|
| **Fess Parker Wine Country Inn & Spa** | | (21) | F | OP |
| 2860 Grand Ave | 805-688-7788 | $260– | R | T |
| www.fessparker.com | 800-446-2455 | $360 | | |
| grassy area, 15 minutes to park | pet fee $50/day | | | |

| C = coffee GP = guest pass to L = lounge<br>CB = continental      fitness center M = microwave<br>    breakfast    IP = indoor pool OP = outdoor pool<br>F = refrigerator   IS = in-room spa R = restaurant<br>FB = full breakfast K = full kitchen S = sauna/steam<br>FR = fitness room (k) = kitchenette T = spa or hot tub | (# of units)<br>& rates | food<br>& drink | pool, sauna<br>& hot tub |
|---|---|---|---|
| **Los Osos** | | | |
| **Megan's Friends B & B**     805-544-4406<br>1355 5th St     800-804-2040<br>www.bnbmegansfriends.com: click "Los Osos" and<br>"Beautiful Home," dogs by advance reservation only,<br>lawn, 1 block to boardwalk, 3 blocks to dog beach | (1)<br>$124 | FB | |
| **Sea Pines Golf Resort**     805-528-5252<br>1945 Solano St     888-732-7463<br>www.seapinesgolfresort.com     pet fee $15/day<br>dogs under 35 lbs allowed in smoking rooms only | (44)<br>$89–<br>$159 | C<br>M/F<br>R/L | T<br>FR |
| **Lost Hills** | | | |
| **Days Inn**     661-797-2371<br>14684 Aloma St     800-329-7466<br>www.daysinn.com     pet fee $6/day<br>grassy area, 2 miles to park | (76)<br>$45–<br>$80 | CB<br>M/F | OP |
| **Motel 6**     661-797-2346<br>14685 Warren St     800-466-8356<br>www.motel6.com     open field, 1½ miles to park | (105)<br>$38–<br>$44 | C | OP |
| **Loyalton** | | | |
| **Country Cookin' Restaurant & Inn**     (6)<br>820 Main St     530-993-1162<br>well-behaved small dogs only, private rooms, shared<br>baths, community kitchen, lawn and open field | (6)<br>$45–<br>$55 | C<br>M/F<br>K<br>R | |
| **Golden Motel**     530-993-4467<br>711 Main St (Hwy 49)     open field for walking dogs | (14)<br>$57 | R/L | |
| **Lucerne** | | | |
| **Beachcomber Resort**     707-274-6639<br>6345 E Hwy 20     800-319-9000<br>www.beachcomberresort.net<br>dogs by manager's approval, shaded lakefront lawn | (9)<br>$54–<br>$90 | K<br>M/F | |

| | | | | |
|---|---|---|---|---|
| **Riviera Motel** | 707-274-1032 | (3) | C | |
| 6900 E Hwy 20 | | $50– | K | |
| small dogs by manager's approval, lawn, trail, lake | | $90 | M | |
| **Starlite Motel** | 707-274-5515 | (20) | F | |
| 5960 E Hwy 20 | pet fee $10/stay | $45 | | |
| small dogs in smoking rooms only, lawn, lake | | | | |

## Madera

| | | | | |
|---|---|---|---|---|
| **Best Western Madera Valley Inn** | 559-664-0100 | (93) | CB | OP |
| 317 North G St | 800-528-1234 | $59– | M/F | FR |
| www.maderavalleyinn.com | pet fee $15/stay | $109 | R/L | |
| grassy sidewalk strips, 1 mile to park | | | | |
| **Days Inn** | 559-674-8817 | (49) | CB | OP |
| 25327 Avenue 16 | 800-329-7466 | $55– | M/F | |
| www.daysinn.com | each pet $10/day | $65 | | |
| lawn walking areas, 1 mile to park | | | | |
| **Motel 6** | 559-675-8697 | (40) | C | IP |
| 22683 Avenue 18½ | 800-800-8000 | $56– | | S |
| www.motel6.com | grassy walking area | $68 | | T |
| **Super 8 Motel** | 559-661-1131 | (80) | CB | OP |
| 1855 W Cleveland Ave | 800-800-8000 | $55– | M/F | |
| www.super8.com | each pet $5/day | $65 | | |
| lawn and open field, 1½ miles to park | | | | |

## Malibu

| | | | | |
|---|---|---|---|---|
| **Malibu Riviera Motel** | 310-457-9503 | (13) | C | T |
| 28920 Pacific Coast Hwy | | $89– | F | |
| small grassy area, 9 miles to dog-friendly beach | | $120 | | |
| **Topanga Ranch Motel** | 310-456-5486 | (30) | F | |
| 18711 Pacific Coast Hwy | | $75– | | |
| 1920s motor court, small grassy areas, near beach | | $95 | | |

## Mammoth Lakes

| | | | | |
|---|---|---|---|---|
| **Convict Lake Resort** | 760-934-3800 | (29) | K | IS |
| RR 1 Box 204 | pet fee $15/stay | $99– | | |
| www.convictlake.com | | $680 | | |
| cabins/vacation homes sleep 2 to 34, lawn, wooded | | | | |
| lakeside trail, 5 miles to natural hot springs | | | | |

| C = coffee<br>CB = continental<br>      breakfast<br>F = refrigerator<br>FB = full breakfast<br>FR = fitness room | GP = guest pass to<br>      fitness center<br>IP = indoor pool<br>IS = in-room spa<br>K = full kitchen<br>(k) = kitchenette | L = lounge<br>M = microwave<br>OP = outdoor pool<br>R = restaurant<br>S = sauna/steam<br>T = spa or hot tub | (# of units)<br>& rates | food<br>& drink | pool, sauna<br>& hot tub |
|---|---|---|---|---|---|
| **Mammoth Lakes (continued)** | | | | | |
| **Crystal Crag Lodge**<br>307 Crystal Crag Dr<br>www.crystalcraglodge.com<br>studio to 4 bdrm cabins, open late May to early<br>October, lakeside walking area | 760-934-2436<br>pet fee $9/day | | (21)<br>$85–<br>$265 | K | |
| **Econo Lodge Wildwood Inn**<br>3626 Main St<br>www.mammotheconolodge.com<br>wooded walking area, close to hiking trails | 760-934-7819<br>pet fee $10/day | | (32)<br>$69–<br>$199 | CB<br>M/F | OP<br>T |
| **Edelweiss Lodge**<br>1872 Old Mammoth Rd<br>www.edelweiss-lodge.com<br>cabins/suites, pet boarding service, vacant lot for<br>walking dogs, close to trails | 760-934-2445<br>877-233-3593<br>each pet $10/day | | (10)<br>$125–<br>$350 | C<br>K<br>M/F | T |
| **Innsbruck Lodge**<br>913 Forest Trail<br>www.innsbrucklodge.com<br>dogs allowed by manager's advance approval only,<br>next to park | 760-934-3035<br>pet fee $10/day | | (17)<br>$50–<br>$200 | C<br>K<br>F | T |
| **Mammoth Creek Inn**<br>663 Old Mammoth Rd<br>www.mammothlodges.com<br>afternoon refreshments and pet treats, woods with<br>creek and running path, across street to park | 760-934-6162<br>866-466-7000<br>pet fee $15/day | | (27)<br>$95–<br>$295 | CB<br>K<br>F | S<br>T |
| **Mammoth Mountain Chalets**<br>1 Minaret Rd<br>www.mammothmtnchalets.com<br>1–4 bdrm chalets sleep up to 10, wooded walking<br>areas, close to hiking trails | 760-934-8518<br>800-327-3681 | | (20)<br>$170–<br>$490 | K | |

| | | | | |
|---|---|---|---|---|
| **Mammoth Premiere Reservations** 760-934-6543<br>89 Laurel Mountain Rd 800-336-6543<br>www.mammothpremiere.com each pet $25/stay<br>1–2 dogs only, 1–3 bdrm condos sleep up to 10,<br>lawn and wooded walking areas, near hiking trails | (10)<br>$130–<br>$260 | K | OP<br>T |
| **Mammoth Reservation Bureau** 760-934-2528<br>94 Old Mammoth Rd 800-462-5571<br>www.mammothReservationBureau.com<br>2 pet-friendly 2 bdrm and 3 bdrm condominiums | (230)<br>$200–<br>$360 | K | IP<br>S<br>T |
| **Motel 6** 760-934-6660<br>3372 Main St 800-466-8356<br>www.motel6.com woods and hillside trail | (151)<br>$72–<br>$86 | C | OP |
| **Pine Cliff Resort** 760-934-2447<br>150 Woodman<br>www.pinecliffresort.com<br>studio to 2 bdrm cabins, quiet neighborhood and<br>wooded walking area, trail to meadow | (5)<br>$70–<br>$165 | K | |
| **Red's Meadow Resort** 760-934-2345<br>Hwy 203 800-292-7758<br>www.redsmeadow.com<br>duplex/rustic cabins sleep up to 6, woods, trails | (8)<br>$75–<br>$125 | (k) | |
| **Rodeway Inn Sierra Nevada** 760-934-2515<br>164 Old Mammoth Rd 800-824-5132<br>www.mammothsnri.com pet fee $12/day<br>lawn walking area, close to hiking trails | (156)<br>$69–<br>$499 | CB<br>K | OP<br>S<br>T |
| **Royal Pines Resort** 760-934-2306<br>3814 View Point Rd 800-457-1997<br>www.royalpines.com each pet $5/day<br>grassy areas and woods | (28)<br>$69–<br>$125 | C<br>K | T |
| **Shilo Inn** 760-934-4500<br>2963 Main St 800-222-2244<br>www.shiloinns.com each pet $15/day<br>walking trail | (70)<br>$69–<br>$219 | CB<br>M/F | IP<br>S<br>T<br>FR |
| **Sierra Lodge** 760-934-8881<br>3540 Main St 800-356-5711<br>www.sierralodge.com each pet $10/day<br>wooded walking areas, 1 mile to park | (36)<br>$69–<br>$179 | CB<br>(k) | T |

| C = coffee | GP = guest pass to | L = lounge |
|---|---|---|
| CB = continental | fitness center | M = microwave |
| breakfast | IP = indoor pool | OP = outdoor pool |
| F = refrigerator | IS = in-room spa | R = restaurant |
| FB = full breakfast | K = full kitchen | S = sauna/steam |
| FR = fitness room | (k) = kitchenette | T = spa or hot tub |

## Mammoth Lakes (continued)

| | | (# of units) & rates | food & drink | pool, sauna & hot tub |
|---|---|---|---|---|
| **Summit Condominiums**<br>3253 Meridian Blvd<br>www.summitcondominiums.com   pet fee $10/day<br>1–2 dogs only, 1–2 bdrm condos, woods, trails | 760-934-3000<br>800-255-6266 | (90)<br>$97–<br>$446 | K | OP<br>T<br>FR |
| **Swiss Chalet Motel**<br>3776 Viewpoint Rd<br>www.mammoth-swisschalet.com   each pet $5/day<br>1–2 dogs only, woods, trail, near dog-friendly ski area | 760-934-2403<br>800-937-9477 | (20)<br>$65–<br>$110 | C<br>(k)<br>F | S<br>T |
| **Travelodge**<br>54 Sierra Blvd<br>www.travelodge.com   pet fee $10/day<br>open walking area | 760-934-8240<br>888-500-4754 | (40)<br>$69–<br>$109 | CB<br>M/F | S<br>T |

## Manhattan Beach

| | | | | |
|---|---|---|---|---|
| **Residence Inn**<br>1700 N Sepulveda Blvd<br>www.marriott.com<br>   pet fee $8/day plus $75–$100 cleaning fee<br>Mon–Thur beverages and light dinner, pet relief<br>area, 1½ blocks to park | 310-546-7627<br>800-331-3131 | (176)<br>$139–<br>$209 | FB<br>K | OP<br>T<br>FR |

## Manteca

| | | | | |
|---|---|---|---|---|
| **Best Western Executive Inn**<br>1415 E Yosemite Ave<br>www.centralvalleybwhotels.com   pet fee $25/stay<br>dogs by manager's approval only, 2 miles to park | 209-825-1415<br>800-626-8322 | (101)<br>$69–<br>$84 | CB<br>M/F | OP<br>T |

## Marina

| | | | | |
|---|---|---|---|---|
| **Motel 6 Monterey/Marina**<br>100 Reservation Rd<br>www.motel6.com<br>across street to park | 831-384-1000<br>800-466-8356 | (126)<br>$52–<br>$82 | C | |

| Super 8 Motel | 831-384-1800 | (114) | CB | T |
|---|---|---|---|---|
| 3280 Dunes Rd | 800-550-0055 | $69– | F | |
| www.inncal.com | pet fee $25/day | $109 | | |
| lawn, vacant lot, 5 minute walk to dog-friendly beach | | | | |

### Marina Del Rey

| Ritz-Carlton Hotel | 310-823-1700 | (304) | CB | OP |
|---|---|---|---|---|
| 4375 Admiralty Way | pet fee $200/stay | $299– | F | T |
| www.ritzcarlton.com | | $3,000 | R | FR |
| dogs under 30 lbs only, walkway to marina | | | | |

### Mariposa

| Best Western Yosemite Way Station Inn | | (78) | CB | OP |
|---|---|---|---|---|
| 4999 Hwy 140 | 209-966-7545 | $50– | | T |
| www.yosemite-motels.com | 800-321-5261 | $110 | | |
| creekside trail, next to park | each pet $10/day | | | |

| Haven of Rest B & B | 209-742-4533 | (2) | FB | |
|---|---|---|---|---|
| 4877 Ashworth Rd | 866-400-4533 | $125 | CB | |
| www.havenofrestbnb.com | | | | |
| small housebroken dogs only, 15 mountaintop acres | | | | |

| Mariposa Lodge | 209-966-3607 | (44) | C | OP |
|---|---|---|---|---|
| 5052 Hwy 140 | 800-966-8819 | $59– | M/F | T |
| www.mariposalodge.com | pet fee $10/day | $139 | | |
| hilly roadside walking area, ¼ mile to park | | | | |

| Miners Inn | 209-742-7777 | (78) | CB | OP |
|---|---|---|---|---|
| Hwy 140 & 49 | 888-646-2244 | $49– | (k) | T |
| www.yosemite-rooms.com | pet fee $10/day | $85 | M/F | IS |
| 1–2 dogs only, pet relief area, 4 blocks to park | | | R/L | |

| Mother Lode Lodge | 209-966-2521 | (15) | C | OP |
|---|---|---|---|---|
| 5051 Hwy 140 | 800-398-9770 | $39– | K | |
| www.mariposamotel.com | pet fee $25/stay | $149 | M/F | |
| rooms/3 bdrm condo, creekside walking area | | | | |

| Pelennor B & B | 209-966-2832 | (4) | K | |
|---|---|---|---|---|
| 3871 Hwy 49 S | | $40– | | |
| www.yosemitebnbs.com/p7_pellennor.html | | $45 | | |
| 4 bdrm 2 bath guest building, self-serve breakfast, | | | | |
| on 7 wooded acres with pond and walking path | | | | |

| C = coffee<br>CB = continental<br>  breakfast<br>F = refrigerator<br>FB = full breakfast<br>FR = fitness room | GP = guest pass to<br>  fitness center<br>IP = indoor pool<br>IS = in-room spa<br>K = full kitchen<br>(k) = kitchenette | L = lounge<br>M = microwave<br>OP = outdoor pool<br>R = restaurant<br>S = sauna/steam<br>T = spa or hot tub | (# of units)<br>& rates | food<br>& drink | pool, sauna<br>& hot tub |
|---|---|---|---|---|---|

## Mariposa (continued)

| | | | | | |
|---|---|---|---|---|---|
| **Restful Nest B & B**<br>4274 Buckeye Creek Rd<br>www.restfulnest.com | 209-742-7127<br>800-664-7127<br>on 10 acres of rolling hills | | (4)<br>$95–<br>$125 | FB | OP<br>T |
| **Rockwood Gardens B & B**<br>5155 Tip Top Rd<br>dogs by advance approval only, on 5 park-like acres | 209-742-6817<br>800-859-8862 | | (3)<br>$70–<br>$90 | FB<br>M/F | |
| **Super 8 Motel**<br>5059 Hwy 140<br>www.super8.com<br>lawn and vacant lot, next to park | 209-966-4288<br>800-800-8000 | | (46)<br>$43–<br>$89 | CB<br>M/F | OP |

## Markleeville

| | | | | | |
|---|---|---|---|---|---|
| **Bed, Bike & Bagel**<br>40 Montgomery St<br>1 bdrm cabin sleeps 4, deck overlooking river,<br>bicycles for guest use, wooded walking area | 530-694-9337<br>pet fee $25/stay | | (1)<br>$130–<br>$165 | (k)<br>R | S |
| **J Marklee Toll Station**<br>14856 Hwy 89<br>dog-friendly outdoor dining area in restaurant,<br>1 acre lawn surrounded by forest | 530-694-2507<br>pet fee $15/day | | (5)<br>$65 | C<br>R | |

## Marysville

| | | | | | |
|---|---|---|---|---|---|
| **Best Value Inn**<br>904 E St<br>small dog by manager's approval only, ½ mile to park | 530-743-1531<br>pet fee $5/day | | (40)<br>$59 | M/F | |

## McCloud

| | | | | | |
|---|---|---|---|---|---|
| **Stoney Brook Inn B & B**<br>309 W Colombero Dr<br>www.stoneybrookinn.com<br>2 dog-friendly rooms, garden area and residential<br>streets for walking dogs | 530-964-2300<br>800-369-6118<br>each pet $17/stay | | (17)<br>$89 | FB<br>M/F | S<br>T |

## Meadow Valley

| | | | | |
|---|---|---|---|---|
| **Lakeshore Resort** | 530-283-6900 | (14) | K | T |
| 1100 Bucks Lake Rd | pet fee $25/stay | $95– | R/L | |
| www.buckslake.com | | $145 | | |
| cabins sleep 2 to 8, boat rental, lakeside trails | | | | |

## Mendocino

| | | | | |
|---|---|---|---|---|
| **Abigail's B & B** | 707-937-0934 | (8) | CB | S |
| 951 Ukiah St | 800-531-7282 | $99– | K | T |
| www.abigailsmendocino.com | pet fee $25/stay | $299 | | |
| guest rooms/4 bdrm vacation home with yard, residential streets, close to dog-friendly state park and beach, also see www.vacationrentals.com for "California/Mendocino/White Gate Village Retreat" | | | | |
| **Blair House** | 707-937-1800 | (5) | FB | |
| 45110 Little Lake St | 800-699-9296 | $150– | K | |
| www.blairhouse.com | pet fee $10/day | $175 | | |
| dog allowed in cottage with loft that sleeps 4, yard, 2 blocks to walking trails, 4 blocks to state park | | | | |
| **Delamere Cottages** | 707-964-3175 | (2) | CB | |
| www.delamerecottages.com | | $150– | | |
| 1 bdrm cottages, ocean views, path to beach | | $165 | | |
| **Hill House Inn of Mendocino** | 707-937-0554 | (44) | C | |
| 10701 Palette Dr | 800-422-0554 | $121– | R | |
| www.hillhouseinn.com | pet fee $15/day | $250 | | |
| dogs allowed in first floor rooms only, grassy walking areas, 2 miles to park | | | | |
| **Joshua Grindle Inn** | 707-937-4143 | (1) | K | |
| 44800 Little Lake Rd | 800-474-6353 | $245– | | |
| www.joshgrin.com | pet fee $25/day | $375 | | |
| 2 bdrm house sleeps 4, lawn, ¼ mile to state park, beach access and hiking trail to waterfall | | | | |
| **MacCallum House Inn** | 707-937-0289 | (34) | FB | T |
| 45020 Albion St | 800-609-0492 | $135– | K | IS |
| www.maccallumhouse.com | pet fee $25/day | $265 | R | |
| guest rooms/cottages/vacation homes sleep up to 9, pet bed/bowl/treats, on 2 acres of lawn, close to beach and park | | | | |

| C = coffee  GP = guest pass to  L = lounge  CB = continental  fitness center  M = microwave  breakfast  IP = indoor pool  OP = outdoor pool  F = refrigerator  IS = in-room spa  R = restaurant  FB = full breakfast  K = full kitchen  S = sauna/steam  FR = fitness room  (k) = kitchenette  T = spa or hot tub | (# of units) & rates | food & drink | pool, sauna & hot tub |
|---|---|---|---|

## Mendocino (continued)

| | | | |
|---|---|---|---|
| **McElroy's Inn** 707-937-1734 998 Main St 888-237-0152 www.mcelroysinn.com pet fee $15/day small field, across street to dog-friendly beach, close to hiking trails | (5) $69– $115 | CB F | |
| **Mendocino Seaside Cottage** 707-485-0239 10940 Lansing St 800-944-3278 www.romancebythesea.com luxury Victorian inn overlooking lighthouse and ocean, pet gift basket, next to dog-friendly state park | (4) $187– $391 | C M/F | IS |
| **Stanford Inn by the Sea and Spa** 707-937-5615 44850 Comptche Ukiah Rd 800-331-8884 www.stanfordinn.com pet fee $25/stay yoga and workout room, organic breakfast, 10 acres, paved road on bluff overlooking ocean for walking dogs, ¼ mile to dog-friendly beach | (41) $265– $395 | FB R | IP S T |
| **Sweetwater Spa & Inn** 707-937-4076 44840 Main St 800-300-4140 www.sweetwaterspa.com each pet $15/day 1–2 dogs only, cottages/3 bdrm home, enclosed garden or yard, trails, beach access | (12) $70– $250 | K | S T |

## Merced

| | | | |
|---|---|---|---|
| **Hooper House Bear Creek Inn** 209-723-3991 575 W North Bear Creek Dr pet fee $25/stay www.hooperhouse.com dogs allowed in cottage only, creekside bike trail | (4) $125– $135 | FB K | |
| **Howard Johnson Inn** 209-723-3711 1213 V St 800-937-8376 www.howardjohnson.com each pet $10/day courtyard for walking dogs | (98) $55– $65 | CB M/F | OP |

| | | | | |
|---|---|---|---|---|
| **Motel 6 North**<br>1410 V St<br>www.motel6.com<br>lawn walking area | 209-384-2181<br>800-466-8356 | (77)<br>$48–<br>$56 | C | OP |
| **Travelodge**<br>1260 Yosemite Pkwy<br>www.travelodge.com<br>lawn walking area | 209-722-6224<br>800-578-7878<br>each pet $10/day | (46)<br>$55–<br>$75 | CB<br>M/F | OP |
| **Vagabond Inn**<br>1215 R St<br>www.vagabondinn.com<br>1 block to park | 209-722-2738<br>800-522-1555<br>each pet $5/day | (76)<br>$46–<br>$48 | CB<br>M/F | |

## Mi Wuk Village

| | | | | |
|---|---|---|---|---|
| **Mi-Wuk Village Inn & Resort**<br>24680 Hwy 108<br>www.miwukvillageinn.com<br>log cabin-style rooms, 2 bdrm suites, woodsy area | 209-586-3031<br>800-549-7886<br>pet fee $20/day | (25)<br>$89–<br>$99 | CB<br>K | OP<br>T |

## Middletown

| | | | | |
|---|---|---|---|---|
| **Eagle & Rose Inn**<br>21299 Calistoga St<br>www.eagleandroseinn.com<br>dogs by manager's approval only, lawn walking area | 707-987-7330<br>pet fee $10/day | (17)<br>$49–<br>$85 | M/F | |

## Midpines

| | | | | |
|---|---|---|---|---|
| **Bear Creek Cabins**<br>6993 Hwy 140<br>www.www.yosemitecabins.com/site/index.html<br>woods and creek, close to trails | 209-966-5253<br>888-303-6993 | (5)<br>$89–<br>$129 | K | |
| **Homestead Guest Ranch**<br>mariposa.yosemite.net/homestead/<br>2 story guest house sleeps 7, breakfast supplies,<br>on 23 acres for walking dogs | 209-966-2820 or<br>209-742-2110 | (1)<br>$180–<br>$200 | K | |
| **Muir Lodge Motel**<br>6833 Hwy 140<br>dogs by manager's approval only, on 73 acres with<br>fire roads for walking dogs | 209-966-2468<br>pet fee $6/day | (27)<br>$39–<br>$49 | | |

| C = coffee  GP = guest pass to  L = lounge  CB = continental  fitness center  M = microwave  breakfast  IP = indoor pool  OP = outdoor pool  F = refrigerator  IS = in-room spa  R = restaurant  FB = full breakfast  K = full kitchen  S = sauna/steam  FR = fitness room  (k) = kitchenette  T = spa or hot tub | (# of units) & rates | food & drink | pool, sauna & hot tub |
|---|---|---|---|

## Midpines (continued)

| **Pimentel's B & B**  209-966-6847  6484 Hwy 140  www.pimentel.net  small dogs allowed with advance approval only,  afternoon tea, on 2½ acres of wooded hillsides | (3) $75–$95 | FB R | |

## Mill Creek

| **Childs Meadow Resort**  530-595-3383  41500 Hwy 36 East  888-595-3383  www.childsmeadowresort.com  each pet $5/day  rooms/cabins/2 bdrm chalets, one with private hot  tub, undeveloped walking area, ¼ mile to hiking trail | (26) $60–$175 | K | |
| **Fire Mountain Lodge**  530-258-2938  43500 Hwy 36 East  each pet $5/day  cabins sleep up to 4, closed in winter, woods, trails | (7) $60–$85 | K | |
| **Mill Creek Resort**  530-595-4449  1 Hwy 172  888-595-4449  www.millcreekresort.net  1–2 bdrm cabins sleep up to 6, woods, meadow,  trout stream, close to dirt roads and hiking trails | (9) $60–$85 | K | |

## Mill Valley

| **Acqua Hotel**  415-380-0400  555 Redwood Hwy  888-662-9555  www.acquahotel.com  complimentary pet magazines, lawn and walking  path, parks and waterfront area within 4 miles | (50) $119–$219 | CB M/F | FR |
| **Tam Valley B & B**  415-383-8716  508 Shasta Way  pet fee $10/day  www.tamvalley.net  dogs by advance approval only, cottage sleeps 4,  patio, garden, woodsy area, 10 minute walk to park | (1) $195 | CB M/F | |

| | | | | |
|---|---|---|---|---|
| **Travelodge** | 415-383-0340 | (50) | CB | IS |
| 707 Redwood Hwy | 800-578-8933 | $99– | R | |
| www.travelodge.com | pet fee $10/day | $119 | | |
| walking trails along marsh | | | | |

## Millbrae

| | | | | |
|---|---|---|---|---|
| **Clarion Hotel** | 650-692-6363 | (251) | R/L | OP |
| 401 E Millbrae Ave | 800-252-7466 | $89– | | T |
| www.clarionsfo.com | | $109 | | FR |
| small dogs only, garden, lawn, bayside walking path | | | | |
| **Westin Hotel–San Francisco Airport** | | (390) | F | IP |
| 1 Old Bayshore Hwy | 650-692-3500 | $119– | R/L | T |
| www.westin.com/sanfranciscoairport | 800-937-8461 | $209 | | FR |
| dogs under 40 lbs only, pet bed/bowls, bayfront path | | | | |

## Milpitas

| | | | | |
|---|---|---|---|---|
| **Best Value Inn** | 408-946-8383 | (80) | CB | IS |
| 485 S Main St | 888-315-2378 | $59– | M/F | |
| www.bestvalueinn.com | pet fee varies | $89 | | |
| dogs allowed with manager's approval only | | | | |
| **Best Western Brookside Inn** | 408-263-5566 | (78) | CB | OP |
| 400 Valley Way | 800-995-8834 | $49– | M/F | S |
| www.bestwesterncalifornia.com | pet fee $15/stay | $79 | | |
| large lawn walking area | | | | |
| **Candlewood Suites** | 408-719-1212 | (126) | C | OP |
| 40 Ranch Dr | 888-226-3539 | $59– | K | T |
| www.larkspurhotels.com | | $159 | | FR |
| pet fee $10/day plus $75 cleaning fee | | | | |
| studios/1 bdrm suites, 2 miles to park | | | | |
| **Embassy Suites Hotel** | 408-942-0400 | (266) | CB | IP |
| 901 E Calaveras Blvd | 800-362-2779 | $109– | M/F | T |
| www.embassysuites.com | pet fee $50/stay | $189 | | GP |
| 1 bdrm suites sleep 6, ¼ mile to park · | | | | |
| **Homestead Studio Suites** | 408-433-9700 | (153) | K | FR |
| 330 Cypress Dr | 888-782-9473 | $65– | | |
| www.homesteadhotels.com | pet fee $25/day | $125 | | |
| rooms with outside entrances, lawn walking areas | | | | |

| | | | | # of units & rates | food & drink | pool, sauna & hot tub |
|---|---|---|---|---|---|---|
| C = coffee | GP = guest pass to fitness center | L = lounge | | | | |
| CB = continental breakfast | IP = indoor pool | M = microwave | | | | |
| F = refrigerator | IS = in-room spa | OP = outdoor pool | | | | |
| FB = full breakfast | K = full kitchen | R = restaurant | | | | |
| FR = fitness room | (k) = kitchenette | S = sauna/steam | | | | |
| | | T = spa or hot tub | | | | |

## Milpitas (continued)

| | | | | | |
|---|---|---|---|---|---|
| **Inns of America–San Jose** | 408-946-8889 | (123) | CB | OP | |
| 270 S Abbott Ave | 800-826-0778 | $49– | M/F | GP | |
| www.innsofamerica.com | pet fee $10/stay | $79 | | | |
| large walking area, 2 miles to off-leash dog park | | | | | |
| **Residence Inn** | 408-941-9222 | (120) | FB | OP | |
| 1501 California Cir | 800-831-3131 | $119– | K | T | |
| www.marriott.com | pet fee $75/stay | $159 | | FR | |
| studios/1–2 bdrm suites, Mon–Thur beverages and light dinner, courtyard, short walk to park | | | | | |
| **Sheraton** | 408-943-0600 | (229) | C | OP | |
| 1801 Barber Lane | 800-325-3535 | $79– | R/L | T | |
| www.sheraton.com | | $179 | | | |
| grassy area, 5 miles to park | | | | | |
| **Towneplace Suites by Marriott** | 408-719-1959 | (145) | K | OP | |
| 1428 Falcon Dr | 800-257-3000 | $109– | | FR | |
| www.towneplacesuites.com | pet fee $35/stay | $129 | | | |
| studios/1–2 bdrm suites, 3 miles to park | | | | | |

## Modesto

| | | | | | |
|---|---|---|---|---|---|
| **Best Western Town House Lodge** | 209-524-7261 | (56) | C | OP | |
| 909 16th St | 800-772-7261 | $73– | M/F | T | |
| www.centralvalleybwhotels.com | each pet $10/stay | $79 | | | |
| **Days Inn** | 209-527-1010 | (100) | CB | OP | |
| 1312 McHenry Ave | 800-843-6633 | $84– | M/F | T | |
| www.daysinn.com | pet fee $10/day | $94 | | GP | |
| courtyard area for walking dogs, 5 blocks to park | | | | | |
| **Doubletree Hotel** | 209-526-6000 | (258) | C | OP | |
| 1150 9th St | 800-222-8733 | $69– | M/F | T | |
| www.modesto.doubletree.com | pet fee $20/stay | $169 | R | FR | |
| small well-behaved dogs only, lawn area for walking dogs, 6 blocks to park | | | | | |

| | | | | |
|---|---|---|---|---|
| **Economy Inn** 602 McHenry Ave next to walking trail along canal | 209-524-7374 | (28) $45–$55 | C M/F | OP |
| **Modesto Inn** 807 Needham St 1 block to park | 209-524-9641 pet fee $5/day | (60) $40–$50 | C M/F | |
| **Motel 6 North** 1920 W Orangeburg Ave www.motel6.com | 209-522-7271 800-466-8356 lawn and open field | (100) $57–$68 | C | OP |
| **Shivas Motel** 735 S 9th St lawn walking area, ¼ mile to park | 209-544-3054 pet fee $2.50/day | (33) $40–$55 | CB M/F | FR |
| **Travelodge** 722 Kansas Ave www.travelodge.com large lawn, 2 miles to park | 209-524-3251 800-578-7878 each pet $10/day | (99) $50–$60 | CB M/F | OP |
| **Vagabond Inn** 1525 McHenry Ave www.vagabondinn.com dog must be in travel kennel in room, ½ block to park | 209-521-6340 800-522-1555 pet fee $5/day | (98) $54–$75 | CB R | OP GP |

## Mojave

| | | | | |
|---|---|---|---|---|
| **Best Value Inn** 16352 Sierra Hwy www.bestvalueinn.com lawn and open desert area, 1 mile to park | 661-824-9317 pet fee $5/day | (24) $60–$80 | CB M/F | OP T |
| **Best Western Desert Winds** 16200 Sierra Hwy www.bestwesternmojave.com vacant lot for walking dogs, ¾ mile to park | 661-824-3601 800-528-1234 pet fee $10/stay | (51) $65–$75 | CB M/F | OP T |
| **Desert Inn** 1954 Hwy 58 www.mojavedesertinn.com open field, across street to park | 661-824-2518 800-305-1625 | (19) $42–$59 | CB M/F | |
| **Econo Lodge** 2145 Hwy 58 gravel area and open field, ½ block to park | 661-824-2463 each pet $6/day | (33) $40–$80 | FB | OP |

| C = coffee<br>CB = continental<br>breakfast<br>F = refrigerator<br>FB = full breakfast<br>FR = fitness room | GP = guest pass to<br>fitness center<br>IP = indoor pool<br>IS = in-room spa<br>K = full kitchen<br>(k) = kitchenette | L = lounge<br>M = microwave<br>OP = outdoor pool<br>R = restaurant<br>S = sauna/steam<br>T = spa or hot tub | (# of units)<br>& rates | food<br>& drink | pool, sauna<br>& hot tub |
|---|---|---|---|---|---|

## Mojave (continued)

| | | | | |
|---|---|---|---|---|
| **Mariah Country Inn**<br>1385 Hwy 58<br>www.mariahhotel.com<br>small dogs only, vacant lot, ¼ mile to park | 661-824-4980<br>866-627-4241<br>pet fee $10/stay | (50)<br>$78–<br>$81 | CB<br>M/F<br>R/L | OP<br>T<br>FR |
| **Motel 6**<br>16958 Hwy 58<br>www.motel6.com  open walking area, 2 miles to park | 661-824-4571<br>800-466-8356 | (121)<br>$45 | C | OP |
| **Palm Inn**<br>2128 Hwy 58<br>open desert area, next to park | 661-824-2214 | (15)<br>$35–<br>$40 | C<br>M/F | |
| **White's Motel**<br>16100 Sierra Hwy<br>open walking area | 661-824-2421<br>800-782-4596<br>pet fee $5/day | (50)<br>$42–<br>$52 | C<br>M/F | OP |

## Mokelumne Hill

| | | | | |
|---|---|---|---|---|
| **Hotel Leger**<br>8304 Main St<br>www.hotelleger.com<br>historic "haunted" inn, 1 block to park | 209-286-1401<br>pet fee $20/day | (13)<br>$55–<br>$125 | R | |

## Mono Hot Spring

| | | | | |
|---|---|---|---|---|
| **Mono Hot Springs Resort**<br>72000 Hwy 168<br>www.monohotsprings.com<br>rustic to modern 2 bdrm cabins, woods, hiking trails | 559-325-1710<br>each pet $5/day | (18)<br>$55–<br>$90 | K | T |

## Monrovia

| | | | | |
|---|---|---|---|---|
| **Aztec Hotel**<br>311 W Foothill Blvd<br>www.aztechotel.com<br>small dogs only, designated Route 66 Historic Hotel,<br>residential walking area, 3 blocks to park | 626-358-3231 | (44)<br>$75–<br>$125 | K<br>M/F<br>R | |

| | | | | |
|---|---|---|---|---|
| **Homestead Studio Suites** 930 S Fifth Ave www.homesteadhotels.com grassy walking area, ½ mile to large park | 626-256-6999 pet fee $75/stay | (122) $95– $105 | C K | GP |
| **Oak Tree Inn** 788 W Huntington Dr www.oaktreeinn.com 3 miles to park | 626-358-8981 888-306-0628 | (56) $55– $59 | CB M/F | OP T |

## Montara

| | | | | |
|---|---|---|---|---|
| **Farallone Inn** 1410 Main St www.faralloneinn.com Victorian inn, rooms have private entrances, decks, across street from beach | 650-728-8200 800-818-7319 pet fee $25/day | (9) $75– $195 | CB | IS |

## Monte Rio

| | | | | |
|---|---|---|---|---|
| **Village Inn** 20822 River Blvd www.villageinn-ca.com riverside lawn, 2 minute walk to dog-friendly beach | 707-865-2304 800-303-2303 pet fee $15/day | (11) $75– $195 | CB R/L | |

## Montecito

| | | | | |
|---|---|---|---|---|
| **San Ysidro Ranch** 900 San Ysidro Lane www.sanysidroranch.com cottages, private decks, evening wine reception, 540 acre resort with 17 miles of walking trails | 805-969-5046 800-368-6788 pet fee $100/stay | (38) $599 | CB M/F | OP FR |

## Monterey

| | | | | |
|---|---|---|---|---|
| **Bay Park Hotel** 1425 Munras Ave www.bayparkhotel.com walking trail, ¼ mile to park | 831-649-1020 800-338-3564 pet fee $20/day | (80) $99– $199 | C F R/L | OP T FR |
| **Best Western Beach Resort** 2600 Sand Dunes Dr www.montereybeachresort.com ground floor pet rooms, beachfront walking area | 831-394-3321 800-242-8627 pet fee $25/day | (196) $99– $389 | C F R | OP T FR |

| | | | (# of units) & rates | food & drink | pool, sauna & hot tub |
|---|---|---|---|---|---|
| C = coffee<br>CB = continental breakfast<br>F = refrigerator<br>FB = full breakfast<br>FR = fitness room | GP = guest pass to fitness center<br>IP = indoor pool<br>IS = in-room spa<br>K = full kitchen<br>(k) = kitchenette | L = lounge<br>M = microwave<br>OP = outdoor pool<br>R = restaurant<br>S = sauna/steam<br>T = spa or hot tub | | | |

## Monterey (continued)

| | | | | |
|---|---|---|---|---|
| **Best Western Victorian Inn**<br>487 Foam St<br>www.victorianinn.com<br>waterfront walking area along Cannery Row | 831-373-8000<br>800-937-8376<br>pet fee $35/stay | (12)<br>$165 | CB<br>F | T |
| **Carmel Hill Lodge**<br>1374 Munras Ave<br>www.carmelhilllodge.com<br>dogs under 20 lbs only, park-like area across street | 831-373-3252<br>pet fee $25/stay | (38)<br>$69–<br>$169 | CB<br>M/F | OP |
| **El Adobe Inn**<br>936 Munras Ave<br>www.el-adobe-inn.com | 831-372-5409<br>pet fee $10/day<br>across street to park | (26)<br>$49–<br>$129 | CB<br>M/F | T |
| **Fireside Lodge**<br>1131 10th St<br>www.montereyfireside.com<br>across street to park, ½ mile to dog-friendly beach | 831-373-4172<br>800-722-2624<br>pet fee $10–$20/day | (23)<br>$69–<br>$289 | CB<br>M/F | |
| **Hyatt Hotel & Resort**<br>1 Old Golf Course Rd<br>www.monterey.hyatt.com<br>lawn area, 5 blocks to park, 5 minute drive to beach | 831-372-1234<br>pet fee $50/stay | (500)<br>$250–<br>$375 | C<br>F<br>R | OP<br>T<br>FR |
| **Monterey Bay Lodge**<br>55 Camina Aguajito<br>www.montereybaylodge.com<br>rooms/suites sleep up to 4, across street to lake and dog-friendly park, close to dog-friendly beach | 831-372-8057<br>800-558-1900<br>pet fee $15/day | (45)<br>$69–<br>$259 | R | OP<br>T<br>GP |
| **Motel 6**<br>2124 Fremont St<br>www.motel6.com    small lawn, short drive to park | 831-646-8585<br>800-466-8356 | (52)<br>$76–<br>$95 | C | OP |
| **Resort 2 Me Lodging Reservations**<br>2600 Garden Rd<br>www.lodgingreservations.net<br>15 pet-friendly lodgings from motel rooms to resorts | 831-642-6622<br>800-757-5646<br>pet fee varies | (200)<br>$75–<br>$560 | | |

## Moreno Valley

| | | | | |
|---|---|---|---|---|
| **Econo Lodge** <br> 24412 Sunnymead Blvd <br> www.choicehotels.com <br> ¼ mile to park | 909-247-6699 <br> 800-424-6423 <br> each pet $5/day | (53) <br> $50– <br> $65 | CB <br> M/F | OP <br> T |
| **Regency Inn & Suites** <br> 24810 Sunnymead Blvd <br> small grassy walking area, short drive to park | 909-247-8582 <br> each pet $10/day | (34) <br> $50– <br> $65 | CB <br> M/F | OP |

## Morgan Hill

| | | | | |
|---|---|---|---|---|
| **Best Western Country Inn** <br> 16525 Condit Rd <br> www.bestwesterncalifornia.com <br> each pet $10–$20/day <br> lawn area, 2 miles to park, 5 miles to hiking trails | 408-779-0447 <br> 888-434-1444 | (83) <br> $65– <br> $78 | CB <br> F <br> R | OP |
| **Economy Inn** <br> 15080 Monterey St <br> dogs allowed in smoking rooms only, ½ mile to park | 408-779-5390 <br> pet fee $10/day | (24) <br> $49 | M/F | |
| **Residence Inn** <br> 18620 Madrone Pkwy <br> www.marriott.com <br> studios/1–2 bdrm suites, Mon–Thur beverages and <br> light dinner, pet relief area, 10 minute drive to park | 408-782-8311 <br> 800-331-3131 <br> pet fee $75/stay | (90) <br> $100– <br> $160 | FB <br> K | IP <br> T <br> FR |

## Morro Bay

| | | | | |
|---|---|---|---|---|
| **Adventure Inn, a Bayfront Inn** <br> 1150 Embarcadero <br> www.adventureinn.net <br> dogsitting service, bayfront walking area, close to <br> off-leash dog beach | 805-772-5607 <br> 800-799-5607 <br> each pet $10/day | (16) <br> $55– <br> $129 | CB <br> F | OP <br> T |
| **Best Value Inn** <br> 220 Beach St <br> small grassy walking area, 10 blocks to park | 805-772-3333 <br> pet fee $10/day | (33) <br> $49– <br> $129 | CB <br> M/F | |
| **Best Western El Rancho Motel** <br> 2460 Main St <br> www.bestwesterncalifornia.com   each pet $10/stay <br> yard and large vacant lot | 805-772-2212 <br> 800-628-3500 | (27) <br> $71– <br> $87 | C <br> F <br> R | OP |

| C = coffee<br>CB = continental<br>  breakfast<br>F = refrigerator<br>FB = full breakfast<br>FR = fitness room | GP = guest pass to<br>  fitness center<br>IP = indoor pool<br>IS = in-room spa<br>K = full kitchen<br>(k) = kitchenette | L = lounge<br>M = microwave<br>OP = outdoor pool<br>R = restaurant<br>S = sauna/steam<br>T = spa or hot tub | (# of units)<br>& rates | food<br>& drink | pool, sauna<br>& hot tub |
|---|---|---|---|---|---|

## Morro Bay (continued)

| | | | | |
|---|---|---|---|---|
| **Cabrillo Motel**<br>890 Morro Ave<br>www.cabrillomotel.com<br>sidewalks for walking dogs, 2 blocks to park | 805-772-4435<br>800-222-9915<br>pet fee $10/day | (23)<br>$69–<br>$149 | CB<br>M/F | T |
| **Days Inn**<br>1095 Main St<br>www.daysinn.com<br>lawn area, 2 blocks to harbor, ¾ mile to beach | 805-772-2711<br>800-247-5076<br>each pet $10/day | (58)<br>$79–<br>$235 | CB<br>F | T |
| **Morro Bay Sandpiper Keystone Inn**<br>540 Main St<br>www.morrobaysandpiper.com<br>vacant lot, 2 blocks to harbor | <br>805-772-7503<br>888-900-3629<br>pet fee $10/day | (21)<br>$55–<br>$169 | C<br>M/F | |
| **Motel 6**<br>298 Atascadero Rd<br>www.motel6.com<br>small grassy area, next to park | 805-772-5641<br>800-466-8356 | (70)<br>$46–<br>$81 | C | OP |
| **Pleasant Inn Motel**<br>235 Harbor St<br>www.pleasantinnmotel.com<br>small lawn, open field, 1 block to waterfront | 805-772-8521<br>888-772-8521<br>pet fee $10/day | (10)<br>$55–<br>$115 | C<br>K | |

## Mountain View

| | | | | |
|---|---|---|---|---|
| **Homestead Studio Suites**<br>190 East El Camino Real<br>www.homesteadhotels.com<br>courtyard and walking trail behind hotel | 650-962-1500<br>888-782-9473<br>pet fee $25/day | (133)<br>$55–<br>$105 | K | GP |
| **Residence Inn**<br>1854 W El Camino Real<br>www.marriott.com<br>studios/penthouses, Mon–Thur beverages and<br>light dinner, lawn walking area, 2 miles to park | 650-940-1300<br>800-331-3131<br>pet fee $75/stay | (112)<br>$159–<br>$184 | FB<br>K | FR<br>GP |

| Tropicana Lodge | 650-961-0220 | (60) | CB | OP |
| 1720 W El Camino Real | 888-961-0502 | $70– | M/F | S |
| www.tropicanalodge.net | | $105 | | |
| dogs by manager's approval only, grassy walking area, 1½ miles to off-leash dog park | | | | |

## Mt Laguna

| Laguna Mountain Lodge | 619-473-8533 | (29) | K | |
| 10678 Sunrise Hwy | pet fee $10/stay | $60– | | |
| www.lagunamountain.com | | $90 | | |
| 1–2 bdrm cabins sleep up to 6, national forest land | | | | |

## Mt Shasta

| A-1 Choice Inn | 530-926-4811 | (29) | C | OP |
| 1340 S Mount Shasta Blvd | pet fee $10/day | $59– | M/F | T |
| www.a1choiceinn.com | | $99 | | |
| small dogs only, open yard | | | | |

| Best Western Tree House Motor Inn | | (90) | FB | IP |
| 111 Morgan Way | 530-926-3101 | $95– | F | T |
| www.bestwesterncalifornia.com | 800-545-7164 | $103 | | |
| wooded area, 1½ miles to park | each pet $10/day | | | |

| Dream Inn | 530-926-1536 | (7) | FB | |
| 326 Chestnut St | 877-375-4744 | $80– | | |
| www.dreaminnmtshastacity.com | | $200 | | |
| large yard, 1 mile to park | | | | |

| Econo Lodge | 530-926-3145 | (20) | C | OP |
| 908 S Mount Shasta Blvd | 800-424-6423 | $39– | M/F | T |
| www.mtshasta-econolodge.com | pet fee $7/day | $89 | | |
| alley behind building to walk dogs, 3 blocks to trail | | | | |

| Finlandia Motel | 530-926-5596 | (23) | C | S |
| 1612 S Mount Shasta Blvd | each pet $10/stay | $39– | K | T |
| www.finlandiamotel.com | | $80 | | |
| small planting areas for walking dogs, 1 mile to park | | | | |

| Mountain Air Lodge | 530-926-3411 | (40) | CB | T |
| 1121 S Mount Shasta Blvd | pet fee $7/day | $50– | K | |
| rooms/suites, grassy walking area, 2 miles to park | | $80 | M/F | |

| C = coffee<br>CB = continental<br>breakfast<br>F = refrigerator<br>FB = full breakfast<br>FR = fitness room | GP = guest pass to<br>fitness center<br>IP = indoor pool<br>IS = in-room spa<br>K = full kitchen<br>(k) = kitchenette | L = lounge<br>M = microwave<br>OP = outdoor pool<br>R = restaurant<br>S = sauna/steam<br>T = spa or hot tub | (# of units)<br>& rates | food<br>& drink | pool, sauna<br>& hot tub |
|---|---|---|---|---|---|
| **Mt Shasta (continued)** | | | | | |
| **Mt Shasta Cabins**     530-926-5396<br>418 S Mount Shasta Blvd    pet fee $10/day<br>www.mtshastacabins.com<br>rustic cabins to 4 bdrm homes that sleep up to 12,<br>walking areas, near hiking, fishing, x-country skiing | | | (10)<br>$90–<br>$205 | K | T |
| **Mt Shasta Ranch B & B**    530-926-3870<br>1008 W. A. Barr Rd    each pet $10/stay<br>www.stayinshasta.com<br>rooms/suites/2 bdrm cottage, rural walking area | | | (10)<br>$60–<br>$115 | FB<br>K | |
| **Strawberry Valley Inn**    530-926-2052<br>1142 S Mount Shasta Blvd    pet fee $10/day<br>grassy walking area, 15 minute walk to park | | | (27)<br>$75–<br>$375 | CB<br>M/F | |
| **Swiss Holiday Lodge**    530-926-3446<br>2400 S Mount Shasta Blvd    pet fee $8/day<br>www.snowcrest.net/swissholidaylge<br>community kitchen, lawn and open field | | | (21)<br>$50–<br>$150 | CB<br>(k)<br>M/F | OP<br>T |
| **Myers Flat** | | | | | |
| **Myers Inn**    707-943-3259<br>12913 Avenue of the Giants    800-500-6464<br>www.myersinn.com    pet fee $25/stay<br>well-groomed dogs allowed by manager's approval<br>only, open field | | | (10)<br>$125–<br>$200 | CB | |
| **Napa** | | | | | |
| **Beazley House B & B Inn**    707-257-1649<br>1910 1st St    800-559-1649<br>www.beazleyhouse.com    pet fee $25/stay<br>dogs by advance approval only, lawn, gardens,<br>historic neighborhood for walking dogs | | | (11)<br>$180–<br>$375 | FB | IS |

| | | | |
|---|---|---|---|
| **Daughters Inn** 707-253-1331<br>1938 1st St 866-253-1331<br>www.daughtersinn.com pet fee $25/day<br>dogs allowed by advance approval only, lawn walking<br>area, 2 miles to dog park | (10)<br>$230–<br>$395 | FB | |
| **Discovery Inn** 707-253-0892<br>500 Silverado Trail each pet $15/day<br>www.napadiscoveryinn.com<br>small dogs by manager's approval, lawn walking area | (15)<br>$65–<br>$150 | C<br>M/F | |
| **Hillview Country Inn B & B** 707-224-5004<br>1205 Hillview Lane<br>www.hillviewinnnapa.com<br>dogs by advance approval only, lawn and private road<br>along vineyard for walking dogs | (4)<br>$125–<br>$200 | FB | OP<br>T |
| **Napa Inn B & B** 707-257-1444<br>1137 Warren St 800-435-1144<br>www.napainn.com pet fee $20/day<br>Queen Anne Victorian mansion, shady garden patio,<br>evening refreshments, 5 minute walk to park | (15)<br>$160–<br>$250 | FB | IS |
| **Napa River Inn** 707-251-8500<br>500 Main St 877-251-8500<br>www.napariverinn.com pet fee $25/stay<br>pet supplies, open field, 5 blocks to park | (66)<br>$159–<br>$459 | FB<br>F | T<br>GP |
| **Napa Valley Redwood Inn** 707-257-6111<br>3380 Solano Ave 877-872-6272<br>www.napavalleybudgetinn.com pet fee $10/stay<br>lawn and open field | (58)<br>$62–<br>$115 | CB<br>F | OP |

## Needles

| | | | |
|---|---|---|---|
| **AHC Temporary Housing and Vacation Rentals**<br>3520 Needles Hwy 702-813-4646<br>park model homes, desert walking area along river | (3)<br>$75–<br>$125 | K | |
| **Best Value Inn** 760-326-4501<br>1102 E Broadway St 888-315-2378<br>www.rf1102@frontiernet.net pet fee $5/day<br>shaded grassy walking area | (30)<br>$53–<br>$125 | CB<br>F | OP |

| C = coffee  GP = guest pass to  L = lounge<br>CB = continental  fitness center  M = microwave<br>breakfast  IP = indoor pool  OP = outdoor pool<br>F = refrigerator  IS = in-room spa  R = restaurant<br>FB = full breakfast  K = full kitchen  S = sauna/steam<br>FR = fitness room  (k) = kitchenette  T = spa or hot tub | (# of units) & rates | food & drink | pool, sauna & hot tub |
|---|---|---|---|

## Needles (continued)

| | (# of units) & rates | food & drink | pool, sauna & hot tub |
|---|---|---|---|
| **Best Western Colorado River Inn**  760-326-4552<br>2371 W Broadway  800-937-8376<br>www.bestwesterncalifornia.com<br>dogs in smoking rooms only, gravel walking area | (63)<br>$68 | C<br>M/F | IP<br>T |
| **Best Western Royal Inn**  760-326-5660<br>1111 Pashard St  800-937-8376<br>small dogs allowed in smoking rooms only | (50)<br>$68 | C<br>M/F | OP<br>S |
| **Fender's River Road Resort & Motel**<br>3396 Needles Hwy  760-326-3423<br>www.fendersriverroadresort.com  each pet $5/day<br>boat launch, grassy walking area along river | (9)<br>$55–<br>$65 | (k) | |
| **Motel 6**  760-326-3399<br>1420 J St  800-466-8356<br>www.motel6.com<br>lawn area, 3 blocks to park | (81)<br>$42–<br>$46 | C | OP |
| **Relax Inn**  760-326-4445<br>2208 Needles Hwy  each pet $5/day<br>dogs allowed in smoking rooms only, lawn walking<br>area, 2 miles to park | (25)<br>$36–<br>$46 | F | |
| **River Valley Motor Lodge**  760-326-3839<br>1707 W Broadway St  800-346-2331<br>2 blocks to park  pet fee $5/day | (30)<br>$30–<br>$35 | M/F | OP |
| **Royal Palms Motel**  760-326-3881<br>1910 Needles Hwy  each pet $5/day<br>grassy walking area, 1 mile to park | (38)<br>$25–<br>$35 | C<br>M/F | OP |
| **Travelers Inn**  760-326-4900<br>1195 3rd St<br>dogs in smoking rooms only, open field,<br>¼ mile to park | (119)<br>$55–<br>$95 | C<br>F | OP<br>T |

## Nevada City

| | | | | |
|---|---|---|---|---|
| **Flume's End B & B** | 530-265-9665 | (6) | FB | |
| 317 S Pine St | pet fee $30/day | $175– | (k) | |
| www.flumesend.com | | $195 | | |
| well-behaved dogs by advance approval, walking path | | | | |
| **Nevada City Inn** | 530-265-2253 | (27) | CB | |
| 760 Zion St | 800-977-8884 | $69– | K | |
| www.nevadacityinn.com each pet $10/day | | $160 | | |
| rooms/studio/2 bdrm cabins, park-like setting | | | | |
| **Outside Inn** | 530-265-2233 | (14) | C | OP |
| 575 E Broad St | pet fee $10/day | $69– | K | |
| www.www.outsideinn.com | | $150 | | |
| 1 small dog only, unique theme rooms, landscaped grounds, residential neighborhood, close to park | | | | |

## Newark

| | | | | |
|---|---|---|---|---|
| **E-Z8 Motel** | 510-794-7775 | (141) | C | OP |
| 5555 Cedar Ct | | $44 | F | T |
| www.ez8motels.com | | | | |
| residential streets for walking dogs | | | | |
| **Homewood Suites** | 510-791-7700 | (192) | FB | OP |
| 39270 Cedar Blvd | | $89– | K | T |
| www.homewoodsuites.com | | $109 | | FR |
| pet fee $10/day plus $50 cleaning fee | | | | |
| dogs under 40 lbs only, studios/1–2 bdrm suites, Mon–Thur beverages and appetizers, small field behind building, 1 mile to park | | | | |
| **Motel 6** | 510-791-5900 | (217) | C | OP |
| 5600 Cedar Ct | 800-466-8356 | $44– | | |
| www.motel6.com | | $52 | | |
| small dogs only, grassy area, 10 minute drive to park | | | | |
| **Residence Inn** | 510-739-6000 | (168) | FB | OP |
| 35466 Dumbarton Ct | 800-331-3131 | $79– | K | T |
| www.marriott.com | | $159 | | FR |
| pet fee $10/day plus $75 cleaning fee | | | | |
| studios/1–2 bdrm suites, Mon–Thur beverages and light dinner, lawn walking area, ½ mile to park | | | | |

| C = coffee      GP = guest pass to   L = lounge<br>CB = continental       fitness center   M = microwave<br>    breakfast     IP = indoor pool    OP = outdoor pool<br>F = refrigerator    IS = in-room spa    R = restaurant<br>FB = full breakfast   K = full kitchen     S = sauna/steam<br>FR = fitness room   (k) = kitchenette    T = spa or hot tub | (# of units)<br>& rates | food<br>& drink | pool, sauna<br>& hot tub |
|---|---|---|---|
| **Newark (continued)** | | | |
| **Towneplace Suites**         510-657-4600<br>39802 Cedar Blvd        pet fee $75/stay<br>www.towneplacesuites.com<br>studios/1–2 bdrm suites, lawn, short drive to park | (127)<br>$69–<br>$104 | (k) | OP<br>FR |
| **W Hotel Silicon Valley**      510-494-8800<br>8200 Gateway Blvd         877-946-8357<br>www.whotels.com/newark<br>      pet fee $25/day plus $100 cleaning fee<br>dogs under 80 lbs only, pet supplies, open field,<br>½ mile to waterfront, trails | (172)<br>$89–<br>$209 | M/F<br>R/L | OP<br>T<br>FR |
| **Woodfin Suites**            510-795-1200<br>39150 Cedar Blvd         888-433-9404<br>www.woodfinsuites.com    pet fee $50/stay<br>1–2 bdrm suites, Mon–Thur evening beverages and<br>appetizers, small grassy walking areas | (153)<br>$109–<br>$169 | FB<br>K | OP<br>T |
| **Newbury Park** | | | |
| **Clarion Palm Garden Hotel**    805-716-4200<br>495 N Ventu Park Rd       888-816-0002<br>www.palmgardenhotel.com<br>lawn area, 5 minute walk to park | (154)<br>$99–<br>$139 | FB<br>M/F | OP<br>T<br>FR |
| **Premier Inns Thousand Oaks**   805-499-0755<br>2434 W Hillcrest Dr        877-913-1191<br>www.premierinns.com<br>pet relief area, 1 mile to park | (128)<br>$40–<br>$50 | CB<br>M/F | OP<br>T |
| **Newport Beach** | | | |
| **Balboa Inn**              949-675-3412<br>105 Main St            877-225-2629<br>www.balboainn.com<br>      pet fee $50/1st day, $25 each additional day<br>lawn, boardwalk and beach for walking dogs | (34)<br>$139–<br>$429 | CB<br>F | OP<br>T<br>IS |

| | | | | |
|---|---|---|---|---|
| **Four Seasons Hotel** | 949-759-0808 | (295) | F | OP |
| 690 Newport Center Dr | 800-332-3442 | $340 | R/L | T |
| www.fourseasons.com/newportbeach | | | | FR |
| dogs under 25 lbs, lawn, short drive to dog park and dog-friendly beach | | | | |
| **Sutton Place Hotel** | 949-476-2001 | (435) | R/L | IP |
| 4500 MacArthur Blvd | 866-378-8866 | $129 | | T |
| www.suttonplace.com | pet fee $50/stay | | | FR |
| lawn area, 10 minute drive to off-leash dog park | | | | |

### Nipomo

| | | | | |
|---|---|---|---|---|
| **Kaleidoscope Inn** | 805-929-5444 | (4) | FB | |
| 130 E Dana St | 866-504-5444 | $125 | | |
| www.kaleidoscopeinn.com | large lawn | | | |

### North Fork

| | | | | |
|---|---|---|---|---|
| **South Fork Motel** | 559-877-2237 | (4) | C | |
| 57714 Road 225 | | $45– | F | |
| small gravel and grassy areas, 1 mile to park | | $55 | | |

### North Highlands

| | | | | |
|---|---|---|---|---|
| **Motel 6** | 916-973-8637 | (63) | C | |
| 4600 Watt Ave | 800-466-8356 | $57– | | |
| www.motel6.com    small courtyard, 2 miles to park | | $63 | | |

### North Hills

| | | | | |
|---|---|---|---|---|
| **Motel 6** | 818-894-9341 | (114) | | OP |
| 15711 Roscoe Blvd | 800-466-8356 | $56– | | |
| www.motel6.com    small lawn, 10 minutes to park | | $68 | | |

### North Palm Springs

| | | | | |
|---|---|---|---|---|
| **Motel 6** | 760-251-1425 | (96) | C | OP |
| 63950 20th Ave | 800-466-8356 | $46– | | |
| www.motel6.com    lawn, open desert, 4 miles to park | | $50 | | |

### Norwalk

| | | | | |
|---|---|---|---|---|
| **Motel 6** | 562-864-2567 | (55) | C | |
| 10646 Rosecrans Ave | 800-466-8356 | $59– | | |
| www.motel6.com | | $66 | | |
| small dogs only, grassy area, 1½ miles to park | | | | |

| C = coffee<br>CB = continental<br>    breakfast<br>F = refrigerator<br>FB = full breakfast<br>FR = fitness room | GP = guest pass to<br>    fitness center<br>IP = indoor pool<br>IS = in-room spa<br>K = full kitchen<br>(k) = kitchenette | L = lounge<br>M = microwave<br>OP = outdoor pool<br>R = restaurant<br>S = sauna/steam<br>T = spa or hot tub | (# of units)<br>& rates | food<br>& drink | pool, sauna<br>& hot tub |
|---|---|---|---|---|---|
| **Novato** | | | | | |
| **Inn Marin**<br>250 Entrada Dr<br>www.innmarin.com<br>lawn, 1 block to hiking trails, 5 miles to off-leash park | 415-883-5952<br>800-652-6565<br>each pet $20/stay | | (69)<br>$89–<br>$219 | CB<br>M/F<br>R/L | OP<br>T<br>FR |
| **Novato Days Inn**<br>8141 Redwood Blvd<br>www.daysinn.com<br>open field, 10 minute drive to off-leash dog park | 415-897-7111<br>800-329-7466<br>pet fee $10/day | | (57)<br>$59–<br>$119 | CB<br>R | OP<br>T<br>FR |
| **Travelodge**<br>7600 Redwood Blvd<br>www.travelodge.com<br>lawn walking area, 6 blocks to park | 415-892-7500<br>800-578-7878<br>each pet $10/day | | (55)<br>$59–<br>$109 | CB<br>M/F | OP<br>T<br>FR |
| **O'Brien** | | | | | |
| **Holiday Harbor**<br>20061 Shasta Caverns Rd<br>www.lakeshasta.com<br>houseboats sleep 6 to 16, shoreline for walking dogs | 530-238-2383<br>800-776-2628 | | (70)<br>$175–<br>$550 | K | |
| **Oak View** | | | | | |
| **Oakridge Inn**<br>780 Ventura Ave<br>www.oakridgeinn.com<br>small dogs only, lawn and open field, 4 blocks to<br>hiking trails | 805-649-4018<br>pet fee $10/day | | (33)<br>$60–<br>$295 | CB<br>K | OP<br>T |
| **Oakdale** | | | | | |
| **Holiday Inn**<br>950 East F St<br>www.holiday-inn.com<br>1 small dog allowed in smoking rooms only, small<br>lawn and vacant lot, ¼ mile to park | 209-847-7023<br>800-546-3516<br>pet fee $10/day | | (32)<br>$48–<br>$58 | CB<br>M/F | OP |

## Oakhurst

| | | | | |
|---|---|---|---|---|
| **Best Western Yosemite Gateway Inn** | | (123) | C | IP |
| 40530 Hwy 41 | 559-683-2378 | $49– | M/F | OP |
| www.bestwesterncalifornia.com | 800-545-5462 | $102 | R | T |
| natural park-like setting on 6 acres, | | | | FR |
| **Chateau Du Sureau** | 559-683-6860 | (11) | FB | OP |
| 48688 Victoria Lane | pet fee $75/stay | $410– | R | T |
| www.chateausureau.com | | $550 | | |
| clean well-behaved small to medium dog by advance approval only, pet treats/bowls, on 9 wooded acres | | | | |
| **Comfort Inn** | 559-683-8282 | (114) | CB | OP |
| 40489 Hwy 41 | 800-321-5261 | $60– | F | T |
| www.choicehotels.com | each pet $10/day | $90 | | |
| paved walking area, 4 blocks to trail, 6 blocks to park | | | | |
| **Pine Rose Inn B & B** | 559-642-2800 | (9) | FB | IS |
| 41703 Road 222 | 866-642-2800 | $95– | K | |
| www.pinroseinn.com | each pet $10/day | $179 | | |
| rooms/log cabins sleep up to 8, patios, small pet relief area across street, dirt road for walking dogs | | | | |
| **Sierra Sky Ranch Resort** | 559-683-8040 | (22) | CB | OP |
| 50552 Road 632 | pet fee $25/day | call | R | |
| dogs allowed in bunkrooms only, creek, meadow and wooded walking area | | for rates | | |

## Oakland

| | | | | |
|---|---|---|---|---|
| **Best Western Inn at the Square** | 510-452-4565 | (100) | C | OP |
| 233 Broadway | 800-633-5973 | $99– | M/F | FR |
| www.innatthesquare.com | pet fee $20/day | $129 | | |
| dogs under 25 lbs only, sidewalks for walking dogs, 2½ blocks to public square and meadow | | | | |
| **Hilton Oakland Airport** | 510-635-5000 | (365) | C | OP |
| 1 Hegenberger Rd | 800-445-8667 | $99– | F | FR |
| www.oaklandairport.hilton.com | | $159 | R/L | |
| dogs under 20 lbs only, courtyard and grassy area, 2 blocks to waterside trail, 5 minute drive to park | | | | |

| C = coffee  GP = guest pass to  L = lounge<br>CB = continental  fitness center  M = microwave<br>breakfast  IP = indoor pool  OP = outdoor pool<br>F = refrigerator  IS = in-room spa  R = restaurant<br>FB = full breakfast  K = full kitchen  S = sauna/steam<br>FR = fitness room  (k) = kitchenette  T = spa or hot tub | (# of units) & rates | food & drink | pool, sauna & hot tub |
|---|---|---|---|
| **Oakland (continued)** | | | |
| **Homewood Suites by Hilton**  510-663-2700<br>1103 Embarcadero  800-225-5466<br>www.homewoodsuites.com  pet fee $50/stay<br>Mon–Thur complimentary beverages and light<br>dinner, waterfront walking path | (132)<br>$109–<br>$139 | FB<br>K | OP<br>T<br>FR |
| **La Quinta Inn**  510-632-8900<br>8465 Enterprise Way  800-426-7866<br>www.lq.com<br>small dogs only, 5 minute drive to park | (148)<br>$89 | CB | OP<br>T |
| **Motel 6 Oakland Airport**  510-638-1180<br>8480 Edes Ave  800-466-8356<br>www.motel6.com<br>lawn area, 2 miles to park | (285)<br>$55–<br>$60 | C | OP |
| **Motel 6 Oakland Embarcadero**  510-436-0103<br>1801 Embarcadero  800-466-8356<br>www.motel6.com<br>lawn, waterfront park and walking path | (97)<br>$72 | C | T |
| **Trident Holdings Vacation Rentals & Sales**<br>5021 Woodminster Lane  510-632-4480<br>www.tridentholdings.com<br>condos/homes sleep up to 12, near mountain trails | (60)<br>$99–<br>$999 | K | T |
| **Occidental** | | | |
| **Inn at Occidental**  707-874-1047<br>3657 Church St  800-522-6324<br>www.innatoccidental.com  pet fee $25/day<br>2 bdrm suites, residential street and walking trails | (17)<br>$325–<br>$625 | FB<br>K | IS |
| **Negri's Occidental Hotel**  707-874-3623<br>3610 Bohemian Hwy  877-867-6084<br>www.occidentalhotel.com  pet fee $8/day<br>open field, 2 blocks to park | (26)<br>$59–<br>$119 | C<br>M/F<br>R/L | OP |

## Oceanside

| | | | | |
|---|---|---|---|---|
| **Best Western Marty's Valley Inn** 3240 Mission Ave www.bwmartys.com pet fee $10/day 1 mile to park, 2 miles to dog-friendly beach | 760-757-7700 800-528-1234 | (107) $89–$99 | CB M/F | OP T FR |
| **Econo Lodge** 1403 Mission Ave close to park | 760-721-6663 800-553-2666 | (79) $69–$79 | C | OP |
| **Motel 6** 3708 Plaza Dr www.motel6.com small grassy walking area | 760-941-1011 800-466-8356 | (136) $56–$70 | C | OP |
| **Motel 6 Downtown** 909 N Coast Hwy www.motel6.com small grassy walking area | 760-721-1543 800-466-8356 | (106) $66–$86 | C | OP |
| **Oceanside Inn & Suites** 1820 S Coast Hwy 1 block to dog-friendly beach | 760-433-5751 pet fee $15/day | (22) $69–$119 | K M/F | |
| **La Quinta Inn** 937 N Coast Hwy www.lq.com dogs under 25 lbs, pet relief area, 5 blocks to park | 760-450-0730 800-531-5900 | (39) $89–$99 | CB M/F | |

## Ocotillo

| | | | | |
|---|---|---|---|---|
| **Ocotillo Motel** 14 E Agate Rd small dogs in smoking rooms only, lawn, desert area | 760-358-7559 | (4) $37–$65 | C M/F | OP |

## Ojai

| | | | | |
|---|---|---|---|---|
| **Best Western Casa Ojai** 1302 E Ojai Ave small lawn, ½ mile to park | 805-646-8175 800-255-8175 each pet $10/day | (44) $72–$115 | CB M/F | OP T GP |
| **Blue Iguana Inn** 11794 N Ventura Ave www.blueiguanainn.com lawn, walking trail | 805-646-5277 pet fee $20/day | (12) $95–$229 | CB K | T |

| C = coffee  GP = guest pass to  L = lounge<br>CB = continental      fitness center  M = microwave<br>    breakfast  IP = indoor pool  OP = outdoor pool<br>F  = refrigerator  IS = in-room spa  R  = restaurant<br>FB = full breakfast  K = full kitchen  S  = sauna/steam<br>FR = fitness room  (k) = kitchenette  T  = spa or hot tub | (# of units)<br>& rates | food<br>& drink | pool, sauna<br>& hot tub |
|---|---|---|---|

## Ojai (continued)

| **Capri Motel**<br>1180 E Ojai Ave<br>www.ojaicaprimotel.com<br>lawn and walking trail | 805-646-4305<br>877-589-560<br>pet fee $5/day | (30)<br>$70–<br>$150 | CB<br>M/F | OP<br>T<br>IS |
|---|---|---|---|---|
| **Lavender Inn**<br>210 E Matilija St<br>www.moonsnestinn.com<br>dogs by manager's approval only, 1874 schoolhouse,<br>cottage with fenced yard, ½ block to park and trail | 805-646-6635 | (8)<br>$130–<br>$300 | FB | T |

## Olancha

| **Rustic Oasis Motel**<br>2055 S Hwy 395<br>rooms/cabin that sleeps 5, open desert area | 760-764-2209 | (10)<br>$30–<br>$60 | CB<br>K | |
|---|---|---|---|---|

## Old Station

| **Hat Creek Resort**<br>12533 Hwy 44 & 89<br>www.hatcreekresort.com<br>1–3 bdrm cabins, pet relief area, woods and creek | 530-335-7121 | (9)<br>$73–<br>$123 | K | |
|---|---|---|---|---|
| **Rim Rock Ranch**<br>13275 Hwy 89<br>www.rimrockcabins.com<br>rooms/cabins sleep up to 9, woods, trails near creek | 530-335-7114<br>pet fee $5/day | (10)<br>$45–<br>$105 | K | |

## Olema

| **Olema Inn & Restaurant**<br>10000 Sir Francis Drake Blvd<br>www.theolemainn.com<br>walking trails, 12 miles to dog-friendly beach | 415-663-9559 | (6)<br>$165–<br>$185 | CB<br>R | |
|---|---|---|---|---|

## Ontario

| | | | | |
|---|---|---|---|---|
| **AmeriSuites** 909-980-2200<br>4760 Mills Cir 800-833-1516<br>www.amerisuites.com pet fee $50/stay<br>dogs under 20 lbs only, grassy sidewalk areas,<br>3 miles to park | (125)<br>$99–<br>$134 | CB<br>M/F | OP<br>FR | |
| **Baymont Inn & Suites** 909-987-5940<br>4395 Ontario Mills Pkwy 877-229-6668<br>www.baymontinns.com<br>dogs under 50 lbs only, sidewalks, 2 miles to park | (105)<br>$99–<br>$139 | CB<br>M/F | OP<br>T<br>FR | |
| **Best Western Ontario Airport** 909-937-6800<br>209 N Vineyard Ave 800-937-8376<br>www.bestwesterncalifornia.com each pet $10/day<br>small dogs only, grassy walking area, 4 miles to park | (154)<br>$69–<br>$189 | CB<br>M/F | OP<br>T | |
| **Country Inn & Suites** 909-937-6000<br>231 N Vineyard Ave pet fee $50/stay<br>www.countryinns.com/ontarioca<br>rooms/2 bdrm suites, lawn area, 2 miles to park | (120)<br>$79–<br>$159 | CB<br>K<br>M/F | OP<br>T<br>FR | |
| **Doubletree Hotel–Airport** 909-937-0900<br>222 N Vineyard Ave<br>www.doubletree.com lawn, 5 miles to park | (484)<br>$99–<br>$172 | C<br>M/F<br>R/L | OP<br>T<br>FR | |
| **GuestHouse International Inn** 909-984-9655<br>1120 E Holt Blvd pet fee $10/day<br>dogs under 30 lbs only, lawn, vacant lot, close to park | (65)<br>$55–<br>$72 | CB<br>M/F | OP | |
| **Hilton Ontario Airport** 909-980-0400<br>700 N Haven Ave 800-445-8667<br>www.ontarioairport.hilton.com<br>dogs under 20 lbs only, sidewalks and grassy areas | (306)<br>$129–<br>$159 | C<br>F<br>R/L | OP<br>T<br>FR | |
| **Holiday Inn Airport** 909-466-9600<br>3400 Shelby St 800-642-2617<br>www.holiday-inn.com/ontarioca pet fee $25/stay<br>dogs under 25 lbs only, open walking area | (150)<br>$110–<br>$190 | FB<br>M/F | OP<br>T<br>FR | |
| **La Quinta Inn & Suites** 909-476-1112<br>3555 Inland Empire Blvd 800-531-5900<br>www.lq.com<br>dogs under 25 lbs only, open field, 2 miles to park | (144)<br>$95–<br>$135 | CB<br>M/F | OP<br>T<br>FR | |

| C | = coffee | GP | = guest pass to | L | = lounge |
|---|---|---|---|---|---|
| CB | = continental | | fitness center | M | = microwave |
| | breakfast | IP | = indoor pool | OP | = outdoor pool |
| F | = refrigerator | IS | = in-room spa | R | = restaurant |
| FB | = full breakfast | K | = full kitchen | S | = sauna/steam |
| FR | = fitness room | (k) | = kitchenette | T | = spa or hot tub |

## Ontario (continued)

| | | (# of units) & rates | food & drink | pool, sauna & hot tub |
|---|---|---|---|---|
| **Motel 6 Ontario East**<br>1560 E 4th St<br>www.motel6.com<br>pet relief area, ½ block to park | 909-984-2424<br>800-466-8356 | (59)<br>$50–<br>$60 | C | OP |
| **Nites Inn**<br>1801 East G St<br>www.nitesinnontario.com<br>dogs under 25 lbs only, grassywalking areas,<br>2 blocks to park | 909-983-3604<br>pet fee $10/day | (160)<br>$53–<br>$63 | CB<br>M/F | OP |
| **Ontario Airport Marriott**<br>2200 E Holt Blvd<br>www.marriott.com<br>grassy walking area, 2 block to park | 909-975-5000<br>pet fee $50/stay | (299)<br>$95–<br>$149 | C<br>F<br>R/L | OP<br>T<br>FR |
| **Red Roof Inn**<br>1818 E Holt Blvd<br>www.redroof-ontario-airport.com<br>1 dog under 80 lbs only, open field | 909-988-8466<br>800-733-7663 | (108)<br>$60–<br>$110 | C<br>M/F | OP<br>T |
| **Residence Inn–Ontario Airport**<br>2025 E Convention Center Way<br>www.residenceinn.com<br>     pet fee $6/day plus $75–$100 cleaning fee<br>pet relief area, cleanup bags, short drive to park | 909-937-6788<br>800-331-3131 | (200)<br>$149–<br>$179 | FB<br>K<br>M/F | OP<br>T<br>FR |
| **Sheraton Ontario Airport Hotel**<br>429 N Vineyard Ave<br>www.sheraton.com<br>10 minute drive to park | 909-937-8000<br>800-582-2946 | (164)<br>$99–<br>$225 | R | OP<br>T<br>FR |

## Orange

| | | (# of units) & rates | food & drink | pool, sauna & hot tub |
|---|---|---|---|---|
| **Crazy 8 Motel**<br>1300 E Katella Ave<br>lawn walking area | 714-639-2500<br>pet fee $10/day | (29)<br>$50–<br>$55 | M/F | OP |

| | | | | |
|---|---|---|---|---|
| **Days Inn** | 714-771-6704 | (28) | CB | T |
| 279 S Main St | 800-329-7466 | $67– | M/F | |
| www.daysinn.com | pet fee $20/stay | $79 | | |
| small dogs only, small grassy areas, 3 blocks to park | | | | |
| **Motel 6** | 714-634-2441 | (150) | | OP |
| 2920 W Chapman Ave | 800-466-8356 | $46– | | |
| www.motel6.com | | $56 | | |
| lawn walking area | | | | |

### Orick

| | | | | |
|---|---|---|---|---|
| **Green Valley Motel** | 707-488-2341 | (20) | C | |
| 120784 Hwy 101 | | $40– | M/F | |
| www.orick.net | | $50 | | |
| pet relief area, ¼ mile to walking trail | | | | |

### Orland

| | | | | |
|---|---|---|---|---|
| **Amber Light Inn** | 530-865-7655 | (40) | C | OP |
| 828 Newville Rd | each pet $5/day | $45– | M/F | |
| small dogs only, grassy walking area, ½ mile to park | | $52 | | |
| **Orland Inn** | 530-865-7632 | (40) | CB | OP |
| 1052 South St | 877-767-5263 | $48– | M/F | |
| www.orlandinn.com | each pet $5/stay | $53 | | |
| lawn area, 1 mile to park | | | | |

### Orleans

| | | | | |
|---|---|---|---|---|
| **Sandy Bar Ranch Riverside Cabins & Nursery** | | (4) | K | S |
| 797 Ishi Pishi Rd | 530-627-3379 | $68 | | |
| www.sandybar.com | | | | |
| cabins sleep up to 5, sauna and bathhouse, riverside | | | | |
| lawn, trails and quiet rural road | | | | |

### Oroville

| | | | | |
|---|---|---|---|---|
| **Best Value Inn** | 530-533-7070 | (69) | CB | IS |
| 580 Oro Dam Blvd East | 888-534-7282 | $59– | M/F | |
| www.bestvalueinnoroville.com | pet fee $6/day | $80 | | |
| open field, ¼ mile to park | | | | |
| **Budget Inn** | 530-533-2121 | (25) | M/F | |
| 1475 Feather River Blvd | pet fee $5/day | $38 | | |
| grassy walking area | | | | |

| C = coffee  GP = guest pass to  L = lounge<br>CB = continental    fitness center  M = microwave<br>   breakfast  IP = indoor pool  OP = outdoor pool<br>F = refrigerator  IS = in-room spa  R = restaurant<br>FB = full breakfast  K = full kitchen  S = sauna/steam<br>FR = fitness room  (k) = kitchenette  T = spa or hot tub | (# of units)<br>& rates | food<br>& drink | pool, sauna<br>& hot tub |
|---|---|---|---|

### Oroville (continued)

| **Comfort Inn**<br>1470 Feather River Blvd<br>www.choicehotels.com<br>dogs by advance reservation only, dirt field for<br>walking dogs, 5 minute walk to park and lake | 530-533-9673<br>800-626-1900<br>pet fee $5/day | (54)<br>$85–<br>$150 | CB<br>M/F | OP<br>S<br>T<br>FR |
| **Motel 6**<br>505 Montgomery St<br>www.motel6.com | 530-532-9400<br>800-466-8356<br>open field | (101)<br>$44–<br>$48 | C | OP |
| **Sunset Inn**<br>1835 Feather River Blvd<br>dogs allowed in smoking rooms only, lawn area | 530-533-8201<br>pet fee $7/day | (42)<br>$50–<br>$55 | CB<br>M/F | OP |

### Oxnard

| **Best Western Oxnard Inn**<br>1156 S Oxnard Blvd<br>www.bestwesterncalifornia.com<br>dirt walking area behind building, 5 blocks to park | 805-483-9581<br>800-937-8376<br>pet fee $20/stay | (105)<br>$85–<br>$120 | CB<br>M/F | OP<br>T<br>FR |
| **Casa Sirena Hotel & Marina**<br>3605 Peninsula Rd<br>www.casasirenahotel.com<br>all rooms have balconies, some with harbor views,<br>waterfront walking area and park | 805-985-6311<br>800-447-3529<br>pet fee $50/stay | (250)<br>$80–<br>$90 | C<br>M/F<br>R/L | OP<br>S<br>T<br>FR |
| **Regal Lodge Motel**<br>1012 S Oxnard Blvd<br>    pet fee $10/1st day, $4/each additional day<br>lawn walking areas | 805-486-8383 | (29)<br>$54–<br>$108 | M/F | |
| **Residence Inn**<br>2101 W Vineyard Ave<br>www.residenceinn.com<br>studios/penthouses sleep up to 5, Mon–Thur<br>beverages and light dinner, lawn, ½ mile to park | 805-278-2200<br>800-331-3131<br>pet fee $75/stay | (252)<br>$119–<br>$159 | FB<br>K | OP<br>T<br>FR |

| | | | | |
|---|---|---|---|---|
| **Vagabond Inn**   805-983-0251<br>1245 N Oxnard Blvd   800-522-1555<br>www.vagabondinn.com   pet fee $5/day<br>lawn walking areas, across street to park | (70)<br>$71–<br>$75 | CB<br>M/F | OP |
| **Wagon Wheel Motel**   805-485-3131<br>2751 Wagon Wheel Rd<br>rooms/suites sleep up to 3, small grassy areas | (85)<br>$54–<br>$130 | C<br>(k)<br>M/F | OP |

## Pacific Grove

| | | | | |
|---|---|---|---|---|
| **Andril Fireplace Motel**   831-375-0994<br>569 Asilomar Blvd   pet fee $14/day<br>www.andrilcottages.com<br>rooms/cottages sleep up to 14, private decks,<br>across street from state park | (20)<br>$78–<br>$149 | C<br>K | T |
| **Anton Inn**   831-373-4429<br>1095 Lighthouse Ave   888-242-6866<br>www.antoninn.com   pet fee $25/day<br>dogs under 40 lbs only allowed in newly remodeled<br>nonsmoking rooms with tile floors, ¼ mile walk to<br>dog-friendly beach | (11)<br>$100–<br>$250 | CB | |
| **Bide-A-Wee Inn**   831-372-2330<br>221 Asilomar Ave<br>www.bideaweeinn.com<br>    pet fee $10/day up to 50 lbs, $15/day over 50 lbs<br>1 block trail to off-leash dog beach | (19)<br>$59–<br>$149 | CB<br>M/F | |
| **Butterfly Grove Inn**   831-373-4921<br>1073 Lighthouse Ave   800-337-9244<br>www.butterflygroveinn.com   pet fee $20/day<br>rooms/suites, lawn, 4 blocks to dog-friendly beach | (29)<br>$79–<br>$299 | C<br>M/F | OP<br>T<br>IS |
| **Gate House Inn**   831-649-8436<br>225 Central Ave   800-753-1881<br>www.gatehouse-inn.com<br>small yard, paved bike path to dog-friendly beach | (8)<br>$100–<br>$225 | FB<br>M/F | |
| **Lighthouse Lodge & Suites**   831-655-2111<br>1150 Lighthouse Ave   800-858-1249<br>www.lhls.com   pet fee $25/day<br>nightly BBQ dinner, 1 block to dog-friendly beach | (60)<br>$79–<br>$189 | FB<br>M/F | OP<br>T |

| C = coffee   GP = guest pass to   L = lounge<br>CB = continental     fitness center   M = microwave<br>    breakfast    IP = indoor pool   OP = outdoor pool<br>F = refrigerator    IS = in-room spa   R = restaurant<br>FB = full breakfast   K = full kitchen   S = sauna/steam<br>FR = fitness room   (k) = kitchenette   T = spa or hot tub | (# of units)<br>& rates | food<br>& drink | pool, sauna<br>& hot tub |
|---|---|---|---|
| **Pacific Grove (continued)** | | | |
| **Olympia Motor Lodge**       831-373-2777<br>1140 Lighthouse Ave       888-745-6343<br>           pet fee $25/stay<br>¼ mile to walking trail, ½ mile to dog-friendly beach | (38)<br>$88–<br>$140 | CB<br>K | OP |
| **Sea Breeze Inn & Cottages**       831-372-7771<br>1100 Lighthouse Ave       800-525-3373<br>           each pet $25/day<br>dogs allowed in cottages only, small lawn, 2 blocks<br>to dog-friendly beach, parks within 1 mile, 10 minute<br>drive to off-leash beach | (34)<br>$99–<br>$149 | CB | |
| **Sea Breeze Lodge**       831-372-3218<br>204 Grove Acre Ave       800-525-3373<br>www.montereyinns.com       each pet $25/stay<br>small lawn, 2 blocks to dog-friendly beach, parks<br>within 1 mile, 10 minute drive to off-leash beach | (30)<br>$89–<br>$159 | CB<br>F | OP<br>T |
| **Pacifica** | | | |
| **Pacifica Motor Inn**       650-359-7700<br>200 Rockaway Beach Ave       800-522-3772<br>www.pacificamotorinn.com       each pet $10/day<br>½ block to beach access | (42)<br>$65–<br>$150 | CB<br>M/F | |
| **Palm Desert** | | | |
| **Best Western Palm Desert Resort**<br>74695 Hwy 111       760-340-4441<br>www.bestwesterncalifornia.com       800-231-8675<br>pet relief area | (152)<br>$59–<br>$169 | FB<br>F | OP<br>T<br>FR |
| **Casa Larrea Inn**       760-568-0311<br>73771 Larrea St       800-829-1556<br>www.casalarrea.com<br>uniquely decorated rooms with private patios,<br>vacant lot for walking dogs, 6 miles to dog park | (11)<br>$69–<br>$129 | CB<br>M/F | OP<br>T |

| | | | | |
|---|---|---|---|---|
| **Comfort Suites**  39-585 Washington St  www.palmdesertcomfort.com          pet fee $15/stay  large lawn and vacant lot, 2 miles to park and hiking  trails, 4 miles to dog park | 760-360-3337  800-517-4000 | (72)  $79–  $169 | CB  K  M/F | OP  IS  FR |
| **Desert Patch Inn**  73758 Shadow Mountain Dr  www.desertpatch.com  fenced lawn for walking dogs | 760-346-9161  800-350-9758 | (14)  $69–  $124 | CB  K | OP  T |
| **Fairfield Inn**  72322 Hwy 111  www.marriott.com  small dogs only, small lawn, 2 blocks to dog park | 760-341-9100  800-228-2800 | (112)  $69–  $159 | CB  M/F | OP  T  FR |
| **Inn at Deep Canyon**  74470 Abronia Trail  www.inn-adc.com          pet fee $10/day  greenbelt walking area, ¾ mile to dog park | 760-346-8061  800-253-0004 | (32)  $74–  $261 | CB  (k)  M/F | OP  T |
| **Motel 6**  78100 Varner Rd  www.motel6.com  small lawn, open desert area | 760-345-0550  800-466-8356 | (82)  $52–  $56 | C | OP |
| **Palm Desert Lodge**  74-527 Hwy 111  www.palmdesertlodge.com  dogs under 80 lbs only, vacant lot, 1 mile to trails | 760-346-3875  800-300-3875 | (31)  $49–  $139 | CB  K  M/F | OP  T |
| **Residence Inn**  38305 Cook St  www.residenceinnpalmdesert.com          pet fee $10/day plus $75 cleaning fee  Mon–Thur beverages and light dinner, lawn walking  areas, 10 minute drive to dog park | 760-776-0050  800-331-3131 | (130)  $109–  $229 | FB  K | OP  T  FR |

## Palm Springs

| | | | | |
|---|---|---|---|---|
| **A Place in the Sun Hotel**  754 E San Lorenzo Rd  www.aplaceinthesunhotel.com          pet fee $15/day  rooms/1 bdrm bungalows, private patios, lawn  walking area, ½ mile to dog park | 760-325-0254  800-779-2254 | (16)  $89–  $299 | CB  K | OP  T |

| C = coffee  GP = guest pass to  L = lounge |
| CB = continental       fitness center  M = microwave |
| breakfast  IP = indoor pool  OP = outdoor pool |
| F = refrigerator  IS = in-room spa  R = restaurant |
| FB = full breakfast  K = full kitchen  S = sauna/steam |
| FR = fitness room  (k) = kitchenette  T = spa or hot tub |

| | (# of units) & rates | food & drink | pool, sauna & hot tub |
|---|---|---|---|

## Palm Springs (continued)

| | | | |
|---|---|---|---|
| **Caliente Tropics Resort**  760-327-1391 | (90) | CB | OP |
| 411 E Palm Canyon Dr  866-468-9595 | $75– | M/F | T |
| www.calientetropics.com | $295 | GP | |
| pet fee $20/day for 1 dog, $30/day for 2 dogs | | | |
| pet supplies, residential streets for walking dogs, | | | |
| 3 miles to dog park | | | |
| **Casa Cody B & B**  760-320-9346 | (23) | CB | OP |
| 175 S Cahuilla Rd  pet fee $10/day | $59– | K | T |
| www.casacody.com | $149 | | |
| lawn walking area, 10 minute drive to park | | | |
| **Casa de Camero Hotel**  760-320-1678 | (9) | F | OP |
| 1480 N Indian Canyon Dr | $60– | | |
| dogs allowed by owner's approval only, mountain | $70 | | |
| views, vacant lot, 10 minute drive to dog park | | | |
| **Chase Hotel at Palm Springs**  760-320-8866 | (26) | CB | OP |
| 200 W Arenas Rd  877-532-4273 | $69– | (k) | |
| www.chasehotelpalmsprings.com  pet fee $10/day | $159 | | |
| great walking neighborhood, 1½ miles to dog park | | | |
| **Coyote Inn**  760-327-0304 | (7) | K | OP |
| 234 S Patencio Rd  pet fee $15/day | $79– | | IS |
| www.coyoteinn.net | $199 | | |
| small to medium dogs only, residential walking area, | | | |
| 2 miles to dog-friendly park | | | |
| **Del Marcos Hotel**  760-325-6902 | (16) | CB | IP |
| 225 W Baristo Rd  800-676-1214 | $109– | K | OP |
| www.delmarcoshotel.com  pet fee $15/day | $350 | L | |
| dogs allowed by manager's approval only, historic | | | |
| hotel, patios or balconies, landscaped grounds, | | | |
| 4 blocks to walking trail | | | |

| | Phone | (#) Rate | | |
|---|---|---|---|---|
| **Desert Fountain Inn** 1777 N Palm Canyon Dr www.desertfountaininn.com  pet fee $10/day dogs by manager's approval only, no children please, open October–June, private enclosed patios, small grass areas, 1½ miles to dog-friendly park | 760-323-0203 877-373-6864 | (14) $109– $229 | CB M/F | OP T |
| **Desert Riviera Hotel** 610 E Palm Canyon Dr  pet fee $10/day www.desertrivierahotel.com 3 miles to dog-friendly park | 760-327-5314 | (10) $75– $95 | CB K | OP T |
| **El Rancho Lodge** 1330 E Palm Canyon Dr  each pet $10/day www.elrancholodge.com pet bed/bowls, pet relief area, 2 miles to dog park | 760-327-1339 | (79) $59 | CB K F | OP T |
| **Hilton Palm Springs Resort** 400 E Tahquitz Canyon Way www.hiltonpalmsprings.com  pet fee $20/stay dogs under 80 lbs only, grassy walking areas, 1 mile to dog-friendly off-leash park | 760-320-6868 800-522-6900 | (260) $99– $259 | R | OP T FR |
| **Hotel California** 424 E Palm Canyon Dr www.palmspringshotelcalifornia.com  pet fee $15/stay small dogs by manager's approval only, residential walking area, 1½ miles to dog-friendly park | 760-322-8855 800-642-7079 | (17) $79– $250 | CB M/F | OP T |
| **Indian Palm Villa** 247 W Stevens Rd #7 well-behaved dogs by advance approval only, 2 bdrm condominium, patio, lawn walking area | 760-325-2269 | (1) $125– $275 | K | IP OP T |
| **La Mancha Villas & Spa Resort** 444 N Avenida Caballeros www.moonstonehotels.com  each pet $25/day 1–3 bdrm villas sleep up to 8, private pools or spas, 10 acres landscaped grounds, close to walking trails | 760-323-1773 866-673-7501 | (51) $129– $799 | R | OP |
| **Motel 6 Downtown** 660 S Palm Canyon Dr www.motel6.com small grassy area, short drive to dog-friendly park | 760-327-4200 800-466-8356 | (148) $46– $64 | C | OP |

| C = coffee　　GP = guest pass to　L = lounge<br>CB = continental　　　fitness center　M = microwave<br>　　breakfast　IP = indoor pool　OP = outdoor pool<br>F = refrigerator　IS = in-room spa　R = restaurant<br>FB = full breakfast　K = full kitchen　S = sauna/steam<br>FR = fitness room　(k) = kitchenette　T = spa or hot tub | (# of units)<br>& rates | food<br>& drink | pool, sauna<br>& hot tub |
|---|---|---|---|

### Palm Springs (continued)

| | | | |
|---|---|---|---|
| **Motel 6 East**　　　　　　　　760-325-6129<br>595 E Palm Canyon Dr　　　　800-466-8356<br>www.motel6.com<br>large grassy areas for walking dogs | (125)<br>$46–<br>$60 | C | OP |
| **Musicland Hotel**　　　　　　760-325-1326<br>1342 S Palm Canyon Dr　　　pet fee $3/day<br>dogs allowed in smoking rooms only, residential<br>walking area, 1 mile to dog-friendly park | (43)<br>$45–<br>$99 | (k)<br>F | OP<br>T |
| **Palm Grove Hotel**　　　　　760-323-4418<br>2135 N Palm Canyon Dr　　pet fee $10/day<br>all rooms face swimming pool, some have private<br>patios, open lot for walking dogs, 3 miles to park | (15)<br>$50–<br>$189 | F | OP |
| **Palm Springs Inn**　　　　　760-320-0705<br>2525 N Palm Canyon Dr　　pet fee $20/stay<br>lawn and open desert area | (25)<br>$35–<br>$45 | K | OP |
| **Palm Springs Riviera Resort**　760-327-8311<br>1600 N Indian Canyon Dr　　800-444-8311<br>www.psriviera.com　　　　pet fee $20/stay<br>dogs under 40 lbs only, lawn area | (475)<br>$79–<br>$229 | C<br>F<br>R | OP<br>FR |
| **Quality Inn Resort**　　　　760-323-2775<br>1269 E Palm Canyon Dr　　800-472-4339<br>2 acre park behind resort | (144)<br>$49–<br>$189 | C<br>M/F<br>R/L | OP<br>T |
| **Ramada Inn**　　　　　　　760-323-1711<br>1800 E Palm Canyon Dr　　800-245-6907<br>www.ramada.com　　　　pet fee $20/day<br>dogs under 25 lbs only, lawn, ½ mile to hiking trails | (255)<br>$60–<br>$170 | C<br>F<br>R/L | S<br>T<br>FR |
| **Resort at Palm Springs**　　760-320-2700<br>701 E Palm Canyon Dr　　　800-854-4345<br>lawn, 5 minute drive to park　pet fee $50/stay | (192)<br>$79–<br>$99 | C<br>F<br>R | OP<br>T |

| | | | | |
|---|---|---|---|---|
| **7 Springs Inn & Suites** <br> 950 N Indian Canyon Dr <br> www.www.7springs.info <br> rooms to townhouses, small lawn, ½ mile to park | 760-320-9110 <br> 800-585-3578 <br> each pet $15/day | (50) <br> $49– <br> $599 | CB <br> K <br> M/F | OP <br> T |
| **Stardust Motel** <br> 1610 S Via Entrada <br> residential walking area, 2 miles to dog-friendly park | 760-322-5057 <br> pet fee $10–$20/day | (10) <br> $45– <br> $55 | M/F | OP |
| **Super 8 Motel** <br> 1900 N Palm Canyon Dr <br> www.super8.com <br> vacant lot, 5 miles to dog park | 760-322-3757 <br> 800-800-8000 <br> pet fee $10/stay | (62) <br> $58– <br> $74 | C <br> F | OP <br> T |
| **Vagabond Inn** <br> 1699 S Palm Canyon Dr <br> www.vagabondinn.com <br> small dogs only, grassy area, short drive to park | 760-325-7211 <br> 800-522-1555 <br> each pet $10/day | (120) <br> $45– <br> $90 | CB <br> M/F | OP <br> T |
| **Villa Rosa Inn** <br> 1577 S Indian Trail <br> www.villarosainn.com <br> 1940s hacienda–style rooms/studios/1 bdrm suites <br> facing pool and patio, residential walking area | 760-327-5915 <br> pet fee $10/day | (6) <br> $89– <br> $165 | K | OP |
| **Village Inn** <br> 855 N Indian Canyon Dr <br> www.palmspringsvillageinn.com <br> rooms/1–2 bdrm suites, covered patio, grassy <br> walking areas, 1½ miles to dog park | 760-320-8622 <br> 866-320-8622 | (16) <br> $47– <br> $189 | CB <br> K <br> M/F | OP |
| **Wyndham Hotel Palm Springs** <br> 888 E Tahquitz Canyon Way <br> www.wyndham-palmsprings.com <br> small dogs allowed in smoking rooms only, vacant <br> lot, 1 mile to off-leash dog park, 2 miles to trails | 760-322-6000 <br> pet fee $35/stay | (410) <br> $79– <br> $279 | R/L | OP <br> T <br> FR |

## Palmdale

| | | | | |
|---|---|---|---|---|
| **E-Z8 Motel** <br> 430 W Palmdale Blvd <br> www.ez8motels.com <br> short drive to dog-friendly park | 661-273-6400 <br> pet fee $25/stay | (112) <br> $49– <br> $58 | C <br> F | OP <br> T |

| C = coffee<br>CB = continental<br>    breakfast<br>F = refrigerator<br>FB = full breakfast<br>FR = fitness room | GP = guest pass to<br>    fitness center<br>IP = indoor pool<br>IS = in-room spa<br>K = full kitchen<br>(k) = kitchenette | L = lounge<br>M = microwave<br>OP = outdoor pool<br>R = restaurant<br>S = sauna/steam<br>T = spa or hot tub | (# of units)<br>& rates | food<br>& drink | pool, sauna<br>& hot tub |
|---|---|---|---|---|---|
| **Palmdale (continued)** | | | | | |
| **Holiday Inn Palmdale Lancaster**   661-947-8055<br>38630 5th St W          800-465-4329<br>www.hipalmdale.com      pet fee $50/stay<br>dogs under 25 lbs only, lawn, 5 minute walk to park | | | (149)<br>$109 | M/F<br>R/L | OP<br>T<br>FR |
| **Motel 6**                661-272-0660<br>407 W Palmdale Blvd        800-466-8356<br>www.motel6.com<br>small grassy walking areas, 10 minute drive to park | | | (103)<br>$52–<br>$60 | C | OP |
| **Ramada Inn**           661-273-1200<br>300 W Palmdale Blvd        800-272-6232<br>www.ramada.com        pet fee $20/stay<br>small to medium dogs only, small grassy walking<br>area, 3 blocks to park | | | (131)<br>$75–<br>$116 | CB | OP<br>T |
| **Residence Inn**       661-947-4204<br>514 W Ave P/Rancho Vista Blvd    800-331-3131<br>www.marriott.com      pet fee $75/stay<br>1–2 dogs under 25 lbs only, Mon–Thur beverages<br>and light dinner, pet relief area, 5 miles to park | | | (90)<br>$145–<br>$180 | FB<br>K | IP<br>T<br>FR |
| **Palo Alto** | | | | | |
| **Crowne Plaza Cabana**    650-857-0787<br>4290 El Camino Real        800-227-6963<br>www.crowneplaza.com/cppaloalto   pet fee $25/stay<br>dogs under 25 lbs only, small grassy areas, trails | | | (194)<br>$129–<br>$169 | F<br>R/L | OP<br>T<br>FR |
| **Days Inn**              650-493-4222<br>4238 El Camino Real        800-329-7466<br>www.daysinnpaloalto.com     each pet $10/day<br>3 miles to shoreline park | | | (23)<br>$79 | CB<br>M/F | T |

| | | | | |
|---|---|---|---|---|
| **Garden Court Hotel** 520 Cowper St www.gardencourt.com dogs under 20 lbs by manager's approval, pet supplies, walking map to local dog-friendly parks | 650-322-9000 800-824-9028 pet fee $50/stay | (62) $299– $599 | CB | |
| **Motel 6** 4301 El Camino Real www.motel6.com small grassy areas, ¼ mile to park | 650-949-0833 800-466-8356 | (72) $52– $66 | C | OP |
| **Palo Alto Travelodge** 3255 El Camino Real www.travelodge.com small dogs only, 2 blocks to park | 650-493-6340 800-578-7878 pet fee $30/stay | (30) $80– $90 | CB M/F | OP |
| **Quality Inn** 3901 El Camino Real www.qistanford.com | 650-493-2760 pet fee $15/stay residential walking area | (54) $70– $75 | CB M/F | GP |
| **Sheraton** 625 El Camino Real phmhotels.com/sheratonpa.html dogs up to 80 lbs only, Stanford campus across street | 650-328-2800 800-325-3535 | (346) $129– $309 | M/F R/L | OP FR |
| **Stanford Motor Inn** 3305 El Camino Real dogs by manager's approval only, 1 block to park | 650-493-3153 each pet $20/stay | (35) $69 | CB M/F | OP |
| **Westin Hotel** 675 El Camino Real www.westin.com/paloalto dogs under 90 lbs only, small lawn, 5 minutes to park | 650-321-4422 800-937-8461 | (188) $189– $289 | F R/L | OP T FR |

### Palomar Mountain

| | | | | |
|---|---|---|---|---|
| **Bailey's Palomar Resort** 33691 Bailey Meadow Rd www.baileyspalomarresort.com historic cabins/house, 60 acres, meadow and woods | 760-742-1859 | (25) $100– $125 | K | |

### Paradise

| | | | | |
|---|---|---|---|---|
| **Comfort Inn** 5475 Clark Rd www.meyercrest.com on 10 wooded acres with walking paths | 530-876-0191 800-626-1900 pet fee $10/day | (62) $67– $80 | CB M/F | OP T FR |

| C = coffee<br>CB = continental<br>  breakfast<br>F = refrigerator<br>FB = full breakfast<br>FR = fitness room | GP = guest pass to<br>  fitness center<br>IP = indoor pool<br>IS = in-room spa<br>K = full kitchen<br>(k) = kitchenette | L = lounge<br>M = microwave<br>OP = outdoor pool<br>R = restaurant<br>S = sauna/steam<br>T = spa or hot tub | (# of units)<br>& rates | food<br>& drink | pool, sauna<br>& hot tub |
|---|---|---|---|---|---|

### Paradise (continued)

| | | | | | |
|---|---|---|---|---|---|
| **Lantern Inn**<br>5799 Wildwood Lane<br>www.now2000.com/lantern/<br>vacant lot, 3 blocks to walking trail and park | | 530-877-5553<br>pet fee $10/day | (16)<br>$60–<br>$75 | CB<br>M/F | OP |
| **Paradise Inn**<br>5423 Skyway<br>pet relief area, 1 mile to park | | 530-877-2127<br>each pet $10/day | (17)<br>$49–<br>$79 | C<br>M/F | OP |
| **Paulson's Motel**<br>6445 Pentz Rd<br>1 dog only, grassy walking areas along stream | | 530-877-2379<br>pet fee $5/day | (8)<br>$60 | C<br>(k) | |
| **Ponderosa Gardens Motel**<br>7010 Skyway<br>www.now2000.com/ponderosa<br>open field, 1 block to park | | 530-872-9094<br>888-727-3423<br>pet fee $6/day | (48)<br>$68–<br>$95 | CB<br>M/F | OP<br>T |

### Parker Dam

| | | | | | |
|---|---|---|---|---|---|
| **Big Bend Resort**<br>501 Parker Dam Rd<br>small dogs only, rooms/trailers/cabins sleep up to 8,<br>waterfront walking area | | 760-663-3755 | (22)<br>$75–<br>$200 | K<br>R | |

### Pasadena

| | | | | | |
|---|---|---|---|---|---|
| **Quality Inn**<br>3321 E Colorado Blvd<br>www.qualityinn.com<br>dogs allowed in smoking rooms only, 1 mile to park | | 626-796-9291<br>pet fee $10/day | (70)<br>$53–<br>$81 | CB<br>F | OP<br>S<br>T |
| **Ritz-Carlton Huntington Hotel**<br>1401 S Oak Knoll Ave<br>www.ritz-carlton.com<br>dogs under 30 lbs only, on 25 acres, gardens, lawn | | 626-568-3900<br>pet fee $125/stay | (400)<br>$189–<br>$290 | F<br>R/L | OP<br>T |

| | | | | |
|---|---|---|---|---|
| **Sheraton** 626-449-4000<br>303 Cordova St<br>www.sheratonpasadena.com<br>dogs under 60 lbs, small lawn, 1 mile to park | (317)<br>$129–<br>$189 | R/L | OP<br>FR |
| **Super 8 Motel** 626-449-3020<br>2863 E Colorado Blvd 800-800-8000<br>www.super8.com pet fee $10/day<br>dogs under 10 lbs in smoking rooms, 2 miles to park | (70)<br>$56–<br>$59 | CB<br>M/F | OP |
| **Vagabond Inn** 626-449-3170<br>1203 E Colorado Blvd 800-522-1555<br>www.vagabondinn.com each pet $10/day<br>dogs under 50 lbs only, lawn area, 2 miles to park | (54)<br>$65–<br>$95 | CB<br>M/F | OP<br>GP |
| **Westin Hotel** 626-792-2727<br>191 N Los Robles Ave<br>www.westin.com/pasadena<br>dogs under 80 lbs only, pet bowls/beds, 3 blocks to<br>park, list of local dog-friendly parks and trails | (350)<br>$139–<br>$169 | F<br>R/L | OP<br>FR |
| **Westway Inn** 626-304-9678<br>1599 E Colorado Blvd pet fee $10/day<br>dogs allowed in smoking rooms only, residential area | (61)<br>$63 | CB<br>F | OP |

## Paso Robles

| | | | | |
|---|---|---|---|---|
| **Dancing Horse Ranch & Retreat** 805-237-2900<br>www.dancinghorse.net pet fee $15/day<br>well-behaved dogs by advance approval only, lodge<br>sleeps 24, cottages sleep 6, deck, waterfalls, 41 acres<br>woods, meadows and trails, horse boarding available | (3)<br>$175–<br>$650 | CB<br>K | T |
| **Farmhouse Motel** 805-238-1720<br>425 Spring St each pet $5/day<br>small lawn walking areas, 5 blocks to park | (24)<br>$35–<br>$65 | M/F | |
| **Hampton Inn** 805-226-9988<br>212 Alexa Ct<br>www.hamptoninn.com<br>dogs under 20 lbs only, lawn and field | (81)<br>$105–<br>$125 | CB<br>M/F | OP<br>T<br>FR |
| **Motel 6** 805-239-9090<br>1134 Black Oak Dr 800-466-8356<br>www.motel6.com<br>small lawn, 12 blocks to park | (121)<br>$46–<br>$63 | C | OP |

| C = coffee<br>CB = continental<br>    breakfast<br>F = refrigerator<br>FB = full breakfast<br>FR = fitness room | GP = guest pass to<br>    fitness center<br>IP = indoor pool<br>IS = in-room spa<br>K = full kitchen<br>(k) = kitchenette | L = lounge<br>M = microwave<br>OP = outdoor pool<br>R = restaurant<br>S = sauna/steam<br>T = spa or hot tub | (# of units)<br>& rates | food<br>& drink | pool, sauna<br>& hot tub |
|---|---|---|---|---|---|

## Paso Robles (continued)

| | | | | |
|---|---|---|---|---|
| **Travelodge**<br>2701 Spring St<br>www.travelodge.com<br>pet relief area, 2 miles to park | 805-238-0078<br>pet fee $10/day | (31)<br>$59–<br>$129 | C<br>M/F | OP |

## Pearblossom

| | | | | |
|---|---|---|---|---|
| **Pearblossom Motel**<br>13250 Pearblossom Hwy<br>open desert walking area | 661-944-3565<br>pet fee $10/day | (6)<br>$45 | C<br>M/F | OP |

## Pebble Beach

| | | | | |
|---|---|---|---|---|
| **Lodge at Pebble Beach**<br>1700 17 Mile Dr<br>www.pebblebeach.com<br>lawn, dog-friendly beach | 831-624-3811<br>800-654-9300 | (169)<br>$555–<br>$755 | C<br>M/F<br>R/L | OP<br>T<br>FR |

## Pescadero

| | | | | |
|---|---|---|---|---|
| **Pescadero Lodging**<br>www.pescaderolodging.com<br>cabin sleeps 6, large deck, wooded walking area,<br>5 miles to ocean, close to hiking trails | 650-879-0868 | (1)<br>$150–<br>$250 | K | |

## Petaluma

| | | | | |
|---|---|---|---|---|
| **Motel 6**<br>1368 N McDowell Blvd<br>www.motel6.com<br>lawn area, 2 miles to park | 707-765-0333<br>800-466-8356 | (121)<br>$46–<br>$66 | C | OP |
| **Quality Inn**<br>5100 Montero Way<br>www.lokhotels.com<br>grassy area, close to walking trails, 3 miles to park | 707-664-1155<br>pet fee $15/day | (109)<br>$95–<br>$200 | CB<br>M/F | OP<br>T<br>FR |

## Phelan

| | | | | |
|---|---|---|---|---|
| **Best Western Cajon Pass Inn** | 760-249-6777 | (46) | CB | OP |
| 8317 Hwy 138 | 866-292-2566 | $65– | M/F | T |
| www.bestwesterncalifornia.com | | $100 | | |
| dogs under 10 lbs only, gravel walking area | | | | |

## Philo

| | | | |
|---|---|---|---|
| **Anderson Valley Inn** | 707-895-3325 | (7) | K |
| 8480 Hwy 128 | pet fee $20/stay | $85– | |
| www.avinn.com | | $100 | |
| rooms/cabins, rural road, 3 miles to state park | | | |

| | | | |
|---|---|---|---|
| **Philo Pottery Inn** | 707-895-3069 | (5) | FB |
| 8550 Hwy 128 | pet fee $15/day | $140 | |
| www.philopotteryinn.com | | | |
| dogs by advance approval, near river and state park | | | |

## Pico Rivera

| | | | | |
|---|---|---|---|---|
| **Days Inn** | 562-942-1003 | (100) | F | OP |
| 6540 Rosemead Blvd | 800-329-7466 | $50 | R/L | T |
| www.daysinnpicorivera.com | pet fee $8/day | | | |
| lawn walking area, 1 mile to park | | | | |

## Pine Grove

| | | | | |
|---|---|---|---|---|
| **Pine Acres Resort** | 209-296-4650 | (8) | C | OP |
| 13026 Tabeau Rd | each pet $5/day | $49– | (k) | |
| www.volcano.net/~pineacre | | $54 | | |
| motel rooms, woods and trails, close to small park | | | | |

## Pine Mountain

| | | | |
|---|---|---|---|
| **Jennings Resort Rentals** | 661-242-6100 | (18) | K |
| 16218 Mil Potrero Hwy | 800-747-1772 | $110– | |
| www.jenningsresortrentals.com | | $120 | |
| pet-friendly 3 bdrm cabin, woods and hiking trails | | | |

## Pine Valley

| | | | |
|---|---|---|---|
| **Pine Valley Inn** | 619-473-8560 | (22) | M/F |
| 28944 Old Hwy 80 | pet fee $10/day | $50– | |
| www.pinevalleyinn.com | | $60 | |
| meadow, trails, near park | | | |

| C = coffee<br>CB = continental<br>    breakfast<br>F = refrigerator<br>FB = full breakfast<br>FR = fitness room | GP = guest pass to<br>    fitness center<br>IP = indoor pool<br>IS = in-room spa<br>K = full kitchen<br>(k) = kitchenette | L = lounge<br>M = microwave<br>OP = outdoor pool<br>R = restaurant<br>S = sauna/steam<br>T = spa or hot tub | (# of units)<br>& rates | food<br>& drink | pool, sauna<br>& hot tub |
|---|---|---|---|---|---|
| **Pinecrest** | | | | | |
| **Pinecrest Chalet Resort**<br>500 Dodge Ridge Rd<br>www.pinecrestchalet.com<br>dogs by advance approval only, cabins/townhouses,<br>wooded walking area | 209-965-3276<br>pet fee $20/stay | | (24)<br>$55–<br>$150 | K | OP |
| **Pinole** | | | | | |
| **Motel 6**<br>1501 Fitzgerald Dr<br>www.motel6.com<br>grassy walking area | 510-222-8174<br>800-466-8356 | | (101)<br>$56–<br>$69 | C | OP |
| **Pioneertown** | | | | | |
| **Pioneertown Motel**<br>5040 Curtis Rd<br>open desert walking area | 760-365-4879<br>pet fee $10/day | | (19)<br>$70 | C<br>M/F | |
| **Rimrock Ranch Cabins**<br>50857 Burns Canyon Rd<br>www.rimrockranchcabins.com<br>1–2 dogs only, 1–2 bdrm cabins with courtyards, pet<br>supplies, 35 acres of high desert, walking paths | 760-228-1297<br>each pet $10/day | | (4)<br>$100–<br>$150 | K | OP |
| **Piru** | | | | | |
| **Heritage Valley Inn**<br>691 N Main St<br>www.heritagevalleyinn.com<br>small dogs only, 3 blocks to park | 805-521-0700 | | (10)<br>$130–<br>$185 | R | |
| **Pismo Beach** | | | | | |
| **Adams Motel**<br>1000 Dolliver St<br>dogs allowed in summer only, 1–2 bdrm units,<br>patio, large yard for walking dogs | 805-773-2065<br>pet fee $20/day | | (12)<br>$50–<br>$95 | C<br>K<br>M/F | |

| | | | | |
|---|---|---|---|---|
| **Cliffs Resort** <br> 2757 Shell Beach Rd <br> www.cliffsresort.com <br> dogs allowed in ground floor rooms with outside <br> entrances, lawn and private beach | 805-773-5000 <br> 800-826-7827 | (165) <br> $199– <br> $399 | FB <br> F <br> R/L | OP <br> S <br> T <br> FR |
| **Cottage Inn by the Sea** <br> 2351 Price St <br> www.cottage-inn.com <br> lawn and gardens, close to dog-friendly beach | 805-773-4617 <br> 800-440-8400 <br> each pet $10/day | (80) <br> $99– <br> $269 | CB <br> M/F | OP <br> T |
| **Motel 6** <br> 860 4th St <br> www.motel6.com <br> grassy walking area, 4 miles to dog-friendly beach | 805-773-2665 <br> 800-466-8356 | (136) <br> $54– <br> $74 | C | OP |
| **Oxford Suites** <br> 651 Five Cities Dr <br> www.oxfordsuites.com <br> dogs under 50 lbs only, beverages and appetizers, <br> small grassy area, 1½ miles to dog-friendly beach | 805-773-3773 <br> 800-982-7848 <br> pet fee $5/day | (133) <br> $89– <br> $179 | FB <br> M/F | OP <br> T |
| **Sandcastle Inn** <br> 100 Stimson Ave <br> www.sandcastleinn.com <br> dog-friendly beachfront walking area | 805-773-2422 <br> 800-822-6606 <br> each pet $10/day | (75) <br> $169– <br> $269 | CB <br> F | T |
| **Sea Gypsy Motel** <br> 1020 Cypress St <br> www.seagypsymotel.com <br> beachfront walking area | 805-773-1801 <br> 800-592-5923 <br> each pet $15/day | (77) <br> $50– <br> $200 | C <br> K | OP <br> T |
| **Shell Beach Motel** <br> 653 Shell Beach Rd <br> www.shellbeachmotel.com <br> 2½ blocks to dog-friendly beach | 805-773-4373 <br> 800-549-4727 <br> pet fee $15/day | (10) <br> $59– <br> $159 | C <br> M/F | OP |
| **Spyglass Inn** <br> 2705 Spyglass Dr <br> www.spyglassinn.com <br> 1 block to dog-friendly beach | 805-773-4855 <br> 800-824-2612 <br> pet fee $10/day | (82) <br> $119– <br> $179 | C <br> F <br> R/L | OP <br> T |

| C = coffee  CB = continental  breakfast  F = refrigerator  FB = full breakfast  FR = fitness room | GP = guest pass to fitness center  IP = indoor pool  IS = in-room spa  K = full kitchen  (k) = kitchenette | L = lounge  M = microwave  OP = outdoor pool  R = restaurant  S = sauna/steam  T = spa or hot tub | (# of units) & rates | food & drink | pool, sauna & hot tub |
|---|---|---|---|---|---|

## Pittsburg

| Motel 6 | 925-427-1600 | (180) | C | OP |
|---|---|---|---|---|
| 2101 Loveridge Rd | 800-466-8356 | $52 | | |
| www.motel6.com | small walking areas, near parks | | | |

## Placentia

| Residence Inn | 714-996-0555 | (112) | FB | OP |
|---|---|---|---|---|
| 700 W Kimberly Ave | 800-331-3131 | $99– | K | T |
| www.marriott.com | pet fee $75/stay | $159 | | FR |
| 1–2 dogs only, Mon–Wed beverages and light dinner, pet relief area, short drive to park | | | | |

## Placerville

| Best Western Placerville Inn | 530-622-9100 | (107) | CB | OP |
|---|---|---|---|---|
| 6850 Green Leaf Dr | 800-854-9100 | $90– | M/F | T |
| www.placervilleinn.com | pet fee $20/day | $110 | R | FR |
| open walking area | | | | |

| Gold Trail Motor Lodge | 530-622-2906 | (24) | C | |
|---|---|---|---|---|
| 1970 Broadway | | $48– | | |
| lawn walking area | | $58 | | |

| Hangtown Motel | 530-622-0637 | (10) | C | |
|---|---|---|---|---|
| 1676 Broadway | pet fee $5/day | $45 | F | |
| dogs allowed in smoking rooms only, open field | | | | |

| Mother Lode Motel | 530-622-0895 | (21) | C | OP |
|---|---|---|---|---|
| 1940 Broadway | each pet $10/day | $52– | M/F | IS |
| vacant lot, 10 miles to park | | $68 | | |

## Pleasant Hill

| Residence Inn | 925-689-1010 | (126) | CB | OP |
|---|---|---|---|---|
| 700 Ellinwood Way | 800-331-3131 | $129– | K | T |
| www.marriott.com | pet fee $75/stay | $219 | | FR |
| studios/1–2 bdrm suites, Mon–Thur beverages and light dinner, pet relief area, 1 mile to park | | | | |

| | | | | |
|---|---|---|---|---|
| **Summerfield Suites** | 925-934-3343 | (142) | FB | OP |
| 2611 Contra Costa Blvd | 800-996-3426 | $109– | (k) | T |
| www.wyndham.com | pet fee $100–$200/stay | $199 | | FR |
| dogs under 75 lbs only, studios/1–2 bdrm suites, grassy walking area, 1 block to jogging trail | | | | |

### Pleasanton

| | | | | |
|---|---|---|---|---|
| **Crowne Plaza** | 925-847-6000 | (244) | C | OP |
| 11950 Dublin Canyon Rd | each pet $50/stay | $79– | F | T |
| www.crowneplaza.com | | $144 | R/L | FR |
| dogs allowed in first floor smoking rooms only, lawn, walking path | | | | |
| **Guest House Inn & Suites** | 925-846-2742 | (34) | CB | OP |
| 2025 Santa Rita Rd | pet fee $10/day | $59– | M/F | |
| www.guesthouseintl.com | | $79 | | |
| dogs by manager's approval only, park across street | | | | |
| **Motel 6** | 925-463-2626 | (76) | C | OP |
| 5102 Hopyard Rd | 800-466-8356 | $61– | | |
| www.motel6.com | | $56 | | |
| grassy area, short drive to walking trail | | | | |
| **Ramada Inn** | 925-463-1300 | (102) | C | OP |
| 5375 Owens Ct | 800-272-6232 | $49– | F | T |
| www.ramada.com | | $89 | | GP |
| small lawn, 1½ miles to park | | | | |
| **Residence Inn** | 925-227-0500 | (135) | FB | OP |
| 11920 Dublin Canyon Rd | 800-331-3131 | $79– | K | T |
| www.marriott.com | pet fee $75/stay | $149 | | FR |
| studios/1–2 bdrm suites, Mon–Thur beverages and light dinner, pet relief area, 5 minute drive to park | | | | |
| **Sierra Suites Hotel** | 925-730-0000 | (112) | CB | OP |
| 4555 Chabot Dr | pet fee $100/stay | $69– | K | FR |
| www.sierrasuites.com | | $119 | | |
| small grassy area, 1 mile to park | | | | |
| **Summerfield Suites Pleasanton** | 925-730-0070 | (128) | FB | OP |
| 4545 Chabot Dr | pet fee $150/stay | $89– | K | T |
| www.summerfieldsuites.com | | $184 | | FR |
| 1–2 bdrm suites, pet relief area, 2 blocks to park | | | | |

| C = coffee          GP = guest pass to    L = lounge | | | # of units)<br>& rates | food<br>& drink | pool, sauna<br>& hot tub |
|---|---|---|---|---|---|
| CB = continental         fitness center    M = microwave<br>  breakfast      IP = indoor pool     OP = outdoor pool<br>F = refrigerator   IS = in-room spa     R = restaurant<br>FB = full breakfast   K = full kitchen     S = sauna/steam<br>FR = fitness room   (k) = kitchenette     T = spa or hot tub | | | | | |

## Pleasanton (continued)

| **Wyndham Garden Hotel**          925-463-3330 | (171) | C | OP |
|---|---|---|---|
| 5990 Stoneridge Mall Rd          800-996-3426 | $59– | F | T |
| www.wyndham.com          pet fee $25/stay | $179 | R/L | FR |
| dogs under 75 lbs only, lawn and open walking areas | | | |

## Plymouth

| **Far Horizons 49er Village**          209-245-6981 | (11) | CB | IP |
|---|---|---|---|
| 18265 Hwy 49          800-339-6981 | $95– | K | OP |
| www.49ervillage.com | $175 | R | T |
| 1–2 dogs in studio/1 bdrm cottage, porch or deck,<br>on 20 acres of lawn/trees/resort roads to walk dogs | | | |

| **Plymouth House Inn**          209-245-3298 | (7) | FB | IS |
|---|---|---|---|
| 9525 Main St | $75– | L | |
| www.plymouthhouseinn.com | $175 | | |
| Gold Country Victorian inn, rooms with outside<br>entrances, decks, residential streets, ½ block to park | | | |

## Point Arena

| **Seashell Motel**          707-882-2000 | (32) | C | |
|---|---|---|---|
| 135 Main St | $50– | M/F | |
| grassy creekside walking area | $75 | | |

## Point Reyes Station

| **Annie's Garden Cottage**          415-663-8143 | (1) | K | |
|---|---|---|---|
| 180 3rd St | $170– | | |
| www.anniesgardencottage.com | $190 | | |
| breakfast supplies, large garden, creekside trail | | | |

| **Berry Patch Cottage**          415-663-1942 | (1) | C | |
|---|---|---|---|
| 68 Mesa Rd          888-663-1942 | $100– | K | |
| www.coastalgetaways.com          each pet $5/day | $150 | | |
| cottage and surroundings completely pesticide-free,<br>breakfast supplies, on secluded acre, short drive to<br>dog-friendly beach and off-leash dog park | | | |

| | | | |
|---|---|---|---|
| **Knob Hill Cottage** 415-663-1784<br>www.knobhill.com 888-663-1784<br>dogs allowed by owner's advance approval only,<br>cottage sleeps 2, on 2 acres for walking dogs,<br>close to dog-friendly beaches | (3)<br>$90–<br>$100 | C<br>F | |
| **Old Point Reyes Schoolhouse Compound**<br>www.oldpointreyesschoolhouse.com 415-663-1166<br>dogs by advance approval only each pet $50/stay<br>Barn Loft sleeps 3, continental breakfast basket;<br>Gray's Retreat sleeps 6, coffees and teas only;<br>Jasmine Cottage sleeps 4, organic breakfast basket;<br>gardens, meadow, close to dog-friendly shore areas | (3)<br>$185–<br>$245 | C<br>K<br>CB<br>FB | T |
| **One Mesa B & B** 415-663-8866<br>31 Mesa Rd 866-663-8866<br>www.onemesa.com pet fee $25/stay<br>1 bdrm cottage, gardens, field, country road | (4)<br>$175 | FB<br>CB<br>K | T |
| **Point Reye's Country Inn** 415-663-9696<br>12050 State Route 1 pet fee $25/day<br>www.ptreyescountryinn.com<br>1 dog only, cottages sleep 2, breakfast supplies,<br>waterfront walking area | (2)<br>$185 | C<br>K | |
| **Point Reyes Station Inn** 415-663-9372<br>11591 Hwy 1<br>www.pointreyesstationinn.com<br>dog allowed in 1 room with outside entrance, garden<br>sitting area, close to park and dog-friendly seashore | (5)<br>$135–<br>$165 | CB | T |
| **West Marin Network Lodging Service**<br>11431 State Route 1 #15 415-663-9543<br>booking service for rooms/cottages/B & Bs/homes<br>in and near Point Reyes Seashore Park | (70)<br>$70–<br>$350 | | |

## Pollock Pines

| | | | |
|---|---|---|---|
| **Best Western Stagecoach Motor Inn**<br>5940 Pony Express Trail 530-644-2029<br>www.bestwesterncalifornia.com 800-937-8376<br>pet fee $7/day<br>dogs under 15 lbs only, gravel walking area, 1 mile<br>to lake | (26)<br>$99–<br>$119 | CB<br>M/F | OP |

| C = coffee  GP = guest pass to  L = lounge<br>CB = continental  fitness center  M = microwave<br>  breakfast  IP = indoor pool  OP = outdoor pool<br>F = refrigerator  IS = in-room spa  R = restaurant<br>FB = full breakfast  K = full kitchen  S = sauna/steam<br>FR = fitness room  (k) = kitchenette  T = spa or hot tub | (# of units)<br>& rates | food<br>& drink | pool, sauna<br>& hot tub |
|---|---|---|---|
| **Pollock Pines (continued)** | | | |
| **Westhaven Motor Inn** 530-644-7800<br>5658 Pony Express Trail  800-424-9928<br>www.westhaveninn.com  pet fee $10/stay<br>small dogs only, small grassy area and open field | (21)<br>$69–<br>$98 | CB<br>M/F | |
| **Pomona** | | | |
| **Lemon Tree Motel** 909-623-6404<br>1700 Gillette Rd  800-884-6304<br>lawn for walking dogs | (67)<br>$55 | C | OP |
| **Motel 6** 909-591-1871<br>2470 S Garey Ave  800-466-8356<br>www.motel6.com<br>1 well-behaved dog, small grassy area, ½ mile to park | (120)<br>$46–<br>$62 | C | OP |
| **Sheraton Suites** 909-622-5042<br>601 W McKinley Ave  800-722-4055<br>www.sheraton.com<br>dog beds, across street to large park | (247)<br>$95–<br>$209 | C<br>M/F<br>R | OP<br>S<br>T<br>FR |
| **Shilo Inn** 909-598-0073<br>3200 W Temple Ave  800-222-2244<br>www.shiloinns.com  pet fee $10/day<br>small grassy area, 2 blocks to college campus | (150)<br>$110–<br>$130 | CB<br>M/F | OP<br>T<br>FR |
| **Porterville** | | | |
| **Best Western Porterville Inn** 559-781-7411<br>350 W Montgomery Ave  877-781-7411<br>www.bestwesterncalifornia.com  pet fee $25/stay<br>across street to dog-friendly jogging trail | (114)<br>$73–<br>$84 | CB<br>F<br>R | OP<br>T<br>FR |
| **Motel 6** 559-781-7600<br>935 W Morton Ave  800-466-8356<br>www.motel6.com<br>lawn walking area, 1 block to park | (107)<br>$42–<br>$46 | C | OP |

## Portola

| | | | | |
|---|---|---|---|---|
| **Lake Davis Resort** 530-832-1060 7582 Buckbrush Dr pet fee $6/day www.lakedavisresort.com dogs allowed in motel rooms but not in cabins, wooded walking areas, ¼ mile to lake | (4) $73– $80 | C M/F | | |
| **Sierra Motel** 530-832-4223 380 E Sierra St each pet $11/day wooded walking areas, paved riverside trail | (23) $56– $70 | C M/F | | |
| **Sleepy Pines Motel** 530-832-4291 74631 State Route 70 www.sleepypinesmotel.com rooms/cabins sleep up to 6, grassy walking areas, across road to river, 1 mile to riverside walking trail | (17) $59– $76 | C M/F | | |

## Poway

| | | | | |
|---|---|---|---|---|
| **Best Western Country Inn** 858-748-6320 13845 Poway Rd 800-648-6320 pet relief area pet fee $15/stay | (44) $79– $85 | CB M/F | OP T |
| **Ramada Ltd Inn** 858-748-7311 12448 Poway Rd 800-272-6232 www.ramada.com pet fee $10/day hillside walking area, 1 mile to dog-friendly park | (47) $99– $129 | CB M/F | OP T |

## Quincy

| | | | | |
|---|---|---|---|---|
| **Bucks Lake Lodge** 530-283-2262 16525 Bucks Lake Rd each pet $10/day www.buckslakelodge.com 1–2 dogs only, 1–3 bdrm cabins sleep up to 8, surrounded by national forest land | (11) $74– $115 | K R/L | |
| **Gold Pan Motel** 530-283-3686 200 Crescent St 800-804-6541 pet fee $6/day small dogs only, walking path, ½ mile to park | (56) $61– $87 | CB M/F | IS |
| **Paxton Lodge** 530-283-1141 32160 Paxton Rd community kitchen, wooded riverside walking area | (9) $45– $60 | C K | |

| C = coffee  GP = guest pass to  L = lounge | | |
|---|---|---|

| | (# of units) & rates | food & drink | pool, sauna & hot tub |
|---|---|---|---|

Key: C = coffee, GP = guest pass to fitness center, L = lounge, CB = continental breakfast, IP = indoor pool, M = microwave, OP = outdoor pool, F = refrigerator, IS = in-room spa, R = restaurant, FB = full breakfast, K = full kitchen, S = sauna/steam, FR = fitness room, (k) = kitchenette, T = spa or hot tub

## Quincy (continued)

| Lodging | Contact | # / rates | food | pool |
|---|---|---|---|---|
| **Pine Hill Motel** 42075 Hwy 70 www.pinehillmotel.com  pet fee $5/day rooms/2 bdrm vacation home sleep up to 6, lawn walking area, ¼ mile to park | 530-283-1670 866-342-2891 | (12) $150 | C K | |
| **Spanish Creek Motel** 233 Crescent St  pet fee $10/stay lawn walking area, 2 blocks to park | 530-283-1200 | (28) $55–$60 | C M/F | |

## Rancho Cordova

| Lodging | Contact | # / rates | food | pool |
|---|---|---|---|---|
| **AmeriSuites** 10744 Gold Center Dr www.amerisuites.com dog treats, lawn and open field, ¾ mile to park, 5 miles to off-leash dog park | 916-635-4799 | (128) $89–$129 | CB (k) M/F | OP FR |
| **Best Western Heritage Inn** 11269 Point East Dr www.bestwesterncalifornia.com  pet fee $25/stay open field, 10 minute drive to park | 916-635-4040 800-641-1076 | (123) $89 | FB F | OP T |
| **Cordova Inn** 10701 Folsom Blvd large yard for walking dogs | 916-631-0373 | (80) $40–$45 | C M/F | OP |
| **Crossland Economy Studios** 11299 Point East Dr www.extendedstay.com  pet fee $25/day, up to maximum of $75 close to bike trail, 3 miles to park | 916-859-0280 800-398-7829 | (129) $55 | K | |
| **Inns of America** 12249 Folsom Blvd www.innsofamerica.com grassy area, ¼ mile to trails, 5 miles to off-leash park | 916-351-1213 | (122) $75 | CB M/F | OP |

| | | | | |
|---|---|---|---|---|
| **Motel 6** | 916-635-8784 | (68) | C | |
| 10694 Olson Dr | 800-466-8356 | $50– | | |
| www.motel6.com | | $58 | | |
| 1 dog only, small grassy areas, 3 miles to park | | | | |
| **Residence Inn** | 916-851-1550 | (90) | FB | IP |
| 2779 Prospect Park Dr | 800-331-3131 | $90– | K | T |
| www.marriott.com | | $125 | | FR |
| pet fee $10/day plus $100 cleaning fee | | | | |
| studios/1–2 bdrm suites, Mon–Thur beverages and | | | | |
| light dinner, lawn and walking area, ½ mile to park | | | | |

## Rancho Cucamonga

| | | | | |
|---|---|---|---|---|
| **Christmas House B & B Inn** | 909-980-6450 | (6) | FB | |
| 9240 Archibald Ave | | $155– | | |
| www.christmashouseinn.com | | $195 | | |
| dogs by advance approval only, in ground floor | | | | |
| rooms with outside entrances, large yard | | | | |

## Rancho Mirage

| | | | | |
|---|---|---|---|---|
| **Lodge at Rancho Mirage** | 760-321-8282 | (240) | F | OP |
| 68900 Frank Sinatra Dr | 866-518-6870 | $99– | R | T |
| www.rockresorts.com | pet fee $75/stay | $1,000 | | FR |
| dogs under 30 lbs only, lawn and desert area | | | | |
| **Motel 6** | 760-324-8475 | (103) | C | OP |
| 69570 Hwy 111 | 800-466-8356 | $46– | | |
| www.motel6.com | | $66 | | |
| vacant lot, 1 mile to park | | | | |
| **Westin Mission Hills Resort** | 760-328-5955 | (512) | C | OP |
| 71333 Dinah Shore Dr | 800-335-3545 | $99– | (k) | T |
| www.westin.com/missionhills | | $254 | R/L | FR |
| dogs under 40 lbs, private patios or balconies, on | | | | IS |
| 360 acres landscaped grounds and jogging trail | | | | |

## Rancho Santa Fe

| | | | | |
|---|---|---|---|---|
| **Inn at Rancho Santa Fe** | 858-756-1131 | (88) | C | OP |
| 5951 Linea Del Cielo | each pet $125/stay | $210– | M/F | T |
| www.theinnatrsf.com | | $230 | R | FR |
| wooded country walking area | | | | |

| C = coffee<br>CB = continental<br>　　breakfast<br>F = refrigerator<br>FB = full breakfast<br>FR = fitness room | GP = guest pass to<br>　　fitness center<br>IP = indoor pool<br>IS = in-room spa<br>K = full kitchen<br>(k) = kitchenette | L = lounge<br>M = microwave<br>OP = outdoor pool<br>R = restaurant<br>S = sauna/steam<br>T = spa or hot tub | (# of units)<br>& rates | food<br>& drink | pool, sauna<br>& hot tub |
|---|---|---|---|---|---|

## Rancho Santa Fe (continued)

| **Rancho Valencia Resort**<br>5921 Valencia Cir<br>www.ranchovalencia.com<br>lawn and walking paths | 858-756-1123<br>800-548-3664<br>each pet $75/day | (49)<br>$470–<br>$875 | (k)<br>R | OP<br>S<br>T<br>FR |
|---|---|---|---|---|

## Randsburg

| **Cottage Hotel B & B**<br>130 Butte Ave<br>www.randsburg.com<br>1 well-behaved dog by manager's approval only,<br>rooms/cottage sleep up to 5, high desert trails | 760-374-2285<br>pet fee $5/day | (5)<br>$85 | FB<br>K | T |
|---|---|---|---|---|

## Red Bluff

| **Best Value Inn & Suites**<br>30 Gilmore Rd<br>vacant lot, short drive to park | 530-529-2028<br>888-315-2378<br>pet fee $6/day | (60)<br>$55 | CB<br>M/F | OP |
|---|---|---|---|---|
| **Cinderella Riverview Motel**<br>600 Rio St<br>large riverside lawn area | 530-527-5490<br>800-549-7778<br>pet fee $5/day | (40)<br>$45–<br>$50 | CB<br>M/F | OP |
| **Days Inn**<br>5 John Sutter St<br>www.daysinn.com<br>large open walking areas, ½ mile to park | 530-527-6130<br>800-329-7466<br>pet fee $10/day | (47)<br>$47–<br>$66 | CB<br>M/F | OP |
| **Econo Lodge**<br>1142 N Main St<br>www.choicehotels.com<br>dogs in smoking rooms only, dog-friendly park | 530-528-8890<br>800-424-6423<br>pet fee $5/day | (29)<br>$45–<br>$100 | CB<br>M/F | OP |
| **Lamplighter Lodge**<br>210 S Main St<br>www.lamplighterlodge.us<br>dogs by manager's approval only, all rooms have<br>outside entrances, ¼ block to riverside park | 530-527-1150 | (50)<br>$55–<br>$65 | CB<br>M/F | OP |

| | | | | |
|---|---|---|---|---|
| **Motel 6**<br>20 Williams Ave<br>www.motel6.com  lawn, field, short drive to park | 530-527-9200<br>800-466-8356 | (61)<br>$44–<br>$50 | C | OP |
| **Sky Terrace Motel**<br>99 Main St<br>across street from park | 530-527-4145<br>pet fee $5/day | (30)<br>$40 | C<br>M/F | OP |
| **Sportsman's Lodge**<br>768 Antelope Blvd<br>www.rbsportsmanlodge.com  open field and trails | 530-527-2888<br>pet fee $7/day | (20)<br>$50–<br>$65 | C<br>M/F | OP |
| **Super 8 Motel**<br>203 Antelope Blvd<br>www.super8.com  each pet $5/day<br>pond and aviary, pet relief area and walking trail | 530-527-8882<br>800-800-8000 | (68)<br>$63–<br>$70 | CB<br>M/F | OP |
| **Travelodge**<br>38 Antelope Blvd<br>www.travelodge.com  each pet $6/day<br>first floor rooms, courtyard, riverside walking area | 530-527-6020<br>800-578-7878 | (41)<br>$55–<br>$60 | CB<br>M/F | OP |
| **Triangle Motel**<br>1175 Montgomery Rd  pet fee up $10/day<br>large yard, across street to park | 530-527-4542 | (10)<br>$35 | C<br>F | OP |
| **Villager Lodge**<br>250 S Main St<br>lawn, 2 blocks to park  each pet $5/day | 530-527-3545<br>888-865-2946 | (34)<br>$45–<br>$50 | CB<br>M/F | OP |
| **Redcrest** | | | | |
| **Redcrest Resort**<br>26459 Avenue of the Giants  pet fee $5/day<br>www.redcrestresort.com<br>motel rooms/1–2 bdrm cabins, dog run, hiking trails | 707-722-4208 | (10)<br>$45–<br>$110 | K | T |
| **Redding** | | | | |
| **Americana Lodge**<br>1250 Pine St  pet fee $5/day<br>lawn area, close to park | 530-241-7020 | (58)<br>$40 | C<br>M/F | OP |
| **Best Western Hospitality House**<br>532 N Market St<br>www.bestwesterncalifornia.com  pet fee $10/day<br>2 blocks to riverside park | 530-241-6464<br>800-700-3019 | (62)<br>$55–<br>$63 | CB<br>M/F | OP<br>T |

| C = coffee    GP = guest pass to   L = lounge<br>CB = continental       fitness center   M = microwave<br>    breakfast    IP = indoor pool    OP = outdoor pool<br>F = refrigerator    IS = in-room spa    R = restaurant<br>FB = full breakfast   K = full kitchen     S = sauna/steam<br>FR = fitness room   (k) = kitchenette     T = spa or hot tub | (# of units)<br>& rates | food<br>& drink | pool, sauna<br>& hot tub |
|---|---|---|---|
| **Redding (continued)** | | | |
| **Best Western Ponderosa Inn**    530-241-6300<br>2220 Pine St                  800-626-1900<br>across street to park       pet fee $15–25/day | (59)<br>$73 | CB<br>M/F | OP |
| **Budget Inn**                530-243-4231<br>1055 Market St          pet fee $5/day<br>lawn walking area, across street to riverside park | (45)<br>$45 | M/F | OP |
| **Capri Motel**             530-241-1156<br>4620 Westside Rd      pet fee $5/day<br>large lawn for walking dogs | (64)<br>$48 | C<br>M/F | |
| **Comfort Inn**            530-221-6530<br>2059 Hilltop Dr      pet fee $15/stay<br>rooms/suites with outside entrances, open walking<br>area behind building, short drive to park | (88)<br>$72–<br>$80 | CB<br>M/F | OP |
| **Deluxe Inn**             530-243-5141<br>1135 Market St         pet fee $5/day<br>dogs allowed in smoking rooms only, small lawn,<br>2 blocks riverside park | (35)<br>$40 | C<br>M/F | OP |
| **Economy Inn**          530-246-9803<br>525 N Market St       pet fee $10/day<br>small grassy walking area, 3 blocks to park | (28)<br>$40–<br>$45 | C<br>M/F | OP |
| **Fawndale Lodge & RV Resort**   530-275-8000<br>15215 Fawndale Rd       800-381-0941<br>www.fawndale.com       pet fee $6/day<br>rooms/cabins sleep up to 6, grassy walking areas | (8)<br>$69–<br>$200 | CB<br>K<br>M/F | OP |
| **Grand Manor Inn**       530-221-4472<br>850 Mistletoe Lane       800-530-3324<br>www.grandmanorinn.com   pet fee $10/day<br>dogs under 25 lbs only, walking area in paved<br>parking lot, 5 miles to park | (71)<br>$98 | CB<br>M/F | OP<br>T<br>FR |

| | | | | |
|---|---|---|---|---|
| **Hilltop Lodge** 2240 Hilltop Dr dirt walking area, 4 miles to park | 530-221-5432 pet fee $10/day | (74) $50 | C | OP |
| **Holiday Inn Express** 1080 Twin View Blvd www.hiexpress.com walking trail, 5 minute drive to riverside trails | 530-241-5500 800-465-4329 pet fee $20/stay | (80) $72– $79 | C F | OP T |
| **Howard Johnson Express Inn** 2731 Bechelli Lane www.howardjohnson.com small dirt walking area, short drive to park | 530-223-1935 800-354-5222 pet fee $10/day | (75) $50– $60 | CB | OP |
| **Jones Valley/Lakeview/Sugarloaf Resorts** 22300 Jones Valley Marina Dr  530-275-7950 www.houseboats.com  877-474-2782 or 800-223-7950 houseboats sleep 10–18, accessible from 3 Shasta Lake resorts, dogs must be leashed while onshore | | (92) $568– $1,282 | K | |
| **La Quinta Inn** 2180 Hilltop Dr www.lq.com lawn walking area, 1 mile to park | 530-221-8200 800-531-5900 | (141) $75– $90 | CB | OP T FR |
| **Lake Shasta's Bed & Breakfast** 215 Lake Blvd www.lakeshasta-inn.com rooms or entire home that sleeps 12 ($500/day), on 80 acres overlooking canyon, trails for walking dogs | 530-238-2388 800-774-8783 | (3) $100– $225 | CB M/F | |
| **Motel 6 Redding Central** 1640 Hilltop Dr www.motel6.com lawn area, 2 miles to park | 530-221-1800 800-466-8356 | (80) $46– $66 | C | OP |
| **Motel 6 Redding North** 1250 Twin View Blvd www.motel6.com lawn area, 5 miles to park | 530-246-4470 800-466-8356 | (97) $46– $66 | C | OP |
| **Motel 6 Redding South** 2385 Bechelli Lane www.motel6.com small park area | 530-221-0562 800-466-8356 | (105) $53– $66 | C | OP |

| C = coffee  GP = guest pass to  L = lounge<br>CB = continental  fitness center  M = microwave<br> breakfast  IP = indoor pool  OP = outdoor pool<br>F = refrigerator  IS = in-room spa  R = restaurant<br>FB = full breakfast  K = full kitchen  S = sauna/steam<br>FR = fitness room  (k) = kitchenette  T = spa or hot tub | (# of units)<br>& rates | food<br>& drink | pool, sauna<br>& hot tub |
|---|---|---|---|

## Redding (continued)

| **Oxford Suites** 530-221-0100<br>1967 Hilltop Dr 800-762-0133<br>www.oxfordsuites.com pet fee $25/stay<br>dogs under 25 lbs only, 1–2 bdrm suites, beverages<br>and appetizers, pet relief area, short drive to trails | (139)<br>$85 | FB<br>M/F | OP<br>T<br>FR |
|---|---|---|---|
| **Ramada Ltd** 530-246-2222<br>1286 Twin View Blvd 800-272-6232<br>www.ramada.com pet fee $15/stay<br>large grassy area and vacant lot, short drive to parks | (63)<br>$74–<br>$89 | CB | IP<br>T<br>FR |
| **Red Lion Hotel** 530-221-8700<br>1830 Hilltop Dr 800-733-5466<br>www.redlion.com lawn area, 4 miles to park | (192)<br>$84–<br>$109 | C<br>R | OP<br>T<br>FR |
| **Redding's B & B** 530-222-2494<br>1094 Palisades Ave 877-514-6244<br>www.reddingbedandbreakfast.com pet fee $10/stay<br>unique theme rooms in antique Iowa farmhouse,<br>1 acre lawn and open field, 4 blocks to hiking trail,<br>5 miles to beach and off-leash dog park | (4)<br>$100–<br>$180 | FB | S<br>T<br>IS |
| **River Inn Motor Hotel** 530-241-9500<br>1835 Park Marina Dr 800-995-4341<br>www.reddingriverinn.com pet fee $6/day<br>riverside walking area | (79)<br>$64 | C<br>F<br>R | OP<br>T |
| **Shasta Lodge** 530-243-6133<br>1245 Pine St pet fee $5/day<br>lawn walking area, 5 blocks to park | (37)<br>$35–<br>$39 | C<br>M/F | OP |
| **Stardust Motel** 530-241-6121<br>1200 Pine St pet fee $10/day<br>1 mile to park | (42)<br>$39–<br>$42 | C<br>M/F | OP |
| **Travel Inn** 530-243-4900<br>1040 Market St pet fee $5/day<br>vacant lot, 1½ blocks to large park | (30)<br>$39–<br>$49 | M/F | OP |

| | | | |
|---|---|---|---|
| **Vagabond Inn**    530-223-1600<br>536 E Cypress Ave    800-522-1555<br>www.vagabondinn.com    pet fee $10/day<br>small lawn, residential street for walking dogs,<br>short drive to dog park | (71)<br>$50–<br>$59 | CB<br>M/F | OP |

## Redlands

| | | | |
|---|---|---|---|
| **Best Western Sandman Motel**    909-793-2001<br>1120 W Colton Ave    800-528-1234<br>www.bestwesterncalifornia.com<br>small dogs only, 2 miles to park | (66)<br>$59–<br>$65 | CB<br>M/F | OP<br>T<br>FR |
| **Dynasty Suites**    909-793-6648<br>1235 W Colton Ave    800-842-7899<br>www.dynastysuites.com    each pet $10/day<br>dogs under 20 lbs allowed for AAA members only,<br>1 mile to park | (54)<br>$75–<br>$145 | CB<br>M/F | OP<br>T<br>GP |

## Redondo Beach

| | | | |
|---|---|---|---|
| **Best Western Redondo Beach Inn**<br>1850 S Pacific Coast Hwy    310-540-3700<br>www.bwredondobeachinn.com    800-528-1234<br>pet fee $50/stay<br>lawn walking area, ½ mile to dog-friendly beach | (110)<br>$75–<br>$129 | C<br>F<br>R | OP<br>S<br>T<br>FR |
| **Ramada Inn**    310-540-5998<br>435 S Pacific Coast Hwy    pet fee $10/day<br>www.ramada.com<br>small dogs only, 1 block to beach | (40)<br>$69–<br>$79 | CB<br>M/F | T<br>IS |
| **Redondo Pier Inn**    310-318-1811<br>206 S Pacific Coast Hwy    800-841-9777<br>www.rpinn.com    pet fee $25/day<br>dogs under 30 lbs allowed in smoking rooms only,<br>residential area, short drive to dog-friendly park | (37)<br>$69–<br>$89 | CB<br>M/F | OP<br>T |

## Redway

| | | | |
|---|---|---|---|
| **Dean Creek Resort**    707-923-2555<br>4112 Redwood Dr    877-923-2555<br>www.deancreekresort.com    pet fee $5/day<br>1 dog allowed only in smoking rooms with outside<br>entrances and private patios, riverside walking area | (11)<br>$57–<br>$130 | C<br>M/F | OP<br>T |

| | | | (# of units) & rates | food & drink | pool, sauna & hot tub |
|---|---|---|---|---|---|
| C = coffee<br>CB = continental<br>breakfast<br>F = refrigerator<br>FB = full breakfast<br>FR = fitness room | GP = guest pass to<br>fitness center<br>IP = indoor pool<br>IS = in-room spa<br>K = full kitchen<br>(k) = kitchenette | L = lounge<br>M = microwave<br>OP = outdoor pool<br>R = restaurant<br>S = sauna/steam<br>T = spa or hot tub | | | |

## Redwood City

| | | | | | |
|---|---|---|---|---|---|
| **Days Inn**<br>2650 El Camino Real<br>www.daysinn.com<br>small dogs by advance reservation only, large lawn | | 650-369-9200<br>800-453-7070<br>pet fee $10/day | (70)<br>$63–<br>$68 | CB<br>M/F | OP<br>T<br>FR |
| **Hotel Sofitel at Redwood Shores**<br>223 Twin Dolphin Dr<br>www.sofitel.com<br>rooms/1 bdrm suites facing lagoon, directions to<br>local dogfriendly parks and walking trails | | 650-598-9000<br>800-763-4835 | (421)<br>$129–<br>$309 | M/F<br>R/L | OP<br>FR |
| **Towneplace Suites by Marriott**<br>1000 Twin Dolphin Dr<br>www.towneplacesuites.com<br>each pet $10/day plus $75 cleaning fee<br>walking trail | | 650-593-4100<br>800-257-3000 | (95)<br>$129 | CB<br>K | T<br>FR |

## Reedley

| | | | | | |
|---|---|---|---|---|---|
| **Edgewater Inn**<br>1977 W Manning Ave<br>well-trained dogs only, walking area | | 559-637-7777<br>800-479-5855<br>pet fee $8/day | (50)<br>$69–<br>$79 | CB<br>M/F | OP |
| **Reedley Country B & B**<br>43137 Road 52<br>www.reedleycountryinnbedandbreakfast.com<br>small dogs only, rooms with enclosed private patios<br>and gardens, on 20 acre working plum farm | | 559-638-2585 | (5)<br>$85–<br>$95 | FB | T |

## Rialto

| | | | | | |
|---|---|---|---|---|---|
| **Best Western Empire Inn**<br>475 W Valley Blvd<br>www.bestwesterncalifornia.com  pet fee $5–$10/day<br>lawn walking areas, 7 miles to park | | 909-877-0690<br>800-937-8376 | (100)<br>$79 | C | OP<br>T |

## Ridgecrest

| | | | | |
|---|---|---|---|---|
| **Best Western China Lake Inn** 760-371-2300 400 S China Lake Blvd 800-937-8376 www.bestwesterncalifornia.com pet fee $10/stay dogs under 40 lbs only, dirt field for walking dogs | (52) $85– $100 | CB M/F | OP T | |
| **Carriage Inn** 760-446-7910 901 N China Lake Blvd 800-772-8527 www.carriageinn.biz pet fee $25/stay small grassy area and vacant lots, ¾ mile to park | (160) $79– $105 | C M/F R/L | OP S T FR | |
| **Desert Motel** 760-375-1371 339 W Church Ave www.desertmotelsuites.com dogs by manager's approval, 1 block to large park | (16) $25– $45 | M/F K | OP | |
| **Econo Lodge** 760-446-2551 201 W Inyokern Rd fenced area for walking dogs off-leash | (85) $55– $69 | CB M/F | OP | |
| **Heritage Inn** 760-446-6543 1050 N Norma St 800-843-0693 next to park | (169) $75– $95 | FB M/F | OP T | |
| **Motel 6** 760-375-6866 535 S China Lake Blvd 800-466-8356 www.motel6.com fenced area, 2 blocks to park | (76) $38– $40 | C | OP | |
| **Quality Inn** 760-375-9731 507 S China Lake Blvd pet fee $20/stay www.qualityinn.com lawn area, 2 blocks to park | (57) $59– $74 | CB M/F | OP | |
| **Rodeway Inn** 760-384-3575 131 W Upjohn Ave 888-424-6423 www.choicehotels.com ½ mile to park | (30) $38– $43 | CB M/F | | |
| **Rose Garden Inn & Suites** 760-375-6777 329 E Ridgecrest Blvd www.rosegardeninn.com open area, 1 mile to park | (61) $27 | C K M/F | OP | |
| **Vagabond Inn** 760-375-2220 426 S China Lake Blvd pet fee $10–$15/stay www.vagabondinn.com open desert area, 3 blocks to park | (35) $49 | CB M/F | OP T | |

| C = coffee  GP = guest pass to  L = lounge<br>CB = continental    fitness center  M = microwave<br>    breakfast  IP = indoor pool  OP = outdoor pool<br>F = refrigerator  IS = in-room spa  R = restaurant<br>FB = full breakfast  K = full kitchen  S = sauna/steam<br>FR = fitness room  (k) = kitchenette  T = spa or hot tub | (# of units)<br>& rates | food<br>& drink | pool, sauna<br>& hot tub |
|---|---|---|---|
| ### Rio Dell | | | |
| **Humboldt Gables Motel**          707-764-5609<br>40 W Davis St                each pet $10–$20/day<br>1–2 small well-behaved dogs allowed with owner's<br>approval only, pet relief area, next to park | (18)<br>$50–<br>$90 | C<br>M/F | |
| ### Rio Vista | | | |
| **Rio Sands Lodge**              707-374-6374<br>205 Hwy 12<br>large lawn, 1½ blocks to riverbank and open field | (20)<br>$58 | C<br>M/F | OP |
| **Vista Motel**                707-374-6341<br>640 Hwy 12                    each pet $5/day<br>walking area behind building, ½ mile to park | (16)<br>$45–<br>$50 | M/F | |
| ### Riverside | | | |
| **Best Western Inn**             909-359-0770<br>10518 Magnolia Ave              800-937-8376<br>www.bestwesterncalifornia.com    each pet $10/day<br>small lawn for walking dogs, 2 miles to park | (59)<br>$68–<br>$89 | CB<br>M/F | OP<br>T |
| **Budget Inn of Riverside**         909-686-8888<br>1911 University Ave            each pet $5/day<br>www.budgetinn.com<br>well-mannered dogs only, breakfast on weekends,<br>lawn and landscaped areas, 3 parks within 1 mile | (36)<br>$50–<br>$70 | CB<br>K<br>M/F | |
| **Dynasty Suites**              909-369-8200<br>3735 Iowa Ave                  800-842-7899<br>www.dynastysuites.com            pet fee $10/day<br>dogs under 25 lbs allowed for AAA members only,<br>2 blocks to park | (34)<br>$75–<br>$82 | CB<br>M/F | OP<br>GP<br>IS |
| **Econo Lodge**                909-351-2424<br>10705 Magnolia Ave              pet fee $5/day<br>3 miles to park | (30)<br>$59–<br>$69 | C<br>M/F | OP<br>T |

| | | | | |
|---|---|---|---|---|
| **Motel 6 Riverside East**<br>1260 University Ave<br>www.motel6.com<br>small grassy area, ½ mile to park | 909-784-2131<br>800-466-8356 | (60)<br>$48–<br>$54 | C | |
| **Motel 6 Riverside South**<br>3663 La Sierra Ave<br>www.motel6.com<br>1 dog only, open field, 2 blocks to park | 909-351-0764<br>800-466-8356 | (121)<br>$46–<br>$52 | C | OP |
| **Motel 6 Riverside West**<br>6830 Valley Way<br>www.motel6.com<br>grassy walking area | 909-681-6666<br>800-466-8356 | (108)<br>$46–<br>$58 | C | OP |

## Rocklin

| | | | | |
|---|---|---|---|---|
| **Howard Johnson Inn**<br>4420 Rocklin Rd<br>www.howardjohnsonrocklin.com   pet fee $20/stay<br>Mon–Thur beverages and appetizers, lawn walking<br>area, 2 blocks to park | 916-624-4500<br>800-462-2400 | (124)<br>$90–<br>$105 | FB<br>M/F | OP<br>T<br>FR |
| **Ramada Ltd**<br>4480 Rocklin Rd<br>www.ramada.com   each pet $25/stay<br>grassy area, 1 block to hiking trail | 916-632-3366<br>877-733-5616 | (100)<br>$77 | CB<br>M/F | OP<br>T |
| **Rocklin Park Hotel**<br>5450 China Garden Rd<br>www.rocklinpark.com   pet fee $75/stay<br>small lawn and walking path, 1 mile to small park | 916-630-9400<br>888-630-9400 | (67)<br>$139–<br>$159 | C<br>M/F<br>R | OP<br>S<br>T<br>FR |

## Rohnert Park

| | | | | |
|---|---|---|---|---|
| **Best Western Inn**<br>6500 Redwood Dr<br>www.bestwesterncalifornia.com<br>small dogs only, grassy areas, short drive to park | 707-584-7435<br>800-937-8376 | (144)<br>$86–<br>$104 | CB<br>M/F | OP<br>T |
| **Doubletree Hotel**<br>1 Doubletree Dr<br>www.dtsonoma.com   each pet $15–$25/day<br>close to pond and residential walking area | 707-584-5466<br>800-222-8733 | (245)<br>$129–<br>$179 | C<br>R/L | OP<br>T<br>FR |

| C = coffee  GP = guest pass to  L = lounge<br>CB = continental  fitness center  M = microwave<br>  breakfast  IP = indoor pool  OP = outdoor pool<br>F = refrigerator  IS = in-room spa  R = restaurant<br>FB = full breakfast  K = full kitchen  S = sauna/steam<br>FR = fitness room  (k) = kitchenette  T = spa or hot tub | (# of units)<br>& rates | food<br>& drink | pool, sauna<br>& hot tub |
|---|---|---|---|

### Rohnert Park (continued)

| **Motel 6**  707-585-8888<br>6145 Commerce Blvd  800-466-8356<br>www.motel6.com<br>small grassy area in parking lot, short drive to park | (127)<br>$46–<br>$56 | C | OP |
|---|---|---|---|

### Rosamond

| **Devonshire Inn Motel**  661-256-3454<br>2076 W Rosamond Blvd  pet fee $10/day<br>www.devonshireinn.com<br>vacant lot for walking dogs, ¼ mile to park | (30)<br>$74–<br>$83 | CB<br>F | OP<br>T |
|---|---|---|---|

### Roseville

| **Best Western Roseville Inn**  916-782-4434<br>220 Harding Blvd  800-255-4747<br>www.bestwesterncalifornia.com  pet fee $10/day<br>grassy walking area, 2 blocks to park | (122)<br>$75–<br>$99 | CB<br>M/F | OP<br>IS |
|---|---|---|---|
| **Oxford Suites Hotel**  916-784-2222<br>130 N Sunrise Ave  800-882-7848<br>www.oxfordsuites.com  pet fee $25/stay<br>beverages and appetizers, lawn, 2 miles to park | (480)<br>$89 | FB<br>M/F | OP<br>T<br>FR |
| **Residence Inn**  916-772-5500<br>1930 Taylor Rd  800-331-3131<br>www.marriott.com<br>  pet fee $10/day plus $100 cleaning fee<br>dogs under 40 lbs only, studios/1–2 bdrm suites,<br>Mon–Thur beverages and light dinner, small lawn,<br>1 mile to fenced off-leash dog park | (90)<br>$120–<br>$155 | FB<br>K | IP<br>T<br>FR |

### Rowland Heights

| **Motel 6**  626-964-5333<br>18970 E Labin Ct  800-466-8356<br>www.motel6.com<br>small grassy walking area | (124)<br>$46–<br>$60 | C | OP |
|---|---|---|---|

## Running Springs

| | | | | |
|---|---|---|---|---|
| **Giant Oaks Lodge** 32180 Hilltop Blvd www.runningsprings.com          pet fee $20/stay walking trails and country roads for walking dogs | 909-867-2231 800-786-1689 | (14) $79 | C M/F | OP T |
| **Rainbow View Lodge** 2726 View Dr www.rainbowviewlodge.com open field and residential walking area | 909-867-1810 888-868-1810 | (6) $89 | C M/F | |

## Sacramento

| | | | | |
|---|---|---|---|---|
| **Best Western Expo Inn** 1413 Howe Ave dogs in smoking rooms only, 5½ acres for walking dogs, 3 blocks to 30 mile long riverside bike trail | 916-922-9833 800-643-4422 | (127) $85– $150 | CB K | OP T FR |
| **Canterbury Inn** 1900 Canterbury Rd small grassy walking area | 916-927-3492 pet fee $10/day | (150) $69 | CB M/F | OP |
| **Clarion Hotel Mansion Inn** 700 16th St www.sacramentoclarion.com          pet fee $35/stay 5 blocks to park with gardens and walking paths | 916-444-8000 800-443-0880 | (106) $69– $109 | C M/F R/L | OP FR GP |
| **Clarion Hotel–Cal Expo** 2600 Auburn Blvd www.choicehotels.com          pet fee $20/day lawn walking area, across street to park | 916-487-7600 800-424-6423 | (177) $79 | C M/F R/L | OP GP |
| **Doubletree Hotel Sacramento** 2001 Point West Way www.doubletree.com          pet fee $50/stay small dogs only, grassy walking areas, 1 mile to park | 916-929-8855 800-222-8733 | (448) $110– $175 | C R | OP T FR |
| **Econo Lodge** 711 16th St dogs allowed in smoking rooms only, small lawn walking area, 6 blocks to park | 916-443-6631 each pet $6/day | (40) $59– $65 | C M/F | |
| **Forty-Niners Motor Lodge** 2730 Auburn Blvd lawn walking area | 916-972-9749 pet fee $5/day | (32) $50 | M/F | OP |

| C = coffee   GP = guest pass to   L = lounge<br>CB = continental      fitness center   M = microwave<br>    breakfast    IP = indoor pool   OP = outdoor pool<br>F = refrigerator   IS = in-room spa   R = restaurant<br>FB = full breakfast   K = full kitchen   S = sauna/steam<br>FR = fitness room   (k) = kitchenette   T = spa or hot tub | (# of units) & rates | food & drink | pool, sauna & hot tub |
|---|---|---|---|
| **Sacramento (continued)** | | | |
| **Hawthorn Suites Hotel**   916-441-1200<br>321 Bercut Dr      800-767-1777<br>www.hawthorn.com<br>studios/2 bdrm suites, on 7 acres for walking<br>dogs, 1 block to riverside trail | (272)<br>$89–<br>$119 | FB<br>M/F<br>R | OP<br>FR<br>IS |
| **Holiday Inn Express Downtown**   916-444-4436<br>728 16th St      800-993-1883<br>www.hiexsacramento.com    pet fee $35/stay<br>pet supplies, 5 blocks to park with gardens and paths | (132)<br>$79–<br>$119 | CB<br>M/F | OP<br>FR<br>GP |
| **Holiday Inn Sacramento NE**   916-338-5800<br>5321 Date Ave      800-338-2810<br>www.holiday-inn.com    pet fee $25/stay<br>lawn walking area, 7 minute walk to park | (230)<br>$134 | C<br>M/F<br>R | OP<br>T<br>FR |
| **Homestead Studio Suites**   916-564-7500<br>2810 Gateway Oaks Dr      888-782-9473<br>www.homesteadhotels.com    pet fee $25/day<br>rooms/suites with outside entrances, lawn and<br>vacant lot, 1½ miles to park | (144)<br>$69–<br>$79 | C<br>K<br>M/F | |
| **Host Airport Hotel**   916-922-8071<br>6945 Airport Blvd      800-903-4678<br>www.hostairporthotel.com    pet fee $50/stay<br>small grassy areas, 8 miles to park | (89)<br>$129 | CB | |
| **La Quinta Inn Downtown**   916-448-8100<br>200 Jibboom St      800-531-5900<br>www.lq.com    lawn area, riverside trail | (165)<br>$81–<br>$95 | CB<br>F | OP<br>T<br>FR |
| **La Quinta Inn North**   916-348-0900<br>4604 Madison Ave      800-531-5900<br>www.lq.com    open field | (127)<br>$95 | CB<br>F | OP<br>T<br>FR |
| **Madison Inn**   916-334-7430<br>4317 Madison Ave<br>www.madisoninnandsuites.com    2 miles to park | (120)<br>$45–<br>$50 | CB<br>M/F<br>R | OP |

| | | | | |
|---|---|---|---|---|
| **Motel 6 Downtown** 1415 30th St www.motel6.com | 916-457-0777 800-466-8356 10 miles to park | (94) $50–$64 | C | OP |
| **Motel 6 North** 5110 Interstate Ave www.motel6.com | 916-331-8100 800-466-8356 1 dog under 35 lbs, small lawn | (81) $50–$70 | C | |
| **Motel 6 Old Sacramento North** 227 Jibboom St www.motel6.com | 916-441-0733 800-466-8356 small lawn, close to park | (105) $50–$64 | C | OP |
| **Motel 6 Sacramento Central** 7850 College Town Dr www.motel6.com parking lot walking area, 2 blocks to college campus | 916-383-8110 800-466-8356 | (118) $50–$64 | C | OP |
| **Motel 6 South** 7407 Elsie Ave www.motel6.com | 916-689-6555 800-466-8356 lawn, 3 miles to park | (122) $50–$70 | C | OP |
| **Motel 6 Southwest** 7780 Stockton Blvd www.motel6.com | 916-689-9141 800-466-8356 small lawn, 1 mile to park | (59) $50–$70 | C | |
| **Motel 6 West** 1254 Halyard Dr www.motel6.com 1 dog under 40 lbs only, 2 miles to park | 916-372-3624 800-466-8356 | (116) $52–$56 | C | OP |
| **Radisson Hotel Sacramento** 500 Leisure Lane dogs under 25 lbs only www.radissonsac.com small lawn walking area, short drive to large park | 916-922-2020 800-333-3333 pet fee $50/stay | (300) $119–$159 | C F R/L | OP T FR |
| **Ramada Ltd** 350 Bercut Dr www.ramada.com 1 block to park | 916-442-6971 800-952-5516 pet fee $20/stay | (99) $74 | CB F | OP T |
| **Red Lion Hotel** 1401 Arden Way www.redlion.com private patios, landscaped courtyard, large grassy areas, 1 mile to off-leash dog park | 916-922-8041 800-733-5466 pet fee $25/stay | (350) $89–$129 | FB M/F R/L | OP T FR |

| C = coffee  GP = guest pass to  L = lounge<br>CB = continental      fitness center  M = microwave<br>  breakfast   IP = indoor pool   OP = outdoor pool<br>F = refrigerator  IS = in-room spa  R = restaurant<br>FB = full breakfast  K = full kitchen  S = sauna/steam<br>FR = fitness room  (k) = kitchenette  T = spa or hot tub | (# of units)<br>& rates | food<br>& drink | pool, sauna<br>& hot tub |
|---|---|---|---|

### Sacramento (continued)

| | | | |
|---|---|---|---|
| **Red Roof Inn**              916-927-7117<br>3796 Northgate Blvd          800-733-7663<br>www.redroof.com<br>1 small dog only, lawn areas, short drive to park | (132)<br>$60 | C<br>F | OP<br>T |
| **Residence Inn**             916-649-1300<br>2410 W El Camino Ave         800-331-3131<br>www.marriott.com<br>pet fee $6/day plus $50 cleaning fee<br>studios/2 bdrm suites sleep 6, Mon–Thur beverages<br>and light dinner, pet relief area, short drive to park | (126)<br>$144–<br>$174 | FB<br>K | OP<br>T<br>FR |
| **Residence Inn–Cal Expo**    916-920-9111<br>1530 Howe Ave                800-331-3131<br>www.marriott.com        pet fee $100/stay<br>dogs under 50 lbs only, studios/2 bdrm penthouses,<br>Mon–Thur beverages and light dinner, pet relief area | (176)<br>$144–<br>$184 | FB<br>K | OP<br>T<br>FR |
| **Sheraton Grand Sacramento** 916-447-1700<br>1230 J St                    800-325-3535<br>www.starwood.com<br>1–2 dogs under 80 lbs only, pet bed/bowls/treats,<br>list of local pet businesses and services, 1 block to<br>park | (503)<br>$99–<br>$675 | C<br>R | OP<br>FR |
| **Super 8 Motel**             916-427-7925<br>7216 55th St                 800-800-8000<br>www.super8.com           pet fee $10/day<br>small landscaped walking area | (61)<br>$50–<br>$78 | CB<br>M/F | |
| **Tahsoe Motel**              916-383-0400<br>8581 Folsom Blvd<br>dogs by manager's approval in smoking rooms only,<br>grassy walking areas behind building | (25)<br>$38–<br>$42 | | |

| | | | | |
|---|---|---|---|---|
| **Vagabond Executive Inn** | 916-446-1481 | (100) | CB | OP |
| 909 3rd St | 800-522-1555 | $89 | M/F | T |
| www.vagabondinn.com | pet fee $10/day | | | FR |
| dogs under 20 lbs only, lawn, 1½ miles to park | | | | |
| **Vagabond Inn** | 916-454-4400 | (82) | CB | OP |
| 1319 30th St | pet fee $10/day | $50 | | |
| www.vagabondinn.com | | | | |
| dogs in smoking rooms only, small grassy areas | | | | |

## Salinas

| | | | | |
|---|---|---|---|---|
| **Inns of California** | 831-424-1741 | (96) | C | OP |
| 555 Airport Blvd | 800-549-5024 | $85– | M/F | |
| www.innsofcal.com | each pet $10/day | $125 | | |
| grassy walking area, close to golf course | | | | |
| **Motel 6 North** | 831-753-1711 | (121) | C | OP |
| 140 Kern St | 800-466-8356 | $46– | | |
| www.motel6.com | | $60 | | |
| walking area in parking lot | | | | |
| **Motel 6 South** | 831-757-3077 | (128) | C | OP |
| 1257 De La Torre St | 800-466-8356 | $46– | | |
| www.motel6.com | | $60 | | |
| small grassy walking areas | | | | |
| **Residence Inn** | 831-775-0410 | (107) | FB | IP |
| 17215 El Rancho Way | 800-331-3131 | $109– | K | T |
| www.marriott.com | | $159 | | FR |
| pet fee $15/day plus $150 cleaning fee 1–2 dogs only, studios/1–2 bdrm suites, Mon–Thur nonalcoholic beverages and light dinner, lawn and sidewalks for walking dogs, 1 mile to park | | | | |
| **Travelodge** | 831-424-8661 | (107) | CB | OP |
| 808 N Main St | 800-578-7878 | $55– | | |
| www.travelodge.com | | $129 | | |
| across street to park | | | | |
| **Vagabond Inn** | 831-758-4693 | (70) | CB | OP |
| 131 Kern St | 800-522-1555 | $49– | M/F | |
| www.vagabondinn.com | pet fee $10/day | $200 | | |
| grassy walking area, ½ mile to park | | | | |

| C = coffee<br>CB = continental<br>breakfast<br>F = refrigerator<br>FB = full breakfast<br>FR = fitness room | GP = guest pass to<br>fitness center<br>IP = indoor pool<br>IS = in-room spa<br>K = full kitchen<br>(k) = kitchenette | L = lounge<br>M = microwave<br>OP = outdoor pool<br>R = restaurant<br>S = sauna/steam<br>T = spa or hot tub | (# of units)<br>& rates | food<br>& drink | pool, sauna<br>& hot tub |
|---|---|---|---|---|---|
| **Samoa** | | | | | |
| **Samoa Airport B & B**<br>900 New Navy Base Rd<br>www.northcoast.com/airbb<br>beachfront lawn and open field | 707-445-0765<br>each pet $15/stay | | (1)<br>$90 | FB<br>F | |
| **San Andreas** | | | | | |
| **Courtyard B & B**<br>334 W Saint Charles St<br>gardens and lawn, 3 blocks to park | 209-754-1518 | | (2)<br>$95–<br>$105 | FB | T |
| **Robin's Nest B & B**<br>247 W Saint Charles St<br>www.robinest.com<br>pet-friendly ground floor room opens onto patio,<br>outdoor kitchen, on 1½ acres, grassy walking area | 209-754-1076<br>888-214-9202 | | (9)<br>$125–<br>$155 | FB<br>K<br>F | T |
| **San Bernardino** | | | | | |
| **Budget Lodge**<br>668 Fairway Dr<br>open field | 909-825-8600<br>each pet $5/day | | (144)<br>$39 | | |
| **Days Inn**<br>1386 E Highland Ave<br>www.daysinn.com<br>lawn area, ½ mile to park | 909-881-1702<br>800-329-7466<br>pet fee $10/day | | (46)<br>$59 | CB<br>M/F | OP |
| **E-Z8 Motel**<br>1750 S Waterman Ave<br>www.ez8motels.com<br>dogs under 15 lbs only, walking area in parking lot | 909-888-4827 | | (119)<br>$32–<br>$80 | C<br>F | OP<br>T |
| **Econo Lodge**<br>606 North H St<br>dogs allowed with manager's approval only | 909-383-1188 | | (52)<br>$45–<br>$50 | CB<br>M/F | OP |

| | | | | |
|---|---|---|---|---|
| **Hilton San Bernardino** | 909-889-0133 | (250) | R/L | OP |
| 285 E Hospitality Lane | 800-445-8667 | $109– | | T |
| www.sanbernardino.hilton.com  each pet $50/stay | | $199 | | FR |
| lawn walking area, 2 miles to park | | | | |
| **La Quinta Inn** | 909-888-7571 | (153) | CB | OP |
| 205 E Hospitality Lane | | $106 | M/F | |
| www.lq.com | | | | |
| dogs allowed in smoking rooms only, grassy areas | | | | |
| **Motel 6** | 909-887-8191 | (104) | C | OP |
| 1960 Ostrems Way | 800-466-8356 | $46– | | |
| www.motel6.com | | $56 | | |
| grassy walking area | | | | |
| **Motel 6 South** | 909-825-6666 | (120) | C | OP |
| 111 W Redlands Blvd | 800-466-8356 | $44– | | |
| www.motel6.com | | $54 | | |
| small grassy walking area | | | | |

### San Bruno

| | | | | |
|---|---|---|---|---|
| **Regency Inn** | 650-589-7535 | (32) | CB | |
| 411 San Bruno Ave E | 877-777-3436 | $69 | | |
| www.regencyinnsfo.com  pet fee $15/day | | | | |
| dog allowed in one smoking room only | | | | |
| **Staybridge Suites Hotel** | 650-588-0770 | (94) | CB | OP |
| 1350 Huntington Ave | pet fee $150/stay | $99– | K | |
| www.staybridge.com | | $139 | | |
| short drive to park | | | | |

### San Carlos

| | | | | |
|---|---|---|---|---|
| **Homestead Studio Suites** | 650-368-2600 | (103) | K | |
| 3 Circle Star Way | 888-782-9473 | $60– | | |
| www.homesteadhotels.com  pet fee $75/stay | | $100 | | |
| 1 small dog only | | | | |

### San Clemente

| | | | | |
|---|---|---|---|---|
| **Country Plaza Inn** | 949-498-8800 | (99) | CB | OP |
| 35 Via Pico Plaza | 800-874-0860 | $99 | M/F | |
| www.countryplazainn.com  pet fee $15/day | | | | |
| dogs in first floor rooms only, 1 mile to beach | | | | |

| C = coffee  GP = guest pass to  L = lounge<br>CB = continental  fitness center  M = microwave<br>  breakfast  IP = indoor pool  OP = outdoor pool<br>F = refrigerator  IS = in-room spa  R = restaurant<br>FB = full breakfast  K = full kitchen  S = sauna/steam<br>FR = fitness room  (k) = kitchenette  T = spa or hot tub | (# of units) & rates | food & drink | pool, sauna & hot tub |
|---|---|---|---|
| ### San Clemente (continued) | | | |
| **Holiday Inn** 949-361-3000<br>111 Avenida De La Estrella  each pet $10/day<br>www.holiday-inn.com<br>grassy walking area, 1 mile to dog-friendly beach | (72)<br>$139–<br>$219 | M/F<br>R | OP<br>T<br>FR |
| **Sea Horse Resort** 949-492-1720<br>602 Avenida Victoria<br>www.seahorsesanclemente.com<br>studios/1–2 bdrm suites, small lawn, across street to<br>dog-friendly beach (limited summer hours) | (11)<br>$159–<br>$215 | C<br>K<br>M/F | |
| **Villa Del Mar Inn** 949-498-5080<br>612 Avenida Victoria<br>www.villasanclemente.com<br>1 bdrm suites, small lawn, dog-friendly beach | (11)<br>$159–<br>$295 | C<br>K<br>M/F | |
| ### San Diego | | | |
| **Beach & Bayside Vacations** 858-488-8827<br>2757 Mission Blvd  800-553-2284<br>www.beachnbayside.com<br>2 bdrm vacation homes, oceanside walking areas | (3)<br>$80–<br>$125 | | |
| **Beach Haven Inn** 858-272-3812<br>4740 Mission Blvd  800-831-6323<br>www.beachhaveninn.com  each pet $10/day<br>dogs under 25 lbs allowed September 15–June 1<br>only, rooms/suites, 1 block to beach | (23)<br>$75–<br>$130 | CB<br>K | OP<br>T |
| **Beach Place** 619-225-0746<br>2158 Sunset Cliffs Blvd<br>www.beachplace.us  1 bdrm cottages near beach | (4)<br>$69 | K | T |
| **Best Western Americana Inn** 619-428-5521<br>815 W San Ysidro Blvd  800-553-3933<br>www.bestwesterncalifornia.com  pet fee $10/day<br>small dogs only, on 4 acres of open walking area | (120)<br>$59–<br>$89 | CB<br>M/F | OP<br>T |

| | | | | |
|---|---|---|---|---|
| **Best Western Lamplighter Inn** | 619-582-3088 | (61) | CB | OP |
| 6474 El Cajon Blvd | 800-545-0778 | $74– | | |
| www.lamplighter-inn.com | each pet $10/day | $200 | | |
| 1–2 dogs only, ½ block to park | | | | |
| **Bristol Hotel** | 619-232-6141 | (102) | C | FR |
| 1055 1st Ave | 800-662-4477 | $99– | F | |
| www.thebristolsandiego.com | | $219 | R/L | |
| dogs under 50 lbs, close to harbor | | | | |
| **Budget Inn–Miramar** | 858-578-4350 | (60) | CB | OP |
| 92126 Kearny Mesa Rd | each pet $20/day | $50– | M/F | |
| 1 mile to park | | $130 | | |
| **Crown Point View Suites Hotel** | 858-272-0676 | (19) | FB | |
| 4088 Crown Point Dr | pet fee $75/stay | $125– | K | |
| www.crownpoint-view.com | | $185 | | |
| quiet neighborhood, 10 minutes to park and beach | | | | |
| **Doubletree Club Hotel** | 619-881-6900 | (216) | CB | OP |
| 1515 Hotel Cir S | 800-486-5315 | $119– | F | T |
| www.doubletreeclubsd.com | | $149 | R/L | FR |
| dogs under 50 lbs only, walking area, ¾ mile to park | | | | |
| **Doubletree Hotel San Diego** | 619-297-5466 | (300) | CB | OP |
| 7450 Hazard Center Dr | 800-222-8733 | $119– | R | IP |
| www.sandiegomissionvalley.doubletree.com | | $199 | | S |
| | pet fee $50/stay | | | FR |
| landscaped grounds, paths, near off-leash dog parks | | | | |
| **E-Z8 Motel Central** | 619-294-2512 | (127) | C | OP |
| 4747 Pacific Hwy | | $45– | F | T |
| www.ez8motels.com | | $80 | | |
| dogs under 35 lbs only, ¾ mile to park | | | | |
| **E-Z8 Motel South Bay** | 619-575-8808 | (89) | C | OP |
| 1010 Outer Rd | | $44– | F | T |
| www.ez8motels.com | | $49 | | |
| small dogs only, lawn, 10 minute drive to park | | | | |
| **Ebb Tide Motel** | 619-224-9339 | (22) | K | |
| 5082 W Point Loma Blvd | | $50– | | |
| next to off-leash dog beach | | $75 | | |

| C = coffee  GP = guest pass to  L = lounge  CB = continental  fitness center  M = microwave  breakfast  IP = indoor pool  OP = outdoor pool  F = refrigerator  IS = in-room spa  R = restaurant  FB = full breakfast  K = full kitchen  S = sauna/steam  FR = fitness room  (k) = kitchenette  T = spa or hot tub | (# of units) & rates | food & drink | pool, sauna & hot tub |
|---|---|---|---|

### San Diego (continued)

| | | | |
|---|---|---|---|
| **Friendship Hotel**  619-298-9898  3942 8th Ave  3 blocks to park with fenced off-leash area | (74)  $29–  $42 | M/F | |
| **Glory's Holiday House B & B**  619-225-0784  3330 Ingelow St  pet fee $10/day  1 dog-friendly room with outside entrance, fenced  yard, residential neighborhood | (2)  $100–  $115 | FB | OP  T |
| **Hampton Inn Seaworld Airport**  619-299-0514  3888 Greenwood St  800-426-7866  www.hamptoninnsandiego.com  pet fee $25/stay  small grassy walking areas, 5 miles to park | (197)  $145–  $179 | CB  M/F | OP  T  FR |
| **Harbor View Hotel & Suites**  619-233-7799  550 W Grape St  www.stayanight.com/harborinnsdca  1 block to dog park | (24)  $44–  $189 | CB  M/F | |
| **Holiday Inn on the Bay**  619-232-3861  1355 N Harbor Dr  800-877-8920  www.ihgonline.com  pet fee $25/stay  1–2 dogs under 25 lbs, small lawn, waterfront path | (617)  $136–  $189 | C  F  R/L | OP  FR |
| **Holiday Inn Rancho Bernardo**  858-485-6530  17065 W Bernardo Dr  800-465-4329  www.holiday-inn.com  grassy walking area | (389)  $109 | FB | OP  T  FR |
| **Homestead Studio Suites**  619-299-2292  7444 Mission Valley Rd  888-782-9473  www.homesteadhotels.com  pet fee $25/day  lawn, 15 minute drive to park | (140)  $90–  $110 | K | |
| **Homestead Studio Suites**  858-623-0100  9880 Pacific Heights Blvd  888-782-9473  www.homesteadhotels.com  pet fee $25/day  small lawn and vacant lots, 1½ miles to park | (134)  $76–  $149 | K | |

| Listing | Contact | # / Price | Codes |
|---|---|---|---|
| **Horton Grand Hotel** <br> 311 Island Ave <br> www.hortongrand.com  pet fee $100/stay <br> dogs under 20 lbs only, 2 blocks to park | 619-544-1886 <br> 800-542-1886 | (130) <br> $169– <br> $269 | C |
| **Imperial Motel** <br> 6624 El Cajon Blvd  pet fee $50/stay <br> dogs by manager's approval only, dirt walking area, <br> 2 blocks to off-leash park, 5 miles to lakeside trails | 619-463-9245 | (33) <br> $58– <br> $88 | K  OP |
| **Inn Suites Hotels San Diego** <br> 2223 El Cajon Blvd <br> www.innsuites.com  pet fee $25/stay <br> grassy walking areas, 6 blocks to park | 619-296-2101 <br> 877-343-4648 | (129) <br> $94– <br> $165 | CB  OP <br> M/F  T <br> FR |
| **Kasa Korbett** <br> 4050 Front St <br> www.kasakorbett.com  dogs by advance approval | 619-291-3962 <br> 800-757-5272 | (4) <br> $99 | CB |
| **Key Suites Inc** <br> 7049 Jackson Dr <br> www.keysuitesinc.com  pet fee $200/stay <br> dogs by advance approval only, lawn and gravel area | 619-465-9999 <br> 877-999-5397 | (N) <br> $89– <br> $199 | C  OP <br> K  S <br> L  FR <br> M/F |
| **La Quinta Inn** <br> 10185 Paseo Montril <br> www.lq.com <br> dogs under 50 lbs, walking area, 1½ miles to park | 858-484-8800 <br> 800-531-5900 | (120) <br> $80– <br> $94 | CB  OP <br> F |
| **Marina Inn Hotel** <br> 1943 Pacific Hwy <br> www.marinainnsd.com  pet fee $10/day <br> lawn walking area | 619-232-7551 <br> 800-525-9055 | (38) <br> $60– <br> $70 | CB  OP |
| **Motel 6 San Diego Downtown** <br> 1546 2nd Ave <br> www.motel6.com  1 mile to park, 8 blocks to harbor | 619-236-9292 <br> 800-466-8356 | (105) <br> $56– <br> $76 | C |
| **Motel 6 San Diego Hotel Circle** <br> 2424 Hotel Cir N <br> www.motel6.com  8 miles to beach | 619-296-1612 <br> 800-466-8356 | (204) <br> $56– <br> $66 | C  OP |
| **Motel 6 San Diego North** <br> 5592 Clairemont Mesa Blvd <br> www.motel6.com  lawn, walking trail to park | 858-268-9758 <br> 800-466-8356 | (65) <br> $66– <br> $76 | C |

| C = coffee  CB = continental breakfast  F = refrigerator  FB = full breakfast  FR = fitness room | GP = guest pass to fitness center  IP = indoor pool  IS = in-room spa  K = full kitchen  (k) = kitchenette | L = lounge  M = microwave  OP = outdoor pool  R = restaurant  S = sauna/steam  T = spa or hot tub | # of units & rates | food & drink | pool, sauna & hot tub |
|---|---|---|---|---|---|

### San Diego (continued)

| | | | | |
|---|---|---|---|---|
| **Motel San Diego**  4780 Mission Bay Dr  www.motel6.com  lawn area and riverside bike trail | 858-273-6533  800-466-8356  pet fee $10/day | (28)  $55 | M/F | |
| **Ocean Beach Hotel**  5080 Newport Ave  www.obhotel.com  private patios, 5 blocks to dog-friendly beach | 619-223-7191  each pet $20/day | (56)  $90–$129 | M/F | |
| **Ocean Villa Inn**  5142 W Point Loma Blvd  www.oceanvillainn.com  lawn walking area, off-leash dog-friendly beach | 619-224-3481  800-759-0012  pet fee $25/stay | (55)  $66–$130 | CB  K | OP |
| **Old Town Inn**  4444 Pacific Hwy  www.oldtown-inn.com  1–2 dogs, small grassy area, dog-friendly beaches | 619-260-8024  800-643-3025  each pet $10/day | (74)  $59–$200 | CB  (k) | OP |
| **Omni San Diego Hotel**  675 6th Ave  www.omnihotels.com  dogs under 40 lbs only, vacant lot, 2 blocks to waterfront, 2 miles to off-leash park, 3 miles to beach | 619-231-6664  pet fee $50/stay | (511)  $179–$349 | C  R/L | OP  T  FR |
| **Pacific Inn Hotel & Suites**  1655 Pacific Hwy  www.pacificinnsd.com  lawn walking area, 1 mile to park | 619-232-6391  800-5712933  each pet $10/day | (34)  $60–$130 | CB | OP |
| **Pacific Shores Inn**  4802 Mission Blvd  www.pacificshoresinn.com      pet fee $25/stay under 50 lbs, $35/stay over 50 lbs  lawn, park, ½ block to dog-friendly beach (dogs allowed after 6 PM only) | 858-483-6300  888-478-7829 | (56)  $70–$125 | CB  K | OP |

| | | | | |
|---|---|---|---|---|
| **Premier Inns** | 619-291-8252 | (111) | CB | OP |
| 2484 Hotel Circle Pl | 800-711-6676 | $48– | F | T |
| www.premierinns.com | | $70 | | |
| riverside area, near parks | | | | |
| **Premier Inns** | 619-223-9500 | (119) | CB | OP |
| 3333 Channel Way | 877-992-9500 | $46– | F | T |
| www.premierinns.com | | $69 | | |
| near riverside walking area and dog-friendly beach | | | | |
| **Radisson Hotel** | 619-260-0111 | (260) | C | OP |
| 1433 Camino Del Rio S | 800-333-3333 | $119– | R | T |
| www.radisson.com/sandiegoca   pet fee $50/stay | | $149 | | FR |
| lawn walking area, 5 miles to parks and beach | | | | |
| **Radisson Suite Hotel Rancho Bernardo** | | (180) | FB | OP |
| 11520 W Bernardo Ct | 858-451-6600 | $99– | M | T |
| www.radisson.com | 800-333-3333 | $149 | R/L | FR |
| dogs under 30 lbs, walking trails, short drive to park | | | | |
| **Red Lion Hanalei Hotel** | 619-297-1101 | (417) | C | S/T |
| 2270 Hotel Cir N | 800-882-0858 | $109– | M/F | OP |
| www.hanaleihotel.com | pet relief area | $169 | R/L | FR |
| **Residence Inn** | 858-635-5724 | (95) | FB | OP |
| 12011 Scripps Highland Dr | 800-331-3131 | $109– | K | T |
| www.residenceinn.com/sannm   pet fee $75/stay | | $149 | | FR |
| Mon–Thur beverages and light dinner, lawn, trail, | | | | |
| 2 blocks to park | | | | |
| **Residence Inn–Mission Valley** | 619-881-3600 | (192) | FB | OP |
| 1865 Hotel Cir S | 800-228-9290 | $159– | (k) | T |
| www.residenceinnsd.com   pet fee $75/stay | | $259 | | FR |
| Mon–Thur beverages and snacks, lawn, walking path | | | | |
| **Residence Inn–Rancho Bernardo** | 858-673-1900 | (124) | CB | OP |
| 11002 Rancho Carmel Dr | 800-331-3131 | $149– | | T |
| www.residenceinn.com   pet fee $75/stay | | $199 | | FR |
| Mon–Thur beverages and light dinner, pet relief area | | | | |
| **Residence Inn–San Diego Central** | 858-278-2100 | (144) | CB | OP |
| 5400 Kearny Mesa Rd | 800-331-3131 | $149– | K | T |
| www.residenceinn.com   pet fee $75/stay | | $269 | | FR |
| 1–2 dogs under 65 lbs, Mon–Thur beverages and | | | | |
| light dinner, lawn, 20 minute drive to beach | | | | |

| C = coffee<br>CB = continental<br>    breakfast<br>F = refrigerator<br>FB = full breakfast<br>FR = fitness room | GP = guest pass to<br>    fitness center<br>IP = indoor pool<br>IS = in-room spa<br>K = full kitchen<br>(k) = kitchenette | L = lounge<br>M = microwave<br>OP = outdoor pool<br>R = restaurant<br>S = sauna/steam<br>T = spa or hot tub | # of units<br>& rates | food<br>& drink | pool, sauna<br>& hot tub |
|---|---|---|---|---|---|

## San Diego (continued)

| | | | | | |
|---|---|---|---|---|---|
| **Residence Inn–San Diego Downtown**<br>1747 Pacific Hwy        619-338-8200<br>www.residenceinn.com    800-331-3131<br>        pet fee $75/stay<br>dogs under 65 lbs only, Mon–Thur beverages and<br>light dinner, grassy areas, 3 miles to off-leash park,<br>8 miles to dog-friendly beach | | | (121)<br>$179–<br>$399 | FB<br>K | OP<br>T<br>FR |
| **Residence Inn–Sorrento Mesa**   858-552-9100<br>5995 Pacific Mesa Ct       800-331-3131<br>www.marriott.com/sanaa   pet fee $75/stay<br>Mon–Thur beverages and light dinner, lawn walking<br>area, 7 miles to dog-friendly beach | | | (150)<br>$99–<br>$149 | FB<br>K | OP<br>T<br>FR |
| **San Diego Marriott Hotel**      619-234-1500<br>333 W Harbor Dr         800-228-9290<br>www.marriott.com<br>next to boardwalk and marina | | | (1,358)<br>$260 | F<br>R/L | OP<br>T |
| **San Diego Marriott Mission Valley**<br>8757 Rio San Diego Dr     619-692-3800<br>www.marriott.com        800-228-9290<br>close to walking trail     pet fee $50/stay | | | (350)<br>$129–<br>$149 | R | OP<br>T<br>FR |
| **Santa Clara Motel**        858-488-1193<br>839 Santa Clara Pl<br>dogs by manager's approval only, bayfront walking<br>area | | | (17)<br>$45–<br>$125 | K | |
| **Shelter Pointe Hotel & Marina**  619-221-8000<br>1551 Shelter Island Dr     800-566-2524<br>www.shelterpointe.com   pet fee $50/stay<br>dogs under 50 lbs only, private patios, bayfront park | | | (205)<br>$119–<br>$239 | M/F<br>R | OP<br>T |
| **Sheraton Hotel**         858-485-9250<br>11611 Bernardo Plaza Ct   888-627-8576<br>small lake and walking trail | | | (209)<br>$105–<br>$239 | C<br>M/F<br>R/L | OP<br>T<br>FR |

| | | | | |
|---|---|---|---|---|
| **Sheraton San Diego Hotel & Marina** | | (1,064) | CB | OP |
| 1590 Harbor Island Dr | 619-291-2900 | $99– | F | T |
| www.sheraton.com | 800-325-3535 | $235 | R | FR |
| 1 dog under 80 lbs only, bayside walking area | | | | |
| **Sheraton Suites** | 619-696-9800 | (264) | M/F | IP |
| 701 A St | 800-325-3535 | $169– | R/L | T |
| www.sheraton.com | | $320 | | FR |
| dogs by advance reservation only, 1 bdrm suites, pet supplies, ½ mile to park, 20 minute drive to beach | | | | |
| **Sommerset Suites Hotel** | 619-692-5200 | (80) | CB | OP |
| 606 Washington St | 800-962-9665 | $89– | K | T |
| www.sommersetsuites.com | pet fee $35/stay | $199 | | |
| dogs under 35 lbs only, studios/1 bdrm suites, grassy walking areas, 2 miles to dog-friendly park | | | | |
| **Staybridge Suites** | 858-453-5343 | (131) | FB | OP |
| 6639 Mira Mesa Blvd | 800-238-8000 | $149– | (k) | FR |
| www.staybridge.com | pet fee $75/stay | $229 | | |
| 1–2 bdrm suites, 2 miles to park | | | | |
| **Staybridge Suites Downtown** | 619-795-4000 | (68) | CB | FR |
| 1110 A St | 800-238-8000 | $169– | K | |
| www.staybridge.com | pet fee $150/stay | $229 | | |
| rooftop terrace, ¼ mile to dog-friendly park | | | | |
| **Staybridge Suites Hotel Carmel** | 858-487-0900 | (116) | FB | OP |
| 11855 Avenue of Industry | 800-238-8000 | $130– | CB | FR |
| www.staybridge.com | pet fee $150/stay | $180 | (k) | |
| 1–2 dogs under 50 lbs only, studios/1–2 bdrm suites, Tue-Thur beverages and appetizers, walking areas | | | | |
| **Surfer Motor Lodge** | 858-483-7070 | (52) | C | OP |
| 711 Pacific Beach Dr | 800-787-3373 | $95– | (k) | T |
| www.surfermotorlodge.com | pet fee $25/stay | $155 | | |
| dogs under 10 lbs only, grassy area, close to parks | | | | |
| **Travelodge** | 858-487-0445 | (49) | CB | OP |
| 16929 W Bernardo Dr | 800-578-7878 | $79– | M/F | |
| www.travelodge.com | each pet $10/day | $89 | | |
| small grassy walking areas, 1 mile to park | | | | |

| C = coffee<br>CB = continental<br>    breakfast<br>F = refrigerator<br>FB = full breakfast<br>FR = fitness room | GP = guest pass to<br>    fitness center<br>IP = indoor pool<br>IS = in-room spa<br>K = full kitchen<br>(k) = kitchenette | L = lounge<br>M = microwave<br>OP = outdoor pool<br>R = restaurant<br>S = sauna/steam<br>T = spa or hot tub | (# of units)<br>& rates | food<br>& drink | pool, sauna<br>& hot tub |
|---|---|---|---|---|---|

## San Diego (continued)

| | | | | | |
|---|---|---|---|---|---|
| **Travelodge–Mission Valley**<br>1201 Hotel Cir S<br>www.missionvalleyhotel.com<br>lawn and gravel walking areas, 3–5 miles to parks<br>and beach | | 619-297-2271<br>each pet $10/day | (102)<br>$59–<br>$99 | C<br>M/F<br>R/L | OP<br>T |
| **U S Suites**<br>10439 Roselle St<br>www.ussuites.com<br>1 dog by advance reservation only, 1–2 bdrm<br>condominiums, next to park, 10–15 minute drive<br>to dog-friendly beaches | | 858-554-0300<br>800-877-8483<br>pet fee $200/stay | (30)<br>call<br>for<br>rates | K | OP<br>T<br>FR |
| **Vagabond Inn**<br>625 Hotel Cir S<br>www.vagabondhc.com<br>lawn walking area, 5 miles to park | | 619-297-1691<br>800-522-1555<br>each pet $10/day | (88)<br>$49–<br>$189 | CB<br>M/F | OP<br>T |
| **Vagabond Inn Point Loma**<br>1325 Scott St<br>www.vagabondinn.com<br>lawn, 15 minute drive to off-leash dog beach | | 619-224-3371<br>800-522-1555<br>pet fee $10/day | (40)<br>$45–<br>$120 | CB<br>(k) | OP |
| **W Hotel San Diego**<br>421 W B St<br>www.whotels.com/sandiego<br>dogs under 80 lbs only, dog-sitting/dogwalking<br>services, pet supplies, list of local pet-friendly parks,<br>2 blocks to bayfront walking area, 1 mile to park | | 619-231-8220<br>866-837-4147 | (259)<br>$225 | C<br>M/F<br>R/L | OP<br>FR |
| **Westgate Hotel**<br>1055 2nd Ave<br>www.westgatehotel.com<br>1 dog under 25 lbs only, 8 blocks to waterfront,<br>12 blocks to off-leash dog park | | 619-238-1818<br>800-221-3802 | (223)<br>$315–<br>$395 | R/L | FR |

| | | | | |
|---|---|---|---|---|
| **Westin Horton Plaza**   619-239-2200 <br> 910 Broadway Cir    800-937-8461 <br> www.westin.com/hortonplaza <br> dogs under 40 lbs only, "Heavenly Dog Beds" | (450) <br> $359 | R/L | OP <br> T <br> FR | |

### San Dimas

| | | | |
|---|---|---|---|
| **Motel 6**    909-592-5631 <br> 502 W Arrow Hwy    800-466-8356 <br> www.motel6.com <br> lawn, 2 blocks to park | (118) <br> $50–<br>$60 | C | |
| **Red Roof Inn**    909-599-2362 <br> 204 Village Ct <br> www.redroof-san-dimas.com <br> dogs under 80 lbs only, small lawn, ¾ mile to park | (134) <br> $59–<br>$99 | C <br> M/F | OP <br> T |

### San Francisco

| | | | |
|---|---|---|---|
| **Absolutely Accommodations**    415-252-1277 <br> www.lodgingincalifornia.com    888-982-2632 <br> referral service for dog-friendly hotels, B & Bs and <br> vacation rentals throughout California | call <br> for <br> rates | K | |
| **American Marketing Systems Inc.** <br> 2800 Van Ness Ave    415-447-2000 <br> www.amsires.com    800-747-7784 <br> studios to 4 bdrm rental homes | (200) <br> $100–<br>$400 | K | |
| **Belvedere House B & B**    415-731-6654 <br> 598 Belvedere St    877-226-3273 <br> www.belvederehouse.com <br> dogs by advance approval, 5 minute walk to park | (6) <br> $85–<br>$125 | FB <br> F | |
| **Beresford Arms Hotel**    415-673-2600 <br> 701 Post St    800-533-6533 <br> www.beresford.com    3 blocks to Union Square | (95) <br> $99–<br>$189 | C | GP |
| **Beresford Hotel**    415-673-9900 <br> 635 Sutter St    800-533-6533 <br> www.beresford.com    2 blocks to Union Square | (114) <br> $82–<br>$89 | CB <br> F | GP |
| **Best Western Civic Center Inn**    415-621-2826 <br> 364 9th St    800-444-5829 <br> www.renesonhotels.com <br> small walking areas, 4 blocks to park | (57) <br> $89–<br>$135 | CB <br> M/F <br> R | OP |

| C = coffee   GP = guest pass to   L = lounge<br>CB = continental        fitness center   M = microwave<br>    breakfast   IP = indoor pool   OP = outdoor pool<br>F = refrigerator   IS = in-room spa   R = restaurant<br>FB = full breakfast   K = full kitchen   S = sauna/steam<br>FR = fitness room   (k) = kitchenette   T = spa or hot tub | (# of units) & rates | food & drink | pool, sauna & hot tub |
|---|---|---|---|
| ### San Francisco (continued) | | | |
| **Best Western Tuscan Inn**                 415-561-1100<br>425 N Point St                                    800-648-4626<br>www.tuscaninn.com                        pet fee $25/stay<br>pet supplies and list of local dog-friendly places,<br>lawn walking area, 6 blocks to waterfront park | (221)<br>$129–<br>$189 | C<br>R | GP |
| **Bristol Hotel**                                 415-296-0980<br>56 Mason St<br>dogs in smoking rooms only, 4 blocks to park | (60)<br>$60 | | |
| **Campton Place Hotel**                   415-781-5555<br>340 Stockton St                                  800-235-4300<br>www.camptonplace.com              each pet $35/day<br>across street to Union Square, 15 minute walk to<br>park in Chinatown | (110)<br>$335–<br>$445 | R | FR |
| **Cartwright Hotel**                           415-421-2865<br>524 Sutter St                                      800-919-9779<br>www.cartwrighthotel.com<br>small dogs only, 1 block to Union Square | (114)<br>$89–<br>$169 | CB<br>F | GP |
| **Chateau Tivoli B & B**                   415-776-5462<br>1057 Steiner St                                  800-228-1647<br>www.chateautivoli.com<br>2 bdrm suites on ground floor with outside entrance,<br>1 block to Alamo Square park | (9)<br>$135–<br>$160 | FB<br>CB<br>(k) | |
| **Crowne Plaza**                              415-398-8900<br>480 Sutter St<br>www.crowneplaza.com<br>dogs under 20 lbs only, 3 blocks to small park | (403)<br>$115–<br>$229 | CB<br>R | FR |
| **Executive Hotel Vintage Court**   415-392-4666<br>650 Bush St                                        800-654-1100<br>evening wine reception, restaurant open for dinner<br>only, 4 blocks to park on Nob Hill | (107)<br>$115–<br>$199 | CB<br>R | GP<br>IS |

| | | | | |
|---|---|---|---|---|
| **Fairmont San Francisco** 950 Mason St www.fairmont.com pet fee $25/stay dogs under 20 lbs only, walking distance to parks | 415-772-5000 800-441-1414 | (653) $150 | F R/L | T FR |
| **Fitzgerald Hotel** 620 Post St www.fitzgeraldhotel.com Victorian hotel, 2 blocks to Union Square, 15 minute drive to dog-friendly park | 415-775-8100 877-662-4455 | (50) $49– $245 | CB | GP |
| **Four Seasons Hotel** 757 Market St www.fourseasons.com/sanfrancisco dogs under 15 lbs only, across street to garden area, 1½ blocks to Union Square | 415-633-3000 800-332-3442 | 277 $299– $439 | M/F R/L | |
| **Golden Gate Hotel** 775 Bush St www.goldengatehotel.com    2 blocks to small park | 415-392-3702 800-835-1118 | (25) $85– $115 | CB | |
| **Halcyon Hotel** 649 Jones St www.halcyonsf.com    pet fee $5/day dogs under 40 lbs only, 7 blocks to park | 415-929-8033 800-627-2396 | (25) $85– $115 | (k) | |
| **Harbor Court Hotel** 165 Steuart St www.harborcourthotel.com pet supplies, next to YMCA, 1½ blocks to park | 415-882-1300 800-346-0555 | (131) $159– $259 | C | GP |
| **Hayes Valley Inn** 417 Gough St www.hayesvalleyinn.com    no pet fee for 1–2 day stay, $20–$50 for longer stay 4 blocks to off-leash dog park | 415-431-9131 800-930-7999 | (27) $53– $66 | CB K | FR |
| **Holiday Inn Civic Center** 50 8th St www.holiday-inn.com    pet fee $75/stay small dogs only, 1 block to lawn walking area | 415-626-6103 800-243-1135 | (390) $179– $209 | C | OP FR |
| **Holiday Inn Golden Gateway** 1500 Van Ness Ave www.holiday-inn.com | 415-441-4000 pet fee $50/stay 2 blocks to park | (499) $134– $154 | C R/L | OP FR |

| | | | |
|---|---|---|---|
| C = coffee | GP = guest pass to | L = lounge | |
| CB = continental | fitness center | M = microwave | |
| breakfast | IP = indoor pool | OP = outdoor pool | |
| F = refrigerator | IS = in-room spa | R = restaurant | |
| FB = full breakfast | K = full kitchen | S = sauna/steam | |
| FR = fitness room | (k) = kitchenette | T = spa or hot tub | |

## San Francisco (continued)

| | | (# of units)<br>& rates | food<br>& drink | pool, sauna<br>& hot tub |
|---|---|---|---|---|
| **Holiday Inn Select Downtown** 415-433-6600 | | (565) | FB | OP |
| 750 Kearny St | 800-424-8292 | $99– | CB | FR |
| www.hiselect.com/sfo-dwntn&spa   pet fee $50/stay | | $189 | F | |
| dogs under 20 lbs only, 4 blocks to park | | | R/L | |
| **Hotel Argonaut** | 415-563-0800 | (252) | R | IS |
| 495 Jefferson St | 866-415-0704 | $169– | | |
| www.argonauthotel.com | | $699 | | |
| small to medium dogs allowed in smoking rooms | | | | |
| only, next to Victorian Park | | | | |
| **Hotel Cosmo** | 415-673-6040 | (144) | L | |
| 761 Post St | 800-794-6011 | $99– | | |
| www.hotel-cosmo.com | | $129 | | |
| pet supplies, patio, guide to local pet-friendly parks | | | | |
| and beaches, 6 blocks to park | | | | |
| **Hotel Diva** | 415-885-0200 | (131) | C | FR |
| 440 Geary St | 800-553-1900 | $99– | | |
| www.hoteldiva.com   pet fee $50/stay | | $195 | | |
| 1 block to Union Square | | | | |
| **Hotel Juliana** | 415-392-2540 | (107) | C | FR |
| 590 Bush St | 800-328-3880 | $129– | | |
| www.julianahotel.com | | $189 | | |
| dogs under 50 lbs only, close to grassy walking areas | | | | |
| **Hotel Metropolis** | 415-775-4600 | (105) | C | FR |
| 25 Mason St | 800-553-1900 | $85– | R | |
| small lawn, 4 blocks to park   pet fee $50/stay | | $155 | | |
| **Hotel Monaco** | 415-292-0100 | (201) | C | FR |
| 501 Geary St | 800-214-4220 | $179– | R | |
| www.monaco-sf.com | | $399 | | |
| yoga and "doga" programs, dogwalking service, 2 | | | | |
| blocks to Union Square, 15 minute walk to large park | | | | |

| | | | | |
|---|---|---|---|---|
| **Hotel Nikko San Francisco**<br>222 Mason St<br>www.hotelnikkosf.com<br>2 blocks to Union Square | 415-394-1111<br>800-645-5687 | (532)<br>$179–<br>$219 | CB<br>R/L | IP<br>FR |
| **Hotel Palomar**<br>12 4th St<br>www.hotelpalomar.com<br>well-behaved dogs welcome, dogsitting/dogwalking<br>services, pet massage and aerobics, 6 blocks to park | 415-348-1111<br>877-294-9711 | (214)<br>$169–<br>$269 | C<br>F<br>R/L | FR<br>FP |
| **Hotel Serrano**<br>405 Taylor St<br>www.serranohotel.com<br>4 blocks to park | 415-885-2500<br>877-294-9709 | (236)<br>$139–<br>$339 | C<br>R | S<br>FR |
| **Hotel Triton**<br>342 Grant Ave<br>www.hoteltriton.com<br>15 minute drive to Golden Gate Park | 415-394-0500<br>800-800-1299 | (140)<br>$139–<br>$179 | CB<br>R | FR |
| **Hotel Villa Florence**<br>225 Powell St<br>www.villaflorence.com<br>next to Union Square, 6 blocks to park | 415-397-7700<br>800-553-4411 | (183)<br>$119–<br>$229 | C<br>R | GP |
| **Inn 1890**<br>1890 Page St<br>www.inn1890.com<br>adult dogs allowed by advance reservation only,<br>1 block to Golden Gate Park | 415-386-0486<br>888-466-1890 | (16)<br>$89–<br>$159 | FB<br>(k) | |
| **Inn San Francisco**<br>943 S Van Ness Ave<br>www.innsf.com<br>well-mannered dogs allowed but must never be left<br>alone in room, 4 blocks to large park | 415-641-0188<br>800-359-0913 | (21)<br>$75–<br>$225 | FB | T<br>IS |
| **Invented City Home Exchange**<br>www.invented-city.com<br>unique "house-swapping" program, see website | 415-846-7588 | | | |
| **Ivy Hotel**<br>539 Octavia St<br>4 blocks to small park | 415-863-6388 | (32)<br>$42–<br>$60 | | |

| C = coffee | GP = guest pass to | L = lounge |
|---|---|---|
| CB = continental | fitness center | M = microwave |
| breakfast | IP = indoor pool | OP = outdoor pool |
| F = refrigerator | IS = in-room spa | R = restaurant |
| FB = full breakfast | K = full kitchen | S = sauna/steam |
| FR = fitness room | (k) = kitchenette | T = spa or hot tub |

## San Francisco (continued)

| | | (# of units) & rates | food & drink | pool, sauna & hot tub |
|---|---|---|---|---|
| **Kensington Park Hotel** | 415-788-6400 | (90) | CB | FR |
| 450 Post St | 800-553-1900 | $110– | | |
| www.kensingtonparkhotel.com | pet fee $50/stay | $160 | | |
| social hour beverages, ½ block to Union Square | | | | |
| **Laurel Inn** | 415-567-8467 | (49) | CB | GP |
| 444 Presidio Ave | 800-552-8735 | $155– | (k) | |
| www.thelaurelinn.com | | $190 | | |
| pet supplies, 5 blocks to park | | | | |
| **Mandarin Oriental Hotel** | 415-276-9888 | (158) | R | FR |
| 222 Sansome St | 800-622-0404 | $260– | | |
| www.mandarinoriental.com | pet fee $25/day | $3,000 | | |
| dogs under 25 lbs only, 4 blocks to waterfront park | | | | |
| **Marina Motel** | 415-921-9406 | (38) | K | |
| 2576 Lombard St | pet fee $10/day | $79– | | |
| www.marinamotel.com | | $99 | | |
| 10 minute walk to dog beach | | | | |
| **Monticello Inn** | 415-392-8800 | (91) | C | GP |
| 127 Ellis St | 800-669-7777 | $99– | M/F | |
| www.monticelloinn.com | evening wine reception | $159 | R/L | |
| **Noe's Nest B & B** | 415-647-5510 | (6) | FB | IS |
| 3973 23rd St | 888-663-6378 | $99– | | |
| www.noesnest.com | | $179 | | |
| backyard walking area | | | | |
| **Ocean Park Motel** | 415-566-7020 | (24) | C | T |
| 2690 46th Ave | each pet $10/day | $85– | K | |
| www.oceanparkmotel.citysearch.com | | $105 | M/F | |
| backyard walking area, 2 blocks to beach | | | | |
| **Omni San Francisco Hotel** | 415-677-9494 | (362) | C | FR |
| 500 California St | 800-843-6664 | $159– | M/F | |
| www.omnisanfrancisco.com | pet fee $50/stay | $329 | R | |
| dogs under 25 lbs only, ½ mile to waterfront | | | | |

| | | | | |
|---|---|---|---|---|
| **Pacific Heights Inn** <br> 1555 Union St <br> www.pacificheightsinn.com   pet fee $10–$15/day <br> 1½ blocks to dog park, 2 blocks to pet daycare | 415-776-3310 <br> 800-523-1801 | (40) <br> $79– <br> $140 | CB | IS |
| **Pacific Motor Inn** <br> 2599 Lombard St <br> www.pacificmotorinn.com   each pet $10/day <br> 1–2 dogs only, 3 blocks to park, 5 blocks to beach | 415-346-4664 <br> 800-536-8446 | (62) <br> $78– <br> $178 | CB | |
| **Palace Hotel** <br> 2 New Montgomery St <br> www.sfpalace.com <br> dogs under 50 lbs only, 1 mile to dog-friendly park | 415-512-1111 <br> 800-325-3535 | (552) <br> $179– <br> $529 | F <br> R/L | IP <br> S <br> T |
| **Pan Pacific Hotel** <br> 500 Post St <br> www.panpacific.com   pet fee $75/stay <br> dogs under 25 lbs in smoking rooms only | 415-771-8600 <br> 800-533-6465 | (229) <br> $209– <br> $360 | FB <br> R | FR <br> GP |
| **The Parsonage** <br> 198 Haight St <br> www.theparsonage.com <br> dogs by advance reservation only, small enclosed <br> garden, 5 minute drive to off-leash dog park | 415-863-7722 <br> 888-763-7722 | (5) <br> $140– <br> $250 | FB | |
| **Prescott Hotel** <br> 545 Post St <br> www.prescotthotel.com <br> evening wine reception, 1½ blocks to park | 415-563-0303 <br> 800-283-7322 | (164) <br> $189– <br> $475 | C <br> F | GP |
| **Ritz-Carlton San Francisco** <br> 600 Stockton St <br> www.ritzcarlton.com <br> dogs under 10 lbs only, ¼ mile to park | 415-296-7465 <br> 800-241-3333 | (336) <br> $360– <br> $395 | C <br> F <br> R/L | IP <br> S <br> FR |
| **San Francisco Marriott** <br> 1250 Columbus Ave <br> www.marriott.com/sfofw   pet fee $100/stay <br> dogs under 50 lbs, 4 blocks to Washington Square | 415-775-7555 <br> 800-228-9290 | (285) <br> $149– <br> $209 | R/L | S <br> FR |
| **Sheraton Fisherman's Wharf** <br> 2500 Mason St <br> www.sheratonatthewharf.com <br> dogs under 80 lbs only, ½ mile to waterfront park | 415-362-5500 <br> 800-325-3535 | (529) <br> $189– <br> $209 | R | OP <br> FR |

| C = coffee  GP = guest pass to  L = lounge<br>CB = continental　　　fitness center  M = microwave<br>　　breakfast　IP = indoor pool  OP = outdoor pool<br>F = refrigerator  IS = in-room spa  R = restaurant<br>FB = full breakfast  K = full kitchen  S = sauna/steam<br>FR = fitness room  (k) = kitchenette  T = spa or hot tub | (# of units) & rates | food & drink | pool, sauna & hot tub |
|---|---|---|---|

## San Francisco (continued)

| | | | | |
|---|---|---|---|---|
| **Sir Francis Drake Hotel** | 415-392-7755 | (417) | CB | GP |
| 450 Powell St | 800-227-5480 | $149– | F | FR |
| www.sirfrancisdrake.com | | $189 | R/L | |
| pet supplies, dogwalking guide to the city, 1 block to Union Square, 3 blocks to park at top of Nob Hill | | | | |
| **Stanford Court Hotel** | 415-989-3500 | (393) | C | FR |
| 905 California St | 800-228-9290 | $179– | R/L | |
| www.renaissancehotels.com | | $279 | | |
| dogs under 20 lbs only, 1 block to park | | | | |
| **Travelodge by the Bay** | 415-673-0691 | (72) | C | |
| 1450 Lombard St | 800-578-7878 | $69– | M/F | |
| www.travelodge.com　　　　pet fee $20/day | | $145 | | |
| dogs in smoking rooms only, 10 blocks to park | | | | |
| **Travelodge Central** | 415-621-6775 | (84) | CB | |
| 1707 Market St | 800-578-7878 | $68– | M/F | |
| www.sanfranciscocentralhotel.com　pet fee $10/day | | $80 | | |
| 15 minute drive to Golden Gate Park | | | | |
| **Twenty-Four Henry Guesthouse** | 415-864-5686 | (10) | CB | |
| 24 Henry St | 800-900-5686 | $65– | | |
| www.24henry.com | | $119 | | |
| dogs allowed with manager's approval only, 1 block to DuBoce Park | | | | |
| **W Hotel San Francisco** | 415-777-5300 | (423) | R/L | IP |
| 181 3rd St | 888-627-8391 | $299– | | T |
| www.whotels.com/sanfrancisco　　pet fee $25/day | | $399 | | FR |
| dogs under 80 lbs, special "Woof-Meow" package includes pet toy/bed/bowls/treats/cleanup bags/ ID tag/list of local pet-friendly parks, dogsitting and dogwalking services available, across street to park and gardens | | | | |

| | | | | |
|---|---|---|---|---|
| **Washington Square Inn**<br>1660 Stockton St<br>www.washingtonsquareinnsf.com   each pet $10/day<br>dogs under 25 lbs only, evening wine & appetizers | 415-981-4220<br>800-388-0220 | (15)<br>$115–<br>$245 | CB | |
| **Westin St Francis**<br>335 Powell St<br>www.westin.com/stfrancis<br>dogs under 40 lbs, pet treats/beds, across street to<br>Union Square, 10 minute walk to gardens | 415-397-7000<br>800-937-8466 | (1,200)<br>$169–<br>$335 | F<br>R/L | FR |
| **York Hotel**<br>940 Sutter St<br>www.yorkhotel.com<br>dogs under 15 lbs only, 12 blocks to park | 415-885-6800<br>800-808-9675 | (93)<br>$69–<br>$149 | CB<br>R/L | FR |

### San Jose

| | | | | |
|---|---|---|---|---|
| **Best Western Gateway Inn**<br>800-437-88552585 Seaboard Ave<br>www.bestwesterncalifornia.com<br>small dogs only, gravel area, 5 minute drive to park | 408-435-8800 | (148)<br>$69–<br>$79 | CB<br>F | OP<br>FR |
| **Days Inn**<br>2460 Fontaine Rd<br>www.daysinn.com<br>lawn walking area | 408-270-7666<br>800-329-7466 | (53)<br>$79–<br>$89 | CB<br>M/F | OP |
| **E-Z8 Motel**<br>1550 N 1st St<br>www.ez8motels.com<br>paved area for walking dogs, 3 miles to park | 408-453-1830 | (81)<br>$45–<br>$95 | C<br>F | OP<br>T |
| **E-Z8 Motel**<br>2050 N 1st St<br>www.ez8motels.com<br>lawn and gravel walking areas, 2 miles to park | 408-436-0636 | (88)<br>$47–<br>$50 | C<br>F | OP<br>T |
| **Executive Inn Suites**<br>3930 Monterey Hwy<br>dogs under 20 lbs, 3 miles to off-leash park | 408-281-8700 | (25)<br>$79–<br>$89 | CB<br>M/F | IS |
| **Executive Inn/Airport**<br>1310 N 1st St<br>dogs under 20 lbs only, large walking area, 3 blocks<br>to small park, short drive to larger parks and beach | 408-453-1100<br>800-877-1331 | (59)<br>$69–<br>$89 | CB<br>M/F | OP<br>T |

| C = coffee<br>CB = continental<br>  breakfast<br>F = refrigerator<br>FB = full breakfast<br>FR = fitness room | GP = guest pass to<br>  fitness center<br>IP = indoor pool<br>IS = in-room spa<br>K = full kitchen<br>(k) = kitchenette | L = lounge<br>M = microwave<br>OP = outdoor pool<br>R = restaurant<br>S = sauna/steam<br>T = spa or hot tub | (# of units)<br>& rates | food<br>& drink | pool, sauna<br>& hot tub |
|---|---|---|---|---|---|

## San Jose (continued)

| | | | | |
|---|---|---|---|---|
| **Fairmont Hotel San Jose**<br>170 S Market St<br>www.fairmont.com<br>dogs under 20 lbs only, across street to park | 408-998-1900<br>800-441-1414<br>pet fee $25/day | (805)<br>$149 | F<br>R | OP<br>S<br>FR<br>GP |
| **Hilton San Jose & Towers**<br>300 Almaden Blvd<br>www.sanjose.hilton.com<br>lawn area, 1 block to park | 408-287-2100<br>800-345-6565 | (354)<br>$139–<br>$269 | C<br>M/F<br>R/L | OP<br>T<br>FR |
| **Homestead Studio Suites**<br>1560 N 1st St<br>www.homesteadhotels.com<br>lawn and paved walking areas, 3 miles to park | 408-573-0648<br>888-782-9473<br>pet fee $25/day | (152)<br>$100 | C<br>K | |
| **Homewood Suites**<br>10 W Trimble Rd<br>www.homewoodsuites.com<br>4 blocks to park | 408-428-9900<br>800-225-5466 | (140)<br>$79–<br>$149 | FB<br>K | OP<br>T<br>FR |
| **Hotel De Anza**<br>233 W Santa Clara St<br>www.hoteldeanza.com<br>short walk to parks | 408-286-1000<br>800-843-3700<br>pet fee $30/stay | (100)<br>$109–<br>$250 | C<br>R/L | FR |
| **Howard Johnson Express Inn**<br>1215 S 1st St<br>www.www.hojo.com<br>small lawn walking area, ½ mile to park | 408-280-5300<br>800-446-4656<br>pet fee $5/stay | (29)<br>$59–<br>$119 | FB<br>(k)<br>M/F | T<br>GP |
| **Motel 6 San Jose Airport**<br>2081 N 1st St<br>www.motel6.com<br>small dogs only, lawn, 20 minute drive to park | 408-436-8180<br>800-466-8356 | (74)<br>$50–<br>$72 | C | |
| **Motel 6 San Jose South**<br>2560 Fontaine Rd<br>www.motel6.com<br>lawn, 3 miles to park | 408-270-3131<br>800-466-8356 | (202)<br>$49–<br>$56 | C | OP |

| | | | | |
|---|---|---|---|---|
| **Residence Inn San Jose South** 408-226-7676 6111 San Ignacio Ave 800-331-3131 www.marriott.com     pet fee $10/day plus $75 cleaning fee pet relief area, 5 miles to walking trails | (150) $79– $159 | FB K M/F | OP FR T | |
| **Sierra Suites Hotel** 408-453-3000 55 E Brokaw Rd 800-474-5773 www.sierrasuites.com     pet fee $5/day plus $100 cleaning fee dogs under 75 lbs only, Mon–Thur beverages and appetizers, pet relief area, 1 mile to park | (138) $79– $149 | FB K | OP T FR | |
| **Summerfield Suites Hotel** 408-436-1600 1602 Crane Ct     pet fee $150/stay www.staybridge.com 1–2 bdrm suites, Tue-Thur beverages and appetizers, lawn walking area, 3 miles to park | (114) $129 | CB K | OP T FR | |
| **Towneplace Suites by Marriott** 408-984-5903 440 Saratoga Ave 800-257-3000 www.towneplacesuites.com     pet fee $75/stay studios/1–2 bdrm suites, lawn, 1 mile to park | (101) $79– $119 | CB K | OP T FR | |
| **Travelodge San Jose Convention Center** 1415 Monterey Hwy 408-993-1711 www.travelodge.com dogs by manager's approval only | (26) $75– $95 | CB M/F | | |
| **Vagabond Inn** 408-453-8822 1488 N 1st St 800-522-1555 www.vagabondinn.com     pet fee $20/stay residential neighborhood, 4 blocks to park | (76) $54– $69 | CB M/F | OP T | |
| **Valley Inn** 408-241-8500 2155 The Alameda small dogs only, open field, 1½ miles to park | (26) $59 | CB M/F | | |

## San Juan Bautista

| | | | | |
|---|---|---|---|---|
| **San Juan Inn** 831-623-4380 Hwy 156     pet fee $10/day lawn walking area, 4 blocks to park | (43) $79– $89 | C M/F | OP T | |

| C = coffee<br>CB = continental<br>    breakfast<br>F = refrigerator<br>FB = full breakfast<br>FR = fitness room | GP = guest pass to<br>    fitness center<br>IP = indoor pool<br>IS = in-room spa<br>K = full kitchen<br>(k) = kitchenette | L = lounge<br>M = microwave<br>OP = outdoor pool<br>R = restaurant<br>S = sauna/steam<br>T = spa or hot tub | (# of units)<br>& rates | food<br>& drink | pool, sauna<br>& hot tub |
|---|---|---|---|---|---|

## San Juan Capistrano

| | | | | | |
|---|---|---|---|---|---|
| **Best Western Capistrano Inn**<br>27174 Ortega Hwy<br>www.capoinn.com<br>1½ miles to park | 949-493-5661<br>800-441-9438<br>pet fee $25/stay | (108)<br>$80–<br>$130 | CB<br>M/F | OP<br>T |
| **Mission Inn B & B**<br>26891 Ortega Hwy<br>www.missioninnsjc.com<br>shaded grassy walking areas | 949-234-0249<br>866-234-0249<br>pet fee $20/day | (20)<br>$145–<br>$230 | CB<br>F | OP |

## San Leandro

| | | | | | |
|---|---|---|---|---|---|
| **Islander Motel**<br>2398 E 14th St<br>landscaped areas for walking dogs, 1 mile to park | 510-352-5010<br>pet fee $50/stay | (67)<br>$44–<br>$50 | (k) | |

## San Luis Obispo

| | | | | | |
|---|---|---|---|---|---|
| **Best Western Royal Oak Hotel**<br>214 Madonna Rd<br>www.royaloakhotel.com<br>½ block to dog park | 805-544-4410<br>800-545-4410<br>each pet $10/stay | (99)<br>$74–<br>$139 | CB<br>F | OP<br>T |
| **Coachman Inn Motel**<br>1001 Olive St<br>lawn walking area, ½ block to park | 805-544-0400<br>each pet $10/day | (27)<br>$40–<br>$89 | M/F | |
| **Days Inn**<br>2050 Garfield St<br>www.daysinnslo.com<br>¼ mile to park | 805-549-9911<br>800-544-7250<br>pet fee $10/day | (75)<br>$99–<br>$139 | CB<br>M/F | OP<br>T<br>FR |
| **Heritage Inn**<br>978 Olive St<br>www.heritageinnslo.com<br>dogs by advance arrangement only, creek and<br>garden area for walking dogs | 805-544-7440<br>pet fee $25/stay | (7)<br>$85–<br>$150 | FB | |

| | | | | |
|---|---|---|---|---|
| **Holiday Inn Express**<br>1800 Monterey St<br>www.hiexpress.com/sanluisobispo    pet fee $25/stay<br>small lawn areas, 1 mile to park | 805-544-8600<br>800-465-4329 | (100)<br>$107–<br>$143 | CB<br>M/F | OP<br>T |
| **Motel 6 North**<br>1433 Calle Joaquin<br>www.motel6.com    pet relief area, 1 mile to park | 805-549-9595<br>800-466-8356 | (86)<br>$48–<br>$76 | C | OP |
| **Motel 6 South**<br>1625 Calle Joaquin<br>www.motel6.com    lawn walking area | 805-541-6992<br>800-466-8356 | (117)<br>$46–<br>$76 | C | OP |
| **Petit Soleil Bed et Breakfast**<br>1473 Monterey St<br>www.psslo.com<br>dogs allowed by advance approval only, winetasting<br>and appetizers, close to lawn and school sports field | 805-549-0321<br>800-676-1588 | (15)<br>$129–<br>$189 | FB | |
| **Ramada Inn Olive Tree**<br>1000 Olive St    pet fee $10/day<br>www.ramada.com    grassy area, 1 block to park | 805-544-2800 | (61)<br>$59–<br>$200 | CB<br>M/F<br>R | OP<br>S |
| **San Luis Inn**<br>404 Santa Rosa St<br>www.sanluisinn.com    pet fee $10/day<br>1 block to park | 805-544-0881<br>800-447-8080 | (35)<br>$35–<br>$179 | CB<br>M/F | OP |
| **Sands Suites & Motel**<br>1930 Monterey St<br>www.sandssuites.com    each pet $10/stay<br>rooms/suites sleep 6, lawn area, near walking trails | 805-544-0500<br>800-441-4657 | (75)<br>$69–<br>$169 | CB<br>M/F | OP<br>T |
| **Vagabond Inn**<br>210 Madonna Rd<br>www.vagabondinn.com    pet fee $10/day<br>4 blocks to park | 805-544-4710<br>800-522-1555 | (61)<br>$69–<br>$145 | CB<br>M/F | OP<br>T |

## San Mateo

| | | | | |
|---|---|---|---|---|
| **Best Western San Mateo Inn**<br>2940 S Norfolk St<br>www.bestwesternsanmateo.com<br>small dogs allowed by manager's approval only, lawn<br>and gravel walking areas, 5 blocks to park | 650-341-3300<br>800-528-1234 | (116)<br>$79–<br>$99 | CB<br>M/F | T |

| C = coffee  GP = guest pass to  L = lounge<br>CB = continental    fitness center  M = microwave<br>    breakfast  IP = indoor pool  OP = outdoor pool<br>F = refrigerator  IS = in-room spa  R = restaurant<br>FB = full breakfast  K = full kitchen  S = sauna/steam<br>FR = fitness room  (k) = kitchenette  T = spa or hot tub | (# of units) & rates | food & drink | pool, sauna & hot tub |
|---|---|---|---|
| **San Mateo (continued)** | | | |
| **Homestead Studio Suites**    650-574-1744<br>1830 Gateway Dr    888-782-9473<br>www.homesteadhotels.com   pet fee $75/stay<br>courtyard, small lawn, 2 blocks to park with lake | (137)<br>$70–<br>$90 | C<br>M/F | |
| **Radisson Villa Hotel**    650-341-0966<br>4000 S El Camino Real    800-333-3333<br>www.radissonvilla.com  lawn, 1 mile to bayfront park | (286)<br>$115 | C<br>F<br>R | OP<br>FR |
| **Residence Inn**    650-574-4700<br>2000 Windward Way    800-331-3131<br>www.marriott.com/sfosm   pet fee $75/stay<br>studios/1 bdrm suites, Mon–Thur beverages and<br>light dinner, lawn and miles-long walking path | (159)<br>$89–<br>$109 | FB<br>(k) | OP<br>T<br>FR |
| **San Pedro** | | | |
| **Holiday Inn**    310-514-1414<br>111 S Gaffey St    800-248-3188<br>www.holidayinnsanpedro.com   pet fee $25/day<br>Victorian hotel, quiet street for walking dogs,<br>5 blocks to harbor | (60)<br>$99–<br>$129 | C<br>(k)<br>F<br>R/L | OP<br>T<br>FR |
| **Mirina Hotel**    310-514-3344<br>2800 Via Cabrillo Marina    877-547-6667<br>www.marinahotelsanpedro.com<br>dogs under 25 lbs only, lawn, 10 minute walk to park | (237)<br>$99–<br>$139 | C<br>M/F | OP<br>T<br>FR |
| **San Rafael** | | | |
| **Four Points by Sheraton**    415-479-8800<br>1010 Northgate Dr    800-325-3535<br>www.fourpoints.com/sanrafael<br>open walking areas, 2 blocks to park | (235)<br>$109 | C<br>R/L | OP<br>T<br>FR |

| | | | | |
|---|---|---|---|---|
| **Gerstle Park Inn** | 415-721-7611 | (12) | FB | IS |
| 34 Grove St | 800-726-7611 | $179– | | |
| www.gerstleparkinn.com | | $225 | | |
| dogs by advance approval only, evening wine reception, orchard, lawn and woods for walking dogs | | | | |
| **Panama Hotel & Restaurant** | 415-457-3993 | (14) | FB | |
| 4 Bayview St | 800-899-3993 | $75– | M/F | |
| www.panamahotel.com | pet fee $25/day | $160 | R | |
| theme rooms, private balconies, historic restaurant, residential area for walking dogs | | | | |
| **Villa Inn** | 415-456-4975 | (61) | CB | OP |
| 1600 Lincoln Ave | | $69– | M/F | T |
| small dogs only, lawn walking area, 4 blocks to college campus, short drive to park | | $75 | | |

## San Ramon

| | | | | |
|---|---|---|---|---|
| **Homestead Studio Suites** | 925-277-0833 | (146) | K | GP |
| 18000 San Ramon Valley Blvd | 888-782-9473 | $70– | | |
| www.homesteadhotels.com | pet fee $25/day | $110 | | |
| landscaped gardens for walking dogs | | | | |
| **Residence Inn** | 925-277-9292 | (106) | FB | OP |
| 1071 Market Pl | 800-331-3131 | $113– | K | T |
| www.marriott.com | pet fee $75/stay | $229 | | FR |
| studios/1–2 bdrm suites, Mon–Thur beverages and light dinner, lawn and walking trail | | | | |
| **San Ramon Marriott** | 925-867-9200 | (368) | R/L | OP |
| 2600 Bishop Dr | 800-228-9290 | $79– | | IP |
| www.marriott.com | pet fee $75/day | $179 | | T |
| across street to walking trail | | | | FR |
| **Sierra Suites** | 925-743-1882 | (142) | FB | OP |
| 2323 San Ramon Valley Blvd | 800-474-3772 | $89– | K | T |
| www.sierrasuites.com | | $159 | | FR |
| pet fee $5/day plus $100–$150 cleaning fee pet relief area, walking trail, 3 blocks to park | | | | |

| C = coffee<br>CB = continental<br>  breakfast<br>F = refrigerator<br>FB = full breakfast<br>FR = fitness room | GP = guest pass to<br>  fitness center<br>IP = indoor pool<br>IS = in-room spa<br>K = full kitchen<br>(k) = kitchenette | L = lounge<br>M = microwave<br>OP = outdoor pool<br>R = restaurant<br>S = sauna/steam<br>T = spa or hot tub | (# of units)<br>& rates | food<br>& drink | pool, sauna<br>& hot tub |
|---|---|---|---|---|---|

## San Simeon

| | | | | |
|---|---|---|---|---|
| **Best Western Cavalier Oceanfront Resort**<br>9415 Hearst Dr                    805-927-4688<br>www.cavalierresort.com          800-826-8168<br>1–2 dogs only, patios, 12 oceanfront acres, walking<br>paths down the bluff, off-leash beach access | (90)<br>$79–<br>$279 | C<br>F<br>R | OP<br>T<br>FR |
| **Courtesy Inn**                        805-927-4691<br>9450 Castillo Dr                    800-555-5773<br>www.courtesyinns.com          pet fee $10/day<br>lawn, ½ mile to park | (61)<br>$49–<br>$119 | CB | IP<br>T |
| **Motel 6**                            805-927-8691<br>9070 Castillo Dr                    800-466-8356<br>www.motel6.com    lawn, 3 miles to beach and park | (100)<br>$46–<br>$92 | C | OP |
| **Sea Coast Lodge**                    805-927-3878<br>9135 Hearst Dr                      800-451-9900<br>www.moonstonehotels.com      each pet $25/day<br>afternoon tea, residential walking area, 5 miles to<br>beachfront boardwalk, 15 miles to dog-friendly beach | (57)<br>$79–<br>$199 | CB | OP |
| **Silver Surf Motel**                  805-927-4661<br>9390 Castillo Dr                    800-621-3999<br>www.silversurfmotel.com          pet fee $10/day<br>large lawn, short walk to dog-friendly beach | (72)<br>$49–<br>$186 | FB | IP<br>T |

## San Ysidro

| | | | | |
|---|---|---|---|---|
| **Motel 6**                            619-690-6663<br>160 E Calle Primera                  800-466-8356<br>www.motel6.com    grassy areas, 2 blocks to park | (103)<br>$44–<br>$60 | C | OP |

## Santa Ana

| | | | | |
|---|---|---|---|---|
| **Candlewood Suites**                  949-250-0404<br>2600 Red Hill Ave                each pet $75/stay<br>www.interconti.com<br>studios/1 bdrm suites sleep 4, lawn walking areas | (122)<br>$89–<br>$112 | (k) | |

| | | | | |
|---|---|---|---|---|
| **Motel 6** 1623 E 1st St www.motel6.com lawn, 2 miles to park | 714-558-0500 800-466-8356 | (79) $46–$76 | C M/F | T |
| **Quality Inn** 2701 Hotel Terrace Dr www.qualitysuitessantaana.com Tue–Thur dinner buffet, lawn, 4 miles to dog park | 714-957-9200 800-424-6423 pet fee $25/stay | (177) $89–$119 | CB M/F | OP T GP |
| **Red Roof Inn** 2600 N Main St www.redroof-santa-ana.com dogs under 80 lbs, grassy areas, park, jogging path | 714-542-0311 800-843-7663 | (125) $59–$89 | C M/F | OP T |
| **Red Roof Inn–Irvine** 1717 E Dyer Rd www.redroof.com 1 dog only, small field, 5 miles to large regional park | 949-261-1515 800-733-7663 | (150) $55–$73 | C | OP T |
| **Travelodge–Airport** 1400 SE Bristol St www.travelodge.com grassy area, 5 minute drive to fenced off-leash park | 714-557-8700 | (120) $67–$77 | CB M/F | OP T FR |

## Santa Barbara

| | | | | |
|---|---|---|---|---|
| **Adobe Motel** 26 E Haley St well-behaved small to medium dogs only, ½ block to park, 3½ blocks to beach and wharf | 805-966-5505 pet fee $10/day | (17) $55–$95 | M/F | |
| **Ala Mar Motel** 102 W Cabrillo Blvd small dogs only, across street to dog-friendly beach | 805-962-9208 pet fee $20/stay | (28) $129–$189 | CB K | |
| **Beach House Inn & Apartments** 320 W Yanonali St www.thebeachhouseinn.com rooms/studios/1 bdrm apts, courtyard, 1 block to park, 2 blocks to beach, short drive to off-leash park | 805-966-1126 each pet $10/day | (12) $80–$250 | C K | |
| **Best Western Beachside Inn** 336 W Cabrillo Blvd www.bestwesterncalifornia.com each pet $20/day 5 blocks to park | 805-965-6556 800-932-6556 | (60) $125–$209 | CB R/L | OP |

| C = coffee GP = guest pass to L = lounge<br>CB = continental fitness center M = microwave<br>breakfast IP = indoor pool OP = outdoor pool<br>F = refrigerator IS = in-room spa R = restaurant<br>FB = full breakfast K = full kitchen S = sauna/steam<br>FR = fitness room (k) = kitchenette T = spa or hot tub | (# of units)<br>& rates | food<br>& drink | pool, sauna<br>& hot tub |
|---|---|---|---|
| ## Santa Barbara (continued) | | | |
| **Blue Sands Motel** 805-965-1624<br>421 S Milpas St pet fee $15/day<br>www.bluesandsmotel.com<br>dogs under 30 lbs only, next to dog-friendly beach | (11)<br>$65–<br>$105 | CB<br>F | OP |
| **Casa Del Mar** 805-963-4418<br>18 Bath St 800-433-3097<br>www.casadelmar.com each pet $10/day<br>private entrances, courtyard, gardens, walking paths | (21)<br>$119–<br>$199 | CB<br>K | T |
| **El Encanto Hotel** 805-687-5000<br>1900 Lasuen Rd 800-346-7039<br>www.elencantohotel.com pet fee $100/stay<br>dogs under 35 lbs only, lawn, 3 miles to park | (74)<br>$189–<br>$925 | C<br>F<br>R | OP |
| **Fess Parker's Doubletree Resort** 805-564-4333<br>633 E Cabrillo Blvd 800-559-5124<br>www.fpdtr.com<br>1 large or 2 small dogs only, patios, on 24 acres | (360)<br>$229–<br>$445 | C<br>F<br>R | OP<br>T<br>FR |
| **Fiesta Inn** 805-569-2205<br>1816 State St pet fee $20/stay<br>4 blocks to park, 1 mile to dog-friendly beach | (26)<br>$70–<br>$179 | CB | |
| **Four Seasons Biltmore Hotel** 805-969-2261<br>1260 Channel Dr 888-424-5866<br>www.fourseasons.com/santabarbara<br>9 dog-friendly cottages, 21 landscaped acres, parks | (209)<br>$535–<br>$1,200 | R | OP |
| **Harbor House Inn** 805-962-9745<br>104 Bath St 888-474-6789<br>www.harborhouseinn.com pet fee $15/day<br>breakfast supplies, 1 block to dog-friendly beach | (10)<br>$99–<br>$235 | C<br>K<br>M/F | |
| **Marina Beach Motel** 805-963-9311<br>21 Bath St 877-627-4621<br>www.marinabeachmotel.com pet fee $15/day<br>dogs by advance approval only, ½ block to dog beach | (32)<br>$89–<br>$219 | CB<br>(k) | T |

| | | | |
|---|---|---|---|
| **Montecito Del Mar** 805-962-2006<br>316 W Montecito St 888-464-1690<br>www.montecitodelmar.com each pet $10/day<br>dogs by advance approval only, small lawn,<br>10 minute walk to dog-friendly beaches | (24)<br>$69–<br>$135 | CB<br>K | T |
| **Motel 6 Beach** 805-564-1392<br>443 Corona Del Mar 800-466-8356<br>www.motel6.com lawn, 2 miles to off-leash park | (51)<br>$66–<br>$106 | C | OP |
| **Motel 6 State Street** 805-687-5400<br>3505 State St 800-466-8356<br>www.motel6.com 1 block to park, 2 miles to beach | (59)<br>$56–<br>$92 | C | OP |
| **Pacifica Suites** 805-683-6722<br>5490 Hollister Ave ·800-338-6722<br>www.pacificasuites.com pet fee $10/day<br>dogs in smoking rooms only, lawn, garden, bike path | (87)<br>$159–<br>$199 | FB<br>M/F | OP<br>T |
| **Secret Garden Inn & Cottages** 805-687-2300<br>1908 Bath St 800-676-1622<br>www.secretgarden.com<br>dogs in cottages only, private gardens or decks with<br>hot tubs, paths, 10 minute drive to dog-friendly beach | (11)<br>$121–<br>$255 | FB<br>F | T |
| **Travelers Motel** ˙ 805-687-6009<br>3222 State St pet fee $10/day<br>www.travelersmotelsb.com<br>residential streets, bike path, short drive to beach | (13)<br>$39–<br>$140 | CB<br>M/F | |

### Santa Clara

| | | | |
|---|---|---|---|
| **Candlewood Suites** 408-241-9305<br>481 El Camino Real pet fee $75/stay<br>www.candlewoodsuites.com<br>studios/1 bdrm suites, 4 blocks to park | (122)<br>$98–<br>$120 | (k) | |
| **E-Z8 Motel** 408-246-3119<br>3550 El Camino Real<br>www.ez8motels.com<br>small grassy walking area, short drive to park | (66)<br>$50 | C<br>F | OP<br>T |
| **GuestHouse International Inn & Suites**<br>2930 El Camino Real 408-241-3010<br>www.ghisuites.com 800-334-3928<br>5 minute drive to dog park pet fee $8/day | (70)<br>$79–<br>$180 | CB | OP |

| C = coffee  GP = guest pass to  L = lounge | | |
| CB = continental       fitness center  M = microwave | | |
| breakfast  IP = indoor pool  OP = outdoor pool | | |
| F = refrigerator  IS = in-room spa  R = restaurant | | |
| FB = full breakfast  K = full kitchen  S = sauna/steam | | |
| FR = fitness room  (k) = kitchenette  T = spa or hot tub | | |

## Santa Clara (continued)

| | (# of units) & rates | food & drink | pool, sauna & hot tub |
|---|---|---|---|
| **Madison Street Inn B & B** 408-249-5541 1390 Madison St www.madisonstreetinn.com small dogs only, 1 block to park | (6) $70– $150 | FB M/F | OP T |
| **Mariani's Inn & Restaurant** 408-243-0331 2500 El Camino Real 800-553-8666 www.marianis.com pet fee $25/stay large lawn, close to parks | (142) $79 | FB R | OP T |
| **Motel 6** 408-241-0200 3208 El Camino Real 800-466-8356 www.motel6.com grassy walking area | (99) $53– $60 | C | OP |
| **Ramada Inn** 408-244-8313 1655 El Camino Real pet fee $10/day www.ramada.com lawn, 3 blocks to park | (75) $80 | CB | OP |
| **Santa Clara Marriott** 408-988-1500 2700 Mission College Blvd www.marriott.com lawn, short drive to park | (759) $99– $169 | M/F R | OP T FR |
| **Vagabond Inn** 408-241-0771 3580 El Camino Real 800-522-1555 www.vagabondinn.com pet fee $10/day small lawn, ½ mile to park | (70) $50 | CB M/F | OP |
| **Wellesley Inn** 408-257-8600 5405 Stevens Creek Blvd 800-444-8888 www.wellesleyonline.com dogs under 25 lbs, grassy area, 30 minutes to beach | (95) $69– $74 | C M/F | OP GP |
| **Westin Hotel** 408-986-0700 5101 Great America Pkwy 800-325-3535 www.westin.com/santaclara dogs under 50 lbs only, paved creekside jogging trail | (505) $109– $119 | C F R | OP T FR |

## Santa Clarita

| | | | | |
|---|---|---|---|---|
| **Residence Inn** 25320 The Old Rd www.marriott.com studios/1–2 bdrm suites, Mon–Thur light dinner and beverages, petwalking area, ¼ mile to park | 661-290-2800 800-331-3131 pet fee $75/stay | (90) $129– $159 | FB K | OP T FR |

## Santa Cruz

| | | | | |
|---|---|---|---|---|
| **Bayfront Inn** 325 Pacific Ave www.bayfrontinnsc.com | 831-423-8564 pet fee $10/day | (47) $48– $109 | C M/F | OP |
| **Beach Bungalow Vacation Rentals** www.beachbungalow.com    831-475-4657 1–2 bdrm vacation homes, fenced yards, close to dog-friendly beaches | | (11) $200– $900 | K | T |
| **Coast Santa Cruz Hotel** 175 W Cliff Dr www.coasthotels.com sidewalk to lighthouse, ½ mile to off-leash dog beach | 831-426-4330 800-663-1144 pet fee $10/day | (163) $119– $349 | C F R/L | OP T |
| **Continental Inn** 414 Ocean St www.continentalinn.net lawn, 1 block to park | 831-429-1221 800-343-6941 pet fee $10/stay | (48) $45– $260 | CB M/F | OP T |
| **Edgewater Beach Motel** 525 2nd St www.edgewaterbeachmotel.com    fee $10–$15/stay pet relief area, ½ mile to off-leash dog beach | 831-423-0440 888-809-6767 | (17) $89– $119 | C K M/F | OP |
| **GuestHouse International Pacific Inn** 330 Ocean St www.guesthouseintl.com    each pet $10/day 4½ blocks to dog-friendly beach and boardwalk | 831-425-3722 | (36) $59– $139 | CB M/F | IP T |
| **Motel 6** 370 Ocean St www.motel6.com    pet fee $10/day 1 mile to dog-friendly beach | 831-458-9220 800-466-8356 | (64) $79– $159 | | |

| C = coffee<br>CB = continental<br>breakfast<br>F = refrigerator<br>FB = full breakfast<br>FR = fitness room | GP = guest pass to<br>fitness center<br>IP = indoor pool<br>IS = in-room spa<br>K = full kitchen<br>(k) = kitchenette | L = lounge<br>M = microwave<br>OP = outdoor pool<br>R = restaurant<br>S = sauna/steam<br>T = spa or hot tub | (# of units)<br>& rates | food<br>& drink | pool, sauna<br>& hot tub |
|---|---|---|---|---|---|

## Santa Cruz (continued)

| | | | | |
|---|---|---|---|---|
| **National 9 Motel**<br>1015 Ocean St<br>8 blocks to park | 831-423-8945<br>pet fee $15/day | (40)<br>$60–<br>$109 | M/F | |
| **Ocean Pacific Lodge**<br>120 Washington St<br><br>dogs under 25 lbs in first floor rooms only, outside<br>entrances, lawn, 5 blocks to dog-friendly beach | 831-457-1234<br>800-995-0289<br>pet fee $20/stay | (58)<br>$80–<br>$100 | CB<br>M/F | OP<br>T<br>IS |

## Santa Fe Springs

| | | | | |
|---|---|---|---|---|
| **Motel 6**<br>13412 Excelsior Dr<br>www.motel6.com<br>small grassy area, short drive to park | 562-921-0596<br>800-466-8356 | (79)<br>$46–<br>$56 | C | |

## Santa Maria

| | | | | |
|---|---|---|---|---|
| **Best Value Inn**<br>839 E Main St<br>small lawn, 1 block to park | 805-925-2551<br>888-315-2378<br>pet fee $25/stay | (57)<br>$50–<br>$90 | CB<br>M/F | OP |
| **Best Western Big America Inn**<br>1725 N Broadway<br>www.bigamerica.com<br>dogs under 35 lbs only, rooms with outside<br>entrances, lawn walking area, ¾ mile to park | 805-922-5200<br>800-426-3213 | (106)<br>$109–<br>$131 | CB<br>F<br>R | OP<br>T |
| **Historic Santa Maria Inn**<br>801 S Broadway<br>www.historicsantamariainn.com<br>lawn walking area, rose gardens | 805-928-7777<br>800-462-4276<br>pet fee $50/stay | (164)<br>$99–<br>$159 | C<br>M/F<br>R | OP<br>T<br>FR |
| **Holiday Inn Santa Maria**<br>2100 N Broadway<br>www.holiday-inn.com/santamariaca<br>2 blocks to park | 805-928-6000<br>800-226-6573<br>each pet $10/day | (207)<br>$105–<br>$145 | M/F<br>R | OP<br>T<br>FR |

| | | | | |
|---|---|---|---|---|
| **Motel 6 North** <br> 2040 Preisker Lane <br> www.motel6.com <br> lawn, 1 mile to park | 805-928-8111 <br> 800-466-8356 | (126) <br> $46– <br> $69 | C | OP |

## Santa Monica

| | | | | |
|---|---|---|---|---|
| **Ambrose Hotel** <br> 1255 20th St <br> www.ambrosehotel.com <br> dogs by manager's approval only, garden walking <br> area, several parks within 1 mile | 310-315-1555 <br> 877-262-7673 | (77) <br> $175– <br> $225 | CB <br> F | FR |
| **American Motel** <br> 1243 Lincoln Blvd <br> lawn, ½ block to park | 310-458-1411 | (6) <br> $65 | M/F | |
| **Casa Del Mar** <br> 1910 Ocean Way <br> www.hotelcasadelmar.com/Santa-Monica <br> dogs by manager's approval only, dog-friendly beach | 310-581-5533 | (129) <br> $405– <br> $650 | C <br> F <br> R/L | OP <br> S <br> T <br> IS |
| **Fairmont Miramar Hotel** <br> 101 Wilshire Blvd <br> www.fairmont.com <br> dogs under 25 lbs only, rooms/bungalows with <br> outside entrances, oceanfront and walking trails | 310-576-7777 <br> 800-441-1414 | (302) <br> $249– <br> $400 | CB <br> F <br> R/L | OP <br> T <br> FR |
| **Four Points by Sheraton** <br> 530 Pico Blvd <br> www.starwoodhotels.com <br> gardens and lawn walking areas | 310-399-9344 <br> 800-325-3535 <br> pet fee $50/stay | (309) <br> $239– <br> $269 | F <br> R/L | OP <br> FR |
| **Georgian Hotel** <br> 1415 Ocean Ave <br> www.georgianhotel.com <br> walking path to dog-friendly beach | 310-395-9945 <br> 800-538-8147 <br> pet fee $100/stay | (84) <br> $177 | R | OP <br> T <br> FR |
| **Holiday Motel** <br> 1102 Pico Blvd <br> small lawn, 3 blocks to park | 310-450-9666 | (12) <br> $60 | | |
| **Le Merigot by Marriott** <br> 1740 Ocean Ave <br> www.lemerigothotel.com <br> fenced petwalking area, next to dog-friendly beach | 310-395-9700 <br> 800-228-9290 <br> pet fee $35/stay | (175) <br> $259– <br> $329 | F <br> R | OP |

| C = coffee<br>CB = continental<br>    breakfast<br>F = refrigerator<br>FB = full breakfast<br>FR = fitness room | GP = guest pass to<br>    fitness center<br>IP = indoor pool<br>IS = in-room spa<br>K = full kitchen<br>(k) = kitchenette | L = lounge<br>M = microwave<br>OP = outdoor pool<br>R = restaurant<br>S = sauna/steam<br>T = spa or hot tub | (# of units)<br>& rates | food<br>& drink | pool, sauna<br>& hot tub |
|---|---|---|---|---|---|
| ## Santa Monica (continued) | | | | | |
| **Loews Santa Monica Hotel**   310-458-6700<br>1700 Ocean Ave          800-235-6397<br>www.loewshotels.com<br>lawn walking area, but no dogs allowed on beach in front of hotel, 10 minute drive to off-leash dog park, 45 minute drive to dog-friendly beach | | | (342)<br>$265–<br>$480 | F<br>R | OP<br>T<br>FR |
| **Palm Motel**               310-452-3861<br>2020 14th St          pet fee $40/stay<br>www.palmmotel.homestead.com<br>dogs allowed in smoking units only, Greek-style bungalows, 2 blocks to off-leash park | | | (26)<br>$65–<br>$90 | C | |
| **Pavilions Motel**        310-450-4044<br>2338 Ocean Park Blvd    800-952-3901<br>next to park           pet fee $5/day | | | (20)<br>$60 | | |
| **Travelodge**           310-450-5766<br>3102 Pico Blvd        800-231-7679<br>www.travelodge.com    each pet $10/day<br>dogs under 20 lbs only, 1 mile to park | | | (85)<br>$89–<br>$129 | CB<br>M/F | |
| **Viceroy Hotel**        310-451-8711<br>1819 Ocean Ave       800-622-8711<br>www.viceroysantamonica.com   pet fee $100/stay<br>dogs under 20 lbs only, ½ block to dog-friendly beach | | | (162)<br>$299 | F<br>R/L | OP<br>FR |
| ## Santa Nella | | | | | |
| **Comfort Inn**        209-827-8700<br>28821 Gonzaga Rd    pet fee $10/stay<br>www.choicehotels.com<br>grass and dirt walking areas | | | (64)<br>$76–<br>$86 | FB<br>M/F | OP<br>T |
| **Holiday Inn Express**   209-826-8282<br>28976 Plaza Dr        800-428-3687<br>www.hiexpress.com/santanellaca   open field | | | (100)<br>$80 | CB<br>F | OP<br>T<br>FR |

| | | | | |
|---|---|---|---|---|
| **Motel 6 Santa Nella** 12733 Hwy 33 www.motel6.com open field for walking dogs | 209-826-6644 800-466-8356 | (111) $46 | C | OP |
| **Ramada Inn–Mission De Oro** 13070 Hwy 33 www.ramada.com lawn and open field | 209-826-4444 800-546-5697 pet fee $10/day | (160) $80 | FB F | OP T |

## Santa Rosa

| | | | | |
|---|---|---|---|---|
| **Best Western Garden Inn** 1500 Santa Rosa Ave www.thegardeninn.com 1–2 small dogs only, garden and lawn, 1 mile to park | 707-546-4031 800-929-2771 each pet $15/day | (76) $80– $100 | M/F R | OP |
| **Comfort Inn** 2632 Cleveland Ave www.comfortinnsantarosa.com small grassy area, 2 miles to park | 707-542-5544 800-228-5150 pet fee $15/day | (100) $75– $95 | CB M/F R | OP |
| **Days Inn** 3345 Santa Rosa Ave www.daysinn.com lawn walking area | 707-568-1011 800-329-7466 pet fee $10/day | (104) $89 | M/F | OP |
| **Fountain Grove Inn** 101 Fountain Grove Pkwy www.fountaingroveinn.com 2 miles to off-leash dog park | 707-578-6101 800-222-6101 pet fee $25/day | (124) $99– $169 | CB M/F | OP T GP |
| **Holiday Inn Express** 870 Hopper Ave www.hiexpress.com/santarosaca lawn area, ½ mile to park | 707-545-9000 800-465-4329 pet fee $20/stay | (95) $99– $139 | CB M/F | OP GP |
| **Los Robles Lodge** 1985 Cleveland Ave www.losrobleslodge.com pet relief area, 2 blocks to park | 707-545-6330 800-255-6330 pet fee $15/day | (89) $69– $139 | C F R/L | OP T FR |
| **Motel 6 North** 3145 Cleveland Ave www.motel6.com grassy areas, 1 block to park | 707-525-9010 800-466-8356 | (119) $50– $66 | C | OP |

| C = coffee  GP = guest pass to  L = lounge<br>CB = continental  fitness center  M = microwave<br>breakfast  IP = indoor pool  OP = outdoor pool<br>F = refrigerator  IS = in-room spa  R = restaurant<br>FB = full breakfast  K = full kitchen  S = sauna/steam<br>FR = fitness room  (k) = kitchenette  T = spa or hot tub | (# of units) & rates | food & drink | pool, sauna & hot tub |
|---|---|---|---|
| **Santa Rosa (continued)** | | | |
| **Motel 6 South** 707-546-1500<br>2760 Cleveland Ave  800-466-8356<br>www.motel6.com  lawn, 3 blocks to park | (100)<br>$50–<br>$66 | C | OP |
| **Sandman Hotel** 707-544-8570<br>3421 Cleveland Ave  pet fee $25/stay<br>small grassy walking area,  2 miles to park | (136)<br>$90–<br>$133 | CB<br>M/F | OP<br>T<br>FR |
| **Santa Rosa Motor Inn** 707-523-3480<br>1800 Santa Rosa Ave  pet fee $10–$15/day<br>www.santarosamotorinn.com  ¼ mile to park | (43)<br>$62 | CB<br>F | |
| **Travelodge** 707-542-3472<br>1815 Santa Rosa Ave  800-578-7878<br>www.travelodge.com  pet fee $20/day<br>lawn walking area, 1 mile to park | (31)<br>$59–<br>$99 | CB<br>M/F | OP |
| **Travelodge** 707-544-4141<br>635 Healdsburg Ave  800-578-7878<br>www.travelodge.com  each pet $10/day<br>small to medium dogs only, small lawn,<br>5 minute walk to park | (43)<br>$59 | CB<br>M/F | OP |
| **Santa Ysabel** | | | |
| **Lake Henshaw Resort** 760-782-3501<br>26439 Hwy 76  pet fee $2/day<br>www.lakehenshawca.com<br>cabins sleep 6, shady walking area, close to lakefront | (17)<br>$50–<br>$70 | K | |
| **Scotts Valley** | | | |
| **Hilton** 831-440-1000<br>6001 La Madrona Dr  800-445-3010<br>www.santacruzscottsvalley.hilton.com<br>each pet $25/day<br>dogs under 40 lbs only, landscaped grounds, short<br>drive to walking trails, 3 miles to dog-friendly beach | (180)<br>$169–<br>$229 | C<br>F<br>R/L | OP<br>T<br>FR |

| | | | | |
|---|---|---|---|---|
| **Scott's Valley Best Western Inn** | 831-438-8355 | (58) | C | OP |
| 6020 Scotts Valley Dr | 800-937-8376 | $99– | F | S |
| www.bestwesterncalifornia.com | | $135 | R | T |

### Seal Beach

| | | | | |
|---|---|---|---|---|
| **Pacific Inn** | 562-493-7501 | (71) | FB | OP |
| 600 Marina Dr | 866-466-0300 | $109– | CB | FR |
| www.pacificinn-sb.com | pet fee $50/stay | $189 | M/F | T |
| walking trails, 5 miles to off-leash dog beach | | | | |

### Seaside

| | | | |
|---|---|---|---|
| **Econo Lodge Bay Breeze Inn** | 831-899-7111 | (50) | CB |
| 2049 Fremont Blvd | 800-899-7129 | $50– | M/F |
| dogs under 20 lbs only, open field | | $200 | |

### Sebastopol

| | | | | |
|---|---|---|---|---|
| **Vine Hill Inn** | 707-823-8832 | (4) | FB | OP |
| 3949 Vine Hill Rd | | $135– | F | IS |
| www.vine-hill-inn.com | | $150 | | |
| well-behaved cat-friendly dogs only, rural walking area, 1 mile to bike path | | | | |

### Selma

| | | | | |
|---|---|---|---|---|
| **Best Western Colonial Inn** | 559-891-0300 | (57) | CB | OP |
| 2799 Floral Ave | 800-891-7545 | $69– | M/F | T |
| www.bestwesterncalifornia.com | pet fee $20/day | $89 | | |
| lawn walking area, 1 block to park | | | | |
| **Super 8 Motel** | 559-896-2800 | (39) | CB | OP |
| 3142 Highland Ave | 800-800-8000 | $58– | M/F | |
| www.super8.com | each pet $5/day | $64 | | |
| lawn walking area, 2 blocks to park | | | | |

### Shasta Lake

| | | | | |
|---|---|---|---|---|
| **Shasta Dam Motel** | 530-275-1065 | (14) | CB | OP |
| 1529 Cascade Blvd | pet fee $5–$10/day | $55– | M/F | |
| www.shastadammotel.com | | $67 | | |
| lawn walking area | | | | |

| C = coffee   GP = guest pass to   L = lounge<br>CB = continental      fitness center   M = microwave<br>    breakfast    IP = indoor pool   OP = outdoor pool<br>F = refrigerator    IS = in-room spa   R = restaurant<br>FB = full breakfast   K = full kitchen   S = sauna/steam<br>FR = fitness room   (k) = kitchenette   T = spa or hot tub | (# of units)<br>& rates | food<br>& drink | pool, sauna<br>& hot tub |
|---|---|---|---|
| ### Shaver Lake | | | |
| **Dinkey Creek Inn**        559-841-3435<br>53861 Dinkey Creek Rd     pet fee $25/stay<br>www.dinkeycreek.com<br>chalet cabins sleep 6, woods and creek, trails | (4)<br>$85–<br>$110 | K<br>R | |
| **Shaver Lake Village Hotel**     559-841-8289<br>42135 Tollhouse Rd       pet fee $10/day<br>www.shaverlakevillagehotel.com<br>rooms/cabins, wooded walking area, hiking trails,<br>5 minute drive to lake | (11)<br>$79–<br>$185 | M/F | |
| ### Shelter Cove | | | |
| **Inn of the Lost Coast**      707-986-7521<br>205 Wave Dr         pet fee $10/day<br>www.innofthelostcoast.com<br>grassy field, 1 mile to dog-friendly beach | (18)<br>$125–<br>$135 | C<br>M/F | |
| **Mario's Marina Motel**      707-986-7595<br>533 Machi Rd<br>dogs in smoking rooms only, 2 minute walk to beach | (8)<br>$75–<br>$85 | C<br>M<br>R | |
| ### Sherman Oaks | | | |
| **Best Western Carriage Inn**     818-787-2300<br>5525 Sepulveda Blvd       877-787-2300<br>www.chmhotels.com     lawn walking area | (181)<br>$89–<br>$129 | R | OP<br>T<br>FR |
| ### Shoshone | | | |
| **Shoshone Inn**         760-852-4335<br>Hwy 127<br>natural warm springs swimming pool, open desert | (16)<br>$64–<br>$125 | (k) | OP |
| ### Sierra City | | | |
| **Bassett Station Motel**     530-862-1297<br>100 Gold Lake Rd       pet fee $10/day<br>www.sierracity.com    creekside walking trail | (3)<br>$70–<br>$75 | (k)<br>R | |

| | | | | |
|---|---|---|---|---|
| **Buckhorn Lodge/Buttes Resort**<br>230 Main St<br>www.sierracity.com<br>1–2 bdrm cabins, decks, open walking areas, close to<br>hiking trails, 40 trout lakes in easy driving distance | 530-862-1170<br>800-991-1170 | (11)<br>$80–<br>$125 | K | |
| **Herrington's Sierra Pines**<br>101 Main St<br>www.herringtonssierrapines.com<br>surrounded by national forest land | 530-862-1151<br>800-682-9848 | (20)<br>$64–<br>$125 | K<br>R | |
| **Kokanee Cabins**<br>15 Loganville Lane<br>www.kokaneekabins.com<br>1 dog only, lawn, riverfront walking area, trails | 530-862-1287 | (5)<br>$65 | (k) | |
| **Packer Lake Lodge**<br>3901 Packer Lake Rd<br>cabins sleep up to 8, woods and walking trails | 530-862-1221 | (14)<br>$74–<br>$165 | K | |
| **Yuba River Inn**<br>510 Main St<br>www.yubariverinn.com<br>cabins on 20 wooded acres, ⅓ mile river frontage | 530-862-1122<br>each pet $10/day | (10)<br>$60–<br>$165 | K | OP |

## Simi Valley

| | | | | |
|---|---|---|---|---|
| **Motel 6**<br>2566 Erringer Rd<br>www.motel6.com | 805-526-3533<br>800-466-8356<br>grassy area, 1½ miles to park | (60)<br>$66–<br>$76 | C | OP |

## Skyforest

| | | | | |
|---|---|---|---|---|
| **Storybook Inn Sky Forest**<br>28717 Hwy 18<br>www.storybookinn.com<br>rooms/suites/2 bdrm villa, 3 acres of lawn and<br>woods, gravel road, 1½ miles to Lake Arrowhead | 909-337-0011<br>877-337-0011 | (12)<br>$89–<br>$249 | FB<br>K | IS |

## Smith River

| | | | | |
|---|---|---|---|---|
| **Casa Rubio**<br>17285 Crissey Rd N<br>www.casarubio.com<br>grassy off-leash walking area, off-leash beach | 707-487-4313<br>800-357-6199<br>pet fee $10/stay | (4)<br>$108–<br>$128 | K | |

| | | | | | (# of units) & rates | food & drink | pool, sauna & hot tub |
|---|---|---|---|---|---|---|---|
| C = coffee | GP = guest pass to | L = lounge | | | | | |
| CB = continental | fitness center | M = microwave | | | | | |
| breakfast | IP = indoor pool | OP = outdoor pool | | | | | |
| F = refrigerator | IS = in-room spa | R = restaurant | | | | | |
| FB = full breakfast | K = full kitchen | S = sauna/steam | | | | | |
| FR = fitness room | (k) = kitchenette | T = spa or hot tub | | | | | |

## Smith River (continued)

| | | | (# units/rates) | food | pool |
|---|---|---|---|---|---|
| **Sea Escape Motel** 15370 Hwy 101 N www.seaescape.us studios/1 bdrm apts, patios, on ½ acre with grassy area overlooking ocean and path down to beach | 707-487-7333 pet fee $15/stay | | (7) $55–$95 | C (k) | |
| **Ship Ashore Resort** 12370 Hwy 101 N www.ship-ashore.com dogs under 10 lbs only, pet relief area, close to Redwoods National Park | 707-487-3141 800-487-3141 | | (54) $60–$140 | (k) R/L | IS |

## Solvang

| | | | (# units/rates) | food | pool |
|---|---|---|---|---|---|
| **Hamlet Motel** 1532 Mission Dr small dogs only lawn walking area, 2 blocks to park | 805-688-4413 800-253-5033 pet fee $10/day | | (15) $52–$100 | CB F | |
| **Meadowlark Inn** 2644 Mission Dr (Hwy 246) www.meadowlarkinnsolvang.com       pet fee $15/day dogs by advance reservation only, on 2 acres with grassy walking areas, across street from 2 mile long walking path | 805-688-4631 800-344-9792 | | (21) $95–$150 | CB K F | OP |
| **Royal Copenhagen Inn** 1579 Mission Dr www.royalcopenhageninn.com small grassy area, 3 blocks to park | 805-688-5561 800-624-6604 | | (48) $79–$125 | CB M/F | OP |
| **Viking Motel** 1506 Mission Dr | 805-688-1337 pet fee $10/day | | (13) $45–$54 | CB M/F | |

## Somerset

| | | |
|---|---|---|
| **Barkley Historic Homestead B & B** | (6) | FB |
| 8320 Stoney Creek Rd                530-620-6783 | $99– | |
| www.barkleyhomestead.com          888-708-4466 | $150 | |
| dogs by manager's approval only, 67 wooded acres | | |
| with ponds, seasonal creeks and hiking trails | | |
| **7 Up Bar Ranch**          530-620-5450 | (6) | FB |
| 8060 Fairplay Rd            800-717-5450 | $100– | M/F |
| www.sevenupranch.com | $140 | |
| rooms with outside entrances, 146 acre ranch with | | |
| wildlife so dogs must be under control at all times | | |

## Sonoma

| | | | |
|---|---|---|---|
| **Andrea's Hidden Cottage**          707-939-7070 | (1) | C | T |
| 138 E Spain St Or 40 Cabrillo Plz | $110– | K | |
| www.andreashiddencottage.com | $154 | | |
| small dogs only, fenced patio, ½ block to park, 1½ | | | |
| blocks to walking trail, see website for special rates | | | |
| **The Arbors Vacation Home**          510-719-4619 | (2) | K | OP |
| 19410 Olive Ave | $400– | | |
| dogs by owner's approval only, 1 bdrm apt and | $650 | | |
| 3 bdrm house sleep 12 altogether, on 5 country acres | | | |
| **Best Western Sonoma Valley Inn**     707-938-9200 | (80) | CB | OP |
| 550 2nd St W          800-334-5784 | $139– | | S |
| www.sonomavalleyinn.com | $389 | | T |
| pet fee $30/stay for 1 dog, $45 for 2 dogs | | | FR |
| complimentary wine, pet relief area, 1 block to plaza | | | |
| and park, 4 blocks to fenced off-leash park | | | |
| **Casa Chiquita**          707-996-4890 | (1) | C | |
| 196 West Spain St | $179– | K | |
| www.casachiquita.com | $300 | | |
| 2 bdrm guest house, close to off-leash dog park | | | |
| **Casita Carneros**          707-996-0996 | (1) | M/F | OP |
| 21235 Hyde Rd          pet fee $25/day | $200 | | T |
| www.casitacarneros.com | | | |
| 1 bdrm cottage, lawn and country road | | | |

| C = coffee GP = guest pass to L = lounge CB = continental fitness center M = microwave breakfast IP = indoor pool OP = outdoor pool F = refrigerator IS = in-room spa R = restaurant FB = full breakfast K = full kitchen S = sauna/steam FR = fitness room (k) = kitchenette T = spa or hot tub | (# of units) & rates | food & drink | pool, sauna & hot tub |
|---|---|---|---|
| ## Sonoma (continued) | | | |
| **Clark's Little House** 707-938-3446 1065 East MacArthur dogs by advance approval only, 1 bdrm cottage, fenced deck and yard, walking path, field, orchard | (1) $100–$195 | C M/F | |
| **Cuneo's Stone Cottage** 707-933-3333 391 E Spain St www.cuneocottage.com dogs under 50 lbs by advance approval only, 2 bdrm vacation home, sun porch, deck, fenced yard | (1) $200–$250 | C K | |
| **Dejon Cottage** 707-333-0083 16600 Gehricke Rd dogs by advance approval only, historic schoolhouse converted to 1 bdrm cottage, wine/cheese/breakfast supplies, 360 acre vineyard and horse ranch, lake | (1) $325–$375 | K | T |
| **Ericksen's B & B** 707-938-4654 851 2nd St E rooms/studio with private deck, breakfast supplies, 5 blocks to off-leash dog park | (3) $150 | CB (k) | |
| **Hannah's House & Cottages** 707-939-9553 19235 Carriger Rd www.hannahshouse.com 1 bdrm cottage, private patio, breakfast supplies, 5½ acres with gardens and fields for off-leash walking | (2) $150–$175 | CB K | T |
| **Lodge at Sonoma Renaissance** 707-935-6600 1325 Broadway 800-228-9092 www.thelodgeatsonoma.com pet fee $50/stay walking trail, 1½ miles to park | (182) $289–$369 | F R | OP T FR |

| | | | |
|---|---|---|---|
| **Magliulo's Rose Garden Inn**      707-996-1031<br>681 Broadway                         pet fee $25/stay<br>www.sonomarose.com<br>dogs by advance approval in 1 room with outside<br>entrance, streetside walking area, 3 blocks to park | (4)<br>$95–<br>$150 | CB | |
| **Morningsong Country Lodging**     707-939-8616<br>21725 Hyde Rd                         pet fee $15/day<br>www.morningsonginn.com<br>cottage sleeps 4, breakfast supplies, on 7 acres of<br>orchard and vineyard for walking dogs | (4)<br>$140–<br>$220 | K | |
| **Smith Ranch Retreat**             707-933-9828<br>20419 5th St East<br>2 bdrm guesthouse on 2nd floor of barn, recreation<br>room, private patio, residential neighborhood,<br>10 minute walk to walking path | (1)<br>$200–<br>$250 | K | |
| **Sonoma Country Cottages**         707-481-0700<br>www.sonomacountrycottages.com          866-919-9800<br>                                      pet fee $10/day<br>dogs allowed by advance approval only, hillside<br>cottages, breakfast supplies provided, on 150 acre<br>estate with streams, redwoods and walking trails | (3)<br>$250–<br>$325 | K | T |
| **Stay Sonoma**                     707-996-1888<br>www.staysonoma.com                    866-647-8888<br>referral and booking service for B & Bs, vacation<br>homes, hotels and motels throughout Sonoma<br>Valley, Sonoma County and the Bay area | (215)<br>call<br>for<br>rates | | |
| **Stonegrove B & B**                707-939-8249<br>240 2nd St E                          pet fee $10/day<br>www.stonegrovebb.com<br>dogs allowed by advance reservation in one cottage<br>only, on 2½ hillside acres, bike path, 1 mile to<br>off-leash dog park | (4)<br>$95–<br>$125 | C<br>F | |
| **Susan's Guesthouse**              707-363-2048<br>458 2nd St West<br>dogs by advance approval only, studio/2 bdrm suite,<br>private patios, 1 block to park, 2 blocks to bike path | (2)<br>$150–<br>$200 | C<br>K | |

| C = coffee<br>CB = continental<br>   breakfast<br>F = refrigerator<br>FB = full breakfast<br>FR = fitness room | GP = guest pass to<br>   fitness center<br>IP = indoor pool<br>IS = in-room spa<br>K = full kitchen<br>(k) = kitchenette | L = lounge<br>M = microwave<br>OP = outdoor pool<br>R = restaurant<br>S = sauna/steam<br>T = spa or hot tub | # of units)<br>& rates | food<br>& drink | pool, sauna<br>& hot tub |
|---|---|---|---|---|---|

## Sonoma (continued)

| | | | | |
|---|---|---|---|---|
| **Villa Castillo**<br>1100 Castle Rd<br>www.sonomatown.com<br>1 bdrm cottage, private patio, breakfast supplies,<br>on 3 fenced acres with koi pond and olive grove | 707-996-4616 | (2)<br>$200–<br>$225 | K | OP<br>T |

## Sonora

| | | | | |
|---|---|---|---|---|
| **Barretta Gardens Inn**<br>700 S Barretta St<br>www.barrettagardens.com<br>small dogs only in two rooms with outside entrances,<br>on 1 acre of gardens and paths | 209-532-6039<br>800-206-3333 | (5)<br>$130–<br>$155 | FB | IS |
| **Best Western Sonora Oaks Hotel**<br>19551 Hess Ave<br>www.bwsonoraoaks.com<br>pet relief area, close to state and national parks | 209-533-4400<br>800-532-1944<br>pet fee $20/day | (101)<br>$94–<br>$116 | CB<br>R | OP |
| **Days Inn**<br>160 S Washington St<br>www.sonoradaysinn.com<br>lawn and park | 209-532-2400<br>800-580-4667<br>pet fee $10/stay | (65)<br>$79–<br>$83 | CB<br>M/F | OP |
| **Gold Lodge**<br>480 W Stockton St<br>www.goldlodge.com<br>lawn, across street to fairgrounds and small park | 209-532-3952<br>800-363-2154<br>pet fee $10/stay | (43)<br>$59–<br>$79 | CB<br>M/F | OP<br>T |
| **Kennedy Meadows Resort**<br>Hwy 108<br>www.kennedymeadows.com<br>rustic cabins, riverside walking areas, hiking trails | 209-965-3900 | (18)<br>$58–<br>$135 | K<br>R/L | |
| **Sonora Aladdin Motor Inn**<br>14260 Mono Way<br>www.aladdininn.com<br>open walking area | 209-533-4971<br>800-696-3969<br>each pet $5/stay | (61)<br>$68–<br>$79 | CB<br>M/F | OP<br>T |

## South El Monte

| | | | | |
|---|---|---|---|---|
| **Travelodge** | 626-579-4490 | (55) | CB | OP |
| 1228 Durfee Ave | 877-375-3379 | $60– | F | |
| www.travelodge.com | pet fee $10/day | $70 | | |
| open field, 5 blocks to riverbed and park | | | | |

## South Lake Tahoe

| | | | | |
|---|---|---|---|---|
| **Alder Inn** | 530-544-4485 | (24) | CB | OP |
| 1072 Ski Run Blvd | 800-544-0056 | $65– | F | T |
| www.alderinn.com | each pet $12/day | $135 | | |
| empty lot with grass and trees for walking dogs | | | | |
| **Alpenrose Inn** | 530-544-2985 | (19) | CB | T |
| 4074 Pine Blvd | 800-370-4049 | $60– | | |
| www.alpenroseinntahoe.com | pet fee $10/day | $149 | | |
| dogs allowed in first floor rooms with outside entrances only, deck, garden, access to private beach, open field | | | | |
| **Ambassador Motor Lodge** | 530-544-6461 | (59) | CB | OP |
| 4130 Manzanita Ave | each pet $10/day | $44– | | |
| www.ambassadorcapritahoe.com | | $199 | | |
| dogs under 35 lbs only, open field, 6 blocks to park | | | | |
| **Beachside Inn** | 530-544-2400 | (16) | CB | T |
| 930 Park Ave | 800-884-4920 | $59– | M/F | |
| www.beachsideinntahoe.com | pet fee $20/stay | $199 | | |
| pond and grassy walking area | | | | |
| **Block Hotel** | 530-544-2936 | (50) | C | T |
| 4143 Cedar Ave | 888-544-4055 | $50– | M/F | |
| www.blockattahoe.com | pet fee $30/stay | $160 | | |
| **Blue Jay Lodge** | 530-544-5232 | (65) | CB | OP |
| 4133 Cedar Ave | 800-258-3529 | $49– | M/F | T |
| www.bluejaylodge.com | pet fee $10/day | $99 | | |
| roadside walking area | | | | |
| **Blue Lake Inn** | 530-544-6459 | (68) | CB | OP |
| 944 Friday Ave | pet fee $10/day | $69– | M/F | T |
| www.bluelaketahoe.com | | $119 | | |
| dogs in smoking rooms only, lawn and walking trails | | | | |

| C = coffee          GP = guest pass to  L = lounge<br>CB = continental          fitness center  M = microwave<br>  breakfast     IP = indoor pool   OP = outdoor pool<br>F = refrigerator   IS = in-room spa   R = restaurant<br>FB = full breakfast  K = full kitchen   S = sauna/steam<br>FR = fitness room   (k) = kitchenette   T = spa or hot tub | (# of units) & rates | food & drink | pool, sauna & hot tub |
|---|---|---|---|

## South Lake Tahoe (continued)

| | | | |
|---|---|---|---|
| **Budget Inn**                          530-544-2834<br>3496 Lake Tahoe Blvd          pet fee $5/day<br>www.budgetinnlaketahoe.com   grassy walking area | (28)<br>$35–<br>$69 | CB<br>M/F | OP |
| **Cal-va Rado Motel**                    530-541-3900<br>988 Stateline Ave               877-544-4789<br>www.calvaradomotel.com<br>rooms/cabins sleep 6, grassy walking areas,<br>3 miles to park, 7 miles to lakeside state park | (20)<br>$49–<br>$79 | C<br>M/F | |
| **Capri Motel**                         530-544-3665<br>932 Stateline Ave             each pet $10/day<br>www.ambassadorcapritahoe.com<br>open field nearby, ½ block to park | (25)<br>$44–<br>$199 | CB<br>M/F | OP |
| **Cedar Inn & Suites**                   530-543-0159<br>890 Stateline Ave               888-822-0199<br>www.cedarinntahoe.com          pet fee $10/day<br>5 minute walk to wooded area | (39)<br>$69 | CB<br>M/F | OP |
| **Cedar Lodge**                          530-544-6453<br>4069 Cedar Ave                pet fee $20/stay<br>www.cedarlodgetahoe.com<br>meadow nearby, 5 miles to dog-friendly beach | (54)<br>$65–<br>$85 | CB | OP<br>T |
| **Chateau Inn & Suites**                 530-541-2363<br>965 Park Ave                  each pet $10/day<br>www.chateausuites.com | (33)<br>$35–<br>$84 | CB<br>M/F | T |
| **Cloud Nine Value Inn**                 530-544-3959<br>2659 Lake Tahoe Blvd          pet fee $20/stay<br>www.cloud9tahoe.com<br>dirt walking area behind building, ½ mile to park | (52)<br>$80 | M/F | |
| **Days Inn**                             530-541-4800<br>968 Park Ave                    800-448-0754<br>www.hotellaketahoe.com          pet fee $10/day<br>open fields for walking dogs | (59)<br>$53–<br>$89 | CB<br>F | OP<br>S<br>T |

| | | | |
|---|---|---|---|
| **Fireside Lodge** 530-544-5515<br>515 Emerald Bay Rd 800-692-2246<br>www.tahoefiresidelodge.com each pet $20/day<br>wine and appetizers, kitchen/bikes/kayaks for guest<br>use, woods and paved bike trail, 2 miles to beach | (9)<br>$89–<br>$155 | CB<br>(k) | |
| **High Country Lodge** 530-541-0508<br>1227 Emerald Bay Rd each pet $5/day<br>lawn and dirt walking area, 6 miles to beach | (15)<br>$39–<br>$95 | C<br>M/F | T |
| **Inn at Heavenly B & B Lodge** 530-544-4244<br>1261 Ski Run Blvd pet fee $20/day<br>www.innatheavenly.com<br>8 blocks to trail, 10 minute drive to beach | (13)<br>$99–<br>$145 | CB<br>M/F | T |
| **Inn by the Lake** 530-542-0330<br>3300 Lake Tahoe Blvd 800-877-1466<br>www.innbythelake.com pet fee $20/day<br>first floor rooms with patios, bikes, across street to<br>lakeside walking trail, 6 miles to dog-friendly beach | (100)<br>$132–<br>$188 | CB<br>M/F | OP<br>S<br>T |
| **Lakeland Village Accommodations**<br>2048 Dunlap Dr 530-544-3234<br>www.tahoeres.com 800-544-3234<br>3 bdrm condos/homes sleep 9, lawn walking area,<br>some with fenced yard, close to hiking trails | (5)<br>$230–<br>$335 | K | T |
| **Matterhorn Motel** 530-541-0367<br>2187 Lake Tahoe Blvd 866-541-0367<br>www.angelfire.com/biz6/matmotel pet fee $10/day<br>lawn walking area, 2 miles to dog-friendly beach | (18)<br>$69–<br>$110 | C<br>(k) | OP<br>IS |
| **Midway Motel** 530-544-4397<br>3876 Lake Tahoe Blvd<br>grassy walking area, 10 minute drive to beach | (37)<br>$28–<br>$45 | C<br>M/F | |
| **Montgomery Inn** 530-544-3871<br>966 Modesto Ave pet fee $10/day<br>www.tahoemontgomeryinn.com<br>dogs in smoking rooms only, wooded walking area | (25)<br>$40–<br>$75 | C<br>F | T<br>IS |
| **Motel 6** 530-542-1400<br>2375 Lake Tahoe Blvd 800-466-8356<br>www.motel6.com<br>small meadow, bike path | (143)<br>$46–<br>$69 | C | OP |

| C = coffee | GP = guest pass to | L = lounge |
|---|---|---|
| CB = continental | fitness center | M = microwave |
| breakfast | IP = indoor pool | OP = outdoor pool |
| F = refrigerator | IS = in-room spa | R = restaurant |
| FB = full breakfast | K = full kitchen | S = sauna/steam |
| FR = fitness room | (k) = kitchenette | T = spa or hot tub |

## South Lake Tahoe (continued)

| | | (# of units) & rates | food & drink | pool, sauna & hot tub |
|---|---|---|---|---|
| **Pistante's Coyote Den** | 530-541-2282 | (16) | CB | T |
| 1211 Emerald Bay Rd | 866-461-2282 | $40– | | |
| evening cookies/tea/coffee, open walking area | | $65 | | |
| **Ridgewood Inn** | 530-541-8589 | (12) | (k) | T |
| 1341 Emerald Bay Rd | each pet $10/day | $59– | | |
| www.ridgewoodinn.com | 1–2 dogs only | $149 | | |
| wooded walking area, 3 miles to dog-friendly beach | | | | |
| **Roadside Inn** | 530-544-3369 | (37) | C | |
| 952 Stateline Ave | pet fee $5/day | $39– | | |
| dogs allowed in ground floor rooms with outside | | $99 | | |
| entrances, 3 blocks to walking path | | | | |
| **Rodeway Inn** | 530-541-7150 | (117) | CB | OP |
| 4127 Pine Blvd | 800-822-5976 | $50– | M/F | T |
| www.choicehotels.com | pet fee $15/stay | $90 | | |
| small grassy walking area, 1 mile to lakefront park | | | | |
| **Sandor's Chateau Motel** | 530-541-6312 | (17) | C | IS |
| 1137 Emerald Bay Rd | | $35– | M/F | |
| www.tahoemotel.com | | $65 | | |
| rooms/suites, 2½ acres with open fields and meadow | | | | |
| **Sunshine Inn** | 530-542-3500 | (17) | M/F | |
| 1184 Emerald Bay Rd | | $40– | | |
| small dogs only, large fenced field, 3 miles to | | $45 | | |
| dog-friendly beach | | | | |
| **Super 8 Motel** | 530-544-3476 | (108) | CB | OP |
| 3600 Lake Tahoe Blvd | 800-800-8000 | $45– | | T |
| www.super8.com | pet fee $10/day | $128 | | |
| grassy walking area, 6 miles to dog-friendly beach | | | | |
| **Tahoe Colony Inn** | 530-544-6481 | (90) | CB | OP |
| 3794 Montreal Rd | 800-338-5552 | $45– | | T |
| www.gototahoe.com | | $70 | | |
| next to national forest, 7 miles to dog-friendly beach | | | | |

| | | | | |
|---|---|---|---|---|
| **Tahoe Cottage Inn**    530-541-3411<br>1220 Emerald Bay Rd<br>suites sleep up to 10, fenced dog run and kennel,<br>wooded walking area, 5 miles to dog-friendly beach | (8)<br>$40–<br>$90 | K | | |
| **Tahoe Hacienda Motel**    530-541-3805<br>3820 Lake Tahoe Blvd    pet fee $5–$10/day<br>www.tahoehacienda.com<br>large open lot, 7 minute to dog-friendly beach | (35)<br>$38–<br>$175 | C<br>M/F | OP<br>T | |
| **Tahoe Keys Resort**    530-544-5397<br>599 Tahoe Keys Blvd    800-462-5397<br>www.calltahoe.com    .    each pet $25/stay<br>condos/cabins/1–5 bdrm homes with yards, guest<br>use of pool/spas/private beaches for a small fee,<br>lawns and residential areas for walking dogs | (300)<br>$171–<br>$190 | K | T | |
| **Tahoe Tropicana Lodge**    530-541-3911<br>4132 Cedar Ave    each pet $10/day<br>www.tahoetropicana.com<br>1–2 dogs by manager's approval, 4 blocks to trail | (56)<br>$40–<br>$85 | C<br>M/F<br>R | OP<br>T | |
| **Tahoe Valley Lodge**    530-541-0353<br>2241 Lake Tahoe Blvd    800-669-7544<br>www.tahoevalleylodge.com    pet fee $10/day<br>1 small to medium dog only, large dirt walking area,<br>1½ miles to bike paths, 2 miles to dog-friendly beach | (19)<br>$135–<br>$185 | C<br>M/F | OP<br>T | |
| **Thunderbird Motel**    530-544-5741<br>4123 Laurel Ave    800-350-5741<br>www.tahoebestmotels.com    pet fee $10/day<br>small dogs only, 10 minute walk to wooded area,<br>3 miles to dog-friendly beach | (54)<br>$40–<br>$100 | | | |
| **Travelers Inn & Suites**    530-544-0220<br>3930 Pioneer Trail    pet fee $10/day<br>www.tahoetravelersinn.com<br>walking trail | (22)<br>$30–<br>$150 | CB<br>M/F | IS | |
| **Washoe Motel**    530-541-4223<br>751 Emerald Bay Rd<br>wooded walking area, 2 miles to dog-friendly beach | (16)<br>$59–<br>$79 | C<br>M/F | OP<br>T | |

| C = coffee GP = guest pass to L = lounge<br>CB = continental fitness center M = microwave<br>breakfast IP = indoor pool OP = outdoor pool<br>F = refrigerator IS = in-room spa R = restaurant<br>FB = full breakfast K = full kitchen S = sauna/steam<br>FR = fitness room (k) = kitchenette T = spa or hot tub | (# of units)<br>& rates | food<br>& drink | pool, sauna<br>& hot tub |
|---|---|---|---|
| **South San Francisco** | | | |
| **Deluxe Inn** 650-583-2408<br>920 El Camino Real<br>small dogs allowed in smoking rooms only,<br>½ mile to park | (20)<br>$55–<br>$65 | | |
| **Howard Johnson Express Inn** 650-589-9055<br>222 S Airport Blvd 800-446-4656<br>www.hojosfo.com each pet $10/day<br>small grassy walking area, 2 miles to park | (51)<br>$50–<br>$120 | CB<br>M/F | |
| **La Quinta Inn San Francisco Airport**<br>20 Airport Blvd 650-583-2223<br>www.lq.com 800-531-5900<br>lawn walking area, 5 miles to park | (170)<br>$89–<br>$129 | FB<br>M/F | OP<br>T |
| **Motel 6 Airport** 650-877-0770<br>111 Mitchell Ave 800-466-8356<br>www.motel6.com<br>grassy area, 8 blocks to park | (117)<br>$56–<br>$66 | | |
| **Ramada Inn** 650-589-7200<br>245 S Airport Blvd 800-272-6232<br>www.ramada.com pet fee $25/stay<br>parking lot for walking dogs, 10 minute drive to park | (323)<br>$59–<br>$799 | CB | OP |
| **Residence Inn Oyster Point** 650-837-9000<br>1350 Veterans Way 800-331-3131<br>www.marriott.com pet fee $75/stay<br>1–2 dogs only, dogwalking service, bayfront trail | (152)<br>$99–<br>$159 | FB<br>K | OP<br>S |
| **Springville** | | | |
| **Mountain Top B & B** 559-542-2639<br>56816 Aspen Dr 888-867-4784<br>www.mountaintopbnb.com<br>2 bdrm cabin sleeps 7, wooded walking area, close<br>to hiking trails, 2 miles to fishing stream | (3)<br>$110 | (k) | |

| | | | | |
|---|---|---|---|---|
| **Springville Inn** <br> 35634 Hwy 190 <br> www.springvilleinn.com <br> rooms/1 bdrm suites sleep 4, lawn, across street to <br> park, 30 minutes to Sequoia National Monument | 559-539-7501 <br> 800-484-3466 <br> pet fee $50/stay | (10) <br> $80– <br> $225 | CB <br> F <br> R | |

## St Helena

| | | | | |
|---|---|---|---|---|
| **Auberge Brisebois B & B** <br> 271 Via Monte <br> www.napavalleyreservations.com <br> dogs by advance approval only, rooms with outside <br> entrances and private decks, on 5½ view acres | 707-963-4658 | (2) <br> $175– <br> $185 | FB <br> F | OP |
| **El Bonita Motel** <br> 195 Main St <br> www.elbonita.com <br> lawn and rural walking area | 707-963-3216 <br> 800-541-3284 <br> pet fee $5/day | (48) <br> $89– <br> $279 | CB <br> M/F | OP <br> S <br> T |
| **Harvest Inn** <br> 1 Main St <br> www.harvestinn.com <br> large lawn and gardens, walking path, 10 minute <br> drive to dog park | 707-963-9463 <br> 800-950-8466 <br> pet fee $75/stay | (54) <br> $315 | CB <br> F | OP <br> T <br> GP |
| **Mille Vigne** <br> 4016 Spring Mountain Rd <br> www.millevigne.com <br> secluded Tuscan villa on private vineyard estate, <br> private decks, hundreds of acres for walking dogs | 707-963-1914 <br> pet fee $25/stay | (5) <br> $169– <br> $330 | FB <br> CB <br> K | T <br> IS |

## Stanton

| | | | | |
|---|---|---|---|---|
| **Motel 6** <br> 7450 Katella Ave <br> www.motel6.com <br> small dogs in smoking rooms only, large lawn | 714-891-0717 <br> 800-466-8356 | (205) <br> $42– <br> $56 | C | OP |

## Stinson Beach

| | | | | |
|---|---|---|---|---|
| **Beach Cottage on the Ocean** <br> Calle Del Sierra <br> www.stinsonbeach.com <br> well-behaved dogs by advance reservation only, <br> next to off-leash beach | 415-868-2124 <br> pet fee $25/day | (2) <br> $200– <br> $275 | K | |

| C = coffee<br>CB = continental<br>    breakfast<br>F = refrigerator<br>FB = full breakfast<br>FR = fitness room | GP = guest pass to<br>    fitness center<br>IP = indoor pool<br>IS = in-room spa<br>K = full kitchen<br>(k) = kitchenette | L = lounge<br>M = microwave<br>OP = outdoor pool<br>R = restaurant<br>S = sauna/steam<br>T = spa or hot tub | (# of units)<br>& rates | food<br>& drink | pool, sauna<br>& hot tub |
|---|---|---|---|---|---|

## Stinson Beach (continued)

| | | | | |
|---|---|---|---|---|
| **Ocean Court**<br>18 Arenal Ave<br>www.oceancourt.ws | 415-868-0212<br>each pet $10/day<br>3 blocks to dog-friendly beach | (9)<br>$95–<br>$135 | K | |
| **Redwoods Haus B & B**<br>1 Belvedere Ave & Hwy 1<br>www.stinson-beach.com<br>well-mannered dogs by advance approval, large yard,<br>close to walking trails and dog-friendly beach | 415-868-1034<br>pet fee $15–$25/day | (4)<br>$65–<br>$160 | FB | |

## Stockton

| | | | | |
|---|---|---|---|---|
| **Comfort Inn**<br>2654 W March Lane<br>park with walking trail behind hotel | 209-478-4300 | (122)<br>$53–<br>$79 | C<br>K | OP<br>T |
| **Comfort Inn**<br>3951 Budweiser Ct<br>www.choicehotels.com<br>pet relief area | 209-931-9341<br>800-228-5150<br>pet fee $10/day | (65)<br>$60–<br>$66 | CB<br>M/F | OP |
| **Holiday Inn**<br>111 E March Lane<br>www.holidayinnstockton.com<br>small dogs only, small grassy area, 5 minutes to park | 209-474-3301<br>800-633-3737<br>each pet $20/day | (202)<br>$109–<br>$99 | CB<br>R/L | OP<br>T<br>IS |
| **Howard Johnson Express Inn**<br>33 N Center St<br>www.hojo.com<br>dogs in smoking rooms only, across street park | 209-948-6151<br>800-446-4656<br>pet fee $10/day | (80)<br>$56–<br>$60 | CB<br>F | OP |
| **Ivy Motel**<br>9172 Thornton Rd<br>open field, 1 mile to park | 209-475-0730<br>pet fee $10/day | (11)<br>$50 | (k)<br>M/F | |
| **La Quinta Inn**<br>2710 W March Lane<br>www.lq.com    small grassy area, 1½ miles to park | 209-952-7800 | (151)<br>$85–<br>$91 | CB | OP |

| | | | | |
|---|---|---|---|---|
| **Motel 6 Charter Way West** 817 Navy Dr www.motel6.com small dogs only, small grassy area, 3 miles to park | 209-946-0923 800-466-8356 | (76) $46–$60 | C | OP |
| **Motel 6 I-5 Southeast** 1625 French Camp Turnpike Rd www.motel6.com lawn and dirt walking areas, 2 miles to park | 209-467-3600 800-466-8356 | (125) $46–$58 | C | OP |
| **Motel 6 North** 6717 Plymouth Rd www.motel6.com small grassy walking area, 1½ miles to park | 209-951-8120 800-466-8356 | (76) $50–$58 | C | OP |
| **Residence Inn** 3240 W March Lane www.marriott.com pet fee $75/stay studios/1–2 bdrm suites, Mon–Thur beverages and light dinner, lawn walking area, short drive to park | 209-472-9800 800-331-3131 | (104) $94–$199 | FB K | OP T FR |
| **Stevens Motel** 8722 N Hwy 99 pet fee $10/day dogs in smoking rooms, small grass and dirt areas | 209-931-2607 | (13) $50 | | |

## Strawberry

| | | | | |
|---|---|---|---|---|
| **Rivers Resort** 28635 Herring Creek Lane www.gorrr.com modern cabins sleep 10, riverside areas and trails | 209-965-3278 800-514-6777 | (15) $95–$275 | K | OP |

## Studio City

| | | | | |
|---|---|---|---|---|
| **Nite Inn** 10612 Ventura Blvd pet fee $10/day lawn walking area | 818-508-8022 | (26) $70–$79 | CB F | |

## Sun City

| | | | | |
|---|---|---|---|---|
| **Best Value Inn** 27680 Encanto Dr www.bestvalueinn.com lawn walking area, 1 mile to park | 909-672-1861 pet fee $10/stay | (56) $50–$64 | CB M/F | OP |

| C = coffee<br>CB = continental<br>    breakfast<br>F = refrigerator<br>FB = full breakfast<br>FR = fitness room | GP = guest pass to<br>    fitness center<br>IP = indoor pool<br>IS = in-room spa<br>K = full kitchen<br>(k) = kitchenette | L = lounge<br>M = microwave<br>OP = outdoor pool<br>R = restaurant<br>S = sauna/steam<br>T = spa or hot tub | (# of units)<br>& rates | food<br>& drink | pool, sauna<br>& hot tub |
|---|---|---|---|---|---|
| **Sunnyvale** | | | | | |
| **Four Points by Sheraton**<br>1250 Lakeside Dr<br>www.starwood.com<br>dogs under 5 lbs, lawn, lakeside path, 3 miles to park | 408-738-4888<br>800-543-3322 | | (375)<br>$65–<br>$139 | C<br>F<br>R | OP<br>T<br>FR |
| **Homestead Studio Suites**<br>1255 Orleans Dr<br>www.homesteadhotels.com<br>small dogs only, shady walking area, 2 miles to park | 408-734-3431<br>888-782-9473<br>pet fee $25/stay | | (134)<br>$60–<br>$85 | (k) | |
| **Maple Tree Inn**<br>711 E El Camino Real<br>www.mapletreeinn.com | 408-720-9700<br>800-423-0243<br>large lawn, close to parks | | (180)<br>$69–<br>$109 | CB<br>M/F | OP<br>FR |
| **Motel 6 North**<br>775 N Mathilda Ave<br>www.motel6.com<br>small grassy area, 3 blocks to park | 408-736-4595<br>800-466-8356 | | (146)<br>$54 | C | OP |
| **Motel 6 South**<br>806 Ahwanee Ave<br>www.motel6.com    small grassy area, 1 mile to park | 408-720-1222<br>800-466-8356 | | (58)<br>$56 | C | OP |
| **Quality Inn**<br>1280 Persian Dr<br>www.qisunnyvale.com<br>dogs under 15 lbs only, close to trail, ½ block to park | 408-744-1100<br>800-433-9933<br>pet fee $10–$15/day | | (72)<br>$69–<br>$99 | CB<br>M/F | OP<br>FR |
| **Residence Inn**<br>750 Lakeway Dr<br>www.marriott.com<br>pet fee $10/day plus $75 cleaning fee<br>Mon–Thur beverages and appetizers, lakeside area | 408-720-1000<br>800-331-3131 | | (247)<br>$89–<br>$175 | FB<br>K | OP<br>T<br>FR |
| **Sheraton**<br>1100 N Mathilda Ave<br>www.sheraton.com<br>dogs under 80 lbs only, lawn and garden areas | 408-745-6000<br>800-556-6449 | | (173)<br>$79–<br>$209 | F<br>R | OP<br>T<br>FR |

| | | | | |
|---|---|---|---|---|
| **Staybridge Suites** 408-745-1515 | (136) | FB | OP |
| 900 Hamlin Ct 800-996-3426 | $99– | (k) | T |
| www.staybridge.com pet fee $150/stay | $149 | | FR |
| dogs under 50 lbs only, complimentary Wednesday | | | |
| evening BBQ, small lawn areas, short drive to parks | | | |

| | | | |
|---|---|---|---|
| **Vagabond Inn** 408-734-4607 | (60) | CB | OP |
| 816 Ahwanee Ave 800-522-1555 | $55– | M/F | |
| www.vagabondinn.com pet fee $10/day | $60 | | |
| dogs allowed in first floor rooms only, small grassy | | | |
| area, 3 blocks to large park | | | |

| | | | |
|---|---|---|---|
| **Woodfin Suites** 408-738-1700 | (84) | CB | OP |
| 635 E El Camino Real pet fee $5/day | $109– | K | T |
| www.woodfinsuitehotels.com | $119 | | |
| Mon–Thur beverages and light dinner, close to park | | | |

## Sunset Beach

| | | | |
|---|---|---|---|
| **Beachnest Vacation Rentals** 831-722-0202 | (6) | K | T |
| www.beachnest.com | $225– | | |
| oceanfront vacation cottages in Sunset State Beach, | $375 | | |
| some fenced yards, close to dog-friendly beach and | | | |
| trails, list of local dog-friendly parks and businesses | | | |

## Susanville

| | | | |
|---|---|---|---|
| **America's Best Inns** 530-257-4522 | (34) | CB | |
| 2705 Main St 888-852-4996 | $52– | M/F | |
| pet fee $10/day | $64 | | |
| complimentary Tuesday evening BBQ, lawn and | | | |
| open field, ¼ mile to park | | | |

| | | | |
|---|---|---|---|
| **Budget Host Frontier Inn** 530-257-4141 | (38) | CB | |
| 2685 Main St 800-283-4678 | $40– | M/F | |
| www.budgethost.com pet fee $10/stay | $50 | | |
| lawn, 3 blocks to park and riverside walking trail | | | |

| | | | |
|---|---|---|---|
| **Diamond View Motel** 530-257-4585 | (8) | C | |
| 1529 Main St pet fee $5–$10/stay | $35– | M/F | |
| small lawn, 1 block to park | $40 | | |

| C = coffee  GP = guest pass to  L = lounge<br>CB = continental  fitness center  M = microwave<br>breakfast  IP = indoor pool  OP = outdoor pool<br>F = refrigerator  IS = in-room spa  R = restaurant<br>FB = full breakfast  K = full kitchen  S = sauna/steam<br>FR = fitness room  (k) = kitchenette  T = spa or hot tub | (# of units)<br>& rates | food<br>& drink | pool, sauna<br>& hot tub |
|---|---|---|---|

### Susanville (continued)

| | | | |
|---|---|---|---|
| **Eagle Lake Rentals**    530-825-3105<br>687-880 Magnolia Way<br>www.eaglelakerentals.com<br>dogs by advance approval only, cabins/vacation<br>homes sleep up to 10, large lawn, close to trails | (7)<br>$75–<br>$150 | K | |
| **Motel 9**    530-251-5702<br>1067 Main St    pet fee $10/day<br>www.motel9.com    next to park | (40)<br>$38 | C<br>M/F | |
| **River Inn Motel**    530-257-6051<br>1710 Main St    each pet $5/day<br>quiet street behind motel for walking dogs | (50)<br>$42–<br>$68 | CB<br>M/F | OP |
| **Roseberry House B & B**    530-257-5675<br>609 North St    pet fee $10/day<br>www.roseberryhouse.com<br>well-behaved dogs by owner's approval only, yard<br>and vacant lot, 3 blocks to park | (4)<br>$80–<br>$100 | FB | |
| **Super 8 Motel**    530-257-2782<br>2975 Johnstonville Rd    800-800-8000<br>www.super8.com    each pet $10/day<br>small grassy areas, ½ mile to park | (69)<br>$54–<br>$64 | CB | OP |

### Sylmar

| | | | |
|---|---|---|---|
| **Motel 6 Los Angeles/Sylmar**    818-362-9491<br>12775 Encinitas Ave    800-466-8356<br>www.motel6.com    small grassy area, 1 mile to park | (158)<br>$40–<br>$66 | C | OP |

### Tahoe City

| | | | |
|---|---|---|---|
| **Hauserman Rental Group**    530-583-3793<br>475 N Lake Blvd    800-208-2463<br>www.enjoytahoe.com<br>dogs by approval only, 1 bdrm cabins to 5 bdrm<br>homes sleep up to 12, wooded walking areas | (20)<br>$100–<br>$600 | K | T |

| | | | |
|---|---|---|---|
| **River Ranch Restaurant & Lodge**  530-583-4264<br>Hwy 89 & Alpine Meadows Rd                800-535-9900<br>www.riverranchlodge.com                each pet $15/day<br>1–2 dogs allowed in Spring thru Fall only, riverside<br>bike path | (19)<br>$65–<br>$195 | CB<br>R/L | |

## Tahoe Vista

| | | | |
|---|---|---|---|
| **Holiday House**                              530-546-2369<br>7276 N Lake Blvd                            800-294-6378<br>www.tahoeholidayhouse.com          pet fee $30/stay<br>1–2 bdrm suites sleep 4, decks overlooking lake,<br>beachfront walking area, 5 minute drive to park | (6)<br>$125–<br>$205 | K | T |
| **Rustic Cottages**                            530-546-3523<br>7449 N Lake Blvd                            888-778-7842<br>www.rusticcottages.com                each pet $15/day<br>1920s cottages sleep up to 7, close to walking trails | (39)<br>$69–<br>$159 | K | OP |
| **Woodvista Lodge**                            530-546-3839<br>7699 N Lake Blvd                          pet fee $10/day<br>dogs by manager's approval in smoking rooms only,<br>large lawn, residential streets, 1¼ miles to beach | (17)<br>$60–<br>$135 | C<br>F | OP<br>T |

## Tahoma

| | | | |
|---|---|---|---|
| **Norfolk Woods Inn**                          530-525-5000<br>6941 W Lake Blvd                         each pet $10/day<br>www.norfolkwoods.com<br>rustic 2 bdrm cabins sleep 6, walking trails, across<br>street to dog-friendly beach | (5)<br>$150–<br>$190 | K<br>R | OP<br>T |
| **Tahoe Lake Cottages**                        530-525-4411<br>7030 W Lake Blvd                            800-852-8246<br>www.tahoelakecottages.com          pet fee $10/day<br>1–2 bdrm knotty pine cottages on west shore of Lake<br>Tahoe, on 1½ wooded acres, hiking trails, 2 minute<br>walk to park, 5 minute drive to dog-friendly beach | (13)<br>$70–<br>$185 | K | OP<br>T |
| **Tahoma Lodge**                               530-525-7721<br>7018 W Lake Blvd                            866-819-2226<br>www.tahomalodge.com                each pet $10/day<br>rooms/studios/2 bdrm cabins, large lawn and<br>woods, across street to lake, ¼ mile to state park | (10)<br>$60–<br>$165 | K | OP<br>T |

| C = coffee<br>CB = continental<br>  breakfast<br>F = refrigerator<br>FB = full breakfast<br>FR = fitness room | GP = guest pass to<br>  fitness center<br>IP = indoor pool<br>IS = in-room spa<br>K = full kitchen<br>(k) = kitchenette | L = lounge<br>M = microwave<br>OP = outdoor pool<br>R = restaurant<br>S = sauna/steam<br>T = spa or hot tub | (# of units)<br>& rates | food<br>& drink | pool, sauna<br>& hot tub |
|---|---|---|---|---|---|

### Tahoma (continued)

| **Tahoma Meadows B&B Cottages** 530-525-1553<br>6821 W Lake Blvd                        866-525-1553<br>www.tahomameadows.com            pet fee $10/day<br>rooms/cottages sleep up to 4, wooded walking area,<br>hiking trails, 2 miles to state park | (16)<br>$95–<br>$375 | FB<br>K | |

### Tarzana

| **St George Motor Inn**        818-702-0371<br>19454 Ventura Blvd           800-845-8919<br>www.stgeorgemotorinn.com    pet fee $25/stay<br>dogs in smoking rooms only, rooms/studio/1 bdrm<br>suites, residential neighborhood, 1½ miles to park | (57)<br>$77–<br>$114 | CB<br>K<br>M/F | OP<br>T |
| **Tarzana Inn**               818-345-9410<br>19170 Ventura Blvd          800-347-9410<br>www.tarzanainn.com<br>grassy area, 3 blocks to park | (48)<br>$79–<br>$99 | CB<br>M/F | OP |

### Tehachapi

| **Best Western Mountain Inn**   661-822-5591<br>418 W Tehachapi Blvd          800-937-8376<br>www.bestwesterncalifornia.com<br>landscaped walking area, 1 block to park | (73)<br>$79–<br>$89 | CB<br>M/F | OP<br>T |
| **Golden Hills Motel**          661-822-4488<br>22561 Woodford Tehachapi Rd<br>large grassy walking area, 1 mile to park | (24)<br>$43–<br>$55 | C<br>M/F | |
| **Ranch House Motel**           661-822-4561<br>500 E Tehachapi Blvd<br>lawn, 2 blocks to park | (12)<br>$45 | F | |
| **Tehachapi Summit Travelodge**  661-823-8000<br>500 E Steuber Rd               pet fee $7/stay<br>www.travelodge.com<br>lawn and open field | (76)<br>$67–<br>$75 | C<br>M/F | OP<br>T |

## Temecula

| | | | | |
|---|---|---|---|---|
| **Comfort Inn** | 909-296-3788 | (72) | CB | OP |
| 27338 Jefferson Ave | pet fee $20/day | $70– | M/F | T |
| www.comfortinn.com/hotel/ca143 | | $100 | | |
| vacant lot for walking dogs | | | | |
| **Motel 6** | 909-676-7199 | (135) | C | OP |
| 41900 Moreno Rd | 800-466-8356 | $52– | | |
| www.motel6.com | | $76 | | |
| next to park | | | | |

## Templeton

| | | | |
|---|---|---|---|
| **Country Comfort Bed & Pet Vacation Retreat** | | (1) | K |
| 507 N Main St | 805-434-3900 | $150 | |
| 2 bdrm modular home sleeps 6, covered patio, | | | |
| private fenced back yard, dog run | | | |

## The Sea Ranch

| | | | | |
|---|---|---|---|---|
| **Sea Ranch Escape Vacation Rentals** | | (74) | K | OP |
| 60 Sea Walk Dr | 707-785-2426 | $215– | | S |
| www.888searanch.com | 888-732-7262 | $327 | | T |
| | pet fee varies | | | |
| vacation homes sleep up to 8, oceanfront bluff over- | | | | |
| looking beach, meadow and hillside for walking dogs | | | | |

## Thousand Oaks

| | | | | |
|---|---|---|---|---|
| **Motel 6** | 805-499-0711 | (175) | C | OP |
| 1516 Newbury Rd | 800-466-8356 | $46– | | |
| www.motel6.com | | $60 | | |
| grassy hillside, 2 parks within 500 yards | | | | |
| **Thousand Oaks Inn** | 805-497-3701 | (106) | CB | OP |
| 75 W Thousand Oaks Blvd | 800-600-6878 | $130 | M/F | T |
| www.thousandoaksinn.com | pet fee $75/stay | | R | GP |
| grassy and landscaped areas, 2 miles to park | | | | |

## Thousand Palms

| | | | | |
|---|---|---|---|---|
| **Red Roof Inn** | 760-343-1381 | (114) | CB | OP |
| 72215 Varner Rd | | $57 | M/F | T |
| www.redroof.com | | | | |
| dogs under 80 lbs, grassy areas, 2 blocks to park | | | | |

| C = coffee<br>CB = continental<br>  breakfast<br>F = refrigerator<br>FB = full breakfast<br>FR = fitness room | GP = guest pass to<br>  fitness center<br>IP = indoor pool<br>IS = in-room spa<br>K = full kitchen<br>(k) = kitchenette | L = lounge<br>M = microwave<br>OP = outdoor pool<br>R = restaurant<br>S = sauna/steam<br>T = spa or hot tub | (# of units)<br>& rates | food<br>& drink | pool, sauna<br>& hot tub |
|---|---|---|---|---|---|

## Three Rivers

| | | | | | |
|---|---|---|---|---|---|
| **Buckeye Tree Lodge**<br>46000 Sierra Dr<br>www.buckeyetree.com | 559-561-5900<br>each pet $5/day<br>small grassy yard | | (12)<br>$62–<br>$114 | CB<br>M/F | OP |
| **Cinnamon Creek Ranch**<br>www.cinnamoncreek.com<br>well-behaved dogs and children welcome, suite and<br>cabins sleep up to 6, open fields, walking trails<br>along river and creek, river swimming hole | 559-561-1107<br>pet fee $20/stay | | (3)<br>$150–<br>$180 | K | T |
| **Lazy J Ranch Motel**<br>39625 Sierra Dr<br>rooms/2 bdrm cottages sleep up to 8, riverfront area<br>for walking and swimming | 559-561-4449<br>pet fee $5/stay | | (18)<br>$65–<br>$190 | CB<br>K<br>M/F | OP |
| **Sequoia Village Inn**<br>45971 Sierra Dr<br>www.sequoiavillageinn.com<br>cottages/chalets sleep up to 12, next to national park | 559-561-3652<br>pet fee $5/day | | (8)<br>$69–<br>$259 | C<br>M/F | OP<br>T |
| **Sierra Lodge**<br>43175 Sierra Dr<br>www.sierra-lodge.com | 559-561-3681<br>pet fee $5/day<br>open field | | (22)<br>$46–<br>$112 | CB<br>M/F | OP |

## Tomales

| | | | | | |
|---|---|---|---|---|---|
| **Continental Inn**<br>26985 State Hwy 1<br>www.thecontinentalinn.com<br>breakfast served on weekends only, 1 block to park | 707-878-2396 | | (11)<br>$110–<br>$139 | CB | |

## Torrance

| | | | | | |
|---|---|---|---|---|---|
| **Days Inn South Bay**<br>4111 Pacific Coast Hwy<br>www.daysinn.com<br>dogs under 30 lbs allowed in smoking rooms only,<br>walking area in parking lot, 2 miles to park | 310-378-8511<br>800-753-5399<br>pet fee $10/day | | (92)<br>$64–<br>$69 | CB<br>M/F | OP |

| | | | | |
|---|---|---|---|---|
| **Homestead Studio Suites**<br>3995 W Carson St<br>www.homesteadhotels.com<br>lawn walking area, 5 minute walk to park | 310-543-0048<br>888-782-9473<br>pet fee $25/day | (140)<br>$89–<br>$99 | K | |
| **Residence Inn**<br>3701 Torrance Blvd<br>www.marriott.com<br>studios/1–2 bdrm suites, Mon–Thur beverages and<br>light dinner, lawn area, 1 mile to park | 310-543-4566<br>800-331-3131<br>pet fee $75/stay | (247)<br>$99–<br>$159 | FB<br>K | OP<br>T<br>FR |
| **Staybridge Suites**<br>19901 Prairie Ave<br>www.staybridge.com<br>1–2 bdrm suites, Tue-Thur beverages and light<br>dinner, lawn area, 2 blocks to park | 310-371-8525<br>800-238-8000<br>pet fee $20/day | (144)<br>$129–<br>$159 | FB<br>K | OP<br>T<br>FR |

## Tracy

| | | | | |
|---|---|---|---|---|
| **Best Western Luxury Inn**<br>811 W Clover Rd<br>www.bestwesterncalifornia.com  pet fee $20/stay<br>dogs under 15 lbs, grassy area, 1½ blocks to park | 209-832-0271<br>877-468-7229 | (59)<br>$63–<br>$69 | CB<br>M/F | OP<br>T |
| **Motel 6**<br>3810 N Tracy Blvd<br>www.motel6.com<br>open field, 5 miles to dog park | 209-836-4900<br>800-466-8356 | (111)<br>$46–<br>$62 | C | OP |
| **Phoenix Lodge**<br>3511 N Tracy Blvd<br>dogs under 40 lbs only, lawn, 1 mile to park | 209-835-1335<br>pet fee $20/stay | (60)<br>$50–<br>$60 | M/F | OP |

## Trinidad

| | | | | |
|---|---|---|---|---|
| **Bishop Pine Lodge**<br>1481 Patricks Point Dr<br>www.bishoppinelodge.com<br>studios/2 bdrm redwood cottages, on 5 acres of lawn<br>and gardens, woods, 2 miles to dog-friendly beach | 707-677-3314<br>pet fee $10/day | (12)<br>$80–<br>$120 | C<br>(k) | |
| **Ocean Grove Lodge**<br>480 Patricks Point Dr<br>www.come.to/oceangrove<br>small dogs only, on 10 wooded acres | 707-677-3543<br>pet fee $10/day | (12)<br>$60–<br>$100 | C<br>M/F<br>R/L | |

| C = coffee  GP = guest pass to  L = lounge<br>CB = continental  fitness center  M = microwave<br>  breakfast  IP = indoor pool  OP = outdoor pool<br>F = refrigerator  IS = in-room spa  R = restaurant<br>FB = full breakfast  K = full kitchen  S = sauna/steam<br>FR = fitness room  (k) = kitchenette  T = spa or hot tub | (# of units)<br>& rates | food<br>& drink | pool, sauna<br>& hot tub |
|---|---|---|---|

## Trinidad (continued)

| **Sea Cliff Motel**  707-677-3485<br>1895 Patricks Point Dr<br>www.seacliffhotel-ca.com<br>dogs by advance approval only, on 2½ acres of woods<br>and meadow, close to dog-friendly beach | (4)<br>$45–<br>$85 | C<br>K | |
|---|---|---|---|
| **Trinidad Inn**  707-677-3349<br>1170 Patricks Point Dr  each pet $5/day<br>www.trinidadinn.com<br>walking trail to wooded area | (10)<br>$65–<br>$135 | C<br>K | |

## Trinity Center

| **Ripple Creek Cabins**  530-266-3505<br>Star Route 2 Box 4020  pet fee $10/stay<br>www.ripplecreekcabins.com<br>cabins sleep 2 to 12, private yards, well-behaved dogs<br>are welcome to walk off-leash around the property | (7)<br>$75–<br>$149 | K | |
|---|---|---|---|
| **Trinity Alps Resort**  530-286-2205<br>1750 Trinity Alps Rd<br>www.trinityalpsresort.com<br>cabins sleep 4 to 10, closed October–April, 90 acres<br>with 1 mile of river frontage, woods and trails | (43)<br>$94–<br>$128 | K<br>R | |
| **Wyntoon Resort**  530-266-3337<br>Hwy 3  800-715-3337<br>www.wyntoonresort.com  pet fee $8/day<br>dogs by advance approval only, 1–2 bdrm cabins,<br>woods and road to marina for walking dogs | (19)<br>$100–<br>$155 | K | OP |

## Truckee

| **Inn at Truckee**  530-587-8888<br>11506 Deerfield Dr  888-773-6888<br>www.innattruckee.com  pet fee $11/day<br>grassy walking area, 10 minute walk to lakeside park | (42)<br>$70–<br>$106 | CB<br>F | S<br>T |
|---|---|---|---|

## Tulare

| | | | | |
|---|---|---|---|---|
| **Best Value Inn** 1050 E Rankin Rd www.bestvalueinn.com large grassy walking area | 559-688-6671 pet fee $5/day | (60) $55 | CB M/F | OP |
| **Best Western Town & Country Lodge** 1051 N Blackstone St www.tularebw.com dogs by manager's approval only | 559-688-7537 888-488-5273 pet fee $20/stay | (93) $59– $79 | FB M/F L | OP T FR |
| **Charter Inn & Suites** 1016 E Prosperity Ave www.charterinnandsuites.com grassy walking area behind building, 1 mile to park | 559-685-9500 pet fee $5/day | (70) $68– $75 | FB M/F | OP T |
| **Days Inn** 1183 N Blackstone St www.daysinn.com small grassy walking area, 1 mile to park | 559-686-0985 800-329-7466 each pet $5/day | (90) $62– $67 | CB M/F | OP FR |
| **Motel 6** 1111 N Blackstone St www.motel6.com 5 blocks to park | 559-686-1611 800-466-8356 | (111) $44– $52 | C | OP |
| **Toga's Inn** 26442 N Hwy 99 dogs by manager's approval only, rooms with outside entrances to landscaped courtyard, lawn and 30 acre walnut orchard, 3 miles to lakeside park | 559-688-0501 | (56) $45– $99 | CB M/F | OP |

## Tulelake

| | | | | |
|---|---|---|---|---|
| **Ellis Motel** 2238 Hwy 139 dirt road behind building for walking dogs | 530-667-5242 pet fee $3/day | (11) $45– $50 | C K | |

## Turlock

| | | | | |
|---|---|---|---|---|
| **Best Western Orchard Inn** 5025 N Golden State Blvd www.bestwesterncalifornia.com small grassy areas, 3 miles to park | 209-667-2827 800-521-5025 pet fee $25/stay | (72) $79 | CB M/F | OP |

| C = coffee<br>CB = continental<br>breakfast<br>F = refrigerator<br>FB = full breakfast<br>FR = fitness room | GP = guest pass to<br>fitness center<br>IP = indoor pool<br>IS = in-room spa<br>K = full kitchen<br>(k) = kitchenette | L = lounge<br>M = microwave<br>OP = outdoor pool<br>R = restaurant<br>S = sauna/steam<br>T = spa or hot tub | (# of units)<br>& rates | food<br>& drink | pool, sauna<br>& hot tub |
|---|---|---|---|---|---|

## Turlock (continued)

| | | | | |
|---|---|---|---|---|
| **Motel 6**<br>250 S Walnut Rd<br>www.motel6.com | 209-667-4100<br>800-466-8356<br>grassy walking area | (101)<br>$44–<br>$58 | C | OP |
| **Travelodge**<br>201 W Glenwood Ave<br>www.travelodge.com<br>dogs under 25 lbs only, across street to open field | 209-668-3400<br>800-578-7878 | (91)<br>$58–<br>$74 | CB<br>M/F | OP<br>T |
| **Western Budget Motel**<br>185 N Tully Rd<br>dirt walking area, 3 miles to park | 209-634-2944<br>each pet $5/day | (68)<br>$44–<br>$49 | C<br>F | |

## Twain

| | | | |
|---|---|---|---|
| **Pine Aire Motel Resort**<br>24642 Hwy 70<br>riverside cabins sleep 2 to 6, grassy and wooded<br>areas along river, sandy beaches | 530-283-1730 | (7)<br>$60–<br>$75 | K |

## Twain Harte

| | | | | |
|---|---|---|---|---|
| **El Dorado Motel**<br>22678 Black Hawk Dr<br>grassy area and open field | 209-586-4479<br>pet fee $10/day | (15)<br>$55 | C<br>M/F | OP<br>T |
| **Gables Cedar Creek Inn**<br>22560 Twain Harte Dr<br>www.gablescedarcreekinn.com<br>dogs under 30 lbs by manager's approval only,<br>rooms/house sleep up to 10, lawn, ½ mile to park | 209-586-3008<br>pet fee $10/day | (8)<br>$79–<br>$104 | C<br>K<br>M/F | |
| **Shadow Ridge Vacation Rentals**<br>18752 Cedar Dr<br>www.shadowridge.com<br>cabins/vacation homes sleep 2 to 12, some with hot<br>tubs or fenced yards, quiet residential streets in<br>wooded area, close to lake and ski resort | 209-586-0334<br>800-382-0334<br>pet fee $10/stay | (15)<br>$140–<br>$190 | K | |

## Twentynine Palms

| | | | | |
|---|---|---|---|---|
| **Best Western Gardens Inn** <br> 71487 29 Palms Hwy <br> www.bestwesterncalifornia.com <br> small grassy area and open desert | 760-367-9141 <br> 800-937-8376 <br> each pet $10/day | (84) <br> $71– <br> $119 | CB <br> M/F | OP <br> T <br> FR |
| **Circle C Lodge** <br> 6340 El Rey Ave <br> www.circleclodge.com <br> courtyard, open desert area, across street to park | 760-367-7615 <br> 800-545-9696 <br> each pet $10/day | (12) <br> $84 | CB <br> (k) | OP |
| **Hillview Motel** <br> 73193 29 Palms Hwy <br> www.virtual29.com/a-z/hillview <br> open walking area, 2 miles to park | 760-367-0334 <br> each pet $5/day | (12) <br> $49 | C <br> M/F | |
| **Motel 6** <br> 72562 29 Palms Hwy <br> www.motel6.com    lawn, open desert, 1 mile to park | 760-367-2833 <br> 800-466-8356 | (123) <br> $46– <br> $48 | C | OP |
| **Twentynine Palms Inn** <br> 73950 Inn Ave <br> www.29palmsinn.com <br> adobe bungalows/2 bdrm cottage sleep up to 5, <br> enclosed patios, on 70 acres of lawn and open desert | 760-367-3505 <br> each pet $35/stay | (24) <br> $75– <br> $135 | K <br> R | OP <br> T |

## Twin Peaks

| | | | | |
|---|---|---|---|---|
| **Pine Rose Cabins** <br> 25994 Hwy 189 <br> studio to 7 bdrm cabins, on 5 acres | 909-337-2341 <br> 800-429-7463 <br> pet fee $10/day | (18) <br> $59– <br> $425 | C <br> K | OP <br> T |

## Ukiah

| | | | | |
|---|---|---|---|---|
| **Best Value Inn** <br> 693 S Orchard Ave <br> www.bestvalueinn.com <br> pet relief area, ¼ mile to park, close to lakes | 707-468-9167 <br> 800-794-3551 <br> each pet $5/day | (53) <br> $50– <br> $65 | CB <br> M/F | OP <br> T |
| **Comfort Lodge** <br> 1070 S State St <br> www.comfortlodgeukiah.com | 707-462-6657 <br> pet fee $10/day <br> short drive to park | (103) <br> $55– <br> $79 | CB <br> M/F | OP |
| **Days Inn** <br> 950 N State St <br> www.daysinn.com | 707-462-7584 <br> each pet $10/day <br> open desert, 2 blocks to park | (54) <br> $80– <br> $90 | CB <br> M/F | OP |

| C = coffee CB = continental breakfast F = refrigerator FB = full breakfast FR = fitness room | GP = guest pass to fitness center IP = indoor pool IS = in-room spa K = full kitchen (k) = kitchenette | L = lounge M = microwave OP = outdoor pool R = restaurant S = sauna/steam T = spa or hot tub | (# of units) & rates | food & drink | pool, sauna & hot tub |
|---|---|---|---|---|---|

## Ukiah (continued)

| | | | | | |
|---|---|---|---|---|---|
| **Discovery Inn** 1340 N State St www.lexres.com grass and dirt walking area | | 707-462-8873 pet fee $25/stay | (176) $65– $100 | CB F | OP T |
| **Long Valley Ranch** www.sheepdung.com 4 bdrm home, breakfast supplies, 800 acre ranch, fenced pet area, hiking trails, pond and small lake | | 707-894-5322 pet fee varies | (1) $175– $400 | C K | |
| **Motel 6** 1208 S State St www.motel6.com | | 707-468-5404 800-466-8356 grassy area, 1 mile to park | (70) $46– $63 | C | OP |
| **Robinson Creek B & B Flower Farm** 1901 Boonville Rd www.robinsoncreek.com small dogs indoors by advance approval only, larger dogs stay in shop building, 2 acres, paths and creek | | 707-468-9039 866-772-9401 | (2) $110– $125 | FB | |
| **Rodeway Inn** 1050 S State St www.rodewayinn.com vacant lot, 1 mile to park | | 707-462-2906 pet fee $10/day | (43) $65 | CB M/F | OP |

## Union City

| | | | | | |
|---|---|---|---|---|---|
| **Crowne Plaza Hotel** 32083 Alvarado Niles Rd www.crowneplaza.com 1 mile to park | | 510-489-2200 800-784-1180 each pet $30/day | (268) $119– $139 | R/L | OP T FR |

## Universal City

| | | | | | |
|---|---|---|---|---|---|
| **Sheraton** 333 Universal Hollywood Dr www.sheraton.com grassy hillside, ¼ mile to park | | 818-980-1212 800-325-3535 | (436) $169– $334 | C F | OP T |

## Upper Lake

| | | | | |
|---|---|---|---|---|
| **Narrows Lodge Resort** 707-275-2718 | (19) | K | | |
| 5690 Blue Lakes Rd 800-476-2776 | $55– | | | |
| www.thenarrowsresort.com pet fee $3/day | $125 | | | |
| dogs by manager's approval, rooms/suites/cabins, | | | | |
| on 4½ wooded acres, quiet road for walking dogs | | | | |
| **Super 8 Motel** 707-275-0888 | (34) | C | OP | |
| 450 E Hwy 20 800-800-8000 | $59– | F | IS | |
| www.super8.com pet fee $10/day | $89 | | | |
| dogs by manager's approval only, large grassy area | | | | |
| behind building, ⅛ mile to park | | | | |

## Vacaville

| | | | | |
|---|---|---|---|---|
| **Best Western Heritage Inn** 707-448-8453 | (41) | CB | OP | |
| 1420 E Monte Vista Ave 800-528-1234 | $72– | M/F | | |
| dogs under 25 lbs only, grassy area, 2 miles to park | $90 | | | |
| **Motel 6** 707-447-5550 | (97) | C | OP | |
| 107 Lawrence Dr 800-466-8356 | $46– | | | |
| www.motel6.com | $66 | | | |
| grassy area, 2 miles to park | | | | |
| **Residence Inn** 707-469-0300 | (78) | FB | IP | |
| 360 Orange Dr 800-331-3131 | $130– | K | T | |
| www.marriott.com pet fee $75/stay | $140 | | FR | |
| studios/1–2 bdrm suites, Mon–Thur beverages and | | | | |
| light dinner, lawn, 2 miles to park | | | | |
| **Super 8 Motel** 707-449-8884 | (53) | CB | OP | |
| 101 Allison Ct 800-800-8000 | $57– | M/F | | |
| www.super8.com pet fee $10/stay | $77 | | | |
| grassy walking area, ½ mile to park | | | | |

## Valencia

| | | | | |
|---|---|---|---|---|
| **Best Western Valencia Inn** 661-255-0555 | (122) | C | OP | |
| 27413 Wayne Mills Pl 800-937-8376 | $87– | M/F | | |
| www.bestwesterncalifornia.com pet fee $10/day | $129 | | | |
| pet treats, pet relief area and park | | | | |

| C = coffee<br>CB = continental<br>    breakfast<br>F = refrigerator<br>FB = full breakfast<br>FR = fitness room | GP = guest pass to<br>    fitness center<br>IP = indoor pool<br>IS = in-room spa<br>K = full kitchen<br>(k) = kitchenette | L = lounge<br>M = microwave<br>OP = outdoor pool<br>R = restaurant<br>S = sauna/steam<br>T = spa or hot tub | # of units)<br>& rates | food<br>& drink | pool, sauna<br>& hot tub |
|---|---|---|---|---|---|

## Vallejo

| | | | | | |
|---|---|---|---|---|---|
| **Best Western Inn at Marine World**   707-554-9655<br>1596 Fairgrounds Dr               800-528-1234<br>www.bestwestern.com/innatmarineworld<br>across street to park           pet fee $30/stay | | | (117)<br>$80–<br>$110 | CB<br>M/F | OP<br>T |
| **Holiday Inn**                   707-644-1200<br>1000 Fairgrounds Dr           800-533-5753<br>www.holiday-inn.com      pet fee $25/stay<br>lawn, 2 blocks to park | | | (170)<br>$75–<br>$127 | F<br>R | OP |
| **Motel 6 Marine World Fairgrounds**<br>458 Fairgrounds Dr            707-642-7781<br>www.motel6.com            800-466-8356<br>small grassy walking area | | | (97)<br>$46–<br>$66 | C | OP |
| **Motel 6 Marine World West**     707-643-7611<br>1455 Marine World Pkwy      800-466-8356<br>www.motel6.com     parking lot for walking dogs | | | (54)<br>$52–<br>$69 | C | |
| **Motel 6 Maritime North**       707-552-2912<br>597 Sandy Beach Rd          800-466-8356<br>www.motel6.com    grassy hillside for walking dogs | | | (149)<br>$52 | C | OP |
| **Quality Inn**                   707-643-1061<br>44 Admiral Callaghan Lane     800-228-5151<br>www.qualityinn-vallejo.com    pet fee $25/day<br>short drive to parks | | | (78)<br>$69–<br>$89 | CB<br>M/F | OP |

## Valley Springs

| | | | | | |
|---|---|---|---|---|---|
| **10th Green Inn**             209-772-1084<br>14 Saint Andrews Rd<br>www.10thgreeninn.com       1–2 dogs only | | | (10)<br>$60–<br>$105 | CB<br>M/F | GP |

## Ventura

| | | | | | |
|---|---|---|---|---|---|
| **Bayshore Inn**               805-643-6427<br>3075 E Main St         pet fee $60/stay<br>lawn, close to parks, ½ mile to dog-friendly beach | | | (25)<br>$55–<br>$69 | M/F | |

| | | | | |
|---|---|---|---|---|
| **Brakey House Country Inn** 805-643-3600 411 Poli St      pet fee $20/day www.brakeyhouse.com 1–3 blocks to several parks, 4 blocks to beach | (6) $95 | FB F | T |
| **La Quinta Inn** 805-658-6200 5818 Valentine Rd www.lq.com lawn, 1 mile to park, 6 miles to dog-friendly beach | (142) $96– $106 | CB M/F | OP T |
| **Motel 6–Beach** 805-643-5100 2145 Harbor Blvd      800-466-8356 www.motel6.com small grassy area, 1½ blocks to dog-friendly beach | (200) $52– $72 | C | OP |
| **Motel 6–South** 805-650-0080 3075 Johnson Dr      800-466-8356 www.motel6.com small grassy area | (158) $52– $72 | C | OP |
| **Rex Motel** 805-643-5681 2406 E Thompson Blvd dogs in smoking rooms only, 1 block to school field | (20) $49– $59 | M/F | |
| **Ventura Beach Marriott** 805-643-6000 2055 Harbor Blvd      800-228-9290 www.marriott.com      pet fee $75/stay dogs under 20 lbs only, 1 block to park and beach | (286) $149– $209 | CB M/F R | OP T |
| **Vagabond Inn** 805-648-5371 756 E Thompson Blvd      800-522-1555 www.vagabondinn.com      each pet $5/day 1 to 2 dogs only, grassy walking area, across street to park and dog-friendly beach | (82) $69– $79 | CB M/F | OP T |
| **Victoria Motel** 805-642-2173 2350 S Victoria Ave      pet fee $5/day professional putting green, pet relief area, 1 block to park, short drive to dog-friendly beach | (36) $58– $92 | CB | |
| **Viking Motel** 805-643-3273 2107 E Thompson Blvd alley behind building to walk dogs, 2 miles to park | (18) $65– $98 | K | |

| C = coffee<br>CB = continental<br>    breakfast<br>F = refrigerator<br>FB = full breakfast<br>FR = fitness room | GP = guest pass to<br>    fitness center<br>IP = indoor pool<br>IS = in-room spa<br>K = full kitchen<br>(k) = kitchenette | L = lounge<br>M = microwave<br>OP = outdoor pool<br>R = restaurant<br>S = sauna/steam<br>T = spa or hot tub | (# of units)<br>& rates | food<br>& drink | pool, sauna<br>& hot tub |
|---|---|---|---|---|---|
| **Victorville** | | | | | |
| **Best Western Green Tree Inn**<br>14173 Green Tree Blvd<br>www.bestwesterncalifornia.com | 760-245-3461<br>pet fee $25/stay<br>3 blocks to park | | (200)<br>$80–<br>$96 | C<br>K<br>R/L | OP<br>T |
| **Budget Inn**<br>14153 Kentwood Blvd<br>small dogs only, lawn walking area | 760-241-8010 | | (40)<br>$43–<br>$46 | M/F | |
| **Comfort Suites**<br>12281 Mariposa Rd<br>www.choicehotels.com<br>1 dog only, 4 miles to park | 760-245-6777<br>pet fee $10/day | | (77)<br>$71–<br>$100 | CB<br>M/F | OP<br>T<br>FR |
| **E-Z8 Motel**<br>15401 Park Ave E<br>www.ez8motels.com<br>paved walking area, 1 mile to park | 760-241-7516 | | (68)<br>$49 | C<br>F | OP<br>T |
| **Howard Johnson Express Inn**<br>16868 Stoddard Wells Rd<br>www.hojo.com<br>grassy area behind building, 1 block to park | 760-243-7700<br>800-446-4656<br>pet fee $8/day | | (100)<br>$50–<br>$55 | CB<br>M/F | OP<br>IS |
| **Motel 6**<br>16901 Stoddard Wells Rd<br>www.motel6.com<br>small grassy area, 1 block to park | 760-243-0666<br>800-466-8356 | | (63)<br>$46–<br>$50 | C | OP |
| **Ramada Inn**<br>15494 Palmdale Rd<br>www.ramada.com/victorville11520<br>small dirt walking area, 2 miles to park | 760-245-6565<br>pet fee $25/stay | | (162)<br>$71 | CB<br>M/F | OP |
| **Red Roof Inn**<br>13409 Mariposa Rd<br>www.redroof-victorville.com<br>dogs under 80 lbs only, desert area, 1 mile to park | 760-241-1577 | | (118)<br>$49–<br>$89 | C<br>M/F | OP<br>T |

| | | | | |
|---|---|---|---|---|
| Travelodge | 760-241-7200 | (43) | CB | OP |
| 12175 Mariposa Rd | 800-578-7878 | $56– | M/F | IS |
| www.travelodge.com | pet fee $6/day | $60 | | |
| paved parking lot to walk dogs, short drive to park | | | | |

## Visalia

| | | | | |
|---|---|---|---|---|
| Best Western Visalia Inn | 559-732-4561 | (41) | CB | OP |
| 623 W Main St | 877-500-4771 | $69– | F | |
| www.bestwesterncalifornia.com | pet fee $10/day | $85 | | |
| 1 small dog only, 3 blocks to park | | | | |
| Days Inn | 559-732-5611 | (77) | CB | OP |
| 4645 W Noble Ave | 800-329-7466 | $50– | M/F | |
| www.daysinn.com | pet fee $25/stay | $75 | | |
| lawn area, 2½ miles to park | | | | |
| Holiday Inn | 559-651-5000 | (270) | F | IP |
| 9000 W Airport Dr | 800-465-4329 | $90– | R/L | OP |
| www.holiday-inn.com/visaliaca | pet fee $25/stay | $99 | | T |
| lawn area, across street to park | | | | FR |
| Super 8 Motel | 559-627-2885 | (39) | CB | OP |
| 4801 W Noble Ave | 800-800-8000 | $55– | M/F | |
| www.super8.com | pet fee $5/day | $60 | | |
| lawn and dirt walking areas, 1 mile to park | | | | |

## Vista

| | | | | |
|---|---|---|---|---|
| Best Value Inn & Suites | 760-726-7010 | (72) | C | OP |
| 330 Mar Vista Dr | 888-315-2378 | $55– | M/F | T |
| www.bestvalueinn.com | pet fee $5/day | $70 | | |
| dogs under 30 lbs only, small grassy area | | | | |
| La Quinta Inn | 760-727-8180 | (106) | CB | OP |
| 630 Sycamore Ave | 800-687-6667 | $85– | F | GP |
| www.lq.com | grassy area and open field | $99 | | |

## Volcano

| | | | | |
|---|---|---|---|---|
| St. George Hotel | 209-296-4458 | (20) | CB | IS |
| 16104 Main St | pet fee $20/stay | $83– | R/L | |
| www.stgeorgehotel.com | | $189 | | |
| 1862 historic hotel, on 1 acre of gardens, friendly small town for walking dogs | | | | |

| C = coffee  GP = guest pass to  L = lounge<br>CB = continental  fitness center  M = microwave<br>breakfast  IP = indoor pool  OP = outdoor pool<br>F = refrigerator  IS = in-room spa  R = restaurant<br>FB = full breakfast  K = full kitchen  S = sauna/steam<br>FR = fitness room  (k) = kitchenette  T = spa or hot tub | # of units) & rates | food & drink | pool, sauna & hot tub |
|---|---|---|---|
| **Volcano (continued)** | | | |
| **Volcano Union Inn**          209-296-7711<br>21375 Consolation St<br>www.volcanounioninn.com<br>small friendly dogs only, lawn area and pet-friendly<br>streets for walking dogs, 5 minute walk to park | (4)<br>$90–<br>$160 | FB<br>F<br>R | |
| **Walnut Creek** | | | |
| **Embassy Suites Hotel**          925-934-2500<br>1345 Treat Blvd<br>www.embassysuites.com<br>pet fee $75/1st day, $15/each additional day<br>evening beverages, courtyard, lawn, 3 blocks to park | (249)<br>$139–<br>$199 | FB<br>M/F | IP<br>S<br>T<br>FR |
| **Holiday Inn**          925-932-3332<br>2730 N Main St          800-465-4329<br>www.holiday-inn.com          each pet $25/stay<br>dogs under 40 lbs only, lawn and jogging path | (156)<br>$79–<br>$149 | F<br>R/L | OP<br>T<br>FR |
| **Motel 6**          925-935-4010<br>2389 N Main St          800-466-8356<br>www.motel6.com<br>grassy areas, 1½ miles to park | (71)<br>$54–<br>$81 | C | |
| **Wasco** | | | |
| **Wasco Inn Motel**          661-758-5317<br>1126 Hwy 46<br>dogs by manager's approval only, lawn and field | (35)<br>$45–<br>$50 | | OP |
| **Watsonville** | | | |
| **Best Western Rose Garden Inn**          831-724-3367<br>740 Freedom Blvd          888-685-5760<br>www.bestwesternwatsonville.com          pet fee $10/day<br>pet relief area, cleanup scoopers provided | (45)<br>$99–<br>$149 | CB<br>M/F | OP<br>T<br>FR |

| | | | | |
|---|---|---|---|---|
| **Motel 6** 831-728-4144 125 Silver Leaf Dr 800-466-8356 www.motel6.com grassy area, 8 miles to park | (124) $48–$76 | C | OP |
| **Red Roof Inn** 831-768-1968 1620 W Beach St 800-733-7663 www.redroof-watsonville.com dogs under 60 lbs only, lawn and dirt areas, 6 miles to off-leash dog park | (95) $60–$83 | CB M/F | OP |

## Weaverville

| | | | | |
|---|---|---|---|---|
| **Best Western Weaverville Victorian Inn** 1709 Main St 530-623-4432 open area, ½ mile to park 800-937-8376 | (63) $65–$99 | CB M/F | OP IS |
| **49er Gold Country Inn** 530-623-4937 718 Main St www.goldcountryinn.com dogs by manager's approval only, vacant lot, 1 block to park | (24) $55–$95 | C M/F | OP IS |
| **Motel Trinity** 530-623-2129 1112 Main St moteltrinity.shasta-trinity.com grassy walking area, 3 blocks to park | (25) $55–$60 | C M/F | OP IS |
| **Red Hill Motel & Cabins** 530-623-4331 Red Hill Rd pet fee $5/stay www.redhillresorts.com rooms/cabins/duplexes sleep up to 5, on 1 wooded acre, close to hiking trails | (14) $37–$80 | K | |

## Weed

| | | | | |
|---|---|---|---|---|
| **Hi–Lo Motel** 530-938-2731 88 S Weed Blvd www.hilomotel.com creekside lawn, 1 mile to park | (40) $55 | M/F R | |
| **Holiday Inn Express** 530-938-1308 1830 Black Butte Dr 800-465-4329 www.hiexpress.com/weedca each pet $10/day lawn, 1½ miles to park | (50) $81 | CB M/F | T |

| C = coffee<br>CB = continental<br>    breakfast<br>F = refrigerator<br>FB = full breakfast<br>FR = fitness room | GP = guest pass to<br>    fitness center<br>IP = indoor pool<br>IS = in-room spa<br>K = full kitchen<br>(k) = kitchenette | L = lounge<br>M = microwave<br>OP = outdoor pool<br>R = restaurant<br>S = sauna/steam<br>T = spa or hot tub | (# of units)<br>& rates | food<br>& drink | pool, sauna<br>& hot tub |
|---|---|---|---|---|---|

## Weed (continued)

| **Motel 6**<br>466 N Weed Blvd<br>www.motel6.com | 530-938-4101<br>800-466-8356<br>pet relief area, 1 mile to park | (80)<br>$44–<br>$56 | C | OP |
|---|---|---|---|---|
| **Sis-Q-Inn Motel**<br>1825 Shastina Dr<br>grassy walking area | 530-938-4194<br>pet fee $5/day | (22)<br>$60 | CB<br>M/F | T |
| **Stewart Mineral Springs**<br>4617 Stewart Springs Rd<br>www.stewartmineralsprings.com<br>cabins/rooms/apartments, mineral baths, stream<br>and wooded hillsides for walking dogs | 530-938-2222<br>pet fee $10/day | (15)<br>$69–<br>$74 | C<br>K<br>R | S |
| **Summit Inn & Restaurant**<br>90 N Weed Blvd<br>small grassy hillside area, 2 blocks to park | 530-938-4481<br>pet fee $5/day | (22)<br>$40–<br>$50 | M/F<br>R | |
| **Townhouse Motel**<br>157 S Weed Blvd<br>rooms and suites sleep 6, vacant lot for walking dogs | 530-938-4431<br>pet fee $4/day | (20)<br>$40–<br>$45 | M/F | |
| **Weed Comfort Inn**<br>1844 Shastina Dr<br>4 pet-friendly rooms, open walking area | 530-938-1982<br>pet fee $10/day | (56)<br>$70 | CB<br>F | OP<br>T<br>FR |

## West Covina

| **Hampton Inn**<br>3145 E Garvey Ave N<br>www.wchampton.com<br>near college campus, lawns, sidewalks to walk dogs | 626-967-5800<br>800-224-5922 | (130)<br>$80–<br>$94 | FB<br>M/F | OP<br>GP |
|---|---|---|---|---|

## West Hollywood

| **Chateau Marmont**<br>8221 W Sunset Blvd<br>www.chateaumarmont.com<br>rooms and bungalows, garden area, ½ mile to park | 323-656-1010<br>800-242-8328<br>pet fee $100/stay | (67)<br>$295–<br>$2,200 | R | |
|---|---|---|---|---|

| | | | | |
|---|---|---|---|---|
| **Le Montrose Suite Hotel** 900 Hammond St www.le-montrose.com bicycles for guest use, 5 minute walk to park | 310-855-1115 800-776-0666 pet fee $100/stay | (133) $199 | (k) M/F R | OP T FR |
| **Le Parc Suites** 733 West Knoll Dr www.leparcsuites.com 3 blocks to park | 310-855-8888 800-578-4837 pet fee $75/stay | (154) $165 | (k) R | OP T |
| **Wyndham Bel Age Hotel** 1020 N San Vicente Blvd www.wyndham.com dogs under 40 lbs, small lawn, short drive to park | 310-854-1111 800-996-3426 pet fee $50/stay | (200) $179– $199 | R | OP |

### West Sacramento

| | | | | |
|---|---|---|---|---|
| **Best Western Harbor Inn & Suites** 1250 Halyard Dr www.bestwesterncalifornia.com 15 minute drive to park | 916-371-2100 pet fee $25/day | (130) $89 | CB M/F | OP |
| **Budget Motel** 964 W Capitol Ave 1 mile to park | 916-371-6723 | (25) $149 | (k) | |
| **Silvey's Motel** 1030 W Capitol Ave grassy walking area, 8 blocks to park | 916-371-4601 pet fee $10/day | (28) $45 | K | |

### Westley

| | | | | |
|---|---|---|---|---|
| **Days Inn** 7144 McCracken Rd www.daysinn.com open area behind building | 209-894-5500 800-329-7466 each pet $10/day | (33) $52– $65 | CB M/F | OP T |
| **Econo Lodge** 7100 S McCracken Rd www.choicehotels.com small grassy walking area | 209-894-3900 each pet $10/day | (37) $49– $59 | CB M/F | OP T |
| **Super 8 Motel** 7115 S McCracken Rd www.super8.com lawn walking area | 209-894-3888 800-800-8000 pet fee $10/day | (34) $48– $64 | CB R | OP |

| C = coffee  GP = guest pass to  L = lounge<br>CB = continental  fitness center  M = microwave<br>breakfast  IP = indoor pool  OP = outdoor pool<br>F = refrigerator  IS = in-room spa  R = restaurant<br>FB = full breakfast  K = full kitchen  S = sauna/steam<br>FR = fitness room  (k) = kitchenette  T = spa or hot tub | # of units)<br>& rates | food<br>& drink | pool, sauna<br>& hot tub |
|---|---|---|---|
| ### Westminster | | | |
| **Motel 6 North**  714-895-0042<br>13100 Goldenwest St  800-466-8356<br>www.motel6.com<br>¼ mile to park | (127)<br>$46–<br>$54 | C | OP |
| **Motel 6 South**  714-891-5366<br>6266 Westminster Ave  800-466-8356<br>www.motel6.com<br>grassy areas, short drive to park | (98)<br>$46–<br>$54 | C | OP |
| ### Westmorland | | | |
| **Super 8 Motel**  760-351-7100<br>351 W Main  800-800-8000<br>www.super8.com  each pet $10/day<br>small grassy walking areas | (50)<br>$65 | CB<br>M/F | IP<br>T |
| ### Westport | | | |
| **Dehaven Valley Farm Inn**  707-961-1660<br>39247 N Hwy 1  877-334-2836<br>www.dehavenvalleyfarm.com<br>Victorian farmhouse, cottages sleep 5, deck, on 20<br>acres of meadow and hills, 2 minute walk to beaches | (9)<br>$140–<br>$151 | FB<br>M/F<br>R | T<br>T |
| **Howard Creek Ranch Inn**  707-964-6725<br>40501 N Hwy 1  pet fee $10/day<br>www.howardcreekranch.com<br>dogs allowed by advance reservation only, 1860s inn,<br>rooms/cabins sleep 2, on 60 wooded acres near<br>wilderness area, 2 mile long hiking trail on property,<br>short walk to ocean | (14)<br>$75–<br>$160 | | S<br>T |
| **Westport Inn & Deli**  707-964-5135<br>37040 N Hwy 1<br>open field for walking dogs | (5)<br>$60–<br>$70 | FB<br>CB | |

## Whittier

| | | | | |
|---|---|---|---|---|
| **Motel 6** 8221 Pioneer Blvd www.motel6.com 1 well-behaved dog only, school football field across street for walking dogs | 562-692-9101 800-466-8356 | (98) $46–$56 | C | OP |
| **Vagabond Inn** 14125 Whittier Blvd www.vagabondinn.com | 562-698-9701 pet fee $10/day small lawn | (50) $62–$69 | CB M/F | OP |

## Williams

| | | | | |
|---|---|---|---|---|
| **Comfort Inn** 400 C St www.comfortinn.com small field across street | 530-473-2381 800-228-5150 each pet $5/day | (59) $65–$71 | CB M/F | OP T |
| **Granzella's Inn** 391 6th St www.granzellas.com 1–2 pets only, gravel walking area, 4 blocks to park | 530-473-3310 800-643-8614 pet fee $10/stay | (43) $75–$90 | CB F R | OP T |
| **Holiday Inn Express** 374 Ruggeri Way www.hiexpress.com/williamsca dogs by manager's approval only, lawn and vacant lot | 530-473-5120 888-887-6607 pet fee $25/stay | (51) $65–$69 | CB M/F | FR |
| **Motel 6** 455 4th St www.motel6.com dirt walking area, 6 blocks to park | 530-473-5337 800-466-8356 | (121) $44–$56 | C | OP |
| **Stage Stop Inn** 330 7th St www.stagestopmotel.com open field for walking dogs | 530-473-2281 pet fee $5/day | (25) $45–$50 | C F | OP |

## Willits

| | | | | |
|---|---|---|---|---|
| **Baechtel Creek Inn & Spa** 101 Gregory Lane www.baechtelcreekinn.com dogs under 35 lbs by manager's approval only, vacant lot for walking dogs | 707-459-9063 800-459-9911 pet fee $15/stay | (42) $89–$150 | CB M/F | OP T |

| C = coffee, CB = continental breakfast, F = refrigerator, FB = full breakfast, FR = fitness room, GP = guest pass to fitness center, IP = indoor pool, IS = in-room spa, K = full kitchen, (k) = kitchenette, L = lounge, M = microwave, OP = outdoor pool, R = restaurant, S = sauna/steam, T = spa or hot tub | (# of units) & rates | food & drink | pool, sauna & hot tub |
|---|---|---|---|
| **Willits (continued)** | | | |
| **Beside Still Waters Farm B & B**   707-984-6130<br>30901 Sherwood Rd    877-230-2171<br>www.besidestillwatersfarm.com   each pet $25/stay<br>1–3 dogs only, private cottages/large guesthouse<br>sleep up to 6, dog bed and treats | (3)<br>$179–<br>$265 | FB<br>(k) | IS |
| **Old West Inn**   707-459-4201<br>1221 S Main St   pet fee $15/day<br>www.oldwestinn.com<br>dogs in smoking rooms only, grassy area, park | (19)<br>$59–<br>$159 | CB<br>F | OP |
| **Pepperwood Motel**   707-459-2231<br>452 S Main St   pet fee $10/day<br>www.pacificsites.com/~pepperwood<br>lawn area, close to park | (21)<br>$35–<br>$75 | M/F | |
| **Western Village Inn**   707-459-4011<br>1440 S Main St   pet fee $10/day<br>dogs in smoking rooms only, gravel walking area | (20)<br>$69 | C<br>M/F | |
| **Willow Creek** | | | |
| **Bigfoot Motel**   530-629-2142<br>39039 Hwy 299<br>www.bigfootmotel.com<br>small dogs only, ½ block to open field | (27)<br>$55–<br>$65 | C<br>M/F | OP |
| **Gambi Hill Cabins and RV Park**   530-629-2701<br>40526 Hwy 299   pet fee $10/stay<br>studio to 2 bdrm cabins, lawn area, walking trail<br>next to national forest land | (12)<br>$50–<br>$100 | K | |
| **Willows** | | | |
| **Amerihost Inn & Suites**   530-934-9700<br>199 Humboldt Ave   800-434-5800<br>www.amerihostinn.com   pet fee $10/stay<br>vacant lot, 4 blocks to park | (71)<br>$59–<br>$76 | CB<br>M/F | IP<br>T<br>FR |

| | | | |
|---|---|---|---|
| **Best Western Golden Pheasant Inn**<br>249 Humboldt Ave 530-934-4603<br>www.bestwesterncalifornia.com 800-838-1387<br>on 8 acres for walking dogs pet fee $10/day | (104)<br>$71–<br>$80 | CB<br>M/F<br>R | OP |
| **Blue Gum Motel** 530-934-5401<br>2637 County Road 99w pet fee $5/day<br>www.bluegummotel.com<br>dogs allowed by manager's approval only, walking<br>area along creek | (30)<br>$38–<br>$44 | C<br>M/F | OP |
| **Days Inn** 530-934-4444<br>475 Humboldt Ave 800-329-7466<br>www.daysinn.com pet fee $12/day<br>small dogs only, grassy walking area | (50)<br>$59 | CB<br>M/F | OP |
| **Economy Inn** 530-934-4224<br>435 N Tehama St each pet $5/day<br>www.willowseconomyinn.com<br>small grassy walking area, 4 blocks to park | (20)<br>$42–<br>$45 | M/F | |
| **Motel 6** 530-934-7026<br>452 Humboldt Ave 800-466-8356<br>www.motel6.com<br>no pet fee for 1 dog, $7/day for 2 dogs<br>lawn area, 7 blocks to park | (41)<br>$45–<br>$56 | C<br>M/F | OP |
| **Super 8 Motel** 530-934-2871<br>457 Humboldt Ave 800-800-8000<br>www.super8.com pet fee $10/day<br>dogs allowed in smoking rooms only, grassy walking<br>area, 1 mile to parks | (41)<br>$50–<br>$61 | C<br>M/F | OP |
| **Willows Motel** 530-934-4778<br>725 S Tehama St pet fee $5/day<br>dogs allowed by manager's approval only, lawn,<br>1 block to park | (18)<br>$42–<br>$45 | C<br>F | |

## Winters

| | | | |
|---|---|---|---|
| **Abbey House Inn** 530-795-5870<br>101 Abbey St<br>www.abbeyhouseinn.com<br>dogs by advance approval only, cottage sleeps 2,<br>orchard for walking dogs | (1)<br>$95–<br>$125 | (k) | |

| | | | | (# of units) & rates | food & drink | pool, sauna & hot tub |
|---|---|---|---|---|---|---|
| C = coffee | GP = guest pass to | L = lounge | | | | |
| CB = continental | fitness center | M = microwave | | | | |
| breakfast | IP = indoor pool | OP = outdoor pool | | | | |
| F = refrigerator | IS = in-room spa | R = restaurant | | | | |
| FB = full breakfast | K = full kitchen | S = sauna/steam | | | | |
| FR = fitness room | (k) = kitchenette | T = spa or hot tub | | | | |

## Wofford Heights

| | | | |
|---|---|---|---|
| **Barewood Motel**                    760-376-1910 | (10) | C | IS |
| 7013 Wofford Heights Blvd | $70– | M/F | |
| www.barewoodmotel.com | $91 | | |
| dogs by manager's approval only, rooms/suite sleep up to 3, 1–3 miles to parks | | | |

## Woodlake

| | | | |
|---|---|---|---|
| **Wicky-Up Ranch B & B**              559-564-8898 | (4) | FB | |
| 22702 Avenue 344                  pet fee $10/stay | $99 | | |
| www.wickyup.com | | | |
| dog allowed in 1 cottage that sleep 3, resident dogs, open walking areas on 20 acre organic orange ranch | | | |

## Woodland

| | | | |
|---|---|---|---|
| **Days Inn**                          530-666-3800 | (50) | CB | OP |
| 1524 E Main St                        800-329-7466 | $59– | M | |
| www.daysinn.com                   each pet $10/day | $65 | | |
| small grassy walking area, ½ mile to park | | | |
| **Holiday Inn Express**               530-662-7750 | (68) | CB | IP |
| 2070 Freeway Dr                       800-465-4329 | $109– | M/F | T |
| www.hiexpress.com/woodlandca   pet fee $20/stay | $118 | | FR |
| small grassy areas, ½ miles to park | | | |
| **Motel 6 Woodland/Sacramento**       530-666-6777 | (79) | C | OP |
| 1564 E Main St                        800-466-8356 | $46– | | |
| www.motel6.com          grassy areas, 1 mile to park | $64 | | |

## Woodland Hills

| | | | |
|---|---|---|---|
| **Hilton**                            818-595-1000 | (326) | CB | OP |
| 6360 Canoga Ave                       800-922-2400 | $89– | F | T |
| www.woodlandhills.hilton.com    pet fee $35/stay | $119 | R/L | FR |
| dogs under 10 lbs by manager's approval in smoking rooms only, 3 blocks to park | | | |

| | | | | |
|---|---|---|---|---|
| **Woodland Hills Motor Lodge**<br>22621 Ventura Blvd<br>1 mile to park | 818-224-2222<br>pet fee $10/day | (18)<br>$55–<br>$65 | M/F | OP |

### Wrightwood

| | | | | |
|---|---|---|---|---|
| **Pines Motel**<br>6045 Pine St<br>small dogs only, across street to park | 760-249-9974<br>pet fee $10/day | (14)<br>$79–<br>$119 | K | |

### Yorkville

| | | | | |
|---|---|---|---|---|
| **Sheep Dung Estates**<br>www.sheepdung.com<br>solar-powered 1-room cottages, breakfast supplies,<br>secluded 320 acre ranch, trails, swimming pond | 707-894-5322 | (5)<br>$95–<br>$250 | C<br>K | |

### Yosemite National Park

| | | | | |
|---|---|---|---|---|
| **The Redwoods in Yosemite**<br>8038 Chilnualna Falls Rd<br>www.redwoodsinyosemite.com<br>1–4 bdrm homes, decks, lawn, riverside trails | 209-375-6666<br>888-225-6666<br>each pet $10/day | (125)<br>$156–<br>$487 | K | T |
| **Yosemite's Four Seasons**<br>7519 Henness Cir<br>www.yosemitelodging.com<br>3 bdrm pet-friendly homes, see website for "Alpine<br>Retreat" and "Camp One," close to woods and trails | 209-372-9033<br>800-669-9300 | (2)<br>$259–<br>$430 | K | T |

### Yountville

| | | | | |
|---|---|---|---|---|
| **Vintage Inn–Napa Valley**<br>6541 Washington St<br>www.vintageinn.com<br>dogs in first floor rooms only, lawn, 1 mile to park | 707-944-1112<br>800-351-1133<br>pet fee $30/stay | (82)<br>$215–<br>$500 | CB<br>R | OP<br>T<br>FR |
| **Yountville Inn**<br>6462 Washington St<br>www.yountvilleinn.com | 707-944-5600<br>pet fee $100/stay<br>across street to park | (51)<br>$300–<br>$375 | CB<br>F | OP<br>T<br>GP |

### Yreka

| | | | | |
|---|---|---|---|---|
| **Amerihost Inn**<br>148 Moonlit Oaks Ave<br>www.amerihostinn.com<br>landscaped walking area, 1 mile to park | 530-841-1300<br>800-434-5800<br>pet fee $10/stay | (61)<br>$84–<br>$90 | CB<br>M/F | IP<br>T<br>FR |

| C = coffee   GP = guest pass to fitness center   L = lounge   M = microwave<br>CB = continental breakfast   IP = indoor pool   OP = outdoor pool<br>F = refrigerator   IS = in-room spa   R = restaurant<br>FB = full breakfast   K = full kitchen   S = sauna/steam<br>FR = fitness room   (k) = kitchenette   T = spa or hot tub | (# of units) & rates | food & drink | pool, sauna & hot tub |
|---|---|---|---|

## Yreka (continued)

| | | | |
|---|---|---|---|
| **Ben-Ber Motel**<br>1210 S Main St    530-842-2791   pet fee $5/day | (36)<br>$46–<br>$62 | CB<br>M/F | OP |
| **Best Value Gold Rush Inn**<br>801 N Main St<br>www.bestvalueinn.com    530-842-1940   each pet $5/day   dirt area, ½ mile to park | (18)<br>$39 | CB<br>M/F | |
| **Best Western Miners Inn**<br>122 E Miner St<br>www.bestwesterncalifornia.com<br>lawn, 5 blocks to park    530-842-4355   800-444-1320   pet fee $10/stay | (134)<br>$68–<br>$70 | CB<br>M/F | OP |
| **Comfort Inn**<br>1804 Fort Jones Rd<br>www.comfortinn.com    530-842-1612   pet fee $10/day   gravel area, 1 mile to park | (52)<br>$69–<br>$89 | CB<br>M/F | OP |
| **Econo Lodge**<br>526 S Main St<br>www.econolodge.com    530-842-4404   pet fee $7/day   vacant lot, 1 mile to park | (44)<br>$49–<br>$59 | CB<br>F | OP |
| **Motel 6**<br>1785 S Main St<br>www.motel6.com    530-842-4111   800-466-8356   lawn, 3 blocks to park | (102)<br>$43–<br>$54 | C | OP |
| **Rodeway Inn**<br>1235 S Main St<br>www.rodewayinn.com    530-842-4412   888-424-6423   pet fee $5/day | (44)<br>$45–<br>$70 | CB<br>M/F | |
| **Super 8 Motel**<br>136 Montague Rd<br>www.super8.com<br>pet relief area, ¾ mile to park    530-842-5781   800-800-8000   pet fee $5/day | (61)<br>$49–<br>$66 | CB<br>M/F | OP<br>FR<br>IS |

## Yuba City

| | | | |
|---|---|---|---|
| **Best Western Bonanza Inn**<br>1001 Clark Ave<br>www.bestwesterncalifornia.com    530-674-8824   800-562-5706   pet fee $10/day | (122)<br>$83 | C<br>M/F<br>R/L | OP<br>T |

| | | | | |
|---|---|---|---|---|
| **California Inn**<br>2129 Live Oak Blvd<br>walking trail behind building | 530-674-9670<br>pet fee $5/day | (20)<br>$55 | | |
| **Comfort Inn Yuba City**<br>730 N Palora Ave<br>www.comfortinn.com | 530-674-1592<br>800-228-5150<br>5 minute walk to park | (53)<br>$58–<br>$64 | CB<br>M/F | OP |
| **Days Inn**<br>4228 S Hwy 99<br>www.daysinn.com<br>dogs in smoking rooms only, lawn, 3 miles to park | 530-674-0201<br>800-329-7466<br>each pet $10/day | (61)<br>$63–<br>$81 | CB<br>M/F<br>R/L | OP<br>T |
| **Days Inn**<br>700 N Palora Ave<br>www.daysinn.com<br>schoolgrounds nearby for walking dogs | 530-674-1711<br>800-329-7466<br>pet fee $7–$10/day | (50)<br>$55–<br>$75 | CB<br>M/F | OP |
| **Harkey House B & B**<br>212 C St<br>www.harkeyhouse.com<br>small dogs allowed in cottage that sleeps 3, poolside<br>garden, historical neighborhood, ½ block to park | 530-674-1942 | (4)<br>$185–<br>$195 | (k) | OP<br>T |
| **Motel 6**<br>965 Gray Ave<br>www.motel6.com | 530-790-7066<br>800-466-8356<br>small dogs only, ½ block to park | (86)<br>$53–<br>$63 | C | OP<br>T |

## Yucca Valley

| | | | | |
|---|---|---|---|---|
| **Oasis of Eden Inn & Suites**<br>56377 29 Palms Hwy<br>www.oasisofeden.com<br>dogs under 35 lbs only, high desert area, quiet road | 760-365-6321<br>800-606-6686<br>pet fee $10/day | (38)<br>$59–<br>$99 | CB<br>M/F<br>R | OP<br>T<br>GP |
| **Super 8 Motel**<br>57096 29 Palms Hwy<br>www.super8.com<br>dirt walking area, next to park | 760-228-1773<br>800-800-8000<br>pet fee $20/stay | (48)<br>$64–<br>$109 | CB<br>M/F | OP |
| **Yucca Inn & Suites**<br>7500 Camino Del Cielo Trail<br>www.yuccainn.com<br>rooms/1 bdrm suites, private patios, grass courtyard<br>for walking dogs, 2 miles to park | 760-365-3311<br>800-989-7644 | (73)<br>$60–<br>$129 | CB<br>K<br>R | OP<br>S<br>T |

# A: Business Name Index

Just in case you know the name of a particular lodging but aren't sure in exactly which city (or suburb) it is located, here's a list of all the business names that appear in the main directory on pages 77–377. This list is sorted alphabetically by business name rather than by city, and the page numbers shown here refer back to the appropriate page in the main directory for each detailed listing.

# C

# G

Gables Cedar Creek Inn,
Twain Harte 358
Gambi Hill Cabins and RV Park,
Willow Creek 372
Garden Court Hotel,
Palo Alto 263
Garden Motel, Cloverdale 135
Gardenia Motel,
Crescent City 142
Gardiner's Resort,
Carmel Valley 126
Gate House Inn,
Pacific Grove 255
Gateway Motel, Barstow 92
Georgian Hotel,
Santa Monica 327
Gerstle Park Inn, San Rafael 319
Giant Oaks Lodge,
Running Springs 289
Glass Beach B & B Inn,
Fort Bragg 166
Glenelly Inn, Glen Ellen 174
Glory's Holiday House B & B,
San Diego 298
Gold Country B & B,
La Porte 200
Gold Lodge, Sonora 338
Gold Mine Lodge,
Big Bear Lake 101
Gold Mountain Manor Cabins,
Big Bear City 98
Gold Pan Motel, Quincy 275
Gold Trail Motor Lodge,
Placerville 270
Golden Bear Cottages,
Big Bear Lake 101
Golden Bear Inn, Berkeley 96
Golden Chain Resort Motel,
Grass Valley 177

Golden Eagle Motel, Dorris 150
Golden Gate Hotel,
San Francisco 307
Golden Hills Motel,
Tehachapi 352
Golden West Motel,
El Centro 155
Golden West Motel,
Loyalton 220
Gorda by the Sea, Big Sur 105
Graciela Burbank, Burbank 114
Grafton on Sunset,
Los Angeles 215
Grand Manor Inn, Redding 280
Granzella's Inn, Williams 371
Grass Valley Courtyard Suites,
Grass Valley 177
Gray Eagle Lodge,
Blairsden 108
Gray Eagle Lodge, Graeagle 176
Gray Squirrel Inn,
Lake Arrowhead 203
Green Gables Motel,
Burney 115
Green Valley Motel, Orick 253
Greenwood Pier Inn, Elk 157
Grey Squirrel Resort and
Vacation Rentals,
Big Bear Lake 101
Griffin House, Elk 157
Groveland Hotel, Groveland 178
Gualala Country Inn,
Gualala 179
Guest House Inn & Suites,
Pleasanton 271
GuestHouse International Hotel,
Long Beach 213
GuestHouse International Inn &
Suites, Santa Clara 323

# R

# B: Topics Index

This index contains a cross-referenced list of all the topics related to traveling with your pet, as they appear in the first 75 pages of this book.

# W

walking
    hazards underfoot  35
    on motel grounds  34
warning
    antifreeze  46
    chocolate  50
    electrical cord  48
    open car window  31
    parked car  32, 51
    pickup truck  32
    toilet water  19
water
    diarrhea  51
    distilled  19
    in room  19, 34
    packing  19, 34
    rest stops  32
    upset stomach  50
wounds
    broken bones  43
    cuts & scrapes  48
    external bleeding  44

# Z

zip-top plastic bags
    cleanup  21
    packing  39
    poison sample  45

# Colophon

This book was produced in
PageMaker 7.0 for Macintosh

🐎 Body text: Century Old Style 10 pt.

🐎 Chapter heads: Dominican 34 pt.

🐎 Section heads: Dominican 24 pt.

🐎 Bullet symbols: Classic Mobile 10 pt.

# We hope you enjoyed this travel guidebook!

**Have Dog Will Travel** guidebooks are designed to keep you and your dog traveling throughout the West—all the way from the Canadian border down to the Mexican border, and everywhere in-between!

# Have Dog Will Travel: California Edition

- 2,275 dog-friendly hotels, motels, B & Bs, cabins and vacation homes

- Travel tips, pet etiquette on the road and in your room, packing essentials, lifesaving first aid guide

- Indexed by business name and topic

- 432 pages, 5½" x 8½" perfectbound softcover, black & white line drawings, ISBN 0-9660544-7-4

# Have Dog Will Travel: Northwest Edition

- 2,128 dog-friendly hotels, motels, B & Bs, cabins and vacation homes throughout Oregon, Washington and Idaho

- Travel tips, pet etiquette on the road and in your room, packing essentials, lifesaving first aid guide

- Indexed by business name and topic

- 400 pages, 5½" x 8½" perfectbound softcover, black & white line drawings, ISBN 0-9660544-8-2